The Other Americans in Paris

BUSINESSMEN, COUNTESSES,
WAYWARD YOUTH, 1880-1941

Nancy L. Green

The University of Chicago Press CHICAGO & LONDON

NANCY L. GREEN is professor of history at the École des hautes études en sciences sociales. She is the author or coeditor of several books, including *Ready-to-Wear and Ready-to-Work: A Century of Industry and Immigrants in Paris and New York*, *Jewish Workers in the Modern Diaspora*, and *Citizenship and Those Who Leave*.

The University of Chicago Press, Chicago 60637
The University of Chicago Press, Ltd., London
© 2014 by The University of Chicago
All rights reserved. Published 2014.
Printed in the United States of America

23 22 21 20 19 18 17 16 15 14   1 2 3 4 5

ISBN-13: 978-0-226-30688-9 (cloth)
ISBN-13: 978-0-226-13752-0 (e-book)

DOI: 10.7208/chicago/9780226137520.001.0001

Library of Congress Cataloging-in-Publication Data

Green, Nancy L., author.
The other Americans in Paris : businessmen, countesses, wayward youth, 1880–1941 / Nancy L. Green.
pages ; cm
Includes bibliographical references and index.
ISBN 978-0-226-30688-9 (cloth : alk. paper) — ISBN 978-0-226-13752-0 (e-book)
1. Americans—France—Paris—History—19th century. 2. Americans—France—Paris—History—20th century. 3. France—Civilization—American influences. I. Title.
DC34.5.A44G73 2014
305.813044'361—dc23
2013045373

♾ This paper meets the requirements of ANSI/NISO Z39.48-1992 (Permanence of Paper).

For Pierre, as always,
who made of me an American in Paris

Those were the caviar years.

OLGA GOW

[To] the casual visitor from American . . . [i]t is all exciting and amusing. . . .
Arriving in Paris, to live there, is quite another matter . . .

MARY BROMFIELD

I used to think that there was only two Real Drinks,
and those were Beer and Wisky. . . .
I still think there are only two . . .
Burgundy and Bordeaux.

LANSING WARREN

CONTENTS

"THE AMERICAN COLONY IS NOT WICKED"

FIGURE 2. "The American colony is not wicked." Davis mocked Americans in Paris, among other things, for pretending that they were naughtier than they actually were (from Richard Harding Davis, *About Paris*, with illustrations by Charles Dana Gibson, 1895).

INTRODUCTION

In March 1892, a crowd gathered to fête the departure of the US minister plenipotentiary to France, Whitelaw Reid. A seven-course farewell dinner was organized at the Hôtel Continental by American bankers, lawyers, and the famous dentist Dr. Thomas W. Evans, former confidant of Napoleon III. It was an important get-together of the elite of the American community in Paris. Influential journalists and businessmen such as "silver king" John Mackay and bankers William Seligman and John Harjes were there. Speeches praised the "American colony" itself, "the greatest we have in any foreign city." Toasts were raised to Reid's long, skillful negotiation of the importation of American pork products to France. The French minister of Foreign Affairs admitted, with a touch of humor, that Reid had been able to persuade France to open its borders even "at the risk of seriously displeasing poor little French pigs."[1] Another image of Americans in Paris comes into view, far from that of the Left Bank literati.

There is an untold tale of Americans in the City of Light, a history of expatriation that parallels the story of those who came to France for creative inspiration.[2] But with an important twist. While many Americans came to France in search of (European) civilization, many more came to disseminate the American version of it. Even as the writers and artists of the well-known "Lost Generation" expressed angst over modernity and America's role in it, other Americans overseas were participating in the debate over modernity in another way: by selling it or trying to.

Nine-tenths of the interwar Americans in Paris were gathering not in literary salons but in clubs and organizations important for any internationalized understanding of America's place in the world.[3] From the American Dental Club of Paris discussing the uses of Novocain to a plethora of business groups spreading the word about American cars and airplanes abroad, the story begins in the late nineteenth century and necessarily includes a heterogeneous cast of characters. The majority of Americans who came to Paris during the first half of the twentieth century comprised businessmen, lawyers, and newly minted American countesses married to titled Frenchmen, but also demobilized soldiers (white and black), former Red Cross nurses, and the occasional lost soul or downright crook. Most of them lived on the Right rather than the more artsy Left Bank of the Seine. Some followed spouses: American women married to American businessmen or to dashing foreigners; American Expeditionary Force (AEF) legionnaires who settled in France after World War I with local sweethearts. Many more were entrepreneurs or manufacturers' representatives living in France to peddle their wares. They came to France not to criticize America nor to escape it, but rather to spread its riches while making more. Neither railroad barons like their American counterparts in Mexico nor extraterritorial colonialists like Americans in China, these Americans in Paris created a different type of "colony,"[4] as they called it.

Doing business and busily socializing, the men of the American Chamber of Commerce, the legionnaires, the women of the Daughters of the American Revolution (DAR) chapters, and the members of the American Women's Club of Paris (AWCP) were all expatriates of another sort. They may have been less self-reflexive than the famous writers who wrote about their experience—they left fewer explicit tomes about it, unless you count the American Chamber of Commerce's *Bulletin*. They were nonetheless torn, as we will see, between flag-waving nostalgia for the United States and defense of the France they had made their home. From those who came before World War I to those who left at the outbreak of World War II, these Americans in Paris did not just become Americans there.[5] They brought America with them, they engaged with the locals, and they arguably set the stage for post–World War II "Americanization" abroad.

OLD WORLD AS NEW FRONTIER: "AMERICANIZATION"?

The distance between the Right Bank bankers and the Left Bank writers seems, at first glance, unbreachable. Yet the two banks were linked. As historian Warren Susman precociously suggested, an "economic invasion" of Paris helped form the background for the "cultural pilgrimage."[6] For him, the literary expatriates were part of a larger American interest in international affairs that preceded World War I and then was greatly increased by it; the 1920s were not as isolationist as traditionally described. By effect if not intent, the interwar writers formed part of a larger "American invasion" of Europe that was both military and economic before being cultural. As journalist Eric Sevareid had put it, as the Western frontier "closed," culture and business turned eastward with "the rediscovery of the European frontier."[7] After the Great War, the troops withdrew, but the number of visiting Americans to France grew, as did the permanent community. And the more Americans there were in Paris, the more interest there was back home for news from the European front, helping keep many a Left Bank journalist employed in Paris with time to spare for creativity. Without necessarily meeting in the same salons or cafés, the Left and Right Bank Americans were part of a common time-space capsule—even if for the most part, as we will see, they ignored if not disdained one another. And both cringed at the ubiquitous tourists.

The Right Bank "frontiersmen" furthermore provide a necessary prequel to later twentieth-century debates over "Americanization." The word has had very different meanings, starting from the early days of the American Republic, when it meant rendering American that which had been British. By the 1920s, Americanization in the United States meant vigorously trying to make Americans out of immigrants. Ultimately, however, these domestic definitions of the term have had to compete with a different, international one, referring to the impact of America on other parts of the world. Baudelaire had used the term "Americanized" in a pejorative sense as early as 1855, as part of his more general critique of the modern idea of progress at the world's fair that year. A decade later, the Goncourt brothers were even more explicit when referring to the upcoming Paris World's Fair of 1867: "[T]he Americanization of France" meant "industry prevailing over art, the steam thresher whittling down painting's pride of place."[8] Across the channel, the London *Times* wrote in 1860 "This Americanization is represented to us as the greatest of calamities."[9] However, by 1901 well-known British journalist William Thomas Stead, in *The Americanisation of the World* (immediately translated into German and French), argued that the trend was inevitable, and if you couldn't beat it, you should join it. Still, he ended his otherwise encouraging tome with a phrase from the scriptures: "What shall it profit a man, if he shall gain the whole world, and lose his own soul?"[10]

After World War I, Gertrude Stein was more prosaic. She defined the Americanization of France as "automobiles which kept [the French] from staying at home, cocktails, the worry of spending money instead of saving it . . . the introduction of electric stoves and the necessity of not cooking too long," along with "hygienes [sic], bath-tubs, and sport."[11] Some have suggested that even the literary expatriates did not just describe and decry Americanization; they participated in it by introducing jazz and cocktail parties to the French capital.[12] Malcolm Cowley, one of them, called the writers inadvertent "trade missionaries." But they were well outnumbered by the true manufacturers' representatives. Henry Luce famously called it "the American Century" in his 1941 article, but Gertrude Stein had already proclaimed it in 1931 in her own definitive manner: "America created the twentieth century."[13]

When did "Americanization" begin? By the 1930s the term meant industrialization and standardization, and it was seen as a threat to European economy and culture. Criticism proceeded apace as the deed followed the word. Americanization has been decried but also its limitations probed, its reception analyzed. The historians' debate has largely focused on the post–World War II period.[14] After the vigorous 1960s leftist critique of the seemingly inexorable American military-industrial spread, historians began to point out that Americanization abroad was actually welcomed by some, while it certainly was vigorously combated by others; in either case, it was not a tsunami simply rolling over unsuspecting folk. But the post-1945 attention to Americanization may help explain why the early twentieth-century business elites have been squeezed out of historical memory, between encomiums to the 1920s writers and copious criticism of the Marshall Plan (1948–52). The latter has functioned as a political, economic, and symbolic flash point for "seducing the French," as Richard Kuisel put it,[15] explaining everything from the Cold War to the demise of French film.

Yet the first half of the century was key in laying the groundwork. Interest has recently returned to the pre-1945 period, with the rediscovery of the "American empire" leading scholars to explore earlier periods for understanding the "spread of the American dream," to use Emily Rosenberg's felicitously facetious phrase.[16] French historians have for decades seen World War I as an important starting point for American influence in France.[17] The start of the "American century" depends, after all, on how it is defined: militarily, 1898 (the Spanish-American War); economically, 1900 (the American pavilion at the Paris World's Fair) or 1911 (when US exports to France decisively overtook US imports from France); culturally (Buffalo Bill's hugely successful Wild West Show, touring Europe from 1887 to 1906 and drawing three million people to the Eiffel Tower grounds in 1905); or all of the above in 1917, with US entry into World War I.[18] Older political and military forms of American empire-building were already being replaced in the early twentieth century by a more subtle economic and cultural web that Frank Costigliola has dubbed "awkward dominion." Cotton and oil, the meat and potatoes of nineteenth-century economic exports, were being transformed into what Victoria de Grazia has skillfully analyzed as the "Market Empire," often abetted by eager recipients.[19]

Which is not to say that it was irresistible. Locals put up resistance, while internationalists in the United States had not won the day there either. Britain and France continued to dispute colonial ventures and markets and to worry more about the flexing of German economic and military might. French government and business were by and large notoriously hard to seduce, and the entrance of American goods and way of life was slow and contested. At the same time, within the United States the internationalists were continually challenged throughout the interwar period by those who felt American investment should remain at home.[20] Yet by shifting the timeline and the scope, we can look at America's international reach in a new light. The first half of the twentieth century helps us understand the genesis of Americanization-in-the-making, furthermore in that most reluctant of places, France. At the same time, we can look beyond or below the business histories of large American corporations to follow some of the important facilitators.[21] An important category of actors has been missing, the "traveling salesmen," those manufacturers' representatives who negotiated the early export of goods and models on the ground, while locals put up a fight.

What about the banquets and the balls? While debates about America's "informal empire" have turned around the relative powers of government, business, and culture (the desire of reception), we also need a better understanding of the social relations as well as the tough negotiations encountered by those who accompanied the American Century abroad.[22] Overseas investments do not necessarily require businesspeople to budge: empire can spread through carefully appointed indigenous representatives. Exports, books, magazines, and films, not to mention two world wars and the Marshall Plan, have amply shown how culture and capital can flow without emigrant bearers. Yet, as one French sociologist has put it, "[k]nowing how to travel has always been a prerequisite for knowing how to do business."[23] Americans overseas have been both willing and unwitting participants in the story of America's global reach. Expatriates of all sorts carry their nation and their goods with them. American salesmen and their products were also often transformed in the process of crossing the seas. "Americanization" and its vulnerabilities need to be seen through their activities as well. How else to understand how Sun-Maid Raisins and Shredded Wheat ended up, for better or for worse, in Paris well before the Marshall Plan?

ELITE MIGRANTS

Not all American residents abroad were in the business of Americanizing the world. The creative classes shuddered at the thought. And even among the other nine-tenths of the American community in Paris, there were the idle rich along with the hardworking businessmen. Some were there to spend rather than sell. They were all part of an elite migration that has been largely missing from migration history.[24] The educated and the well-to-do, the rentiers, the professionals, and the managers abroad, along with their own "service" workers (journalists, grocery importers . . .) have been invisible due to their class and culture and due to the ways in which migration history has been defined as working-class history. Yet the executives and the socialites play their parts in a more encompassing history of mobility.

Elite migration has a much longer history than contemporary studies of expatriation imagine. While sociologists and anthropologists today have tracked the movements of the "new elites of globalization," business "expats," or "privileged migrants" retiring to the sun, there has been an assumption that they are a peculiarly late twentieth-century phenomenon.[25] However, globalization itself is hardly new (although everyone seems to have their favorite period for it, most noisily those who insist that it is a recent phenomenon). Globalizations keep being rediscovered, and elite migration has a long, untapped history. From the Roman Empire to Columbus, the great eras of discovery and the subsequent periods of empire-building, it seems naive to imagine that American businessmen and their acolytes invented the mobility of goods and services and a peripatetic way of life. The twentieth-century American exporters and importers follow in a long line of travelers and merchant capitalists who have plied the oceans ever since Marco Polo. At the start of the century, there were already American "emigrant empire-builders," as Donna Gabaccia has called them, in Asia and the Americas. In 1910, Elihu Root, former US secretary of state, heralded a brave new world of travel and business, speaking eloquently about "a new class of citizens traveling or residing abroad." Declining tariffs and the increasing facility of transportation and communication had "set in motion vast armies of travelers who are making their way into the most remote corners of foreign countries to a degree never before known."[26] And they especially headed eastward. Before the jetsetters, the early twentieth-century practitioners staked out new territory crossing the Atlantic by steamer—thrilled at its speed compared to that of the sailing ships that preceded them. European peasants were heading in one direction, American businessmen in the other.

Yet can we call the latter an "immigrant group" like the former? The term, with its lower-class connotation, is, of course, never used with regard to Americans abroad.[27] Three problems arise in calling Americans "immigrants" when they are settled away from home: they have never formed a mass migration; their perceived wealth hardly fits the usual image of "immigrants"; and a heartily proclaimed individualism has largely defied any group analysis. The very notion of Americans overseas as emigrants or immigrants seems, well, foreign. And Americans moving across the Atlantic in the opposite direction from most of their predecessors have surely wanted to distinguish themselves from the mass migrations of US history. Immigrants are ancestors who came to the United States, not people who left it. Or immigrants were the Italians and Poles who came to work in early twentieth-century France. Yet just as neighborhoods, clubs, language, and newspapers have all helped define immigrants *to* the United States or to France, similarly Americans in Paris have moved abroad to work, congregated with each other, set up their own churches and clubs, and often lived in proximity to one another. They certainly fulfilled Tocqueville's expectations of Americans by creating a host of voluntary associations in France. But what Tocqueville argued was an American trait is arguably a characteristic of most immigrant groups.[28] Even if, like most immigrants, many of the Americans in Paris planned to return home, in the meantime and for years on end they did battle with the French administration and the *garçons de café*, all the while pursuing their own agendas of business and social life.

That which does make Americans abroad different is that they are richer than most other foreigners, even if their money and their citizenship are not always shields against dislike or xenophobia. The idea of an elite migration tests our notion of "immigration" itself and questions what defines it. For the most part, a different class has meant a different terminology. *Expatriate*, a term once reserved for the literary bohemians, has evolved into *expats*, which has become a common word of choice to describe Americans and other elite migrants abroad. But in the first half of the twentieth century, Right Bank Americans rejected the term, as we will see. They were just the "American colony."

WHY LEAVE?

Before World War II, Paris housed the largest American community abroad. At its interwar peak in 1926, there were some forty thousand Americans in Paris, although the estimates vary widely.[29] Forty thousand is a sizable group indeed, far larger than most studies of the Lost Generation have envisioned, although tiny compared to the hundreds of thousands of Italians and Poles in France in the same period. Americans were not the only foreigners in Paris, nor were

they necessarily the richest; wealthy South Americans and British and Russian aristocrats all vied for status in the Paris salons.[30] Yet to themselves and
to French observers, the Americans' presence—swollen every summer with
hundreds of thousands of tourists—loomed increasingly large in the 1920s.[31]

The very reasons for Americans to settle in Paris nonetheless seemed contradictory to some astute observers. As Henry James wryly observed in 1878,
if America was really so terrific—as many Americans abroad kept insufferably
insisting—then why had they left?[32] To some it was obvious. Journalists and
writers waxed enthusiastic on the pull of Paris, as did former soldiers after the
war: the mythical attraction of the French capital, the liberty of life, the sense
of art, the beauty of the city. Clichés all. All true. But to explain Americans
abroad, more specific reasons were invoked. In the late nineteenth century, one
participant observer described wealthy Americans in Paris as men of means
and their families who had come to France for pleasure, health, and the education of their children, in that order.[33] By the 1920s journalists delighted
in mocking American culture to explain the departures. Alex Small, caustic
columnist for the *Chicago Tribune European Edition*, proffered a long list of
reasons, from worship of the past to sex. There were those who hankered for
life in a château and those who simply preferred monuments and ruins to skyscrapers and federal post offices. It was easier to be socially successful in Paris
than in Framingham, Massachusetts: no one asked embarrassing questions.
Small castigated the American notion that passion is a disease, and he included
a passing attack on "imbecile laws like the Mann Act" (prohibiting white slavery)! He blamed the problems in America on everything from public-spirited
women, whose pernicious benevolence was mischief-making, to the national
hunt for culture. He mocked public libraries, book clubs, and the hundreds of
so-called colleges and universities, collectively "keeping people in a constant
fever of improvement," which makes "social life an ordeal." Almost last, but not
least, religion, that "national obsession" ranging from intolerant Puritanism
to enlightened sceptics, also had its part in driving "a sane man . . . to France
where people do not touch the question." Small was not alone in mocking
home and praising France by comparison. Another journalist added that "Rotary meetings, searching unsuccessfully for parking places, progress and pep,"
along with the "insane hurry over nothing," were incentives for departure.[34]

Did the businessmen also come over in anticipation of a different lifestyle
away from the hustle and bustle? In the 1880s and 1890s, John Mackay commuted between his Nevada silver mines and his wife's Parisian salon, network-
ing at Franco-American banquets while plotting the cable lines that would
further connect the continents. After World War I, American businessmen

hurried over in great numbers, some to help reconstruct damaged French monuments but many others to take advantage of postwar opportunities and introduce American gadgets. And as the interwar years wore on, they came to sell airplane parts in anticipation of the next war. Adventurers of a new sort, American entrepreneurs, female philanthropists, and librarians combined business with a new lifestyle—and they too were presumably not impervious to Paris's charms. Not to mention, as one socialite added, that nowhere else in the world could the servant question be resolved so easily.[35] There were those who left home to hide from scandal or scrutiny. Others went to seek: work, culture, business opportunities, or bright lights.

Snide observers summed up the interwar motivations in three words: drink, love, money. There were those who went to slake the "Great Thirst" during Prohibition; the Temperance League, after all, *warned* that there were thirty-two thousand cafés, bars, and cabarets in Paris.[36] There were the men who returned to their wartime sweethearts and American women who continued to seek European titles. Then there were the presumed tax evaders, either unhappy after the first income-tax law was passed in 1913 or wanting to avoid Roosevelt's "soak the rich" taxes later. Above all, many went to Paris because it was cheap—as astonishing as that notion may seem today. With the exchange rate climbing from ten francs to the dollar in 1919 to twenty-five francs in 1933, it was a relative bargain to do business and live there—whether romantically starving in a garret, buying antiques to furnish a fancy villa, or hiring employees.

DEALING WITH THE "NATIVES"

Whatever the reasons for going—and staying—and whatever the impact Americans may have had on their new home, the Americans of Paris were never alone. More so than the writers, who kept largely to themselves, or the tourists in their buses, American residents dealt with the French on a daily basis, navigating a city justifiably imbued with its own sense of self-worth, its own divisions, and a changing political and economic landscape. From the false security of the Belle Époque through the shock of World War I, as "America" came into focus as a competitive power if not menace, many French greeted these and other newcomers eagerly, then cautiously and with increasing suspicion in the xenophobic 1930s. True, World War I saviors and even their corporate collaborators were initially welcomed with open arms. In the immediate postwar period France was clearly open to foreign investment. Yet by the mid-1920s Franco-American relations were on a decided roller-coaster, and Americans in Paris lived through fierce disputes over film quotas and the impact of a wildly gyrating dollar. The war debt question—American insistence on French payment; French foot-dragging on moral grounds—was a source of continual political quarreling, while tariff negotiations proved to be an economic battleground. Specific moments of tension alternated with official expressions of great amity. In October 1921, a bomb was sent to American Ambassador Herrick to protest Sacco and Vanzetti's conviction—although the incident was roundly criticized by most Parisians. In July 1926 there was practically a riot against Americans visitors as irate Parisians, infuriated by haughty tourists, chased them off their buses (see chapter 7 below)—it too downplayed in the French press. The following year, rallies—peaceful at first—again protested the fate of Sacco and Vanzetti. On August 23, 1927, the day of their execution, widespread anti-American rioting broke out. Yet that French ire against what was seen as a gross miscarriage of justice was bracketed by the assembling of delirious crowds to acclaim Charles Lindbergh's triumphant arrival at Le Bourget Airport in May of that year and the hearty welcome given to the twenty thousand American Legionnaires who came to the City of Light for their national convention in September (however drunken it turned out).[37]

The Americans of Paris lived through it all. Maybe they were impervious to some of it. How good, after all, was their French? We can assume that the American residents spoke better French than the American tourists, and that the Right Bank businessmen spoke better French than the Left Bank writers who were busy honing their English. According to Samuel Putnam, the hangers-on at Harry's Bar spoke better French than the literary crowd of the Left Bank, "whose French was for the most part execrable"; "[i]t was a standing jest among us that the best French spoken by an American in Paris was to be heard from the Negro bootblack (point of origin Harlem) in the basement of the American Express Company's building in the rue Scribe."[38] We have surprisingly little information on what people spoke (or how badly), but it seems to have varied greatly. The Princesse de Polignac, née Winnaretta Singer, daughter of the sewing-machine mogul, reigned over an avant-garde musical and artistic salon in Paris that would last half a century. Hearing her accent, a young French woman once asked her how long she had been in Paris. "Depuis trente ans je crois" (about thirty years) came the dry reply. [39] In business circles, those Americans with the best French were put forward as particularly valued go-betweens. John H. Spaulding, one of the founders of the American Dental Club of Paris, was appreciated as a "student of the French language" and therefore "one of our first professional ambassadors in France."[40] The American lawyers considered that the figurative and literal translation of law and practice was their stock in trade—and they charged accordingly. And then there were those, such as "dear old Mrs. Parsons, . . . who, after forty years in this country, spoke French with the greatest fluency, but with exactly the same accent with which she spoke American. You had to listen to her for a minute or so to realize whether she was still continuing to speak 'American' or French."[41]

Whatever the language, in salon settings, in business offices, or at the butcher's, national identities melded at best, collided at worst, for Americans living in Paris. Many consciously carried their capital and their culture on their sleeve, interacting with the locals as unremitting "Americanizers" bringing their own vision of modernity to the world. Others may have represented "the varied expressions of Americanism" abroad in spite of themselves, an "offhand imperialism" as Nora Faires called it.[42] As we shall see, it is not always clear who or what they represented—capital or country—and to whom, themselves or others. Many of the Americans worked hard at creating a community (chapter 1). People turned to the consulate in time of need to exercise the power of citizenship (chapter 2). All in all, the consulate records and law-firm archives show that Americans in Paris did not simply hang out in cafés. They worked, doing everything from fixing trucks to giving music lessons to forging business deals (chapters 4 and 5). Whatever their activities, they had to negotiate with the French, in love (chapter 3) as in money (chapter 5), while the poor among them gave the lie to the notion that all Americans are rich (chapter 6). Ultimately, they lived at the crossroads of various visions of Americans, of Americanization, and of their own conflicted ideas about the French (chapter 7). Wending their way between American and French business and social practices, overseas Americans have run the gamut from boisterous boosterism to active assimilation to foreign ways. The expatriate experiences explored here are a necessary complement to Gertrude Stein's inimitable salon.

DR. THOMAS W. EVANS.
From a photograph by Ch. Reutlinger taken about 1875.

To face p. 1.

FIGURE 3. Dr. Thomas Evans. From *The Memoirs of Dr. Thomas W. Evans: Recollections of the Second French Empire*, ed. Edward A. Crane (London: Unwin, 1905).

FIGURE 4. Bricktop. Photograph by Jack Robinson, The Jack Robinson Archive, LLC (http://www.robinsonarchive.com).

CHAPTER 1

The Not So Lost Generation

The "American Colony"

There is only one nation on earth . . .
whose citizens have imagined making
constant use of the right of association in civil life.

ALEXIS DE TOCQUEVILLE (1840)[1]

Benjamin Franklin slept here, Gertrude Stein wrote here, Ernest Hemingway drank here. There are many reminders in Paris that Americans have been coming to the city since Americans became Americans. Franklin, Thomas Jefferson, and John Adams along with Abigail have pride of first place in most anecdotal accounts of Americans in Paris. There could be a walking tour for every interest group: American diplomats and their mistresses, American lesbians of the Left Bank, African American Montmartre musicians, American historians and their archives . . . No commemorative plaque, however, announces that the Chase and Equitable Banks merged here, that Palmolive Société Anonyme was set up here, or that "here lived milk mogul George Hull," who provided the community with pasteurized goods. The working rich made up the largest segment of the Americans in Paris, but their activities were not exactly plaque-making.

True, people on plaques do not a community make. So how can we find the other Americans in Paris in the first half of the twentieth century, those who did not leave famous memoirs or novels? They called themselves and were called "the American colony." The term *colony* was not specific to these potential Americanizers abroad. It was used frequently from the nineteenth century on—until twentieth-century decolonization gave it a bad name—to describe groups of foreigners of all classes, in France and elsewhere. The American residents of Paris embraced the word to distinguish themselves from the ephemeral tourists, there today, gone tomorrow. When a mini-French riot broke out against American tourists flouting their dollars in 1926, the

American residents of Paris hastened to distance themselves from the traveling hordes.[2]

Neither tourists nor immigrants per se, the American residents in Paris nonetheless acted in many ways like other groups of foreigners in the city, busily creating clubs and associations to take care of their own, to socialize or pray together, or to celebrate the Fourth of July thousands of miles from home. Certainly there were many long-term inhabitants who never set foot in any community organization (just like other immigrants), but in good Tocquevillian fashion, the Americans in Paris banded together for everything from (weak) coffee and (layered) cake to lectures on Flaubert or Lafayette. They created organizations to take care of everything from health to welfare to faith but also to promote everything from American cars to planes to dental work. There were two chapters of the Daughters of the American Revolution and an American Dental Club of Paris. Many of the major American institutions existing in Paris today date to the nineteenth or early twentieth century, and, along with guidebooks and newspapers, they defined the American "colony," conscious of self yet not at all self-conscious.

A FAMOUS DENTIST AND CONFLICTING HEAD COUNTS

American travelers heading eastward in the early nineteenth century crossed paths with Alexis de Tocqueville. While this mobile noble Frenchman traveled to the United States in 1830 and scrutinized, approved, yet also warned about the American model of democracy, good American democrats were traveling in the other direction. More than one observer noted the irony of Americans' fascination with the European aristocracy, always delighted to be invited to partake in the pomp.[3]

Paris is "invaded by a crowd of Americans," wrote one mid-nineteenth-century French observer. Yet it is difficult to pin down precise statistics, given the fluctuating character of arrivals and departures. Approximately thirty thousand Americans visited France between 1814 and 1848 (well outnumbered by the British), yet perhaps only three hundred families were settled in Paris in the mid-1840s. A decade later, the American consul there estimated that one to three thousand Americans were residing in or touring the city.[4]

To understand the early American colony in Paris, there is no better hero than a dentist. Thomas W. Evans was a community builder who at the same time epitomizes the American elite hobnobbing with French nobility. Personal dentist to the French emperor, Evans was not the first American dentist in Paris. He went there in 1847 to join the thriving practice of Cyrus Starr Brewster, formerly of South Carolina. But Brewster was out of the office one day when Louis Napoleon Bonaparte got yet another of his frequent toothaches. Evans went to his side. With his discreet, efficient manner and his wonderful gift for relieving toothaches, Evans became not only the regular dentist of the then-president and soon to be self-appointed second emperor of France but his confidant as well. By 1850, Evans had set up his own practice down the street from Brewster's on the fashionable rue de la Paix. The "father of gold fillings"[5] became a Europe-renowned expert for his use of nitrous oxide as an anesthetic and his agility at straightening crooked royal teeth. His access to the mouth—and ear—of Louis Napoleon meant that this Philadelphian was apparently able to discourage Napoleon III (as he became known once he established the Second Empire) from recognizing the Confederacy during the American Civil War, although the majority of Americans in Paris at the time sided with their native South. Evans even made the American consuls and ministers in France a wee bit jealous of his dental-chair diplomacy. His faithfulness to the American republic was equaled only by his fidelity to the French imperial family. In his most shining moment, during the Franco-Prussian War—as recounted ad nauseam afterward to friends and acquaintances—Evans helped the empress escape to England on September 4–5, 1870, after her husband, the First Patient, was captured at Sedan. After the fall of the Second Empire, Evans still retained his royal clientele in Europe, and even the now-republican French forgave him his role in the empress's getaway.

Evans appears again and again not just as dashing dentist but as community leader. In 1868 he created the *American Register*, a newspaper that would last almost fifty years, and he was part of the initiative to set up both major American churches that still throne over Parisian avenues today. Not surprisingly, he began the American Dental Club of Paris. But first he was instrumental in presenting the American ambulance system at the Paris World's Fair of 1867 (although the official American Sanitary Commission considered him to be something of an expatriate arriviste in doing so without having been asked) and then helping implement it during the Franco-Prussian War. The French newspapers were generous in their praise of wealthy Americans who could have fled to safer places but remained to help, and they marveled at the cheerful atmosphere of the American hospital with "its daring reliance on fresh air, since the French were normally paralyzed by the fear of air currents."[6]

When the childless grand man of the American community died in Paris in 1897, several months after his wife, his will generously reflected his Franco-American interests. "Handsome Tom" had taken on a French mistress, one of the *grandes horizontales* (courtesans). But Tom was tolerant, and some of her other lovers had become his friends, such as the French symbolist poet Sté-phane Mallarmé. A handsome sum thus went to Méry Laurent, while 100,000 francs were set aside for Americans stranded in Paris. The bulk of Evans's fortune went to his hometown, Philadelphia, as did he, for burial beside his wife. The resulting dental school and museum at the University of Pennsylvania exist to this day. As an American newspaper had described the transnational dentist: "He has the whiskers of a German, the accent of an Englishman, the manners of a French man [but] he has creditably clung to the nationality that permitted his success."[7]

Friend of French royalty yet creator of American institutions in Paris, Evans represented one of the major contradictions of the early Americans in Paris: democrats' fascination with nobility. Evans's longevity allowed him to span three French regimes, from the short-lived Second Republic (1848–51) through the twenty years of the Second Empire, into the first twenty-five years of the ultimately long-lasting Third Republic. He, like other members of the early American colony, was by turn anxious and alarmed by the jam-packed events of 1870–71. From the declaration of the Third French Republic on September 4, 1870, through the Commune (March 18–May 28, 1871) to the consolidation of the Third Republic, US northerners and southerners, the wealthy American elite invited to court and the more middle-class American residents, reacted in different ways. The court hangers-on, such as Evans, would long be nostalgic for the empire. But Elihu Washburne, the American minister in Paris at the time, was positively thrilled at the declaration of the Third Republic: "I am so tickled at what has taken place that I can hardly contain myself. . . . Only think, breakfasting in an Empire and dining in a Republic, all so quick as to make your head swim."[8] Once the Third Republic settled in, the theme of amity between the French and American Republics would become a staple slogan of the American community in Paris—along with an abiding interest in noble titles.

After the commotion, travel to France resumed, and the American colony grew. If there were some five thousand permanent American residents in Paris in 1870–71, by the turn of the century the *American Register* trumpeted on its undoubtedly overly generous masthead: "30,000 Americans Reside in Paris."[9] The American residents became an ever more visible component of late nineteenth-century Paris, leading one American critic to lament the fact that they stuck to themselves: "They remain what they are, and no matter how long it may have been since they ceased to be Americans, they do not become Frenchmen. They are a race all to themselves; they are the American Colony."[10]

FROM *RENTIERS* TO DOUGHBOYS

Consider a luggage theory of mobility: we are what we pack. If we could peek inside the steamer trunks, we would no doubt see confirmation of the changing social and class composition of Americans traveling to France. Benjamin Franklin's and Thomas Jefferson's trunks included official documents and letters of representation. Edith Wharton's valises were presumably filled with literature and writing books. But there were also the likes of Mrs. Mackay, "bonanza princess" thanks to her husband's silver mines, her trunks filled with gowns and jewels. She became a well-known *salonnière* in Paris before 1900, bringing together American, French, and other European elites in her 17th arrondissement villa.[11] By the early twentieth century, however, more and more suitcases were filled with commercial order books and accounting pads accompanying eager industrialists across the seas.

After World War I, the rentiers of the turn of the century continued to come, but a veritable onslaught of businessmen, artists, writers, and teachers changed the makeup of the American colony. Historian Harvey Levenstein has well described the shifting crowds of American tourists in France, and these shifts would hold true for the residential community as well. After mid-nineteenth-century upper-class single young men set off for months if not years on a Grand Tour for cultural enrichment, increasing numbers of upper-middle-class tourists began making the journey. Mothers and daughters started coming for several months of art, music, and shopping. But already by the 1890s there were complaints that American tourists were everywhere ("vulgar, vulgar, vulgar," commented Henry James).[12] The real change came with World War I. The doughboys, both white and black, led the way for "the invasion of the lower orders."[13] Levenstein tells a tale of changing patterns of tourism in which the elite American tourist metamorphoses into the nouveau-riche and then middle-class shopper in an inexorable march toward tour buses.

While tourists came in droves beginning at the turn of the century, the permanent community also grew. Perhaps as many as 100,000 American tourists visited Paris in 1906, and the number rose to some 300,000 per year in the 1920s.[14] The figures for more permanent residents vary greatly, given that immigration and emigration data rarely coincide, nor did city and national counts. Whereas the French census counted almost 18,000 Americans in France at the peak of their statistical presence (1926), the Paris municipal council had estimated three years earlier that there were 32,000 in Paris alone. This made Americans the sixth largest foreign group in the capital, after Belgians,

Italians, Russians, Swiss, and the British.[15] After the stock market crash sent many Americans scurrying home, the US State Department counted 19,466 Americans in France in 1933, but apparently only 11,878 of them had French residence cards that year.[16] That would mean there were (at least) 7,588 American illegal aliens. Contemporary newspaper reports estimated that there were up to 40,000 Americans settled in Paris in the late 1920s, and that has become the favorite figure of historians.[17]

The changing composition of American visitors, in addition to reflecting social change at home, was due to both technological advances in transatlantic travel and World War I. As steamships replaced sailing ships, the length of time needed to cross the Atlantic plummeted. For the steamer set, "New York's only a week away." And as competition increased, the liners lowered their fares. The shift in the American colony was noticed by American and French observers alike, as salaried men coming for a vacation joined gentlemen of leisure. But business would soon take precedence over pleasure.[18]

Then came the war and free trans-Atlantic crossings—for doughboys. World War I brought yet another social class of Americans to France. As the song goes, "How ya gonna keep 'em down on the farm (after they've seen Paree)," "They'll never want to see a rake or plow / And who the deuce can parleyvous a cow? . . . Imagine Reuben when he meets his Pa / He'll kiss his cheek and holler 'OO-LA-LA!'" The song was not just a joking symbol of postwar malaise. As one veteran explained, once "the first excitement of home-coming was over, and when we ceased to be heroes, thoughts turned toward the fair land of France and the Second American Invasion was on."[19] For black soldiers returning home to American racism, glimpses they'd had of an (imagined?) race-free French society took many of them back to France after the war as well. Not to mention the American women who went over during the war as nurses, canteen workers ("serving doughnuts to doughboys," as Susan Zeiger has put it), YMCA hostesses, or Salvation Army lassies, some of whom also stayed on.[20] The US army's *Stars and Stripes* magazine, after all, had encouraged soldiers to appreciate *la belle France*, the better to win the war, and when transportation bottlenecks meant long delays between the armistice of November 1918 and the return home (as late as August 1919 for some), the US government organized travel tours and enrollment in French civilization classes to occupy the soldiers. Even French department stores did their bit to help US soldiers get along in France; one printed a brochure explaining, among other things, how to pronounce *merci* (Mare-see). After the war, an ever more mixed crowd of energetic doughboys, the occasional nurse, and busy businessmen would constitute the new "vast armies" of industrious Americans abroad.[21]

CREATING COMMUNITY

"The American colony of Paris was an enclave in which everybody knew everybody else and wanted to know everything that happened to them, particularly if it were scandalous."[22] Yet before exploring how the community coalesced through its bricks-and-mortar or stone-and-spire institutions, we do well to take a detour through the guidebooks and directories the Americans published. The books helped to construct the colony through their very compilation. They helped the Americans of Paris recognize one other, find each other, and gossip about each other.

Besides filling the cavities of the colony, Dr. Evans began the list craze, although he was certainly not the first of his social class to want to identify and be identified in a social registry or blue book. His newspaper, the *American Register*, like other social who's whos, printed long lists of Americans, both traveling and in residence throughout Europe. While ship arrival lists tried to capture the "floating" population, as one early traveler aptly called it, other directories tried to pin down the permanent population. Albert Sutliffe, correspondent for the *San Francisco Chronicle*, underlined the new growth of the late nineteenth-century community when he published *The Americans in Paris* in 1887. It listed addresses along with days for calling: the Evanses received on Sundays and Tuesdays, Mrs. Mackay on Tuesdays . . .[23]

The most impressive and comprehensive effort to delineate the American crowd was carried out at the height of the community's presence in interwar France. Not surprisingly, it came from one of the most important American organizations around, the American Chamber of Commerce (ACC), about which more anon. By the time the ACC published its first directory of *Americans in France* in 1925, the complexion of the colony had changed. Whereas Sutliffe had addressed his book to "the lady of fashion as well as to the general reader,"[24] the Chamber of Commerce's listing, not surprisingly, had the businessman more in mind. Of the almost 700 pages of the improved 1926 edition, 130 pages listed American commercial businesses represented in France. A 20-page American Professional List covered eighteen categories from accountants to writers, not to mention two geologists. Even more pages were devoted to a community roster. An impressive list of American clubs and organizations was followed by a 185-page American Residential List, complete with home and business addresses, occasional summer residences, college degrees, and US and French club memberships.[25] The directories, which were published until World War II, show a community-in-the-making while having two audiences in mind. They were a people-locater for the Americans themselves; even the consulate used them when searching for missing persons. The directories clearly aimed at French businessmen as well, serving as a window onto American business opportunities. They thus ultimately provided information on the French for Americans, on Americans for the French, and of course on Americans for Americans.

The directories were an instant success and a profit-maker for the ACC, abundantly illustrated with French and American luxury item advertisements. According to the publication's own humble estimate in its prefaces, it was blazing a new trail to aid American business in France while serving the whole American community and all who came into contact with it. Not to mention latter-day historians. People appear, disappear, and reappear in the directories. Many of the Americans in Paris we know most about are not listed there. Children are largely invisible, by either design or thoughtlessness, or the fact that Paris was really seen as a town for adults. Other silences may be telling. Edith Wharton is included, but the more wandering Ernest Hemingway and F. Scott Fitzgerald are not. Gertrude Stein is listed; Alice B. Toklas is not. African American painter Henry Ossawa Tanner is there, but Josephine Baker is conspicuously absent. As is Ida Treat, resident of Paris for over twenty years, polyglot translator from Russian (D. S. Mirsky's biography of Lenin) and English (Claude McKay's *Banjo*) into French, both in tandem with her husband, French communist leader Paul Vaillant-Couturier. Others whom we know were in Paris (such as my great-uncle) never appear: Alexander Zukovsky, Russian-born concert violinist, apparently preferred playing violin with Prokofiev to being part of the American colony.[26] While the directories purported to be a guide to the entire community, and they served as a way to find Man Ray as well as the head of International Harvester's branch in France, it was not just a question of fame, fortune, or length of stay. One had to want to let one's whereabouts be known. And thousands did.

CREATING VARIETY

However, "[c]olonies are proverbially inharmonious," as Sutliffe complained in 1887.[27] Community creation does not mean that everyone gets along or comes along to every ball or club event—a fact that we need to remember for any community study. The Americans were no exception, and regional, professional, and racial differences divided the Americans in Paris. As John Russell Young, on his travels around the world with General Grant, keenly observed in 1877:

> The [Paris] colony has class distinctions and draws lines. There is the old resident and the new resident; the American in trade; the idle American; the

American who speaks French; the one who does not, but always buys a French newspaper and pretends to read it in public in a dazed condition . . . the American who wears the red ribbon of the Legion of Honor; the democrat, who despises all such aristocratic nonsense, but who would give a good slice of his income to be able to wear it without danger from the police.[28]

Conceding that it was normal that Bostonians largely spent time with Bostonians and Philadelphians with Philadelphians, Sutliffe spent several pages responding to the allegation that Americans were "not sufficiently gregarious" among themselves and admonished those who lapsed into "undignified abuse of one another." Ultimately Sutliffe concluded that "unity in variety" was part of the American national character. But he clearly hoped to remedy internal divisions through the very existence of his directory.[29]

Regional and ethnic variety only grew after World War I. American names ranged from Anderson to Gagliaducci to Zuckerman, "*Mayflower* descendants and Sons of the Steerage."[30] After the mid-nineteenth-century southerners, late-nineteenth-century writers and businessmen alike came more frequently from the Atlantic states. But after 1920, "rootless" expatriates as well as many entrepreneurs came also from the Middle and farther West.[31] Gertrude Stein loved this particular aspect of the world war and "always said the war was so much better than just going to America. Here you were with America in a kind of way that if you only went to America you could not possibly be." The soldiers, in all their geographical diversity, impressed the Radcliffe-trained intellectual: "americans just americans, the kind that would not naturally ever have come to Europe. It was quite a thrilling experience."[32]

However, by the 1920s the greatest divide among Americans in Paris was arguably the Seine. The Left Bank of the river was crawling with American writers and intellectuals, some with means (from Natalie Barney or Nancy Cunard's great wealth to Gertrude Stein's more solidly middle-class fortune) but most without. The Right Bank was where the much more well-heeled crowd defined and largely confined itself. Two caveats regarding this sociogeographical divide must, however, be kept in mind. First, neither the Left Bank literati nor the Right Bank businessmen formed a homogeneous group. If each bank of the Seine had its character, each also had its characters and its rivalries. Left Bank intellectuals were hardly a unified lot, despite what some descriptions of the literary salons would have us believe. Historian Shari Benstock emphasized long ago the *salonnières*' separate circles. Gertrude Stein and Natalie Barney rarely met. French artists and musicians had to tread lightly from one American salon to another. As for the Left Bank men, Miller, who arrived later (in 1930), didn't socialize with the other white American writers. He hated Hemingway (whom he considered a fake hard guy) and disdained Joyce (as too literary). As Claude McKay cogently summed it up: "In Montparnasse generally writers and artists plunged daggers into one another."[33] We will see ample evidence of variety on the Right Bank of the Seine as well.

Second, to state that the river was a divider of Americans does not mean that there were no crossovers. The two social groups represented by the two banks of the Seine did on occasion meet. Walter Berry, "lawyer and man of letters," as Proust called him, encouraged Harry Crosby to give up banking for poetry, which he did.[34] But perhaps no one epitomizes the marriage of money and bohemia better than Peggy Guggenheim, whose collection of artworks was perhaps outdone only by her collection of lovers and husbands (the writer John Holms, the communist Douglas Garman, the playwright Samuel Beckett, the artist Yves Tanguy, the surrealist Max Ernst . . .). Her first husband, the novelist, poet, and painter Laurence Vail, had a father who was a painter and a mother who was a member of the DAR and a pillar of the American colony in Paris. Yet Laurence chose to live *la vie bohème* on the Left Bank, and Peggy followed him there, to her mother's chagrin: she would have preferred that her daughter marry a nice Jewish millionaire. By Peggy's own account, the bohemian life was not for her; after soirées at their place, she would go around the apartment with Lysol, worried about catching some venereal disease.[35]

For the most part, however, Right Bank bankers and Left Bank writers rarely met. "Hemingway and Fitzgerald? Sure. I knew them, but they didn't belong to my world," wrote Thérèse Bonney, famous American photographer of French art and architecture in the interwar period: "I lived in a world where people earned their living."[36] According to Al Laney, who worked for the Paris *Herald* from 1924 to 1930, Americans in Paris were divided into the self-appointed Young Intellectuals of the Left Bank and the "non–Young Intellectuals," also known as Philistines, who were skeptical of the former and their literary reviews whose titles eschewed capital letters.[37] Or as one American doctor in Paris described the Montparnasse expatriates, they "wrote experimental novels that one day would give some of them income-tax headaches."[38] The Americans in Paris were a diverse and divided lot. Activities, social class, race, and age all led them to different parts of the city.

"PARIS NOIR"[39]

If the river largely divided rich American businessmen and rentiers on the Right Bank from the more impecunious writers and artists on the Left Bank, it also separated the white writers in Left Bank Montparnasse from the black musicians in Montmartre. Before World War I, Montmartre had been the French artists' quarter, but after the war avant-garde artists relocated to the Montparnasse area. Montmartre, with its cheap hotels and dubious reputation for drunken dancing and tourist traps that the police chief hoped to clean up, was now "available."[40] African American musicians made it their own and created their own neighborhood there. But even after F. Scott Fitzgerald discovered Montmartre and brought his Montparnasse friends to the cabarets, black and white Americans maintained largely separate existences in Paris.

The history of black Americans in interwar Paris is both the story of those who came and what they did and a double story of race relations: of American blacks and American whites and of American blacks and French whites. American racism in France could mean white Americans sometimes scuffling with blacks on café terraces or their trying to convince the French of the dangers of black-white fraternization. An infamous 1918 wartime memorandum labeled "Secret Information concerning Black American Troops" aimed at convincing French officers that they needed to respect the American idea that the Negro was a menace to the white race. The memo included a series of recommendations, from not shaking hands with Negroes (outside of military service requirements) to preventing any intimacy between white women and black men. The memo was purportedly issued by the French Military Mission, but it was a vehicle for American racism and ultimately denounced as such.[41]

American racism also played itself out in cafés and bars when white Americans objected to the presence of blacks in the restaurants they frequented, especially if they were with white women.[42] They tried to get French restaurateurs to throw them out. Brawls sometimes ensued, and the police were called. In one high-profile incident, the former boxer, war hero, and now Montmartre cabaret manager Eugene Bullard had apparently jostled a white patron at the Café de Paris. A white American officer punched Bullard twice, and Bullard had to be hospitalized. In another incident involving Bullard and two white Americans, the *Chicago Tribune European Edition* concluded: "Dozens of Negroes are now said to be infesting Montmartre."[43] Examples of white Americans' racism in France were repeated over and over. As Josephine Baker recounted to Henry Louis Gates Jr. half a century after the fact: "I was afraid to go into prominent restaurants in Paris. Once I dined in a certain restaurant with friends. An American lady looked at our table and called the waiter. 'Tell her to get out,' the lady said. 'In my country, she is belonging only in the kitchen.' The French management asked the American lady to leave."[44]

To the extent that the French took the side of American blacks, the moral of these stories helped create the image of a color-blind France. It was not the little-surprising news that white Americans "had carried . . . the seeds of their poisonous hate" abroad (McKay).[45] It was the more unexpected fact that the French resisted. While some café and restaurant owners did pander to the racist demands of their big-spending American clientele, and while not all black Americans were Josephine Baker, stories of ordinary restaurateurs defending ordinary black patrons made the rounds. And one oft-quoted comment tells of the French village mayor who, after a group of rowdy white Americans disrupted his town, said: "Take back these soldiers and send us some real Americans, black Americans."[46] The French Parliament had publicly denounced the 1918 military memorandum and ordered copies of it burned. Several years later, an official statement by the French government reminded Americans that they were guests in another country and had to abide by France's rules, which did not permit ejecting people from restaurants because of their color.[47] The French press also often took the side of black Americans. In the first Bullard incident, one French paper editorialized that "[a] Negro has the right to take a beer with everyone else in a café."[48] In 1929, in a pointed critique, French Caribbean writer René Maran returned to the scandalous 1918 circular, warning of the dangers of the "Americanization" of France through the importation of racism.[49]

Whether American blacks (or whites) followed the French press or French law, the reports they sent back home often stressed what they could see and feel on the Paris streets, a marked contrast to Jim Crow America. And it was the meaning and the memory of this difference that stuck. African Americans were unaware of how the French segregated their colonial workers during the war. In France at the height of its colonial power, despite its paternalistic disdain for its colonial subjects, nationality seemed to trump race when it came to black Americans, making them too a sort of "elite migration," privileged by citizenship over color. However "complex and flawed," the myth of a color-blind France would help perpetuate a black pilgrimage there for decades to come.[50]

The fact that many white Americans carried their racism with them abroad undoubtedly played a part in the creation of a separate black American community, as Michel Fabre and Tyler Stovall have shown, from the well-known late nineteenth-century African American painter Henry Ossawa Tanner to the famous post–World War II writers, Baldwin, Wright, and beyond. Tanner was already listed as one of the leading members of the Anglo-American Colony of Paris in a 1905 *Who's Who*; he stayed on after World War I and received the French Legion of Honor.[51] The French experience informed the art of many African American artists who lived for a time in Paris: Hale Woodruff, Lois Mailou Jones, Nancy Elizabeth Prophet, Augusta Savage. Others were inspired by the African and Antilles worlds they encountered in the French capital, and others still lived in Paris without referring to France in their art or writings.[52]

African American writers in the interwar period did not necessarily come to Paris specifically to escape racism (as they did in the 1950s), but as James Weldon Johnson put it in 1905, in an oft-cited phrase, arriving in France gave him the sensation of feeling "free to be merely a man."[53] As Stovall has pointed out, the politicization of American blacks in Paris and a greater awareness of France's own race relations occurred largely after World War II, when a literary community of black writers congregated on the Left Bank around the Café Tournon.[54] The interwar black writers rarely stayed beyond a year or two (like many of the white writers). Countee Cullen, a great Francophile and the most monied of the African Americans in Paris, enrolled at the University of Paris in 1928 and 1929, initially, like others, on a Guggenheim scholarship. Langston Hughes was in Paris only from February through July 1924 and again in 1938. His public image of Paris ("I felt sure I would fall in love with Paris once I saw it") was more muted in his private correspondence, where he initially complained that there was no hot water and no jobs and counseled others not to come. Claude McKay (originally from Jamaica) stayed the longest in France, from 1923 to 1933, although he was in Paris only in 1924 and 1929. His famous novel *Banjo* is set in the sunny south of Marseille, whose "motley" character of "black and brown humanity" he preferred to that of Paris.[55] A Marxist who had previously traveled to Russia, McKay was skeptical of French color-blindness. He was also one of the few African Americans who did frequent the Montparnasse cafés and socialized with white American expatriates, although he did not identify with their angst, since he had plenty of his own. As he put it in his autobiography, "The majority of them were sympathetic toward me. But their problems were not exactly my problems. They were all-white with problems in white which were rather different from problems in black."[56]

At first glance, it seems that Josephine Baker did not have a "black problem." By far the most visible and well-loved African American in interwar Paris, she seemed to revel in the primitivism that, thanks to her signature banana skirt and her talent, made her renowned. Like Edith Wharton or Gertrude Stein and Alice B. Toklas, Baker was one of the Americans in Paris who stayed the longest, and like them, she mixed equally with French society. Famous right from her début in the Revue Nègre in 1925, Baker ultimately became a chic French star dressed in the latest Parisian fashion. She was decorated for her

Resistance work in World War II and hailed, from the French government to French communists, as a symbolic counterweight to American racism. After World War II, she adopted a dozen children of different backgrounds and set up a multicultural utopian community on her property in the Dordogne in center-west France. As Bennetta Jules-Rosette puts it in her wonderful biography of Baker, Baker was not simply used by her lover(s) and manager(s); she staked out her own unique identity in a twentieth-century France coming to grips ever so slowly with its colonial population.[57]

How can we find the other, less well-known African Americans in interwar Paris? Besides the writers and artists, there was, as McKay reported, "an army of school teachers and nurses, Negro students, Negro communists," and a "Negroid elite" in the city in the late 1920s.[58] Tyler Stovall has estimated that there were several hundred African Americans living in Paris between the wars.[59] Few American blacks, however, seem to have signed in to the ACC's *Americans in France* directory or shown up in law firm or consular archives. But then how can we know for sure? African American names are not identifiably "ethnic." It is, however, entirely plausible that black Americans abroad had not come to Paris to spend time with rich white Americans, and that they were even less inclined than the whites to turn to the consulate for help.

Beyond Baker and the writers, Paris provided jobs for jazzmen. The African American community, from down-on-their-luck trumpeters to boldly dressed "chocolate dandies" strutting along the boulevards, was largely centered on the clubs, the cabarets, and the inexpensive residential hotels of Montmartre, painted by some black artists such as Palmer Hayden and Archibald Motley. The nightclubs of Bullard, Ada Smith (known as Bricktop), and Baker formed the heart of the neighborhood: Le Grand Duc, Bricktop's, and Chez Josephine, along with Florence Jones's Chez Florence. As the French became fascinated with jazz for its sound and its meaning—liking jazz was also a way of criticizing American racism—the new music became wildly popular. This drew jazz musicians of renown to Paris and led others to take up the trumpet in order to stay on. But as Bricktop says more than once in her memoirs, black women were few.[60]

The white American writers in Montparnasse eventually "discovered" Montmartre just as the Greenwich Village crowd had discovered Harlem. Cole Porter was one of Bricktop's most faithful fans and customers until he left in 1937. Black musicians played at the American Hospital nurses' graduation, and, as the DAR minutes put it, "a negro orchestra softly played American airs" at one of the chapter meetings.[61] But for the most part, white and black Americans in Paris had separate worlds. As Stovall has argued, black Americans were escaping the American ghetto, yet they re-created their own community in Paris.

OF PRAYERS, BOWLING ALLEYS, AND STETHOSCOPES

The center of the American colony was neither Montmartre nor the Montparnasse of the Lost Generation writers. It was located in the myriad social clubs and organizations that helped "resolve the problem of strangeness"[62] and were situated for the most part on the Right Bank of the Seine, in the more expensive neighborhoods. Many of them would prove amazingly tenacious, lasting until today.

The official headquarters of Americans in Paris of course were and are the embassy and the consulate. Today's building, just off the place de la Concorde, opened in 1934. Not all immigrants frequent their consulates voluntarily—refugees stay away, and some Left Bank writers made it a point of honor not to call on the embassy. However, the American Embassy in Paris served as a center for the colony in two ways: as home to governmental institutions that employed a number of Americans in Paris, and in the person of the ambassador. Titular head of many American organizations, making appearances at balls and talks, serving as official and unofficial counselor to businessmen and clergymen alike, the American ambassador to France has always been an important man[63] about town. The early twentieth-century diplomats were no exception. And the ambassadors carefully alternated their presence at Memorial Day and Thanksgiving services between the two major American churches in town.

Still, it is the impressive plethora of voluntary associations set up by Americans in Paris that are key to understanding the community. Their activities ranged from health to welfare, from birth to death. Most serviced both residents and tourists, with occasional tension between the different needs of these groups. Many were open to the French as visitors or even associate members. Some could best be described as "missionary" institutions seeking converts to the American way of life or business, such as the YMCA and the Rotary Club, almost all of whose members were French.[64] The organizations of interest here, though, are those that structured the American community itself. Created by Americans in Paris for themselves, they are witness to the growth of the colony from which they sprang and which they helped consolidate. Tocqueville, theoretician of Americans' propensity for club-itis, would hardly have been surprised.

"One may live in Paris and feel that he is in a world without souls," worried one of the first American pastors in Paris.[65] True to supposed character, the two earliest American organizations in Paris were churches.[66] Being Protestant in a Catholic country beset by its own recurrent religious conflicts was not easy. The first building permit (21 rue de Berri) for American Protestants was issued in 1857 with the proviso that there be no preaching in the French language, in order to prevent proselytizing to the locals. By 1931 this chapel had become the Protestant ecumenical American Church in Paris, located in a new, imposing, neo-Gothic building on the quai d'Orsay. It included a social hall for residents and tourists and facilities intended to attract students and others: a gym, a theater stage, and a bowling alley—that great symbol of American togetherness, where leagues from the American consulate, the American Express office, the American Legion, and the Bankers' Trust all converged.

But no successful operation is without its competition. In 1859, at the Christmas service on the rue de Berri, an "undignified and unchristian" dispute had broken out, prefiguring tensions that would split the interdenominational church over the form of service to be used. Separate Episcopalian services had been held in Paris since 1847, and in 1859 the parish of the Holy Trinity was formally opened to "all Americans and friends irrespective of church ties at home." The current impressive building on avenue George V (then avenue Alma) was consecrated on Thanksgiving Day 1886, and in 1922 the Church of the Holy Trinity became the American Cathedral of the Holy Trinity. Funeral services for both Edith Wharton (in 1937) and the Jewish-born Gertrude Stein (in 1946) were held at the "very tony" cathedral, testimony to its centrality for the American community, however religiously defined.[67]

The sources are discreet, but there seems to have been a healthy rivalry over American souls between the two major American churches. They both functioned as community centers for American residents as well as travelers, while watching out for errant students and pleasure-seeking expatriates, whom Rev. Cochran chastised from the pulpit for having lost their spirituality in the crossing.[68]

Students in particular, neither tourists nor long-term residents, were ubiquitous in the City of Light. They gathered in the Left Bank Montparnasse area, where art classes were plentiful and apartments cheap. They came, like many of the writers and artists, for several months or a year or two. For the most part they were white, although there were also black students, on fellowships or on their own. (Anna Julia Cooper became the first African American woman to earn a doctorate, at the Sorbonne in 1925, with a dissertation critical of the French attitude toward slavery during the French Revolution.)[69] American students had been coming to Paris since medical students had flocked to the French universities in the mid-nineteenth century. However, by the beginning of the twentieth century, they came especially for the arts. According to a 1903 census, over one thousand American students in Paris had come from all over the country—from Yonkers, New York; to Elgin, Illinois; to Oakland, California. Painting and architecture (for the men), singing and French (for the women), were the most popular areas of study.[70] Students also enrolled in French faculties of arts and letters, encouraged to do so by no less than the famous French sociologist Émile Durkheim. An "ardent apostle of international education" who thereby hoped "to offset German academic influence," Durkheim headed two committees that recommended the recruitment of foreign students, and he proposed a year-long introductory course on French history and civilization, which became a precursor to the Sorbonne's Cours de civilisation française that continues today.[71] American students also attended the new summer programs set up by American universities in the 1920s, and a dormitory for American students, the Fondation des États-Unis, was opened as part of the Cité internationale universitaire de Paris in 1930, although in keeping with the purpose of the CIUP, it was dedicated more to international peace than to purely American socializing.[72]

Yet parents, moralists, and the American churches in Paris worried about their youth abroad. Dr. Evans had helped found a hostel for American women art students in the 1880s. In 1891, Elizabeth Mills (Mrs. Whitelaw) Reid created what would become Reid Hall, to house women art students, a "perfect blending of seriousness and charm," as one French abbot commented. It still serves Americans-abroad programs today.[73] Both of the major American churches set up programs to save the souls of wayward youth from the dangers of the Left Bank. The American Cathedral's efforts in particular ultimately metamorphosed into a veritable Parisian institution, the American Students' and Artists' Center, set up in 1922. By the late 1920s, its Thursday afternoon teas attracted fifty to sixty people—especially after it upgraded the cakes—and Sunday concerts and dances drew good crowds of two to three hundred. Books and records were available on the premises, although, as someone complained, the musical offerings needed to be updated: the most recent record was "Yes, We Have No Bananas."[74] In 1934, the center moved to 261 boulevard Raspail, into the facility that would make it renowned, including a restaurant, a gymnasium, and a swimming pool in the basement, complete with much-appreciated shower facilities. Dances now drew up to four hundred people. Dean Beekman of the cathedral continually insisted on the center's nonsectarian nature, and, in 1931 it was transformed into an independent lay corporation, incorporated in Delaware. The center was seen as "a sort of refuge from corruption by the French, women, or drink." Besides or because of its somewhat provincial and prudish yet at the same time modern aspect, the center was a success. In the depths of the Depression in 1934 it still had some seven hundred members.[75]

Besides student centers, churches competed on everything from building projects to burials. After World War I, both churches decided to expand. Dean Beekman of the cathedral engaged in energetic fundraising to create the American Memorial Battle Cloister and then to expand the American Students' and Artists' Center, while the Reverend Joseph Cochran of the American Church also began fundraising for what would become the new building on the quai d'Orsay. Pledges from Americans in Paris were disappointing, however, and Cochran commented that they were less religious than Americans at home.[76] There was a debate/dispute over architectural style. Everyone agreed on Gothic, but some favored the simpler twelfth-century style while others advocated a more elaborate fifteenth-century style (which won). The cornerstone was laid in 1927, another neo-Gothic testament to the vigor of American Protestantism in Paris.

The Episcopalian Cathedral emphasized over and again that it was a community meeting place and that over half of its attendees were non-Episcopalians. This was also stressed during a small battle over burials. An undated note circa 1928 in the cathedral's files complained about the American consulate's policy of sending bodies to the sexton of the rue de Berri Church, sometimes "against their will and their annoyance and extra expense." The consulate alternated recommendations between the two churches, although the cathedral argued that it normally had eight times more business than the church. The cathedral wanted the consulate to provide both churches' cards, without comment, but the consul general replied that the consulate itself often paid for the interment and that the American Church was charging only half as much as the cathedral. The cathedral agreed to match its rival's fee.[77]

After the soul, the body. Health needs came next in the creation of the colony. There's nothing worse than getting sick in another language. In 1904, two American doctors in Paris decided to create a hospital by Americans for Americans. The founders had both the penniless and the rich in mind when the hospital was built in 1909 in the well-to-do near-western suburb of Neuilly. It had twenty beds for rich and poor: ten individual rooms for those who could afford them and two common rooms for five men and five women each. Importantly, it was to be staffed by "American physicians and surgeons, and American or English nurses, so that the patients are cared for by people speaking their own language."[78] The hospital expanded greatly during the interwar period, but not without a concomitant identity crisis. For one thing, French doctors joined the staff; the French medical association now prohibited foreign doctors who did not have a French medical degree to practice. In 1925 the American College of Surgeons accredited the hospital, a more modern facility was opened in 1926 with 120 beds, and the hospital soon attracted well-to-do patients from all over Europe. The number of in-patients and consultations doubled, to almost seven thousand. However, this upscaling caused debate, given the hospital's original aim of aiding poor Americans. Accommodations still ranged from common rooms to comfortable suites, although, as Bricktop's mother said when she had to go there and refused a private room, "Besides the cost, I [wouldn't] have anyone to talk to." Right Bank and Left Bank Americans were happy to get help in English, and even Hemingway showed up at the emergency room one day, "his head swathed in toilet paper. He had been hit on the head by a lamp, thinking he was pulling the chain of a flush toilet." The Depression strained the hospital's resources—although one patient left her fur coat in payment; gala fundraisers and other support from the American colony helped it get through the hard times.[79] Today it is considered one of the best, but also one of the most expensive, hospitals in town.

TO CHEER UP FELLOW COUNTRYMEN

Not all immigrant communities can build neo-Gothic churches or establish entire hospitals, but all create their own social clubs, small and large, with often overlapping memberships—and internecine squabbles. The Americans were no different, banding together for leisure and business, with the two often intertwined. They created alumni clubs, business organizations, and overseas branches of patriotic organizations. American organizations in Paris might be classified by purpose—social, aid, business, patriotic—or by social class. Two of the community's major organizations, one for the rich, one for the poor— the American Chamber of Commerce and the American Aid Society—will be explored later. The organizations can also be classified by sex: business clubs, veterans groups, and alumni organizations gathered a world of men, while women met in auxiliaries and in their own organizations. The two sexes mingled at their respective social functions. Later chapters will abundantly cover the gatherings of men; suffice it here to mention the rich, the poor, and the drinkers' gathering spots.

The men did not always call theirs men's clubs, of course. Amherst College, Columbia, Cornell, Harvard, Princeton, and Yale all had alumni clubs in Paris by the mid-1920s, hosting regular dinners, luncheons, and football games. The American Club of Paris claims the oldest ancestry of all. Set up in 1904, it traces its origins to Benjamin Franklin's Sunday dinners that sought to cheer up his fellow countrymen in Paris.[80] As an independent, nonpartisan (gentlemen-only) gathering, the American Club was considered to have a more literary and artistic bent than did its "big brother," the American Chamber of Commerce with its more "commercial, economic, business-like, finger-on-the-trigger practicability."[81] The American Club's weekly luncheons served then as now as a popular though exclusive meeting place for community leaders and distinguished French friends. The American Legion Post served a rather different crowd. With over one thousand members in the 1920s, it concentrated on helping down-on-their-luck veterans either find jobs in France or go back home. It also ran the annual Poppy Sale Drive to help disabled soldiers, their wives or widows, and war orphans; its women's auxiliary also did extensive welfare work among Franco-American veterans' families. Its headquarters, Pershing Hall, became another meeting place for the community. The post served as much as an employment agency and a welfare bureau as a social club for AEF veterans. But as historian Warren Susman once commented, it was also, in its own way, "an important advance-guard agency in promoting American enterprise in France."[82]

Last but hardly least, the men had their bar. Harry's Bar, still a living legend at "sank roo doe noo," as its ads proclaim for the linguistically challenged (5 rue Daunou, near the Opéra). It was founded by an American jockey but got its name in 1923, when it was bought by Harry MacElhone, a Scottish native and author of the still available *The ABC of Mixing Cocktails*. The place became a hub for American residents and tourists, not least because one could get the latest sports results while escaping Prohibition. MacElhone set up a registry where Americans passing through could list their hotel for others to find them, and the bar organized (and still carries out) a straw poll for Americans to vote well before they could legally do so from abroad. But on most days Harry's was a place where American men and a few women congregated to mingle and to escape the Great Thirst. The day Prohibition was abolished, the beer was free.[83]

WOMEN OF THE RIGHT BANK

One evening in December 1933, Gertrude Stein gave an impromptu talk at the American Women's Club in Paris. It wasn't really her world. "[H]er Roman emperor's head over stiff garments" and Alice B. Toklas's "enigmatic and dark . . . slight resemblance . . . to a Hebrew prophet" contrasted with the glittering evening gowns of most of the evening's guests. Stein had been invited as a guest of the scheduled speaker, her good friend (and later Vichy collaborator) Bernard Faÿ, who had gotten stuck in a snowstorm. Stein, whose *Autobiography of Alice B. Toklas* had recently been published to acclaim—at last—"stepped manfully into the breach" and agreed to answer questions in what became a lively evening. The *Chicago Tribune European Edition* described it as "Gertrude Stein Meets Hecklers in Art Session at Women's Club" and related that a "notable duel" took place between Stein and Mrs. Harry Lehr. While Stein had long been precociously collecting Picassos, Mrs. Lehr's own abundant art collection was more of the Louis XIV variety. She took objection to Stein's defense of Picasso and Braque, and, "either routed or enraged," she finally left the room "with a swish of black chiffon and a glitter of diamond bracelets."[84]

While the "women of the Left Bank" had bohemian salons but also the prim and proper Reid Hall, the American women of the Right Bank had their own watering holes, notably the American Women's Club of Paris and two chapters of the Daughters of the American Revolution. Each had their own socials; each had their own class of classy American women. The American Women's Club of Paris, where the serge-vs.-silk duel occurred, had been founded in 1921 to serve as an American social center with cozy reading rooms and writing rooms. Women had been forming their own clubs in the United States since a small group of women created the Ladies' Education Society of Jacksonville, Illinois, in 1833. The General Federation of Women's Clubs was founded in New York City in 1890, and the first club overseas was set up in London in 1891. In 1931, the London club convened a meeting that set the stage for a Europe-wide federation of American Women's clubs abroad: the Federation of American Women's Clubs Overseas (FAWCO), still going strong today. By 1933, although the Depression was sending many Americans home, the London and Paris "giant" clubs had fourteen hundred and thirteen hundred members respectively.[85]

Two issues particularly mobilized American women abroad in the interwar years: their legal status and the cause of peace. On the one hand, many of them, having lost their citizenship after the Expatriation Law of 1907 due to marrying a foreigner, joined the fight to regain their full US citizenship. On the other, as FAWCO founder Caroline Curtis Brown believed, American women were especially well equipped to promote peace. Historian Nora Faires has suggested that American women's clubs could exude a "gendered Americanism" that extended American power in a genteel manner.[86] The American Women's Club in Paris, catering largely to women whose husbands were diplomats or businessmen, was, however, not explicitly active on the political front. The members believed in helping to spread peace through understanding, yet they were "not to dabble in politics"; meetings were to avoid "controversial or dangerous subjects." When the club's *Bulletin* did (rarely) evoke politics, its positions ranged from moderate to conservative. One article in the 1920s spoke out against the proposed twentieth "Child Labor Amendment," that, backed by the AFL, "the Russian Reds," and the League of Women Voters, was considered "un-American, unnecessary and will not work." Two articles in the late 1920s reported favorably on Mussolini, highlighting his description of women as that "pleasant parenthesis of life."[87] The club's stand on women's issues was essentially one of pride in women's accomplishments, linked to a strong belief in the importance of motherhood. As the president of the club in the mid-1920s suggested, this was what differentiated the overseas women's groups. While women's clubs in the United States were promoting a "new type of woman, a thoroughly trained university product" establishing welfare bureaus, setting up libraries, or beautifying public buildings, the overseas clubs saw their task as emphasizing "woman's supreme joy," motherhood.[88]

The first purpose of the club was for residents. Regular weekly activities included teas, *thés dansants*, concerts, luncheons, and current events classes, with the occasional fashion show and bridge or mah-jongg tournament. Weekly dances attracted one to two hundred people and fashion shows up to four hundred. One loyal member even paid the entrance fee for her lap dog. Club members willingly aided newly arrived Americans in getting over "the homesick hour." Yet resident women were sometimes seriously annoyed by those just passing through, that "large body of exasperated shoppers who think existence a tragedy because they cannot be shampooed as they were in New York or find ice-cream soda at every stop."[89] In the mid-1920s, the club's Information Bureau handled over fifteen hundred job requests per year, from American and French men and women. Before the crash, it helped some 40–50 percent of them find jobs as governesses, butlers, secretaries, guides, or music, art, or language teachers. The bureau also answered requests (over 1,000 per month during the height of its activity) for information on doctors and dentists, apartments and hotels, barbershops and beauty parlors. It found chaperones for evening parties, advised on the best place for a manicure or where to have one's razors sharpened. People asked for help on matters from purchasing a Normandy château to finding a backgammon teacher in Versailles to writing lyrics for an opera to settling an inheritance claim. There were limits to its helpfulness, however. Several times the chairwoman had "been asked to use my influence to rearrange domestic troubles of all varieties—when husband or wife are wandering from their own fireside," she reported, "but I decided that did not come under the service of our Information Bureau."[90]

Like other American organizations in Paris, the club saw itself as both furthering American community and furthering Franco-American amity. In 1924,
the club moved into a villa of its own at 61 rue Boissière in the posh 16th arrondissement, where there was a restaurant and ultimately forty-four rooms to
rent on a short-term basis to members' acquaintances. Club membership grew
(to 1,300 in 1929), and some twenty thousand registered guests passed through
in 1928. (That figure would be halved after the stock market crash.) Expansion
led to growing pains, however: increased fundraising and necessary bureau-
cratization of house rules (too frequent guests had to become members). Self-
doubt emerged. Have we become more of a social club than a service one? the
president asked members at the 1926 annual meeting.

Clearly marked by the war, the club's politics trumped gender solidarity. Its
activities were open to Allied and neutral citizens alike, but German women
were apparently not welcome. American identity remained paramount. The
restaurant nostalgically offered waffles on Mondays, corn fritters on Tuesdays,
flannel pancakes on Wednesdays, and cornbread every day. The women heralded the introduction of lemon pie, but it was apparently difficult to teach
their French pastry chef how to make a chocolate layer cake. Doubly proud,
as women and as Americans, the club proclaimed repeatedly that its work was
"of American women for American women, by American women." "Only the
American woman has known how to combine in a big social center her vast
service work with her love of social activity." Doing good for others while
doing good for themselves, the women of the club represented to themselves
and to the French another model of America, and of the American woman in
particular.[91]

While the AWCP brought together the wives of the business elite, another
group of American women formed clubs that were even more explicitly patriotic and exclusive. The Daughters of the American Revolution (DAR)
chapters in Paris combined the social with the patriotic while their members
hobnobbed with the French aristocratic elite. The AWCP and the DAR clubs
occasionally frequented each other's events, and chiffon and diamonds were
in ample evidence in both groups' functions. For the most part, however, their
activities seem to have been separate, serving different functions and a largely
different clientele. The Daughters of the American Revolution actually formed
two chapters in Paris, carrying their patriotism overseas while bringing together a Franco-American elite. The avowed purpose of the organization, at
home as abroad, is to perpetuate the memory of American Revolutionary–era
ancestors. Founded in 1890 in the United States, the DAR had 175,000 members at home and abroad in 1934. "The forming of D.A.R. chapters by patriotic

American women in foreign countries has been the most excellent propaganda for our country, its history, and the American way of life."[92] In France, the DAR also included members descended from Frenchmen who had fought for American independence. The first chapter created in France, in 1923, was named after Benjamin Franklin. The second, in 1934 (the result of a split?), was named after General Comte de Rochambeau. No records of the Benjamin Franklin chapter seem to exist; it closed in 1961. But the minutes of the Rochambeau chapter, still active today, tell the tale of talks and teas in the 1930s.[93] The Rochambeau chapter's founders included an American countess (Comtesse de Chilly, née Josephine Munford) and an American princess (Princesse Margaret Boncompagni, née Draper), along with Mrs. Bates-Batcheller. Bates-Batcheller and Draper came from prominent Massachusetts families; their fathers had been great friends. The Paris club maintained close ties with the National Society in the United States and, like other chapters, voted funds for such things as the upkeep of George Washington's mother's grave back home.

The Wreath Committee was particularly active, rain or shine. Memorial activity was hard work, however. The DAR women joined with other patriotic clubs and French guests to celebrate American holidays with ceremonies at statues or tombs. On a sunny Memorial Day in 1938, for example, fifteen members of the Rochambeau chapter attended the service at the American Cathedral before moving on to place a wreath at the tomb of the Unknown Soldier at the Arc de Triomphe. Mrs. Watrous then hosted a "lovely little luncheon" at the Union Interalliée before they reconvened in the afternoon with others at the Suresnes cemetery outside of Paris. From there they motored to Garches, where planes dropped small bouquets in tribute to Franco-American friendship. All of this was followed by a "cosy tea" in town by the officers "to talk it all over." Over a month later, they were not so lucky. When the chapter members valiantly gathered, along with other patriotic societies, on July 4 at Lafayette's tomb, it was pouring rain. They continued from there to the monument in memory of American soldiers in the Great War before heading to Washington's statue and then proceeding, on foot, still "braving the torrents," to Rochambeau's statue. And that was just the morning's activities. Drenched, some dashed home to change before a luncheon for the foreign press and a rousing reiteration of Franco-American friendship.[94]

Headed by women and run by women, the chapter's regular monthly business meetings were followed by a talk and then tea that could bring together up to several hundred guests (men and women, American and French), often at Mrs. Bates-Batcheller's estate in Saint-Cloud, just outside of Paris. Members read aloud from revolutionary-era documents unearthed from private archives on both sides of the Atlantic. Men often gave the lectures, invariably described as very charming or delightful. Two prominent female chapter leaders also occasionally read from their own works. The Comtesse Jean (Pauline) de Pange, the first Frenchwoman to be admitted to the DAR, was a published author with a doctorate from the Sorbonne. Her admiring friend Tryphosa Bates-Batcheller, author of *Une amitié historique*, about French-American relations, was also a concert singer—although according to some musicologists the socialite's wealth was greater than her voice.[95] In 1936 she regaled the membership and guests with a "brilliant concert" and talk on patriotic American songs, noting along the way that "The Star Spangled Banner" was taken from an old French song.

Far from the Left Bank salons of Gertrude Stein and Natalie Barney, the women of the AWCP and the DAR sustained more conventional female roles, all the while reveling in their female-assigned and -assumed roles as tea-givers and wreath layers. The Right Bank women offered, to themselves and to their French acquaintances, a variant on the image of the independent American female, this time with her board meetings, philanthropies, and clubs. Both groups were linked to larger American movements and exuded pride in being American. But they explicitly carved out their own roles overseas as explicit proponents of Franco-American friendship. Whether Americanizers or fervent Franco-American peaceniks, the bejeweled, active, and patriotic countesses and businessmen's wives created places where they could gather among their own.

SO AS NOT TO BE LOST IN TRANSLATION

Like all foreigners, Americans wanted to read in their own language, and like other immigrants, they imported books and newspapers, set up reading rooms, and created their own newspapers. Unlike other foreigners, the Americans early on had two major lending libraries and two daily newspapers, bankrolled by US-based papers, one of which would become an internationally renowned newspaper by the end of the twentieth century, the *International Herald Tribune*—hardly your run-of-the-mill immigrant press. American bookstores and libraries not only provided the reading matter that one could take home to garret or villa but also provided physical spaces for people to congregate in ways less formal than dues-paying club meetings.

Sylvia Beach, "Yankee, young and brave," as James Joyce described her, is the most famous of the interwar American book purveyors. But she was neither the first nor the most long-lasting. Brentano's Bookstore opened in

1895 and has lasted over a century, catering to English-reading travelers and residents. Beach's boisterous bookshop, as she described it, opened in 1919, offering books not available elsewhere because of either censorship or price, and above all promoting the opposite of "train literature." Beach first set up shop in the Latin Quarter on the rue Dupuytren and then moved around the corner to 12 rue de l'Odéon in 1921. Shakespeare and Company remains a staple of Lost Generation memory because of the famous company Beach kept and the most famous of books she published, James Joyce's *Ulysses*. What we forget is that Beach's bookstore was also an active lending library, and it served, like its Right Bank "rival," the American Library in Paris, as a meeting place for Americans. Lending books to impecunious writers who couldn't afford to buy, Beach also hosted literary teas and allowed her shop to serve as a mail drop. Hemingway picked up his mail there, and most of the white expatriate writers frequented the shop, but so did Claude McKay and Gwendolyn Bennett.[96]

Did the business elite seek out Beach's books? There was another option for reading books in English. The American Library in Paris, which to this day serves everyone from American parents delighted with the children's story hour to French students boning up for exams on American civilization, was of course not in direct competition with Shakespeare and Company's much more distinctive collection. Nor was it the only American library serving the Right Bank crowd. The Chamber of Commerce's Franklin Library contained some twenty thousand volumes in English and French relating to commerce, industry, and law. But the American Library in Paris was open to an even wider public. It was set up thanks to a more cheerful legacy of the war—the American Library Association donated thirty thousand books left behind by its War Library Service—and community members expanded the collection. By 1940, the library had 100,000 volumes.[97] It had three goals from the outset: to memorialize the American Expeditionary Force, to promote understanding and knowledge of America, and to provide an example of American library practices. As education scholar Mary Maack has pointed out, "Unlike Beach, the librarians on the Right Bank [largely American women] focused on providing information about the United States and demonstrating effective library practices rather than promoting literature." As one of its early proponents put it, the library would serve as "a missionary for one of America's most cherished ideals, popular education by means of books," and it sought to interpret America to Europe in order to correct misconceptions and prevent misunderstandings.[98]

There was another, more ephemeral, but just as important glue that bound Americans together in Paris: their newspapers. The 1920s produced not just the numerous Left Bank American literary magazines that were as short-lived as they were inventive, lasting several issues to several years if they were lucky. Another "literary" output of Americans in Paris existed in the form of newspapers. They provided news of home, news of the colony, and news of Paris, along with international news, financial reports, sports updates, comics, and that big news item then as now, the weather: resort weather, Paris weather, world weather. Other English-language newspapers existed (*Galignani's Messenger*; *Daily Mail*), but Americans needed their own news, their own gossip. The newspapers detailed the comings and goings of the Right Bank colony, listing births, marriages, deaths, and "yacht movements." And they published, like the *American Register*, long lists of ship arrivals, "an office headache" but "good business." It was hard work covering the balls and salons, concerts and auctions, that "untiring *labeur de fête*" of the American colony (and boring to boot, grumbled William Shirer).[99] The newspapers also provided jobs for the struggling writers of the Left Bank.

The nineteenth-century ancestor, in this as in so many things, was dentist Evans's *American Register*. Mostly produced and written by his colleague Edward A. Crane (himself a long-white-bearded dashing man about town), the paper was distributed widely on steamers and in hotels in Europe and the United States. It eschewed politics as divisive, preferring the lists of Americans in Paris and around Europe. The weekly provided news from home ("ship collision on Lake Erie") and described itself as an advertising medium, as its pages well attest. Indeed, victim of its success, it had to publicize a disclaimer about some usurpers who used the paper's name to reap advertising money on their own.

With the growth in numbers of travelers and residents, two major American newspapers, first one from New York, then one from Chicago, started Paris editions, the first of which rivaled the *Register* in defining "America" abroad. The New York paper owner James Gordon Bennett Jr. started the Paris edition of the *New York Herald*, "FRIEND and GUIDE of Americans Abroad," in 1887. The Evans-Crane *Register* closed in 1915. Other community newspapers appeared during the interwar period, such as the *Paris Times* (1924–29), whose motto was "Class, Character, Cleanliness."[100] But the main competition to Bennett's Paris *Herald* became the Paris edition of the *Chicago Tribune*. Its army edition was founded during the war as a "tent mate of the army," "hopeful that we may add some warmth to the famous spirit of the American armies and speed the fatal bayonet into the heart of German imperialism." The *Tribune* had its popular comic strips to offer, and it aimed explicitly to give Midwestern doughboys and other Americans in Paris something other than a New York paper that furthermore had been corrupted by being in Paris for so long. The Paris (Chicago) *Tribune* eventually became "tainted" in its own way, closer to the Left Bank writers, with more of them on its payroll. Thus while the New York paper became a paper for the Right Bank "lobster-palace Americans," proclaiming its "Assurance, Dignity, Reliability," the Chicago paper advertised its "Personality" and "Character" and did a better job of describing the Left Bank literary activities.[101] If the *Tribune* was the livelier and more high-brow of the two, the *Herald* had more readers and more advertisers and paid more. Both papers reported on American institutions in Paris, and both advertised products that no American family could do without—Erector sets, genuine ice cream soda, typewriters with American keyboards—alongside French products aimed at the lucrative American market. By 1930, the *Herald* "was claiming a circulation of fifty thousand and printing twenty. Modestly, [the *Tribune*] claimed a circulation of twenty and printed eight. Our advertisers believed neither paper." As the American tide retreated in the early 1930s, the *Herald* bought out the *Chicago Tribune*'s European edition middecade, but letters poured in pleading it to keep the *Tribune*'s comic strips.[102]

PARISIAN 'HOODS AND THE "EBB AND FLOW OF TRAVEL" [103]

The American colony did not just congregate in clubs, organizations, and newspaper reading rooms. It also had its own residential neighborhoods. Like many foreigners in the city, Americans tended to cluster. Unlike other foreigners, they had the means to settle in the *beaux quartiers* of the Right Bank. Their ingathering was as much a class phenomenon as an "ethnic" one. While goatherds selling fresh milk still plied the impoverished Left Bank Contrescarpe area where Hemingway lived, Helena Rubinstein, like a good many of her compatriots and social peers, had a fashionable villa in the posh 16th arrondissement.

As Henry James described it in his letters to the *New York Tribune*, the American elite in Paris in 1875 clustered mostly around the Paris Opera area.[104] Extending to the Champs Élysées, the American Quarter was "the gaudiest and most expensive" section in Paris, where "tradesmen paint American coats of arms on their windows, and charge twenty-five per cent more for their wares than their neighbors over the river."[105] By the turn of the century, the center of gravity had moved farther west, closer to the Arc de Triomphe, where "on certain sections of the avenue Kléber or the avenue Mac-Mahon, the Parisian himself feels foreign" in this "little American city."[106] And if the lease for Henry

Blackmer, of Teapot Dome scandal, is any example, in the mid-1930s a wealthy American living near there on the rue de Presbourg would have to promise in his lease, like other well-heeled inhabitants of that part of town, to occupy his spacious multiroom apartment "bourgeoisement," meaning no animals, nothing hanging out the windowsills, neither laundry nor even flowerpots, and he had to avoid any noises or odors that could trouble his neighbors. Deliverymen had to use the service staircase (before 10 a.m.); domestics were forbidden to use the elevator; only Mr. Blackmer, his family, and his visitors could use it, but only to go up, not to go down, maneuvering the levers themselves and only at their own risk. Then as now, the central heating would be turned on only in winter months, and never with any guarantee as to how warm it would get.[107]

The Chamber of Commerce directories provide a striking new map of Americans in Paris for anyone still convinced at this point that they all lived on the Left Bank. The 1926 addresses confirm that over one-half of the Americans listed lived in a golden ghetto in the well-heeled 16th, 8th, and 17th arrondissements. The similarly better-off portion of the Left Bank, the 6th (Stein and Beach) and 7th arrondissements, accounts for another fifth of the Parisian American population. The Montparnasse area (14th *arr.*) is poorly represented in the directory, even if Man Ray signed in.[108]

Nonetheless, there remains a problem with pinning down a permanent population of restless resident wealthy Americans. Even those who considered themselves settled in, and sometimes (but not always) had French residence cards to prove it, divided their time between Paris and the outlying areas. From the businessmen to Josephine Baker and Bricktop, many had country estates to which they could flee in the summer to avoid the tourist crush. They also moved between the Paris region and the Riviera, where many wintered, or between Paris and home in the United States, to which they regularly returned for months on end.

How long does it take to become part of a community rather than be seen as a transient visitor? For Albert Sutliffe, five or ten years sufficed to become a bona fide member of the community, "and the shortest of these two periods is enough to naturalize a good American as a citizen of the American Colony of Paris." He differentiated, like others, between the "permanent American colony" and the "floating elements." But he worried about mobility. In his 1887 guide, Sutliffe defended peripatetic Americans abroad by pointing out that the American's "normal existence is one of movement," due first of all to the expanse of the American continent, but adding that Paris was no farther from New York than San Francisco and cheaper to get to. However, he also expressed concern that this "migratory" pattern not degenerate into a disease, before concluding that when mobility is practiced in moderation, its benefits far outweighed its evil effects.[109] Once the steamships had cut travel time to one week instead of four, transatlantic commuting became frequent. Evans often returned to the United States on dental business. Mrs. Mackay stayed in Paris entertaining while her husband commuted to the West Coast to watch over his silver mines. James called Wharton, who lived in France for thirty years, "the pendulum woman" since she went back to New York every year.[110]

The question of mobility is a question not just of time—length of stay—but also of place. For some, home was a hotel. Five percent of the respondents in the 1926 ACC directory listed a hotel as their calling address. The hotels were often grand—the Ritz, the Plaza Athénée, the Majestic—and well over two-thirds of them were located on the Right Bank. They were mostly inhabited by unaccompanied married women, but also unmarried women, some couples, and single men. (Living long term in apartments in residence hotels was common practice in New York, Chicago, and elsewhere at the time.)[111] By December 1, Paris hotels were empty, the Riviera ones full; the reverse movement occurred in the spring. It was not just the Fitzgeralds. Black Americans followed the flow, playing in the clubs on the Côte d'Azur during the season. In 1927 Alfred Sharon, an enterprising lawyer who apparently dabbled in Riviera real estate, published a short-lived magazine, *Americans on the Côte d'Azur*, in which he helped create the Riviera community by listing Americans who owned villas or were visiting in the hotels there. Mary Cassatt, Mrs. Whitelaw Reid, and Edith Wharton were all noted, not to mention Walter Berry, former president of the ACC, said to be recovering from an appendix operation. Decidedly upbeat, Sharon encouraged people to send in cheerful news items, because "[w]e came to the Côte d'Azur for our pleasure and for the admirable climate." Perhaps all was not perfectly idyllic on the Riviera, as the Fitzgeralds clearly understood. Sharon ran ads for other problems: a Société de Surveillance against break-ins and, in case that didn't work, jewelry insurance.[112] In any case, the frequent mobility of the American community in Paris was a major headache for Alfred M. Brace, the 1920s editor of the *Americans in France* directories. In each preface, he exhorted his informants to help keep the directory up to date so as not to inconvenience themselves and their friends or business associates.

Who counts in defining the American community overseas? There are fundamental ambiguities in even such a deceptively straightforward list of "American" "residents." The community roster, people-finder for contemporaries, boon to the historian, had its limits. Although the directory listed some 5,225 Americans for all of France in 1926, the French authorities counted nearly

18,000 Americans in the census of that year, itself an undoubtedly low number.[113] Almost one-fifth of the Americans gave only a bank or the American Express office as their port of call, not to mention a young art student who simply listed "Café du Dôme, Montparnasse and Raspi [sic], Paris," along with the American Express Company. Sometimes such addresses were sent in because residence was subject to change or because the American-in-France was only an American-in-France-part-of-the-year. In other cases, people split their time between more than one residential address. Isadora Duncan ("a kind of dancing bridge" between the bourgeois Wharton-James era and the avant-garde Stein-Hemingway generation, as Adam Gopnik has cleverly put it)[114] listed both her apartment in the 16th arrondissement and her villa on the Riviera, yet she spent much of her time on tour elsewhere. One couple had four addresses: one in Paris, a horse farm and a château in the country, and a summer place in the south.

Yet the residents knew who they were. And they were adamantly against being confused with tourists. Hemingway hated it when he had to wait for a table because a quaint Parisian restaurant had been listed in an American guidebook as untouched by Americans, leading to the contrary.[115] It was not just inconvenience; it was also a matter of pride. Outraged writer Francis Warrington Dawson defended himself to the French authorities, proclaiming: "I have lived in France for more than ten years, and can scarcely be compared to an 'étranger de passage' [sic, foreigner passing through]."[116] According to a sample of the 1925–40 *Americans in France* directories, about half of those listed stayed one to two years, and the other half remained three years or more.[117] But by dint of listing themselves at all they seem to have had a sense of settledness. As one historian later commented, what united the "survivors" of the nineteenth-century colony around the Étoile, the artists in Montparnasse, and the students in the Latin Quarter was "the snobbery verging on contempt with which they regarded the average American tourist."[118]

I cannot conclude this study of colony-zation without two caveats necessary for any community study: those who opted out and those whose national identity may be ambiguous. Many people sought invisibility or solitude abroad, the opposite of togetherness. The nonjoiners were undoubtedly even more numerous than the joiners—a useful reminder for the study of any group. In one extreme case, when the French authorities rescinded Patrick Waldberg's residence permit in 1934, presumably for having been personal secretary to a French communist deputy, he did not want the US consul general to intervene. The twenty-one-year-old Waldberg had resided most of his life in France, and the consular officer commented that "his viewpoint is that of a young French national." Although "the imprudence of an American national participating actively in French domestic politics was suggested to Mr. Waldberg . . . this feature had never occurred to him."[119] Other Americans, even those who were at the community's center, could fade to its margins. When David Fuller, former consulate employee, died in 1910 of senile decay, he had been in Paris for thirty years and lived alone in the modest Pigalle neighborhood. The consular death certificate states "Family unknown," and he was buried in the Pantin cemetery. Other Americans undoubtedly just kept to themselves, although lack of companionship, whether American or French, could have dire results. Lucinda Farrar, a music student living on the Left Bank, committed suicide by gas inhalation, leaving a note indicating neurasthenia, discouragement in her studies, and weariness of life.[120] There were alarming reports about other depressed American students ending their lives in the City of Light. But more frequently it was homesickness that lurked, leading African American writer Gwendolyn Bennett to speak of a Fourth of July loneliness for home, which, she specified, did not mean that she identified with the crowds of Americans jostling each other at the American Express office.[121] There were many definitions of home and of Americanness for Americans overseas.

Who, after all, is "American"? Winnaretta Singer, aka Princesse Singer-Polignac, born in the United States, one of the twenty-four children (by two wives and at least three mistresses) of her profligate sewing-machine inventor father, was raised in France by her French mother and was described as having "been so thoroughly absorbed into French society that she is rarely seen among Americans."[122] Yet she was seen as "l'Américaine" in France and listed herself in the *Americans in France* directory. There were also a fair number of American LaFleurs, Labouchères, et cetera, in Paris, Americans of French origin whose ancestors had crossed the Atlantic westward two or three generations before. The Americans in France reflected the diverse origins of American society. The overwhelming majority of names in the directories were Anglo-Scottish, but there were also Italian-, German-, Irish-, and Russian-sounding names. The Americans in Paris, "immigrants" to France, mirrored immigration to the United States itself.

Women in particular had changing citizenship identities due to marriage during the interwar period. American women who had foreign husbands were listed in italics in the ACC directories; French women who had become American through marriage were listed under their husbands' names. Many of the latter may have never traveled to the United States, war or business having brought their husbands their way. But how did Yvonne Jocelyn, née Dugas, the wife of a Harvard-educated American (now a poultry farmer settled with her in the north of France), identify herself? She is listed as an American in France, and indeed she was, via marriage. The "Americans" of the directories seem to be identified as such regardless of the nature of citizenship (through birth, naturalization, or marriage) or even, perhaps, the interested party's opinion.

All in all, the "other" Americans in Paris stand out in two ways: in contrast to the Left Bank Lost Generation and in contrast to other foreigners in the city. First, by now it should be abundantly clear that the clubs, organizations, and newspapers provide a group portrait of "Americans in Paris" quite different from that of the literary crowd on the Left Bank. It is the picture of a group huddled in the hotels and villas of well-to-do areas of Paris and its suburbs. The Americans in France ranged from consular officers and soldiers who stayed on to look after American graves to businessmen and lawyers setting up American subsidiaries in France, to Frenchwomen who became American through marriage, to American women who became countesses through the same process. Above all, Right Bank Americans set up numerous organizations for themselves to pray and to play.

Second, with the might of the war effort behind them and the expansion of trade before them, the Americans in France were no ordinary immigrant group. If they set up their own clubs—perhaps no more than those of other immigrant groups—what clearly sets these elite migrants apart is that they had an incomparable advantage. They had the means and the money to create bold buildings visible to all, bespeaking the Americans' physical presence in town, along with a major daily still available today at every newsstand. Money matters, and the two churches, the hospital, the American women's organizations, and the newspapers all existed due to funds from home as well as from the wealthy community in Paris. Many institutions were set up as Delaware or New York corporations, not simply to keep the ties that bind but to be independent, among other things, from French tax authorities. The American organizations were by Americans, for Americans, but they were also some of the most visible signs of the growing overseas presence of the United States in the first half of the twentieth century.

Individuals, institutions, and historians can "make" communities. The American organizations in Paris all started out and remained meeting places for the homesick—immigrant watering holes serving everything from American cocktails at Harry's Bar to homemade waffles at the American Women's Club. They were also the hubs of social and business networks. Americans' worlds were often multiple and decidedly peripatetic, and some people are always invisible to contemporary chroniclers and historians alike. Yet tens of thousands of Americans and their institutions stood still long enough to create an "American village" in Paris beyond the Left Bank.[123]

We can now turn to another important way in which Americans in Paris defined themselves: through their citizenship. The Americans in Paris belonged both to a place on the Seine and to a country far away.

CHAPTER 2

Uses of Citizenship

Tales from the Consulate, or
How Mrs. Baker Got Her Hat Back

That a native-born citizen may be deprived
of the protection inherent in his citizenship
through residence abroad
for whatever time and for whatever reason,
but without the process of law, appears intolerable.

AMERICAN CHAMBER OF COMMERCE IN PARIS (1908)[1]

Americans abroad present a paradox. They can be seen as ambassadors of goodwill or the avant-garde of American capitalism. They can also be considered suspect citizens, ex-patriots in sum. While, as we have seen, Americans in Paris beginning in the late nineteenth century created community institutions unabashedly heralding their American identity, they also sometimes had to prove their bona fide identity to the US government. The relationship of Americans overseas to the government is complex. People go abroad for a variety of reasons, some to work, some to play, some forever, and others just to visit. In the process, their relationship with "home" and particularly the State Department may vary. Some may never set foot in a US consulate; others turn beseechingly to their government to defend them in times of trouble.

The life of the US consulate on the rue des Italiens until it moved with the embassy to the place de la Concorde in 1934 seems like the stuff of a television series. It was where citizens, sometimes fawning, sometimes obstreperous, activated their citizenship rights from abroad, contacting the government as a muscular older brother to help out after an altercation with the French. Americans in Paris have turned to the government for help for the serious and the frivolous, in times of war as in times of peace. They have gone for help over "misunderstandings" about smuggled goods or after imprisonment for child kidnapping. Citizens used the consulate as a mail drop, as a missing person's bureau, as an aid to businessmen, or for help after a run-in with a French shopkeeper. The consulate was where an everyday use of citizenship was brought to bear on everything from the inconvenience of being abroad to more serious tiffs with the French state.

EXPATRIATION: FROM BECOMING AMERICAN TO CITIZENSHIP LOSS TO JUST BEING ABROAD

Before turning to citizens' use of their citizenship as seen through the consular peephole, we need to remember a fundamental ambiguity of being citizens abroad. The term *expatriation* literally means loss of citizenship, while *expatriates* just refers to citizens living abroad. The root concept of expatriation has in fact shifted considerably over the last two centuries. In the early national period, expatriation meant *becoming* American. As the United States affirmed its break from Britain, expatriation was initially heralded as the freedom of emigration to the United States. This meant countering British claims to a "natural law" of perpetual allegiance, binding those born there to the crown. In order to define American independence and citizenship, expatriation from Britain had to be deemed a legal, indeed natural, right chosen by the individual. Over the nineteenth century, the US government increasingly reaffirmed this right to leave other countries in order to become Americans. Two decades after mass immigration from Europe began, Congress enacted the first US Expatriation Act in 1868. It explicitly affirmed the right to renounce one's birthright, thus reassuring European newcomers that expatriation to the United States and acquisition of American citizenship were secure against claims of their native states. By that time other countries were also declaring emigration to be a natural right, and by the late nineteenth century a flurry of bilateral naturalization treaties was signed, recognizing that emigrants had the right to change the legal ties that bind and that one country's expatriate was another's citizen.[2]

By the turn of the twentieth century, however, as increasing numbers of US citizens moved abroad, a new image of expatriation emerged. Clearly Americans were now leaving as well as arriving. After welcoming expatriated foreigners in the nineteenth century, the government now worried about the opposite category of expatriates, those Americans who waded overseas. Jurists had long been calling for a clearer definition of expatriation. The 1868 law had reaffirmed the right of aliens to become American. A 1907 Law of Expatriation sought to define those Americans who became aliens. It made explicit the conditions under which Americans could lose their citizenship: naturalization or an oath of allegiance pledged to a foreign state; extended residence abroad of naturalized American citizens; and marriage of women to foreign citizens. Already as of 1906, naturalized American citizens, although still protected under the law no matter where they roamed, risked losing their new citizenship if they resided for two years in their country of origin or five years in any other foreign state.[3] As of 1907, the presumption of loss of American citizenship due to extended residence abroad could be overcome only if satisfactory evidence were provided that there had been no intent to relinquish American citizenship. Exemptions included residence abroad for business purposes (if coupled with intent to return). Nonetheless, the American Chamber of Commerce businessmen in Paris complained that the 1907 law was "onerous and arbitrary."[4]

The 1907 circular was particularly harsh on women. Their expatriation was effected through marriage.[5] A native-born woman "followed" her husband's nationality and thereby lost her US citizenship, whether she left the United States or continued to reside there. Expatriation could occur without emigration. From its inception, the 1907 expatriation of women caused an outcry, which the Married Women's Independent Citizenship ("Cable") Act of 1922 largely rectified, although women who lived in their husband's country as much as two years would still lose their citizenship, and American women married to Asians, themselves ineligible for citizenship, were still expatriated until 1931. It took until the 1940s for completely equal nationality rights to be reestablished for women.[6]

Yet while American women were losing their citizenship involuntarily, a different image of expatriation was emerging, distinct from the legal category of citizenship loss. The "expatriate" was simply becoming a citizen abroad. The novelists, painters, poets, and musicians who flocked to Paris in the 1920s were expatriates without (legal) expatriation. They lived abroad but never lost their citizenship in the process. The term still had negative connotations in the first half of the twentieth century, however. As Hemingway had one disapproving character define it: "You know what's the trouble with you? You're an expatriate. . . . You've lost touch with the soil. You get precious. Fake European standards have ruined you. You drink yourself to death. You become obsessed by sex. You spend all your time talking, not working. You are an expatriate, see? You hang around cafés."[7] Although Hemingway, Fitzgerald, and other expatriate writers quickly achieved literary fame, many commentators remained skeptical of those who had chosen to leave American shores. Whatever their recognized artistic and literary talent, the flamboyant Americans in Paris were disparaged as being rootless, hedonistic, extravagant, hard-drinking, or homosexual.[8]

Even the wealthy Americans of the Right Bank came in for their share of criticism. Lilian Bell had published a novel titled *The Expatriates* (1900) that seems to be the earliest American use of that noun form. She harshly mocked rich Americans in Paris who, to their financial and even physical peril, succumbed to the sirens of impoverished and scheming titled French men and women. "'Where do you live now?' she demanded. 'In Paris.' 'Expatriates—both of you!' she said, scornfully, turning her glasses on them. . . . Why did this man . . . deliberately live away from her dear country and tacitly repudiate the flag?"[9] Julia Ward Howe went so far as to call the expatriation of Americans to Europe an "obliteration of American democracy and independence."[10] Besides insufficient patriotism, other dubious motives attributed to those living abroad included, as we have seen, leaving home to avoid taxes or to flee Prohibition. Whereas writers may have reveled in their countercultural image, the more posh set of Americans in Paris took umbrage at the term *expatriate*, which they considered derogatory, and they sought to distance themselves from the word as well as from the bohemian types of the Left Bank: "Whenever some thoughtless tourist applied it to a local resident," a member of the American community would write in to the Paris *Herald* "Mailbag" to protest.[11]

Over the course of one and a half centuries, the American image of expatriation had thus shifted from a friendly figure, welcomed to a sparsely populated continent, to a series of suspicious characters: women married to foreigners, expatriate writers, the tax-evading wealthy. By the 1920s, the legal concept of expatriation (although still very much enforceable after 1907) had been displaced in popular parlance by the image of the expatriates, adored by their reading public but suspect in the eyes of the patriotic masses. Yet whatever the criticisms of the writers, drinkers, or tax evaders, they never lost their citizenship in the process, let alone their attachment to America. And who could be more American than businessmen overseas who defended their right to be there precisely in order to sell America abroad? Writers and manufacturers' representatives alike assumed their right to life outside American boundaries, and they clung tenaciously to their citizenship rights.

PROTECTION OF CITIZENS ABROAD

While expatriates of all stripes may have been suspected of questionable loyalties, they generally never questioned the government's duty to come to their aid. Citizens abroad point to one of the conundrums of citizenship: the ways in which ordinary citizens, after leaving their homeland, turn to it in times of need. Americans in Paris turned to the US government at the literal drop of a hat. When Mrs. Baker could not get her new hat back from a Parisian hat-maker, she went to the consulate. She had taken the hat in for adjustment, but the milliner refused to return it until a friend of Mrs. Baker's who had placed an order made good on it. The consular officer went with Mrs. Baker to call on Madame Yvonne, and he got her hat back.[12]

Already in 1877, John Russell Young commented on "the tendency of the American mind to seek his minister upon all occasions when he is overcharged for candles, when he has lost his baggage, when he is homesick, and . . . when the right gloves have not come home from the bazaar." Citizens abroad show how "thin" ties of citizenship can become "thick" when a problem is at hand. Young's theory was that, as taxpayers, Americans had a "sense of possession in dealing with ministers and consuls," so much so that it was just as well, he thought, that the legation should not be too convenient of access![13] The US consulate was not necessarily a miracle worker, and its patience could be tried, but it stood then and now as both symbol and literal locus of the United States abroad. And it was the place where overseas citizens exercised—in both senses of the word, as we will see—their citizenship. Supplicating individuals in Paris insisted that their citizenship status entitled them to a variety of services, from safeguarding their possessions to getting out of town. Or out of prison.

As the number of private citizens abroad increased over the late nineteenth century, well beyond the stranded seamen for whom consulates were first created, the consular officials' functions expanded to take care of everyone from the impecunious to the mentally deranged, and of everything from authenticating documents to dealing with accidents, performing marriages, handling funerals, and arranging for the shipment home of remains. The interwar consulate acted as an all-purpose welfare bureau, investigating the whereabouts of wandering Americans and even on occasion tracking lost luggage. As one official wrote, "Americans are notably careless about their luggage."[14] Americans turned to the consulate for help in retrieving forgotten handbags from taxis or suitcases from the train station check room. This is not to say that all requests were treated with perfect equanimity. There was the category of "ridiculous requests," such as the lengthy, detailed list of questions a California writer sent to complete a book he was writing on France.[15]

There are two schools of thought regarding the protection of nationals: protection as a privilege but not a right of citizenship versus the idea that the consul is duty bound to afford protection once citizenship is unquestionably established.[16] The latter is the general US position, although it was always tempered in the interwar period by limited funds and three provisos: proof of citizenship had to be provided; the US government would not intervene in purely private matters (a list of American lawyers was available, with the caveat that the consulate assumed no responsibility for their services); and all available local legal remedies needed to be pursued first.

WORLD WAR I: TRACKING PEOPLE AND POSSESSIONS

To be caught abroad at the outbreak of a war must be terribly frightening. There are the foresightful and fortunate who have the means to leave, have a place to go, and have already left. There are others who have hemmed and hawed, who have convinced themselves it will never really happen. But when war breaks out, embassies are besieged by their citizens abroad. At the beginning of the Franco-Prussian War, the US legation in Paris issued passports to thirty-three hundred American residents and tourists and provided "protection papers" for Americans to post on their property in the hope that, since the United States did not take sides, villas, apartments, and cars identified as American could be safeguarded from the invader's grasp.[17]

August 1914: Banks were swamped, cable offices crowded. Anxious Americans of all walks of life converged on the American Embassy in Paris, including a distraught retired major trying to leave with his pet bird.[18] Like Elihu Washburne in 1870, the American ambassador, Myron T. Herrick, impressed the French by staying on in Paris even after the French government and almost all of the diplomatic corps left for Bordeaux. "Can it be," he wrote in despair to a friend on September 15, 1914, "that this is really 1914, the age when civilization has reached the highest peak!" Herrick had to find a way to issue identification papers. "Imagine the happy days when nobody needed to have a passport" except to go to Russia or Turkey. But now the French were asking all foreigners to show one, and the embassy came up with a usable certificate of identity. With the halls lined with citizens, Herrick wrote to his son: "We are a bank and a relief society and a railway exchange."[19] The embassy's tasks quadrupled. The consulate posted a notice requesting all citizens to register with the embassy, and approximately five thousand did, either by letter or in person. The embassy then set up a committee of private citizens to assist people in catching trains to the ports and to secure tickets from the Compagnie Générale Transatlantique, the only shipping line still making the crossing. A relief subcommittee advanced cash for passage against proper identification and promissory notes or other security. Leaflets were prepared in French and German, and American flags were distributed, all to be placed on American property as protection if the Germans reached the city.[20]

Besides the Americans who headed home, there were those who stayed, those who wanted to fight, and those who came over to fight. The strain was felt by all who stuck it out, from the distant guns of August through the shelling of Paris by "Big Bertha" in 1918. All of the major American institutions became active in war work and relief activities, as they had during the Franco-Prussian War. The American Hospital set itself up as an "ambulance" hospital for the wounded, but it was suspected by the Germans of being partial, as it was initially filled with mostly French and British wounded. So the staff rounded up a few Germans to treat. The churches' women's guilds prepared tens of thousands of surgical dressings. The first years of the war were particularly nerve-wracking for Americans in France, anxious for the United States to enter the war "for a cause in which America's heart was already enlisted," said Herrick.[21] When the United States finally did join the war, Americans in Paris were relieved. Ultimately there were so many uniformed soldiers present on Sundays that the American Church began calling itself "the Khaki church."[22]

Given the numbers of prewar Americans still in France plus those who had come over to drive an ambulance or otherwise help the war effort, the State Department and the Paris embassy and consulate combined became a frantic hub for both Americans in the United States desperately seeking relatives in France and Americans in France just as frantically looking for help in tracking lost people and lost possessions. Worried Americans at home scrawled handwritten letters to the secretary of state looking for uncles, brothers, cousins, or wayward students, either on the battlefront or on the French home front.

Alice B. Toklas, E. E. Cummings, and John R. Dos Passos all had relatives who turned to the State Department, which relayed the information to the consulate in Paris, which finally traced them. Toklas's father in San Francisco wrote in the fall of 1915, and the consulate made inquiries at 27 rue de Fleurus, where Toklas and Gertrude Stein lived. They found that she had left for Palma de Mallorca on the Spanish Balearic Islands the previous April. They should have known this from their own records. As Gertrude Stein recounted it, she and Alice had gone to the embassy to get passports before leaving for Spain. Two embassy clerks said they did not need passports unless they were going to the United States; their French matriculation papers were sufficient to allow them to stay in France. When Stein insisted, saying that a friend of hers had received one, the embarrassed official said that that was a very special case, to which she replied severely: there could be "no privilege extended to one American citizen which is not to be, given similar circumstances, accorded to any other American citizen." The secretary to the embassy blushed and agreed, and off went Gertrude and Alice to join a friend in Palma de

Mallorca, to "forget the war a little" before doing relief work in the south of France.[23]

More serious were Cummings's and Dos Passos's predicaments. Cummings had gone missing, and his parents had been informed that he was dead. In fact, he had been imprisoned by the French government, as he later recounted rather humorously in *The Enormous Room*. The young Cummings and his friend William Slater Brown had been arrested on charges of treason. Like many other young college men, they had volunteered for the Norton-Harjes Ambulance Corps before the United States had entered the war. But they soon became disillusioned with the ambulance hierarchy. (Their chief of section criticized their fraternization with the French, maintaining: "We're here to show those bastards how they do things in America.")[24] But it was less their insubordination than pacifism that got them arrested. In a letter to a friend, Brown had criticized war itself (a "senescent institution," like "the Church, or marriage"), said he looked forward to revolution in France, and even commented that French soldiers had nothing personally against the Germans—they disliked the English even more. As a result of the intercepted missive, the two buddies were incarcerated for over three months in Normandy. It took a patriotic pleading directly to President Wilson on the part of Cummings's father, a well-connected Harvard professor, "calling to your attention a crime against American citizenship." Cummings *père* complained of ineffective action on the part of the ambassador in Paris and beseeched the president above all on behalf of Cummings's mother: "Pardon me, Mr. President, but if I were President and your son were suffering such prolonged injustice at the hands of France; and your son's mother had been needlessly kept in Hell as many weeks as my boy's mother has, I would do something to make American citizenship as sacred in the eyes of Frenchmen as Roman citizenship was in the eyes of the ancient world.[25]" E. E. was sprung, but Brown spent another three months in prison, given his "vaporings of a youthful mind," undoubtedly influenced by "socialistic literature."[26] The experience did not prevent Cummings from returning to Paris repeatedly during the early 1920s. But the response to his incarceration in the "enormous room" of the French prison, and especially his father's efforts to get him released, showed the belief in the powers of citizenship, especially in times of war.

Six months after Cummings's father, Dos Passos's aunt (his father had died in 1916) also turned to the State Department when she received a cable from Dos Passos saying that he urgently needed a thousand dollars. Dos Passos had volunteered, like Cummings, in the ambulance service. When it was taken over by the army once the United States entered the war, Dos Passos joined the Red Cross as a civilian, never knowing that in the meantime his draft board considered him delinquent. From November 1917 to June 1918, he was posted in Italy, and one of his letters got him too in trouble, although not the letter he later remembered. He subsequently told his biographer that the incriminating letter gave a "too explicit description of the Italian army . . . officers selling the men's rations."[27] However, according to State Department files, it was a different letter, one that he wrote in French to a friend in Madrid. It was his pacifist critique of the "boredom, slavery to all military stupidities . . . and the immense, tragic digression [that is war] in the history of nations" that attracted the censor's eye and got him dismissed from the Red Cross and from Italy. The State Department ultimately found him in Paris and then decided that he was neither un-American nor pro-German: "Department assured he is thoroughly American."[28]

People turned to the government not only to find and protect family but also to protect possessions. American residents of France caught in the United States at the outbreak of the hostilities turned to the State Department to help protect the belongings they had left in Paris. One woman, writing from Connecticut, was desperate: "In view of a possible occupation of Paris by the German army, could not the American Embassy there help me in some way to safeguard my apartment? . . . I am an American. . . . Everything I own in the world is there, relics, furniture, clothes, furs, *everything*. . . . Could you not advise the Embassy there to help me?"[29] In June 1915, a man wrote from Cleveland on Hotel Statler letterhead ("700 rooms 700 baths—The Complete Hotel") enclosing a pawn ticket and money. He wondered if the embassy could redeem a diamond ring that he had left in Paris in 1914. And the embassy did, sending it back to its owner, even specifying for the customs agents that the unaccompanied ring should be exempt from duty.[30]

One category of Americans in France during World War I who had particular need of the embassy's support were those with German-sounding names. Suspected by the French of being enemies, they risked expulsion. At the outset of the war, they turned to the State Department to prove their American credentials. Gustav Adolph Trube, head of the French Westinghouse Air Brake Company, had been living in France since 1912, but he was expelled during World War I as a supposed enemy national. He turned to the US embassy to explain his citizenship to the State Department and thus to the French: his father had been born in Germany only because his grandfather, an American citizen, had been traveling there; his father became naturalized in the United States years before Trube's birth; his mother was American-born, and, he added, her ancestors had fought in the American Revolutionary War. Westinghouse went to bat for this "Francophile to the core," as his wife described him, as did the exclusive Noonday Club in Paris. This club of "distinguished

Americans abroad" signed a petition stressing both Trube's status as an honorable and loyal American and his faithfulness to the French nation.[31] Another woman with a German-sounding name had been denounced as German by a discharged French cook, who "in her ignarance [sic] has not known the difference between a Holland Lady and a German Woman!!" Mrs. Haeften-Hatch wrote to the secretary of state from Cannes in 1916, arguing stridently that the US government should protect "American innocent citizens from the callomnious statements of infurated [sic] servants" and more generally the "infuriated lower classes." She brought all of her ancestry and connections to bear on the matter: born in Holland and well known by Queen Wilhelmina and the Dutch minister currently in Washington; above all, her husband, Mr. Charles P. Hatch, was a Rough Rider, known to Mr. Rooseveldt [sic] himself.[32]

There were also "French" Americans who turned to the embassy for help, even if their upbringing had been essentially French and their connection to the United States had long abated. Thérèse Mayer, born in New York to an American father and a French mother, had lived in France since the age of five. When her house was ransacked and her belongings stolen by the Germans during World War I, she wrote a very polite letter, in French, to the secretary of state, submitting an itemized list of her possessions (piano, Louis XV desk, etc.) and their estimated prices, asking the US government for help in their recovery. She admitted that she had no one else to turn to "because, as an American, I can only turn to you and not to the French government, currently so overburdened with its own citizens."[33]

Yet the US government could also turn a suspicious eye on those who had moved away. In a little-known episode during World War I, it made a (short-lived) attempt at surveillance of Americans abroad. The crisis period raised doubts in some officials' minds about the activities of residents who had stayed in France during the war and civilian aid workers who had gone there to help. The concerns of an intelligence officer prompted a telegram, dated January 8, 1918, from Ambassador Sharp in Paris to the secretary of state:[34]

Major Cabot Ward, Chief of Intelligence Section, line of communication American Expeditionary Force, states that he has been directed by Colonel Nolan, Chief of Staff for Intelligence Section, to obtain a list of all Americans in France and information regarding movements of Americans. He has theretofore requested that the Embassy and Consulate General supply him with records as to Americans suspected of disloyalty to their own or Allied countries; all passport records of Americans journeying in and out of France since August, 1914, and all records necessary to make a complete list of Americans now in

France and to supply such information in the future. He further states that this information is desired with a view to relieving the French. I do not recommend supervising Americans in France and not with idea of causing them annoyance or persecuting them.

The Bureau of Citizenship ("RWF," undoubtedly Richard W. Flournoy Jr.) advised the State Department, on January 23:

> This is the first time I have seen this remarkable telegram.
>
> While I think that something should be done to keep tab on the many Americans going to France (doctors, nurses, relief workers, clerks, laborers employed on military works of various kinds, as well as commercial travelers and others not connected with the Army) and have discussed the matter with Colonel VanDeman, the rather vague plan described in this telegram seems indeed a "large order" and largely impracticable.
>
> As to "disloyal" Americans in France, I think that our consuls have sense enough to report concerning any they hear of.
>
> As to supplying passport records of all Americans who have visited France since 1914, that seems to me an impossible and useless task.
>
> The following steps appear to me to be practicable:
>
> (1) All Americans in France [might be called upon to register] upon pain of expulsion if they fail to do so. The French would have to agree to assist in enforcing this.
>
> (2) All Americans entering France after date set to be required to register. . . .
>
> (3) This Department to furnish Military Intelligence hereafter with daily reports of all Americans to whom passports for France are issued.

In a second memo the following day, RWF was even more circumspect:

> It appears to me that the Embassy ought to be called upon to explain this telegram and the one of January 8. Why has this question become acute all of a sudden? What are the Americans doing in France that causes such apprehension? Before we rush into a census of all Americans who are now in France, and who have visited France since 1914, it appears to me that the Department should be informed more definitely what the trouble is and what is to be accomplished by the proposed census.

On February 5, 1918, the State Department again asked why the question had suddenly become acute, although it nonetheless put pressure on the embassy to compile a list of Americans. In August, Ambassador Sharp expressed the difficulty of the task: we're doing the best we can, he telegraphed. The embassy had gathered a list of almost seven hundred Americans in the Paris area, but many had already left town. No further action seems to have been taken.

HELP IN TIME OF PEACE:
MISSING PERSONS, HATS, AND HANDBAGS

Whereabouts and missing-persons queries were not just wartime concerns. Many of the functions that had an urgent character in time of war continued to occupy the consulate during peacetime, as US citizens at home sought relatives who had wandered afar or business associates who had dropped out of sight. The whereabouts queries provide a window onto what Americans were doing in Paris and how they in turn used the consulate as a general-delivery window to reply to their worried correspondents. The consulate acted at times as a virtual detective agency, its officials writing to local mayors in France, visiting addresses in Paris, talking to concierges or tenants in order to inquire after a missing American. It contacted local police authorities, asked at the American Red Cross and the American Express Company, and even put advertisements in the American papers in Paris: letter waiting at the consulate-general.

And the historian has to admit to shock and awe. Shock, from an early twenty-first-century perspective, at how many Americans turned confidently, insistently, to the government for help for sometimes the slightest of slights. But also unexpected awe at how the consular officers seem to have had the time and the energy to follow up a vast number of inquiries. In this period the ratio of officials to citizens abroad was undoubtedly much greater than it is today. Of course we know of only the cases that left a mark in the archives. Those who stormed out disappointed have left few traces there.

People used the government as a mailbox. The consulate handled thousands of pieces of mail per year for American tourists traveling through Paris. For long-term residents, too, its mail-drop function could involve a circuitous yet often efficient routing: a handwritten letter from a woman in Kansas, addressed directly to the secretary of state, was transferred from the State Department in Washington to the embassy in Paris to the consulate, which made inquiries and responded via the embassy to the State Department back to Kansas reassuring her that her son was safe and sound, just not much of a correspondent. The "missing" in France were sometimes simply laggard letter-writers. As one woman apologized: "I have been shamefully neglecting my correspondence; but I have been on the move through Provence—and writing letters is difficult, considering the rather primitive lighting. . . . I am all right, and know where I am most of the time—which is some achievement for an American wanderer.[35]"

Beyond nudging poor letter-writers on behalf of relatives at home, the consulate officer was called upon, sometimes timidly, sometimes with temerity, for everything from custody cases to lost jewelry with the assumption that the government would help out. When Miss Perkins, after a "gay and expensive life," pawned her jewelry to pay her way home, the consulate helped her recover the jewelry by finding the gentleman who held the pawn ticket. After the forgetful but resourceful Nellie S. Hainer misplaced her watch while changing trains at Lille, she sent a telegram from the next station, got a reply that it had been found, and then wrote directly to the secretary of state to recover it. Sure enough, the consulate sent an official to pick it up and send it back to her.[36]

At times the consulate served in loco parentis. Teens who had come to France not so much to leave their country as to leave their family also turned to their official representatives of home away from home when the money ran out. In 1910, young Warner Miller had run away from home with his violin and forty dollars. Both he and his father used the consulate to negotiate his future. Miller seems to have gone to the consulate for help before his now-repentant father, no longer determined to make a college student and businessman out of his artistically inclined son, had written to the secretary of state. The sixteen-year-old Warner had shown up in Paris cold, hungry, and sans violin, which he had had to sell en route. The American consul general, Frank H. Mason, took him under his wing and, even before any communication from the States had arrived, lent Warner an overcoat and some cash and found a spot for him at an inexpensive boarding house in the student quarter on the Left Bank. His father soon sent word that Warner could stay in Paris for at least one year to take violin lessons, and that he would send him twenty-five dollars per month, but that he should earn some income of his own so as not to be idle. Mr. Miller also sent rather detailed instructions to the consulate, hoping that it could find a suitable school for his son and make sure that he had "good but not expensive clothing. I want him to live in a clean place, but not in an expensive manner." He wanted his son to report weekly to the consulate, which would disburse Warner's allowance judiciously. Mason, who had clearly taken a liking to the "plucky and courageous" young man, was happy to keep him under observation, entrusting him to the care of both Deputy Consul-General Yost and the Reverend Shurtleff, one of the American clergymen looking after American students in the Latin Quarter. Mason advised Mr. Miller that twenty-five dollars per month would not be enough and that the chances of his son's finding work in France with no knowledge of French were slim. The State Department and Mr. Miller corresponded about such matters as the price of violins and music lessons, and Mr. Miller expressed his hearty gratitude to Mason and Yost. However, in April of the following year, when the young Miller took ill, Mason agreed with the father that the young man "should at once be sent home and placed on a ranch or farm where he can have pure air and freedom from all mental labor and excitement."[37] When Consul General Mason, "Gallant Soldier, Successful Journalist, and Distinguished Public Servant," died in 1916, his "sweetness, kindness, gentle courtesy and unfailing thoughtfulness" were greatly mourned by all.[38]

The extent of consular help may have depended on the temperament, energy, and resources of the men on the job. If Vice Consul John R. Wood's 1925 report is any indication, he continued in Mason's energetic steps.[39] Protecting the growing number of Americans abroad and their belongings kept the consulate busy indeed, especially dealing with customs agents and shopkeepers. Of the thirty-nine cases Wood reports, there were several instances of true duress due to accident or arrest. When the Misses Moy and Connors of Boston were in a serious car accident on their way to visit the battlefields, the consulate helped arrange their hospitalization and transportation and then helped to negotiate their insurance claims. After a young woman on a school tour was diagnosed with a "hopeless case of insanity," the consul general helped her father, who came to fetch her, and subsequently arranged for some dresses she had ordered to be forwarded to the United States.

Americans also turned to Wood's office for help when they were accused of smuggling. They generally protested their innocence on the grounds that they did not know enough French to understand the limitations on importing tobacco or exporting cash. Consular officials negotiated lesser fines and the return of impounded goods. They also occasionally had drunks on their hands. After Mr. Robinson was released after being arrested for inebriety, and he could not even remember the name of his hotel, the embassy was contacted. He agreed to spend the night elsewhere and handed over his return ticket to the embassy for safekeeping until he sobered up. However, shortly thereafter, Robinson was arrested again and placed in an insane asylum. A consular officer helped arrange for his discharge and this time secured his prompt dispatch on a train to Cherbourg and thence home by steamer.

Citizens also appealed to the consulate for help in custody cases. Mr. Fulton, an upstanding resident of the American community in Paris, asked the consulate for help in order to contact the US consulate in Florence. His divorced wife had taken his four children there and had apparently abandoned them with a governess but no rent money while she left for the United States with a "young Italian Prince." The children and the governess were returned to Paris. In another case, it was the mother who, after initially leaving her three small children with family in Paris, had been able to have two of them join her in London, but she asked the consulate to help her find the third child, who had been "spirited away by its uncle."[40]

Dealing with customs officials, addressing dire health issues, and negotiating custody cases seem, from an early twenty-first-century perspective, logical arenas for state intervention. More surprising is how Wood reported with equanimity, indeed satisfaction, on how the consulate acted as travel agent, lost-and-found department, and small claims bureau. Citizens turned to it for help with finding and forwarding luggage, settling refunds, getting reimbursements, and recovering a lost handbag from a taxi or a forgotten tie stickpin from a hotel room. Not to mention the book manuscript recovered for a Mr. Smith from a literary agent who was no longer answering Smith's letters. The vice consul himself described one couple's dispute with the firm À La Reine d'Angleterre as "a very interesting and deserving case" in which he helped the Banghofs settle a claim over a defective lambskin coat. And when the stout Mrs. Beardslee was disappointed with a custom-made coat, accusing the dressmaker of fraud and insisting on either a refund or a new garment, a consular official accompanied her to the shop. A new coat was made. The vice consul's report is full of pride, describing how he or one of his representatives responded immediately to a written request or personally accompanied an American to press for redress. As Americans in Paris turned to the consulate for help, the consular officer acted as chivalrous savior, charging off to right wrongs for the citizens in his care, negotiating first in a friendly manner, then firmly if necessary. Undoubtedly, as citizens hoped, the official muscle of Uncle Sam helped convince reluctant insurance agencies and coat makers to reimburse sums or articles due. Not one case reported by Wood was unsuccessful. Through "tactful discussion," he was often able to arrange for a "friendly settlement" to the "satisfaction of all parties concerned." And he proudly if a bit self-aggrandizingly included excerpts from thankful notes from grateful citizens: "It makes one truly proud of being an American citizen to receive such help as you rendered."[41]

TO TRAVEL TO HIDE

Not all American citizens abroad want to be helped, however. Just as not everyone set foot in community institutions, not everyone turned to the consulate for protection or help. Some had left to flee not modernity nor Prohibition nor taxes but merely family or debts. Many of the whereabouts cases involved people who simply did not want to be found. When a company wrote to the State Department during World War I for help in trying to locate a former employee—his wife apparently thought him dead and wanted to collect on the life insurance policy—the consulate found Mr. Jones all right, but he was apparently reluctant to go home.[42] Some of the "missing" abroad were clearly just having too much fun and wanted to be left alone; others were happy to answer, via the consulate: send cash now, I've been too embarrassed to ask. For those who just did not want to be found, once ferreted out, they asked the consulate to take no further action or to withhold their address. The reverse was also true: sometimes when Americans in France got into trouble and the consulate tried to find their nearest of kin in the United States, some families who had bid good riddance to their troublesome relatives did not want to be reached or had no funds to help.

When Gladys F. Brown fled to France in 1913, she definitely had no desire to turn to the consulate. But her parents did, and once again the government was called upon in loco parentis. After the eighteen-year-old ran off with George H. Dutting, approximately forty years old and presumed by her parents to be a married man, a series of telegrams and a valiant consular officer tried to intercept her, while her father got on the next available eastward bound ship. Once the SS *Kaiserin Auguste Victoria* arrived in Cherbourg, a consular agent named Osborne went on board, accompanied by a French police officer. The captain of the vessel had received a wireless en route explaining that, contrary to their representations, Mr. Dutting and his companion were not man and wife, and he "had then separated them and endeavored to keep them apart as much as practicable." Hunting down Brown on the ship, the good Osborne tried to reason with her: "[E]xplaining my mission and authority, [I] made an earnest appeal to her sense of propriety, decency, filial affection, and expediency," arguing that she should disembark in Cherbourg until her father arrived. She absolutely refused. Dutting, for his part, swore that he was not married and intended to marry Miss Brown at the earliest opportunity. Given that the captain was unwilling to force her to go ashore and that the French police commissioner said that it was out of the question that he arrest her on a German steamer, Osborne had to give up hope of getting custody of the "thoroughly self-possessed and aggressive young woman [who] appeared to me to be quite unabashed and unrepentant." Dutting did not impress him favorably either. However, a final letter from the father, after thanking the State Department for its help, reported: "As the persons connected in this case are now married, everything has turned out for the best."[43]

IRATE CITIZENS AND THE LIMITS OF HELP

Wayward youth or their parents, just like unhappy customers, could call upon citizenship ties in hopes of mitigating the dangers of going abroad. However, not everyone was so thrilled with the consulate's services, Miss Brown surely much less so than the young Mr. Miller. True, many citizens at home and abroad were very grateful when they got help and wrote to say so: "My dear Mr. Hull, . . . I can not begin to tell you how deeply I appreciate the effort you made and the interest you and your Department showed in locating my son. . . . You not only relieved a worried mother but you have given me and many others, a new, deep respect and confidence in our country and in your Department."[44] Citizens had their patriotism renewed when the protective function worked. The "splendid attention and sympathetic care" rendered by consular officers induced "pride to be able to let our people know that in the event one of them is found in a distressful condition in foreign lands, there is one of their own who can and will cheerfully and competently lend the aid of this strong arm of our national government."[45]

Others, however, railed with irate disappointment. Their indignation was in direct proportion to their unrequited high expectations of the flag's help. Mid-nineteenth-century American travelers reportedly grumbled about "the languid treatment they received at the American Consulate when they reported lost luggage or being overcharged for candles."[46] In 1910, one American who extravagantly compared himself to the wronged French army captain Dreyfus, insisted that he wanted "to know if I can absolutely rely upon my Gov't or if I must definitely consider myself as abandoned? One thing or the other," although he generously added: "I do not ask my Gov't to protect me blindly or to protect me if I am not worthy of protection."[47] And the amiable Frank Mason, who had taken such good care of young Warner Miller, nevertheless concluded in 1911 with regard to another demanding citizen (who had been arrested for vagrancy):

[Carey seems] to have been under the very common delusion that "as an American citizen" he had some peculiar rights and privileges and should have been tried by American rather than by French laws. Men of this class are also apt to suppose that when under arrest in this country it is within the power of the Embassy or Consulate, by simply making a formal demand, to secure their immediate release. The fact is, however, that the criminal laws of France are very definite and strictly enforced; they treat foreigners precisely the same as French citizens, and any injudicious interference in behalf of an American citizen on trial or under sentence for crime committed in this country may be resented and aggravate rather than ameliorate the case of the accused.[48]

Americans in France could be unruly, insulting, irate, and downright difficult in their demands. As Ambassador Herrick described his needy compatriots in the 1920s, many seemed to believe firmly that he was there to look after their interests or pleasure rather than to deal with the French government and French people.[49] Trying to use the symbolic force of their passports and the actual intervention of the US government to wheedle their way out of prison or debt, various citizens addressed American officials with a mixture of gratitude, insistence, insouciance, and outright fraud. At times the consulate even had to defend the French police against quarrelsome American citizens.

At 5:30 one evening in late August 1938, consular officer Mr. MacArthur received a phone call at home.[50] Moses Wolinsky was in jail, and a friend of Wolinsky's had gotten (wormed?) MacArthur's number from the guard on duty at the embassy. So MacArthur ended up spending most of his Saturday night at the police station, ultimately negotiating Wolinsky's release. Wolinsky's dastardly crime? Driving without a front license plate and then resisting arrest. Stopped a first time, Wolinsky had explained that the plate had fallen off after a minor accident and promised to have it fixed. Bad luck, the same officer spotted him again and later claimed that Wolinsky had sped off, an allegation Wolinsky denied. A third time, Wolinsky had the audacity to thumb his nose at the officer without stopping; Wolinsky's version was that he had simply given the officer a friendly wave. When the policeman finally came upon Wolinsky parking his car one day, still without the front plate, he asked him to accompany him to the police station. Wolinsky refused, the officer tried to handcuff him, and Wolinsky kicked and struck him. This he did not deny. A somewhat defiant and bellicose Wolinsky explained to MacArthur that, true enough, he had not had the plate fixed, since it would have cost the dear amount of six dollars to do so and he was leaving shortly for the United States. After reminding Wolinsky that when in Rome . . . , MacArthur appealed to the police chief to release him, given that otherwise he would have to wait in jail until a hearing on Monday or Tuesday. The police chief said that that was impossible, but with a very French wink suggested that if MacArthur called the head of the Judiciary Police, perhaps something could be done. In the end, the police chief agreed to release Wolinsky because he was American, because the consulate had intervened on his behalf, and because he wished to do his part for Franco-American friendship. Wolinsky would be tried in absentia, and if he had no other problems with the police over the next five years, the matter would be completely dropped. To which Wolinsky responded that he was going to sue for unlawful arrest. MacArthur had to reason with him, and they all returned to other Saturday evening occupations.

But it was not the last time MacArthur heard from Wolinsky. A few days later, a staff member from the Hotel Montana called, stating that Wolinsky had left two checks to pay his bill, saying, when questioned about their soundness, that "his good friend, Mr. MacArthur, at the American Embassy" would vouch for him. MacArthur explained the circumstances under which he had met the man. It turned out that after Wolinsky had borrowed money from the hotel manager and made a phone call to New York after settling his bill, the hotel manager had had to take the ill-tempered guest to the Commissariat. Wolinsky finally left his passport as a guarantee that he would not leave town. And then he promptly left town, returning to the United States. This left another consular officer with the delicate task of recovering Wolinsky's passport at the hotel. The reception was hardly welcoming.

Unhappy Americans who found that their citizenship was not sufficient to extricate them from their troubles in a foreign land escalated their rhetoric quickly, making them standard-bearers for all American citizens abroad. "If the embassy does not protect me and other citizens likely to fall in the same rot, who is going to do it? . . . It is an outrage that nobody seems to be willing to take any action to protect the interest of American citizens."[51] Individual matters quickly became defined as jeopardizing all Americans overseas. One man, François (Frank) Gueydan de Roussel, strenuously claiming his innocence after being accused of manufacturing artificial wine in the south of France in 1907, wrote a 188-page "pamphlet" venting his rage against the French judicial system. But he also voiced his anger and despair at the secretary of the US embassy for letting him down.[52]

Turning to the embassy in expectation of succor and defense, disappointed citizens transferred their ire to it when full satisfaction was not forthcoming. Although the registered letter has always been a favorite form of forceful communication in France, Mark Trepionok also went in person to hound French officials and American embassy personnel alike.[53] A naturalized American citizen born in Russia, Trepionok had settled in France from 1905 to 1911 as an American manufacturers' representative, agent for everything from an ironworks factory in San Francisco to a woven hose and rubber company in Boston. He purchased a press agency at one point and was active in sales in the Russian, Siberian, and Manchurian as well as French markets. He had an epistolary style that alternated supplication with insult. Without quite the literary panache of Gueydan de Roussel, Trepionok too published a brochure ("rather scurrilous," according to the State Department) to publicize his side of the story: *In the Land of Thieves*, subtitled *The "Odyssée" of an American Merchant who while losing his Fortune in Paris lost his Citizenship.* "Dogged by Detectives, snubbed by the French Judges and seconded by Representatives of his own Country," Trepionok was enraged at both governments. It is hard to tell whether his thirty-four-page exposé, "sold in all kiosks of the principal R.R. and SS. Stations," was a bestseller.

Trepionok had had money stolen from him. As he put it discreetly: "On the twentieth of September 1908, putting up at the Hôtel du Centre in Paris, I was robbed of Frs. 12,000 within 15 minutes after my arrival at the hotel." The State Department's investigation of the matter filled in the details. Trepionok had apparently visited a low-class hotel "with a disorderly woman." While in the room, his wallet, in a pocket of his jacket hung on the wall, was "visited" by the woman's accomplice; the hotel owner, by her own admission, got a 10 percent cut, and Trepionok accused her of sharing the profits with the police. Trepionok, "a tough customer," as one State Department official frankly described him, certainly left no stone unturned in his own very proactive defense. He wrote to the presidents of France and the United States—and their wives—and had to be thrown out of the French Chancellery when he insisted on getting a copy of his file. He tracked down Jean Longuet (Karl Marx's grandson), the editor of the socialist newspaper *L'Humanité*, in his country home and waited for him for two hours in the parlor until a servant finally told him that Longuet was hiding in the garden and would not receive him. It took Trepionok a dozen letters and six visits to the Chamber of Deputies to get an audience with "H.S. Majesty" Jean Jaurès, which led nowhere. The editor of a scandal sheet received some fifty letters from him, along with biweekly visits to his editorial offices before Trepionok followed him too to his summer place, where his wife claimed that he was not home. In June 1919, when Wilson was in Paris for the Paris Peace Conference, Trepionok wrote to Mrs. Wilson that as her husband was doing "his best to help the victims of the war to obtain redress, even for the Frenchmen," "I thought it is opportune for me to come out and speak about my misfortune also. . . . I appeal to your kind heart, Madam, and in the name of the same humanity implore for your help." Furious with French judges, lawyers, bailiffs, and journalists but also with the secretary of the American embassy for not coming to his aid, Trepionok nonetheless continued insistently to hope that the US government would right his wrong. That he resorted to "vilification against the embassy" did not help his case. The State Department official reiterated that foreigners had to abide by the laws of the land where they lived, and Trepionok was advised that he had to exhaust all local remedies. But he took his case to Washington, laid siege to politicians there, and opined that it was because he was only a naturalized American that protection from the US government was not forthcoming. He was still pleading for redress some thirteen years after the robbery. A last letter in the State Department file is dated 1921, but as an earlier internal note had commented: "This is from a crank, more scoundrel than crank I think."

Disappointed citizens, disappointed government—perhaps it is a draw in some cases. But citizens' anger against the government was often as great as their (dashed) expectations of help. It was also equal to the scrapes in which they had gotten themselves. Blanche M. Turner had a very different problem from Trepionok's, but she was no less furious with the consulate for not providing the help she expected.[54] Turner had been arrested on October 2, 1934, for complicity in the kidnapping of her granddaughter. She was jailed for two months and turned to the consulate only to have them charge her with passport tampering. Indeed, she and her daughter, Constance Fish Shaw, had abducted the five-year old Andrée from the girl's father's home in Liencourt. Shaw had then registered Andrée on her American passport and sailed with her for New York. Turner, the grandmother, a regular in Paris, remained there "to continue my French studies," as she explained to the secretary of state. The father, a Frenchman, Germain Albert Gay, and Constance Shaw had met in 1929, when Shaw came to Paris while her divorce from Mr. Shaw was under way in the United States. There was some talk of marriage, which never took place, but Gay was duly registered as the birth father, and he argued that Shaw had shown scant interest in little Andrée. He and his subsequent wife had raised her as their own, and they were outraged at her being whisked away to America. The attorney for Shaw claimed that under American law, given that the child had been born prior to her mother's actual divorce from Mr. Shaw, little Andrée was legally the daughter of the estranged couple. Gay argued that according to French law, his legal recognition of the child at birth gave him the right of custody. However, once documentary proof arrived showing that the child's mother had still been married to Mr. Shaw at the time of Andrée's birth, Turner was released from prison.

She was, however, taken into custody a second time. This time it was because the French authorities had noticed that her passport had been altered in several places. How could her daughter, Constance Shaw, have been born in 1901 if Turner claimed to have been born in 1890? Not to mention that every time Turner had applied for a passport she had given different dates for her two marriages. Turner wrote indignantly to Cordell Hull, complaining that "pathetic and frantic appeals from prison brought no aid from the American Consulate. . . . I am ill from this imprisonment through their negligence and their shameful after-math in trying to make an issue of the Passport of a trivial date of marriage twenty-three years ago." Like others, she appealed to the secretary of state on behalf of all "innocent American citizens in Paris" who might come into "tragic circumstances" and be "at the mercy of Consular services and American attorneys." The consulate defended itself to the State Department: it had sent a representative to visit Turner in prison and had consulted with American lawyers in Paris. But the "highly emotional" Turner was convinced that both French and American authorities were persecuting her. The consulate concluded with its own grievance: Turner had absorbed many hours of officers' and clerks' time, and they had only been victims of her persecution complex in return. The irate citizen, bane of consular services yet proof of citizens' expectations.

There were clearly limits to the consulate's largesse and patience in the face of demanding citizens. Suppliants' demands were sometimes considered unreasonable. "Writer seems insane. May we not simply file this?"[55] Limited funds were a major constraint. The State Department was willing to make regular mail inquiries concerning whereabouts at no charge, but it drew the line at telegraphic costs; they had to be reimbursed. Furthermore, the consulate had no funds set aside to help repatriate stranded Americans, however desperate. In other cases the limits had to do with the nature of the problem itself and the limitations of a foreign government's intercession on behalf of its citizens in another country, whether it involved Americans unhappy with French rent laws or an American woman about to enter a French convent and turn her inheritance over to it. Relatives in the latter case protested that she had fallen "into the clutches of the Jesuits," but the consulate concluded that the case was entirely outside its province. The thirty-two-year-old woman could legally do as she wished.[56]

Furthermore, while citizens turned to their country for help, they did not always return the favor. The treasurer of the United States and the embassy carried on considerable correspondence in the months following the 1914 exodus in order to recover loans ranging from $7 to $250 that had been extended by the embassy's wartime Relief Commission. After trying to hunt people down, in one case all the way to Shanghai, to get repayment, all too often the embassy had to write back to the Treasury that the debtor could not be found. By July 1916, loans remained outstanding to some seventy-three people, some of "whose manner of living presupposes a present ability to make payment." "All possible pressure" was to be brought to bear on them, including tagging their file for the next time they sought to extend or amend their passports.[57]

After the war, the consulate most often referred relief requests to two organizations that were set up in the postwar period: the American Legion Paris Post, which had its own welfare committee to help out veterans, and the American Aid Society of Paris. The consulate also routinely handed out its lists of American attorneys and detective agencies in France. When Albina Barre, in Marseille, American through marriage to her French-born but US-naturalized husband Gaston, turned to the consulate asking it to contact the sheriff of Los Angeles in order to have her husband arrested for having run off with the children, the consulate responded that this was a private matter and it could not help. Consular officials had, however, made inquiries, and they reassured her that the children were fine and in school. (Mrs. Barre later wrote that she and her husband had made up and all was well.)[58]

PROVING CITIZENSHIP

There was of course a prerequisite for getting help from the government: proving citizenship. Passports have been studied of late as part of the means by which states exercise both sovereignty and surveillance.[59] In the first half of the century passports were not absolutely required either to leave the United States or to enter France, but they were in the process of becoming the great identifier and the open-sesame for crossing borders. This was not to everyone's liking. Some of the "better classes" and the business community felt the need for identification to be an affront to their respectability.[60] But as we can see through the Paris consulate, the identification function worked two ways. When in doubt, the consulate checked out individuals' citizenship status before helping those who requested aid. But Americans also turned to the US consulate for help in proving their credentials to French authorities. Birth certificates, passports, and affidavits had to be shown or procured through State Department channels to prove eligibility for aid from the US government or to prove to French officials that one was indeed American. Americans used various identification papers and a variety of arguments to prove their citizenship. Claimants often referred to their passport number or American ancestry when writing to the ambassador or the secretary of state. They garnered supporting letters and drew on friends and relations to attest to their bona fide Americanness and reputation as upstanding individuals. One man stressed that not only was he a native-born citizen, but he kept almost the whole of his fortune in the United States, where he traveled frequently. He added a (clinching?) economic argument: monies he had loaned to a French company were sent to him from the United States by his bankers and business partners. Birth, business, and dollars were all stamped American. Furthermore, he concluded that the resolution of his particular problem had consequences for all Americans doing business in France and thus for all American interests there.[61] Again, one expatriate's problems stood for the many.

Yet consular officials could be suspicious of identities due to accent or lifestyle. When there was a question concerning the status of a naturalized American citizen, the consulate may have reaffirmed that official policy was that naturalized and native-born citizens were to be protected alike, but the consular officers sometimes commented on the way an individual spoke or added that the man's wife, incidentally, was a native American citizen. The use of citizenship papers could, furthermore, be a matter of timing. When an American-in-waiting, a German who had filed for US citizenship but whose papers had not yet come during the war, had his property sequestered by the French government as belonging to an enemy alien, the State Department advised that since he was in fact still a German subject at the time when the property was seized, there was nothing the US government could do. The French government itself had taken the position that recently acquired American citizenship did not entitle claimants to the release of property that had been German-owned at the time of custody.[62] Post facto naturalization did not work as a defense of property.

The problem for some naturalized citizens was that the 1907 Law of Expatriation had been passed without their knowledge, while they were away. The consular officer in Lyon sounded a little miffed that Mr. Emil or Emile Supper (born in Germany, naturalized in the United States, living in France) had never contacted the office during his twenty years in that city, but he admitted that Supper was "known and considered" as an American citizen there. Yet neither public reputation-as-American nor his business dealings on behalf of American buyers sufficed in his case against the 1907 law's presumption of expatriation for his having overstayed the five-year limit of residence abroad for naturalized citizens. The State Department refused to consider his claim when he came for help at the beginning of the war. He reverted to being German in both American and French eyes, with disastrous consequences. His private and business goods were confiscated, and he was placed in a French internment camp.[63]

During the interwar period, Americans also turned to the US government for help with getting French ID papers. Grace V. Carpenter had lived in France since 1924, but she had let her French residence permit lapse, thinking it was not really necessary. In 1938, as xenophobic French labor law increasingly tightened against foreigners, she found she could no longer work without the permit. Furthermore, she had been hospitalized for anemia and railed against both the Frenchwoman keeping tabs on her apartment and the US consulate for not helping her. She wrote that she was now without money, without luggage (which had been sent on before she canceled her trip), and added that she had not bought a new dress in fifteen years.[64] Arguments that she hoped, in vain, would convince the consulate to intervene on her behalf with the French authorities. Other Americans wrote directly to the White House to help them with their French papers. When, in July 1939, Mildred Arden Blandy's French identity card was refused, she sent a telegram to an old friend at the White House, Edwin Watson, asking that he "act at once for AULD LANG SYNE." Watson in turn drew on his network, writing to "Dear Summy," George T. Summerlin, chief of protocol, explaining that Mildred Arden, daughter of a very famous American actor, had married his roommate from West Point. A telegram went from the Department of State to the embassy in Paris. Officials there looked into the matter and found that her ID card had been withheld because of a disputed 1933 hotel bill; she was now liable for about $125 in fines and faced possible imprisonment and expulsion for having failed to regularize her situation.[65]

The "cloak of citizenship," a protective shield in time of war or peace, was considered by Americans abroad to be their best defense, whether they were bona fide citizens or not. They drew on their networks and mustered sob stories to convince the consulate to help them. But above all they needed proof of citizenship. It could mean the difference between jail and freedom. The examples are many, but suffice it to look at two final cases of questionable identity: that of a businessman/spy and of a titled American woman, both of whom tried to mobilize their links to the United States while living abroad.

Was Raymond Roy (or Rolfe) Swoboda, who crossed the Atlantic eastward accompanied by five commercial trunks, a bona fide American businessman? After thirty-plus-year-old Swoboda was arrested and interned in France during World War I as a German spy in connection with a fire aboard the French steamship *Touraine*, he tried to extend his passport and thus the US government became involved.[66] The passport had expired while he had been in prison, and the State Department granted that the expiration, at least, was not his fault. Swoboda claimed that he was American, having been born in San Francisco to an American father and Québécois mother. His parents separated shortly after he was born, and he had traveled with his mother all over Europe before they returned to the United States. Later he went to China, returned to New York after a nervous breakdown, and then went back to France, where he had lived for the last decade. His peripatetic life did not simplify his citizenship status, and the State Department considered any number of points in Swoboda's tale questionable. He claimed that he had no birth certificate since everything had burned during the 1906 San Francisco fire and that he had lived all over the world because of his mother's forced independence after his parents' separation. The State Department speculated whether she was a woman of dubious virtue and whether Swoboda was a legitimate manufacturers' representative (some of his business acquaintances in the United States swore to his integrity—and wanted their samples back), a crook, or a spy. The US legation officer in Switzerland, where he had gone after being let out of French prison, was also doubtful about his citizenship. The official peppered his appraisal of Swoboda with a number of observations about his lifestyle: he was living in Switzerland with a woman "whom he claims to be his wife"; "his mother has been a wanderer" and, it was believed, "an adventuress or woman of irregular life." Perhaps worst of all, Swoboda's accent was deemed distinctly German, and his idioms were not those "ordinarily used by native Americans, no matter how long they may have resided abroad." Swoboda defended his accent by saying that he spoke four languages, all with a slight accent. This did not prevent his US passport from being taken away from him, and his being arrested again, in Switzerland, for espionage in 1917.

The seventy-year-old American whose calling card identified her as "Baroness Heckscher Von Hohler," thanks to her naturalized but now deceased husband, had a different kind of problem once the war broke out. She had to remind everyone that she had been born in Ohio, was not a German subject, never claimed to be one, spoke no German, had never lived there, and paid taxes in France, where she had lived for the past twenty years. As the State Department Bureau of Citizenship analyzed the situation, "this is merely the case of a foolish woman who has assumed the title to which her late husband may or may not have been entitled." Instructions were sent to the consul at Nice to register "Mrs. Heckscher" "as an American citizen and continue to protect her as such, upon the understanding that she will drop the German title which she has improperly assumed and will return to this country when it is possible for her to do so"—which was "where she belongs," as her nephew and brother in Ohio insisted anyway.[67]

Many overseas Americans used their citizenship one last time, whether they realized it or not. This last service abroad was one that most citizens never knew about, never requested personally, although perhaps if they had thought about it, they might have hoped it would occur: help with burial arrangements. As the community grew, so did the deaths abroad, leading the consulate to come up with a preprinted form in 1912 to facilitate the transmittal of information. There was concern that between French law and American law, there could be confusion as to who should take care of bodies and belongings. When Theodore Gentil died intestate in France in 1880 without any known heir or legal representative, the American consul general had placed a seal on his apartment, as did the local justice of the peace. The American legation subsequently wrote to the Foreign Office to clarify the matter, stressing that "[t]here are many wealthy Americans residing in Paris" and they should be assured of what would happen to their belongings in the case of death.[68] In 1912, a Supreme Court case (*Rocca v. Thompson*) reaffirmed that there is no federal probate law and that consular officials must act in conjunction with the laws of the state in which the deceased dies.

Some people were foresightful. One person wrote her(?) banker (?) that in case (s)he died in Europe, (s)he had already purchased a plot outside of Paris. But (s)he stressed that this did not mean "that I intend always to reside in Europe—or that I am not an American citizen"; it was simply a matter of convenience.[69] Many, however, died without leaving instructions. When the time came, consular officers helped send citizens to their last resting places (either in France or back home), especially for those who died without close friends or family at hand. Many Americans in fact died in Neuilly, not because they lived there but because that is where the American Hospital is located. Wherever they died, if there was no one else to take care of their affairs, a consular officer called in a locksmith, went to the apartment or hotel room, sent a telegram to the closest of kin, advanced money for the transportation of belongings, tipped the janitor, paid the hospital and the undertaker. The officer would also do a detailed inventory of personal effects, from hairpins to soiled drawers, worn, torn, or newly purchased shirts or skirts, a crucifix here, a rosary there, curling irons and eyeglasses, rhinestone ear-clips, glove stretchers and shoe trees, hat boxes, wigs, items of silk and satin or of cloth or wool, old or new, canceled passports, divorce decrees, writing paraphernalia and books. Scrupulous accounts were rendered at the inventory fee of $2 per $100 value of the estate.[70]

Expatriates could be the most patriotic of all when it came to turning to the embassy. But of course not everyone did so. As with other community institutions, there were a multitude of US citizens in Paris who never called on their government representative. We know about only those who showed up at the gate. And we can speculate that there were those who, due to class or race, did not equally feel that they could exercise their citizenship rights in this manner. Although Eugene Bullard's father wrote to the secretary of state to try to get him sent home during the war, for the most part there are few traces in the consular files of protection cases relating to African Americans.[71] Again, names may be no indication; we do not know for sure that Mr. Miller or Miss Brown was a white rather than black citizen. But we may speculate that certain problems—with hatmakers, for example—were the province of certain particularly self-entitled white American women. It seems more than likely that just as African Americans' relationship to America was fraught with trouble in the United States itself, their relationship with officialdom abroad could be more complex than that of Gertrude Stein or the American Chamber of Commerce in Paris. Similarly, it is logical that Americans who went abroad to escape America would be less inclined to visit the consulate, or any of the other American organizations for that matter. The Left Bank crowd apparently dragged its feet and would cross the river to the embassy only under duress. As Samuel Putnam put it: "At times . . . we would find ourselves alarmingly low in funds and faced with the bleak prospect of having to throw ourselves on the nearest American consul."[72]

But many Americans went to the consulate purposefully, even demandingly, a sign in itself perhaps of how elite migrants may have a sense of entitlement to citizenship rights wherever they live. Mrs. Baker's hat may have been the exception rather than the rule. (Wood was surely putting the consulate's best foot forward in his 1925 report.) We simply do not know how many people went away peeved that the consulate did not succeed in getting a hat back or a dress remade, but we do see that the officials tried. As surprising as it seems today that the consular officials had the energy, the time, and the means to deal with such matters in the first half of the twentieth century, so is the idea that Americans abroad expected it of them.

When overseas, expatriates are subject to the laws of their land of residence. But this has not deterred them from seeking succor from their home state. *Au contraire*. American citizens in Paris who got into trouble clearly turned wherever they could for help. Many had the means to hire a lawyer. By the time citizens turned to the consulate, it was usually with the insistent assumption that protection from the strong arm of their strong government would be forthcoming. The US government in turn considered protection of American citizens among its foremost duties, and the consulate helped track down runaway sons and eloping daughters and had to deal with jailed grandmothers. However, citizenship had to be proved, local remedies exhausted, and in the meantime consular officials sometimes questioned accents and the veracity of citizenship claims.

Not all Americans abroad were upstanding members of the community, setting up hospitals and churches, sewing bandages for the war-wounded.

Do-badders and do-gooders alike sought to exercise their citizenship rights, exercising the consul in the process. Ohio-born (the baroness), naturalized (Trepionok), fake (Swoboda?), and future ex-citizens (Gueydan de Roussel fled to Switzerland and ultimately became a citizen there) alike believed that the United States could help them by virtue of their (supposed) citizenship and the power of the United States itself. Americans in Paris may have been expatriates by residence. They were decidedly citizens by self-assertion and as expressed via vigorous complaint.

COUNT BONI DE CASTELLANE AND HIS COUNTESS, FORMERLY MISS ANNA GOULD OF NEW YORK.
From a photograph by Davis & Sanford, New York.

FIGURE 5. Anna Gould and Boni de Castellane (1899).

CHAPTER 3

For Love or Money

Marriage and Divorce in the French Capital

[Y]ou may have a Baron of moderate quality for about
fifty thousand dollars. A good Count, with an ancient title
and an old historical chateau, is cheap at a hundred thousand;
but then the old chateau always wants a good deal of repairing,
and so too, pretty often, does the husband. You cannot get
a well-authenticated Marquis under two hundred thousand,
and a genuine Duke is scarcely to be had under
half a million of dollars. But if one has a million, my love,
one may soar at anything.

LUCY HAMILTON HOOPER (1880)[1]

When the American heiress Anna Gould married the French count Boniface de Castellane in 1895, the private was inevitably very public, and envy accompanied scorn as worried American patriots imagined pots of gold leaving the United States. Debate raged over "title-itis" and the relationship of love and money. Were not American heiresses squandering good American wealth on European nobility in a dubious exchange of money for status? Not to mention that their noble European husbands were often described as contemptible cads. In Lilian Bell's novel *The Expatriates* (1900), the rich American Maria Hollenden literally dies as a result of her infatuation with the despicable French Marquis d'Auteuil. At the same time, at the other end of the social spectrum, moral tales in the American press decried the dangers lurking for unsuspecting American girls in Paris. Wealthy or not, American females in Paris were seen as weak beings in need of protection from roué Frenchmen.

The love lives of Americans in Paris in the first half of the twentieth century were more complicated than most tales of Parisian romance imply. They could be matches made within the community or crosscultural affairs that even led to citizenship loss. Above all, they put national stereotypes to the test, reminding us that gendered stereotypes of nation or city have never been fixed once and for all. Both the wizened elderly gentleman named Uncle Sam who often represents the sage United States and the bare-breasted French revolutionary female Marianne have competing symbols. What about the stalwart American female Columbia and the proud (indeed insufferable) French *coq* (rooster)? As we will see, a gamut of recombined stereotypes was present in the lives, loves, and losses of American residents of the Right Bank.

Paris is a woman's town. Or so the French capital has so often been portrayed. Yet the image of the city depends upon the viewer. Paris may have been "that feminine and flirtatious refuge from reality" in the male gaze;[2] it has abounded in Latin lovers or alluring aristocrats in women's eyes. If Paris was a woman's town, it was also very much a man's town. The turn-of-the-twentieth-century idea that the French capital was dangerous for young American girls meant that it was filled with Frenchmen of dubious merit, be they impecunious artists mooning after models in the Latin Quarter or heiress hunters haunting Right Bank salons in search of *une riche Américaine*. Before World War I, Edith Wharton described France through the eyes of a status-climbing American woman (*Custom of the Country*, 1913), while Henry James had depicted the tribulations of American men trying to enter French society (*The American*, 1877; *The Ambassadors*, 1903). By the interwar years, lesbians such as Djuna Barnes and Natalie Barney were creating their own city of women on the Left Bank, while Hemingway and Miller and hard-drinking American journalists freed from Prohibition imbibed in a very male, heterosexual carousing across the Seine. Competing stereotypes about sexual mores in the City of Light were evident even to good middle-class American girls on overseas studies programs, often housed in the homes of sheltered and chaperoned *jeunes filles bien élevées*, yet confronted elsewhere with that never-failing eye-opener to Americans, prolific smooching on the streets.[3]

These rival images of a female, male, proper bourgeois, but above all sexual Paris are the inevitable background to the private lives of the American men and women who lived in Paris from the Belle Époque through the interwar years. There were the by now legendary lesbians but also the bankers' wives. Danger versus freedom: the contrast is vivid—and in the eye of the beholder. The idea of a sulfurous city was a well-trodden trope, but one largely constructed by American adults with vulnerable youth in mind. Yet their offspring, loose in the City of Light, very often appreciated a place to play away from the disapproving parental eye. After reviewing the stories of danger and freedom, we will see how marriage and divorce in Paris could encapsulate them all. In some cases France was but a complex backdrop to Americans meeting and parting ways. In other instances it was the place for living in close quarters with a gallant or galling Gallic partner. Dangerous liaisons could turn into legitimate happily-ever-afters. Or not. Then, as now, intercultural relations ranged from platonic amity to steamy affairs both heterosexual and homosexual. The latter have been largely written about in the histories of the Left Bank's famous lesbian couples: Gertrude and Alice, Natalie Clifford Barney and her series of lovers, not to mention the more discreet Janet Flanner and Solita Solano.[4] The heterosexual exchanges explored below involved love and money, aristocratic titles and post–World War I politics. French-American marriages were not just cross-cultural affairs sometimes lost in translation. We have little information on who spoke what language and what *faux amis* or *faux pas* were the cause of hilarity, consternation, or distress. What we do know more about is how mundane matters of money also traversed these unions. Who owns the château, the man, the woman, the French citizen, or the American? From Anna Gould to a former Harvard graduate turned poultry farmer—presumably for the love of his French sweetheart—French-American liaisons show how Americans' close encounters with the natives were intertwined with class and culture.

THE DANGERS OF THE CITY: "NO WORK, NO MONEY, EVIL MEN"

"Was it at all possible, for instance, to like Paris enough without liking it too much?" worries Strether in Henry James's *The Ambassadors*.[5] The problem, of course, was sex. Parents and patriots depicted the City of Light as a city of shadows where American youth might be seduced. "Public liberty, private liberty, high culture, and untrammeled sexuality: these are the components of the myth of Paris in the American imagination."[6] There were the prudish Protestants who felt that the Louvre itself was a bad influence—all that revealing statuary! But by and large, the warnings had to do with life in the garrets. At the turn of the century, the fear of bohemia led to a rash of articles in the American press warning parents about letting their children go adrift in the French capital. Indeed, the dangers of the city were one of the main reasons that upstanding American do-gooders sought to create the protective institutions described above. They tried to provide wholesome places where American students could safely congregate for tea or bowling rather than be drawn to the wilds of the lascivious Left Bank.

Each sex was at risk, alarming reports insisted. Sons could pick up bad habits and lose their bearings upon contact with the Parisian atmosphere.

Residence counted. As one guidebook for American women in Paris warned, the American man residing in Paris became "entirely different from the home variety." Adopting polite surface manners and a little of the French idea about women, "he is likely to have a good many half-baked radical theories about love and probably will want to try them out on you."[7] In another vein, one Anglo-American fortnightly in Paris ran a spoof titled "Parents' Protection Agency": Do you know where your son is? Tongue in cheek, the faux detective replied: You may think he is studying the Old Masters, but he has "broken out with beard, an epidemic of which is sweeping the entire Left Bank of Paris"; his French is fine, "coining new descriptive phrases" to yell at taxi drivers; and his female companionship is flourishing—three French girls, two Americans, one German, two Swedes, and a Turk.[8]

While good American boys and men could be corrupted in Paris, most parents' and moralists' fears focused on the female sex. Wealthy women were berated for squandering their riches, poor girls for endangering their health. Both could be morally suspect. While the legatees were criticized for carting their money off to the Old World, the problem was the reverse for the poor female art students who had not brought enough money with them. The dangers for the likes of Anna Gould could be limited by a good prenuptial agreement, and hers was. The remedy for an art student trying to get by on a shoestring was more complex.

Worries over the "average American girl" in Paris combined moral, material, cultural, and patriotic angst. In a lengthy 1906 article in the *Ladies' Home Journal* titled "Is Paris Wise for the Average American Girl?" Mildred Stapley described the appalling life in cheap hotels full of vermin and dirty gray linen, with fifty-year-old sanitary facilities consisting of "dark little lavatories without running water—and a faucet only on each landing." Renting a studio was no better, since this meant that the girl ate, dressed, slept, worked, and entertained her friends all in the same space. The most "undesirable male element" hung around, "men who are renowned as idlers and 'sponges,' young boys of twenty; old sinners of fifty." And many of them, aspiring artists themselves, of "rakish reputation," would "honor" their girlfriends by asking them to pose for them instead of hiring a model.[9]

The issue was not simply a moral one. Material straits compounded moral weakness, in the view of worried observers. Of course, living in an artist's garret was not the fate of American students alone: all newcomers to Paris, including French youth from the provinces, had difficulty finding their bearings. But American students often arrived with enough money for only one year that they tried to make last for two. As the money ran out, "slack habits, loose morals" set in.[10] In July 1913, one alarmed citizen wrote a handwritten letter to the US secretary of state on the back of Yale University's Sunday service program (inspired by that Sunday's sermon?) saying that he had heard dire tales of distress of young Americans in Paris, and even one death of a young American woman art student. He requested that the consul general in Paris investigate the matter and publish a warning to keep others from going there.[11] The consulate complied, although the resulting report, authored by the stalwart consul general Frank Mason was more sanguine about the situation. Mason criticized as passé the rhetoric of pathos and "sufferings and perils" that kept cropping up in the American press. Over the previous eight years, Mason pointed out, a number of organizations such as the YWCA and the American Girls' Club had been created to help young women. The latter was flourishing, contrary to reports that it had closed. Indeed, if occasional cases of want and suffering still existed, they were "through the ignorance and persistent neglect of the victim to avail herself" of the assistance within reach. A bit miffed perhaps that not everyone sought out the proper avenues of salvation, Mason nonetheless admitted that it was not only the victims' own fault. Certain material dangers did exist, beginning with the rainy, damp, and depressing climate during certain months. Different food, unheated houses, and long flights of stairs could affect young women's health. Furthermore, the cost of living had increased in recent years, and girls should carefully budget their trips before coming over, with enough money for the return trip. Like others, Mason argued that girls need not even come to Paris to learn the rudiments of art; they could do that just as well at home. He further warned against the illusion that they would be able to find work in Paris—unless they had perfect French secretarial skills. As for the few suicides that had occurred, Mason was explicit: they were due to dashed expectations rather than hunger or need. His main advice: urge young women to register at the consulate and get in touch with one of the American organizations in town.[12]

It was not only Mason who blamed the girls themselves. Another *Ladies' Home Journal* article cited the naiveté (worse was not imagined) of the "neat little women, earnest in their good, true little hearts," that led them to succumb to temptation.[13] Moralists had a dim view of the American girl's capacity either for becoming a successful artist or for refusing a foreign man's advances. As one woman raising money for a girls' home in Paris argued, 90 percent of the girls who went to Paris to study art had no business doing so: they had no talent and would probably never be serious artists. In the meantime, "they waste their time, injure their health, grow lax in their moral views and get into slatternly habits through the bohemianism that has such a false glow about it."[14] Their parents too were to blame for letting them go off. The pastor of the American Church complained that for all of the hundreds of letters he received each year asking for advice on hotels, pensions, or schools (to which he invariably gave "cheerful attention"), fewer than a dozen asked for pastoral watch over their offspring.[15]

The biggest culprits, it often went without saying, were the men, of French and other foreign origins. This prompted patriotic pleas for the girls to return to America and their own kind. "The Latin Quarter seethes with ne'er-do-weels."[16] "French, Italians, Russians, Roumanians, Greeks—everything—men whose attitude toward her sex is as unlike an American's (in his own country) as one could possibly imagine."[17] Worries about the deleterious effects of Paris on the "Anglo-Saxon standard of morality" abounded. The proof, ironically, was in the visiting. One only had to go to Paris to see debauched Americans. Stapley worried about the "sorry spectacle" that some American young women were for the French: "her name is a reproach to the [American] Quarter"[18]— bad for the girls, bad for the image of the United States. Misguided young women would be better off staying at home, where they could find everything they needed: art lessons and good responsible American boyfriends.

Although the major spate of articles in this puritanical, patriotic, miserabilist, and moralist vein date to the period before World War I, worries resumed along with transatlantic travel after the war. Extravagant confirmation came from the field. One woman, writing from the visitors' writing room of the American Express office in Paris in 1923, appealed directly to "President Harding, White House, Washington (Thank God)":

> Dear Mr. President,
>   There is an attempt to push an American girl into the underworld in Paris because she is out of funds and cannot speak French.
>   No work—no money—evil men.[19]

The plea combined a measure of paranoid desperation with belief in the power of her citizenship and an ages-long idea that a direct appeal to the head of state would solve the problem. (The consulate did help send her home, thanks to the American Aid Society.) In the meantime, the prelates at both American churches in Paris expanded their youth programs in the interwar period in order to try to keep young Americans safe from "the moral and spiritual dangers they face constantly."[20]

FREEDOM: CITY AIR MAKES ONE FREE

Danger in the eyes of parents, clergymen, and patriotic worrywarts was from another point of view freedom. Perceptions of dangers in Paris implied a fear of too much freedom. It is the lasting legacy of the literati, from the cultivated Wharton and James to the pre–World War I bohemia to the interwar Lost Generation, that Paris was imagined as the place where homo- or heterosexual, racial, and even linguistic freedom could be experienced without the stern gaze of Uncle Sam or Mom and Dad. It was where books with explicit sexual content, banned in the United States, could be printed. It was where Sylvia Beach published James Joyce's *Ulysses* and where Djuna Barnes's *Nightwood* appeared. It was where Nancy Cunard published her *Negro Anthology* and where Gertrude Stein and James Joyce experimented with the English language. Everyone from students to socialites came to France to seek something unavailable at home. Socialite Mrs. Mackay had been snubbed by New York society. Others simply sought titles. For the boys as for the girls, from before World War I but even more so in the interwar period, the city meant a release from home, from the strictures of American society. Just "being abroad" most often held its own attraction.

A more run-of-the-mill version of Parisian freedom was expressed in a very different image of the average American young woman there, one at odds with the idea that she was weak prey to the dangers of the city. As one late nineteenth-century French admirer described her: "[She] has a disheveled independence, but is very honest. . . . She goes out and travels unchaperoned; and when it suits her, she goes out and travels with a male friend"; "[she] creates French styles; Parisian women detest her; provincial women despise her; men of all countries are crazy about her, but they would not allow themselves to marry her unless she is colossally rich."[21] The American girl even danced with a "natural gayness, an easy way about her, a simple and genuine cordiality, without affectation or prudeness, that makes her the most amiable of dance partners."[22] The image was drawn particularly in comparison with young middle-class French women—a contrast between "good girls" of both societies. If American girls could be spotted the minute they got off the train, it was not just because of the outfits they wore that no French girl would be caught dead in. It was because they had that independent air.[23]

The independence of *l'Américaine* was noted by French writers from the 1870s on as writers and novelists began to criticize the strict Catholic upbringing that separated sexes before marriage in France. L'Américaine was seen as more spontaneous, thanks both to her Protestant upbringing and to the American notion of self-government, which put responsibility for good behavior in her own hands.[24] True, French attitudes toward the conduct of single American women in Paris could still vary: while one interwar landlord willingly let her American tenant go out, leaving the key in the mailbox for a late return, another got hysterical after her renter came back late from dancing at the Café du Dôme—with her son.[25] But as the "new woman" was being constructed in France, the American woman was seen as a harbinger of female independence.[26] Some American observers, for their part, noticed the effect of Paris on the young American woman. It was a place where she could "cut herself loose" from "our still persistent though rapidly vanishing Puritanical traditions."[27] This could still worry some, but there was also a growing pride among Americans in the ways of their women and an increased acceptance on the part of the French that such behavior was no longer so unseemly. Neither lesbian *salonnière* nor cropped-haired flapper, the "average" young American woman was increasingly seen as a benign and enviable form of female modernity.

The Left Bank writers and artists were thus not the only ones to appreciate a certain social and sexual liberty in the City of Light. But danger, freedom, and independence depend on who's doing what and who's watching and worrying. The experiences of Americans in Paris could range from those succumbing to the sirens of homo- or heterosexual freedom to the "wholesome" independent young woman demurely enjoying a year abroad. Age, sex, and culture all had their part to play in how men or women, boys or girls, French or Americans viewed proper behavior. Parental worry over too much freedom, for their daughters in particular, contrasted with notions that those same young women were independent. Many young Frenchwomen admired and envied the freedom of their American counterparts, while their mothers complained that their daughters were starting to strut with their hands on their hips. Images of danger and freedom could depend on the viewer and the country, but they also changed over time as corseted ideas about women's roles slowly came unlaced.

LE MARIAGE

American couples came to Paris, and Franco-American couples formed there. Relations between the sexes ranged from free-wheeling coupling on the Left Bank to traditional marriages celebrated at the American Cathedral on the Right Bank. Sex, class, and citizenship all had parts to play in the sometimes dangerous but more often legitimate liaisons that brought couples together but also sometimes tore them apart in the French capital.

Marriage and divorce are not, however, just matters of love and hate. They are also matters of citizenship and money. In any given historical moment, men and women of different class and national backgrounds marry in differing proportions. Americans and French in the first half of the twentieth century did not get together totally randomly in Paris. I will first sketch the demographic makeup of the American community—the men, the women, the single, the married—before looking at three variations on heterosexual coupledom: Americans married to Americans, American women married to French men, and American men married to French women.

Two things in particular set the early twentieth-century American community in Paris apart from other immigrants: its wealth and its women. Thanks to the French census and the busybodies of the American Chamber of Commerce who pestered their compatriots to sign on to their Residential List in the *Americans in France* directories, we have a relative sense of how many women and men there were among the Americans in Paris. Harvey Levenstein has already noted the feminization of travel at the end of the nineteenth century.[28] This was true for the resident American community as well. According to the French census, there were more American women than men officially registered in the French capital for most years (56–59% of the total) for 1901 to 1931; only in 1921 and 1936 were women just less than half of the Americans in the city.[29]

Could this preponderance of women be a sign of elite migration in and of itself? A comparison with the mass of foreign workers in interwar France is telling. Whereas the 760,000 Italians and 300,000 Poles in France in 1926— mineworkers, factory workers, agricultural workers—were overwhelmingly male (60%), only the numerous British in Paris outdid the Americans in the number of women in their mostly well-to-do ranks (56%). Indeed one could argue that the percentage of women in each group is practically shorthand for a group's prosperity—only 2 percent of Africans in France were women—were it not for the fact that the Luxemburger and German women in France also outnumbered their male compatriots because large numbers of those women came to France to work in domestic service.[30] Not all female-predominant migrations are elite.

Beyond the by now well-known lesbian *salonnières*, the American women who lived in interwar Paris were a varied lot: wives, widows, spinsters, divorcées, and countesses. Thanks to the Residential Lists of the Chamber of Commerce directories and the useful if now archaic categories, we know who is a Miss and who is a Mrs., and we know the maiden names of married women.[31] There were the single and the married. The majority of Americans living in Paris in 1926 were there with family: over one-half (53%) of the American women and even more of the men (almost 57%) were listed in the directories as part of a couple or other family unit. This included mothers and daughters or sisters (5%) living together. Mothers brought their daughters for a European education—better to accompany them than to send them off on their own—while shopping and socializing themselves. But there were also working women, the Morgan sisters, for example: the Misses Marguerite, Frances, and Virginia, respectively pianist, violinist, and harpist.

Nonetheless, a significant 46 percent of American women (only 43% of men) were listed as living alone. The registry entries may be misleading. As we have seen, Gertrude Stein is listed but Alice B. Toklas is not, neither with Gertrude nor under her own name. There were the single "Misses" but also "Mrs." on their own—gay divorcées? widows? women separated from their husbands? The singly listed women could range from modest singing teachers or "middle-aged women with small, fixed incomes, who can be comfortable in France on a sum that would mean poverty at home,"[32] to American legatees. Of the Mrs., Madames, or Countesses listed alone, over half (54%) were titled, including, in ascending order of rank, four baronesses, two viscountesses, seventeen countesses, four marquises, two duchesses, and five princesses.

The Residential Lists also give us an idea of who married whom. There were two major options: Americans married to Americans and Americans married to French, not to mention Eleanor McCormick, known as the Countess Tolstoï, who reminds us of a small but significant group of American women married to a Russian count, an English lord, or another member of the international elite residing in the French capital. In the Paris *Tribune*, Josephine Baker was hailed as the "first American colored countess" when rumor had it that she had married her manager, the Italian "count" Pepito de Abatino. While doubters questioned whether he was a count and whether they were really married, she flashed a ring and answered "I sure am and he sure is . . . he's got a great big family tree, lots of coats of arms and everything."[33]

The vast majority of Americans were listed as married to other Americans—perhaps not surprisingly given the source. Some of them may have met in Paris, maybe thanks to the churches' chaperoned affairs or the colony's clubs and banquets. Or perhaps they met where everyone else met, in cafés. But most of the directories' American couples presumably came to Paris together. Businessmen brought their wives. And the same last names appear from the Chamber of Commerce's business listings to the roster of the American Women's Club. In this, as in many other things, the Americans of the Right Bank stuck together. Yet Franco-American marriages inevitably occurred as well, often leading to comment and concern.

MIXED MARRIAGES, FROM HEIRESSES TO SOLDIERS

What about the mixed marriages, those brave souls who conquered language to live lives in another culture? Many Americans were in Paris for love of the

French, literally. "International marriages," as they were called, either the cause or an effect of prolonged presence abroad, constituted over one-quarter (27%) of the couples listed in the 1926 directory, to which could be added those American women listed singly whose French surnames indicate a French spouse past if not present.[34] All in all, 15 percent of all married men and 14 percent of all women who were or had been married had a spouse of another nationality. And those are just the ones we know about. Other binational couples undoubtedly melted into the Parisian *boiseries* (woodwork) without leaving a trace in the American colony's records.[35]

The names are only suggestive, but they give an intriguing peek into the hybrid social, cultural, and legal identities behind a Viscountess Antoine Marie Hector de Chabannes Curton la Palice, known in her former life as May Patterson, or an Ethel Simon who became Mme Mouillefarine. Not to mention, in the other direction, a woman née Marguerite du Bouzet de Roquépine de Poudenas who became Mrs. Benjamin Francis Berry. Although men's names did not get changed in the process, may we assume, for example, that Stephen Perry Jocelyn Jr., the poultry farmer in the Aisne department, who earned a bachelor's degree from Harvard in 1916 and belonged to the American Legion, stayed on for the love of Yvonne Dugas, if not necessarily for the chickens? While the Harvard soldier-turned-poultry-farmer is a little-known "type," the Daisy Polk turned Countess de Buyer-Mimeuvre is a better-known figure.

Together, Countess Daisy Polk and Stephen Perry Jocelyn Jr. represent the two most prominent types of French-American couples living in Paris in the first half of the twentieth century: the American heiress married to a cash-poor French nobleman and the starry-eyed Stars and Stripes soldier who tied the knot with his wartime sweetheart. The asymmetry of the mixed marriages is striking. "French-American marriages" is perforce a heterogeneous category. They not only brought two cultures into close contact. They did so with different sexes at different ends of the social spectrum.

American Heiresses, French Aristocrats

The American female falling for the smooth Frenchman: every girl's dream, every mother's nightmare? Let's face it, girls, Frenchmen may have that little *je ne sais quoi*. Yet are they to be trusted? In their gently humorous guide addressed to American women who might come to live or settle in Paris, Helen Josephy and Mary Margaret McBride wrote in 1929: "[S]ince Europeans generalize by labeling all American men as rich, unimaginative and imbecilically good-natured, why should we not hazard a few light-hearted generalizations about Europeans . . . ?" They noted that the European nobility were "prone to propose excursions to this or that European summer resort," while aristocratic Parisians were "capable of real Platonic friendship tinged with a gentle sentimentality" and frequent sending of flowers. In contrast, the young French bourgeois was "simple-headed." He too sent bouquets, but they tended to be stiff—the flowers that is, like the men.[36] The authors warned that the average young American woman was unlikely actually to meet a French aristocrat. (And clearly not all of the French husbands were aristocrats; Hector Guimard, for example, the famous Art Nouveau artist who married Adeline Oppenheim, was simply a good catch in his own right, described as a brilliant conversationalist with a thick mass of wavy black hair and dark curly beard that apparently appealed as much as his curlicued Metro stops.)[37] But the idea of being swept off one's feet by a French nobleman remained the most visible image of French-American marriages in the early part of the twentieth century.

While some mothers and moralists worried about their daughters losing their virtue in exchange for flowers, others worried about the loss of American money for European titles. The stereotype of the heiress and the aristocrat had been a staple of the American imagination of France well before Anna Gould married that dandy-about-town Boni de Castellane in 1895. Already in 1879, John Russell Young noted: "So long as Americans are vain of title and rank and have marriageable daughters, so long as our petroleum and bonanza dowagers see in a coronet a glory exceeding the glory of the sun, or the moon, or an army with banners, and to be prized even above true, genuine American manhood, so long will our maidens dear be bought and sold in a strange sad way."[38]

The attraction was mutual. To paraphrase Jane Austen: It seems to be a truth universally acknowledged that a single man in lack of a good fortune but in possession of an aristocratic title must be in want of a wealthy wife.[39] In turn-of-the-twentieth-century Europe, it seems that an eligible nobleman with a declining fortune was in want of an American heiress. Some French families seem to have specialized in this form of capital accumulation. Three brothers, the counts Bertrand, Paul, and Jacques d'Aramon, married three American women, who thus became a trio of Countesses d'Aramon. Some American women became serial brides, picking up different titles along the way. After her divorce from Count Boniface de Castellane in 1907, Countess Anna Gould subsequently became Duchesse de Talleyrand, aka Princesse de Sagan, after marrying one of Boni's cousins.

These matches made in money became objects of disapproval and derision. In Lucy Hamilton Hooper's 1880 novel *Under the Tricolor*, one of her characters stated unequivocally that if there were perhaps some decent noblemen in the world, there were not many who frequented the American colony. She suggested facetiously that there should be a price list for dowries. But alas, she continued, "our sex is weak, and shiny boots, perfectly-fitting gloves, and a bow, deep as though the gentleman executing it had a hinge on the middle of his back, too often prove irresistible attractions."[40]

With the Gould–de Castellane marriage in 1895, the critique of this type of expatriation of money and perhaps love reached new heights. American papers could be catty. The *New York Times* titled its article about Isabelle Blanche Singer's marriage to Duc Decazes in 1888 "She Pays All the Bills—He Thinks Himself Cheap at the Price."[41] Lilian Bell's acerbic antiaristocratic, anti-French, patriotic novel *The Expatriates*, published in 1900, was a scathing critique of such mismatches. "It is just pathetic, sordid, and occasionally ridiculous," commented another writer.[42] It took a (male) banker to see some merit in these exchanges of money for title. As William Seligman blithely commented: "There is no harm in this as long as the young wives feel contented and happy in their new aristocratic sphere."[43] Yet rich American women "who 'play[ed] at being' aristocrats by marrying (allegedly) titled foreigners instead of 'men of their own race'" were often castigated on patriotic grounds as having made a particularly loathsome renunciation of American democratic ideals.[44]

The phenomenon was Europe-wide. Maureen Montgomery has well analyzed how transatlantic marriages were part of elite formation on both sides of the ocean, with such American-British entitling marriages peaking from 1895 to 1905.[45] France at least was a republic, but American fascination with French titles remained strong. The political and economic power of the French aristocracy may have been long gone, but as everyone from James to Proust knew, its symbolic power persisted.[46] One could argue that French perspectives on titles-for-money depended on whether the source of American money was male or female. As Henry James portrayed them, French aristocratic families were adamant in their rejection of crass American dollars. But this seems particularly the case when the dollars came from men. When James created the iconic contrast of the uncultured "new" American versus the cultivated "old" European in *The American* (1877), his hero Christopher Newman not only represented business activity versus inherited wealth. He was a man threatening a woman's inherited aristocratic name. And he was ultimately unsuccessful in wooing his way into Claire de Cintré's family.

Wealthy American women, on the other hand, could be beneficial to the continuation of the line. *Their* dollars represented a means of maintaining both the family name and the family castle. In May 1895, just two months after Anna Gould married Boni de Castellane, the conservative high-society French newspaper *Le Gaulois* picked up a "very curious list" from the American press which identified rich American women who had married into the European aristocracy. Of the fifty-two American women listed who had married British, Italian, or French noblemen, fifteen had married into Parisian society. The *Gaulois* listed their names and fortunes somewhat triumphantly, estimating that they had brought a total of 169 million francs to France. Anna Gould's 85 million francs were incomparable; others had brought anything from "only" half a million to 15 million francs. Three of the fortunes came from the American sewing-machine inventor Isaac Merritt Singer's estate alone, thanks to his third wife and two of their daughters.[47] The *Gaulois* was positively complimentary if a bit paternalistic about these bearers of imported American wealth, tickled that they had intelligently understood French aristocratic ways:

> They have all assimilated to French ways with a flexibility and a rare intelligence that have made them gracious ornaments of Parisian society, particularly distinguished due to the generosity that they spread around them.
>
> Some of them have become admirable mothers. . . . Nothing shows better the magnificent and useful role of great wealth than to see it thus allied with grace, distinction and goodness.[48]

While images of these upper-class French-American marriages veered from American sneers to a measured Gallic enthusiasm, the marriages themselves succeeded or failed. Winnaretta Singer's marriage to Prince Edmond de Polignac was snidely described as "the marriage of the sewing machine with the lyre," to which her husband blithely replied, "No, it's the marriage of the dollar with the penny [*sou*]."[49] Together, although each apparently had her or his own same-sex lovers, they seem to have had an amicable arrangement joined by a love of music and the Singer fortune.

While we need not doubt that there were contented couples among the titled set, an aristocratic name was no guarantee of harmonious matrimony. Expectations about love and marriage could be sorely tested where money and title were at stake. A long-buried detective's report yields rare detail on one particularly unhappy marriage. It is a cautionary tale about the perils of infidelity (his) and of citizenship loss (hers). When Mrs. Grey, aka Baronne de Vuillemin du Terroir (the names have been changed to protect the not-so-innocent), married the war-decorated baron in 1920, the *New York Times* society article put it delicately: the bride had made her debut some years earlier. She was in fact thirty-five years old and four years prior had inherited a vast sum of money from her skyscraper-building father. The baron, about thirty years old, came from an eminent French family related to Lafayette. The couple had met in France, where she had been living.[50]

By 1928, the marriage was in difficulty. The baroness contacted an American lawyer in Paris to draw up a will that would exclude her husband from her personal estate and would protect any female beneficiary: her daughter's inheritance should be for her sole use, free from any "control or debts or management or disposition whatsoever of any husband."[51] (Her son and daughter were, respectively, three and six years old at the time.) Early the following year, she asked that the baron be followed. He was returning to France from the United States and was not, his wife believed, alone.

The life of a detective is never easy, and this one's first day of assignment started at 3:30 a.m. in order to get to Le Havre in time for the 7:00 a.m. arrival of the transatlantic steamer. As he reported, the baron had indeed sailed with a female companion, about twenty-eight years old. They had separate cabins, but their frequent drunkenness and one especially loud dispute had drawn the attention of the purser. The detective followed them by train and taxi to the Hôtel California in Paris (8th arrondissement), where they checked in at 12:35 p.m.; the baron finally emerged at 6:30 p.m. For the first day's work alone, the detective charged 1,230.90 francs, including tips to steamer and hotel informants, taxis, and overtime for the early hours. Subsequent surveillance revealed that the baron entered and exited the hotel via the service door, in spite of a violent altercation with the staff, which had instructions not to let him use that exit. With two detectives on the case, one who tailed the baron to the hairdresser's, the shirtmaker's, and the tobacconist's, and another who made inquiries at the hotel, it was determined that his friend was most of the time entirely intoxicated. One day alone, she had ordered ten large glasses of port in the morning and two whiskeys and one cocktail in the afternoon. Outdoors she walked with difficulty, and they saw her slap the baron violently in the face. He had bleeding scratches on his face. She too was covered with bruises. In the back room of a restaurant for dinner, he ordered a Perrier while she continued with a whiskey and at one point "took off her shoes and put same on the table; she took unbecoming positions while the Baron was looking at her very fondly, trying to caress her while she was insulting him!!"[52] They ran up a bill, champagne included, of 600 francs, while the snooping detectives billed 274 francs for their own meal and some informants' tips. Back at the hotel, the maître d'hôtel apparently caught the two lovers in their room in a position so compromising that even the detective couldn't bring himself to describe it other than with three suspension points.[53] By the fifth day either the lawyer or the baroness had had enough, and the detective ceased operations.

Was the poor baroness a victim of differing Franco-American mores? Perhaps not so much of her husband's philandering—hardly unknown in the United States—as of reluctant French witnesses. Her lawyer warned her that "hotel keepers in France like to consider themselves bound by professional secrecy," and "misconduct is exceedingly difficult to establish in France";[54] hotel employees could lose their jobs if they told tales out of rooms. However, as the detective's report and expense statement showed, tips apparently did help loosen tongues—which did not mean that such evidence could be used in court. Infidelity is certainly not the province of the French aristocracy alone, and the baron's behavior in particular did not reflect blithely accepted French norms. Even the French detective was appalled, punctuating his reports with disapproving exclamation marks.

In any case, even with the detectives' findings, the baroness apparently did not press for divorce, and four years later she had her husband followed again. By 1950, still married, she still wished to cut her husband out of her will, although she now wished to favor her son over her (married) daughter. (Perhaps the daughter had not heeded her mother's marital advice.) In any case, Mrs. Grey had by now moved up the aristocratic ladder along with her husband. Title trumps infidelity? The baron's father had died; he became a viscount, and she was now Madame la Vicomtesse.

Marriage and Citizenship

Mrs. Grey's problems were not related to only love and money. They were also related to citizenship. Born American, she had lost her American citizenship in 1920 when she married the baron and became French according to American and French law. She went to the United States in 1939 and stayed there seven and a half years, regaining her US citizenship at that time. Then she returned to Europe in 1947 but never resided more than six months in France. In 1948, she completed formalities for domicile in Switzerland, all the while maintaining a home on the chic avenue Montaigne in Paris. By 1950 she was thus American according to American law but still French according to French law, and the lawyers had to reconsider whether, and under which law, she could completely exclude her husband in her will from the millions she had inherited from her father.[55]

American women married to foreigners risked losing their money. They also risked losing their citizenship. As we have seen, in 1907 the US government passed a law stripping American-born women of their US citizenship if they married a foreigner. According to the theory of coverture, a woman had to follow her husband in life, law, and citizenship. The 1907 Expatriation Law was seen by some jurists as simply regularizing an asymmetrical situation arising from a prior law of 1855. The 1855 law, passed at the height of the first wave of nineteenth-century mass immigration to the United States, allowed foreign women to become US citizens through marriage to an American man. The reverse situation, that of an American woman married to a foreign man, was not made clear. In 1907 that "inequity" was resolved, to women's disadvantage, making all women follow their husband's citizenship. American-born women now lost their US citizenship if they married a foreigner. This was true no matter where they lived. The first case tested under the 1907 law was that of Mrs. Mackenzie, an American woman living in California with her British husband. She had become expatriated under the law without ever having emigrated. The case galvanized American women to fight the 1907 law.

Citizenship alone, however, does not define one's legal status with regard to the state. Legal domicile also counts, although it has been neglected in most analyses of citizenship law. And living abroad was an aggravating factor for American women in the first half of the twentieth century. As we have seen, the Cable Act of 1922 reversed the 1907 law for most but not all American women who married foreigners. A woman would no longer automatically lose her citizenship *unless* her husband was himself ineligible for citizenship (i.e., Asian, adding a racial component to ineligibility); or she formally renounced citizenship (i.e., the choice being the individual's and not the state's); or *she moved abroad*. In this respect the Cable Act treated American women like naturalized citizens. Like them, an American woman married to a foreigner who resided continuously for two years in her husband's home country or five years elsewhere outside the United States would still lose her US citizenship. Living abroad in and of itself prompted the presumption that citizenship had been abandoned, even though residing with her husband, was, after all, the natural thing for a woman to do, as one lawyer commented. He advised his female client to return home periodically and from time to time to allow her passport to expire while in America so that a new one could be issued there. While abroad, she should register at the American consulate and promptly pay all her US income taxes. Otherwise, domicile could trump origin. Only in 1930 was this presumption overturned.[56]

Such thorny citizenship issues only contributed to the general belief that persisted into the interwar period that little could come of "international marriages." When Comtesse de la Tour de Saint-Maurice (aka Corneau d'Addison) addressed the topic in a talk at the American Women's Club of Paris in 1933, she lamented that the world heard too much about unhappy Franco-American matches and not enough of the happy ones. Through the prism of widowhood (her husband had died in her arms during World War I), she argued that even if women lacked legal rights in France, "Frenchmen of the best type—and they are legion—endeavour to give their wives every legal liberty, particularly in cases of international marriages." Everyone worried about her before she married, she said, even her "old negro Polly," who had also heard of the lack of rights for women in France. As the countess recounted the conversation to her white audience (apparently presuming that mimicked dialect would entertain), Polly had warned her as she left for her honeymoon: "Miss Gracie, I hear you am goin' to a country where ladies am got no rights. Honey, you jes' take 'em." But the countess claimed that she never tried nor needed to assert her rights. Her young husband had given her a separate bank account "in spite of a frowning French bank president who quite disapproved, and a worried notary manifestly uneasy." The American countess thus defended the male-breadwinner model entrenched in French law that denied certain rights to married women. She countered the naysayers by emphasizing that "[c]hildren are admirably protected. . . . [T]he whole basic principle of French law in regard to marriage is the protection of the home and family with the responsibility for its welfare vested in the father as master of the household."[57]

From the suffering baroness to the conventional countess, wealthy American women married to French noblemen apparently had to put up with the worst and the best. The Right Bank women often did so with aplomb, defending their rights through lawyers or explaining themselves to other American women. Through mixed marriages, some had forfeited love and/or citizenship for title. Others had it all. But in either case, they seem to be unabashed representatives of more traditional female roles, light years away from the lovers rather than mothers, writers rather than wives of the Left Bank.

American Soldiers, French Wives

What about the converse category of Franco-American marriages, distinct by class and by sex, American men married to French women—a phenomenon that peaked two decades after the high point of the turn-of-the-century aristocratic marriages? Harrowing encounters on the battlefront had reversed the damsel-in-distress model as soldiers-in-distress had awoken in hospitals to solicitous French demoiselles coming to their aid. According to a 1930 newspaper account, there were more American men married to Frenchwomen in France than American women married to Frenchmen, unlike today.[58] The result of war rather than inheritance, these couples had met during the war or after, throughout that long period between demobilization and heading home. For the most part they represent another class of Americans, another class of French, both more modest of means than the newly titled legatees and even their cash-strapped spouses.

In James's *The American*, written while he was still in Paris and published in 1877, Christopher Newman is thwarted by an aristocratic French family. But in James's *The Ambassadors*, published some twenty-five years later, his new American man, Chadwick Newsome, has better luck wooing his upper-class French lover. The French aristocracy had unbent somewhat, and the French-American contrasts in the second book are more nuanced. Lambert Strether comes to France from Massachusetts to rescue Newsome, who has apparently taken up with some Parisian hussy, and get him to come home to family and the family business. However, by the end of the novel Strether is wistful regarding his own paths untaken, and almost all the Americans in the novel have become enamored either of France or of specific persons in France. Chad's woman friend, ten years his elder, turns out to be the elegant Mme de Vionnet, a very fine and very wonderful woman, who is separated from her husband and is living with her young daughter in an apartment described as having "possessions not vulgarly numerous, but hereditary, cherished, charming," with an "air of supreme respectability." Semi-detached from family, she can accept the "newsome" American, as the Americans come to accept what she represents.[59]

Nonetheless, unlike American heiresses, American men who successfully married into French aristocratic society were rare. For the most part, the American men who married Frenchwomen were of more moderate resources; they had first come to Paris during World War I to fight and then stayed to flirt. As one soldier put it rather bluntly years later: "The women were nice looking but no more so than the girls back home but those girls were there and the girls in Paris were here."[60] Given military strictures—American women nurses had officer status and were off limits, as were, theoretically, even the licensed French prostitution houses—more informal French-American encounters were inevitable. But the military officials worried about their men falling on the amorous battleground, and the Frenchwoman was blamed. As one version of the well-known ditty "Mademoiselle from Armentières," otherwise known as "Hinky-Dinky Parlez-Vous," went:

> With her I flirted I confess,
> But she got revenge when she said yes. . . .
> My Froggie girl was true to me,
> She was true to me, she was true to you,
> She was true to the whole damn army too.[61]

The army's official *Stars and Stripes* newspaper, along with more local army papers such as the *Oo La La Times* (in Saint Nazaire), tried to discourage American soldiers from being distracted from home and Mom. This could, after all, lead to changed insurance benefits, not to mention that French wives, under the principle of coverture, became American citizens, eligible for transport to the United States, veterans' benefits, and the like. But although the president, the military, and the YMCA did their utmost to discourage relations between American soldiers and French demoiselles—Wilson urged abstinence as both a patriotic duty and a public health measure; the YMCA cautioned that the Frenchwoman was as dangerous as the German foe; and racists worried about the eventual return of "French-women-ruined Negroes"—the predictable happened: venereal disease for some, an "avalanche" of postwar marriages for others. Some five thousand American soldiers married Frenchwomen after the war, leading to migrations in both directions: Frenchwomen moving to the United States, American soldiers ending up in France.[62]

Both French bride and American groom were a far remove from the American heiress and her French nobleman. Studies of postwar marriage registries by Yves-Henri Nouailhat and Mark Meigs show that most of the French war brides came from modest backgrounds. They were maids, laundresses, waitresses, typists. If their family did have property, it was often a small café or hotel where the couple had first met. The American military paychecks in war-weary France undoubtedly helped things along, but all of the American soldier bridegrooms were enlisted men, with the exception of a couple of officers. And given American army rules against racial fraternization, the grooms, with the flamboyant exception of Eugene Bullard, were white.[63]

Although hurried weddings occurred throughout the period—as one Frenchwoman wrote to the US embassy (in French): "I need your permission very quickly because I need to regularize my situation which is delicate and to do so as soon as possible," confirmed by telegram from her American fiancé: "YOUR REFUSAL ALLOWING US TO MARRY HINDERS MY ACTING HONORABLY UNDER DISTRESSING CIRCUMSTANCES"[64]—Bernhard Ragner, former soldier and managing editor of the Chicago *Tribune* in Paris, himself married to a Frenchwoman, dismissed the idea of widespread shotgun weddings. When he reflected on World War I marriages, he gave examples of his legionnaire buddies' happily settled lives in France and provided an almost classic typology of these Franco-American romantic encounters. There was the major, formerly of Wichita, who married his French landlady's daughter and became a first-class hotel owner in his own right. There was Robert L. Jones, who used to be against binational "mixed marriages," just like the young Frenchwoman he met at a dance on Bastille Day. Until they both changed their minds. Not to mention the couple that met on a beach in Cannes and fell in love although he spoke no French, she no English. A bit more unusual, perhaps, was Myer Agen, formerly of Brooklyn, who met his future bride thanks to a poem he published from the trenches. It moved Mlle Hélène Siegel to write to him; a long correspondence and marriage ensued. Ragner's description of the tranquil, ordinary American men contentedly married in France helped to serve the point of his November 1939 article: the United States should enter World War II sooner rather than later. He defended Franco-American amity in the process and perhaps exaggerated the happy endings just a wee bit. This was not the time to elaborate on those close encounters that had not worked out. Ragner was understandably silent on the subject of desertion and divorce.[65]

LE DIVORCE

Divorce does not fit the usual image of Americans in Paris. And certainly, at both ends of the social scale, many compatible French-American couples lived happily together, even if one of them had an accent. However, "seeking relief from matrimonial infelicity," as one *New York Times* article delicately put it, was also a possible outcome, and this was true from rich to poor, from the famous to the unknown, from American couples to Franco-American ones.[66] When love or money runs out, when cultural differences become too stark, or when someone else comes along, people part ways. The list of reasons is hardly specific to binational unions.

We can turn to two types of split-ups among the Americans of Paris: those of American-American couples and those of Franco-American couples. In the first case, American couples living in the city could be torn apart by the French experience—loss of love or money could occur *because of* being in France, but it could also simply be played out against French scenery. In the second case, Franco-American divorces in the American colony could be among the rich or the poor. Law-firm and consular archives give us a peek into these two sets of stories. Unhappy wealthy American women turned to American lawyers for help with their marital woes or to track down no-good noblemen (although Mrs. Grey, it should be remembered, never divorced). Stories of abandonment that appear in the American consulate files are more revealing of the former soldiers and their French wives. The US consulate became the repository of across-the-seas complaints, with separation and abandonment occurring in both directions. Men and women, American and French, turned to the US government for marital redress. There were American wives in the

United States trying to track down wayward American or French husbands lost in France; there were American husbands back in the United States pining for French wives who had returned with the children to their families in France; at the same time, in France, abandoned French wives also turned to the US consulate to seek husbands who had returned to the United States without leaving a trace, let alone any sort of alimony.

Americans v. Americans

For some Americans in France, Paris may have been the background to divorce more than the immediate cause. But their divorces highlight some of the ways in which living in France provided transnational opportunities for some but heightened alienation and even thwarted divorce proceedings for others. Women in particular seem to have turned to the kindly Archibald of the eponymous law firm to present their case, and thick files show the meltdown of marriages from their point of view. Clara Steichen, wife of the well-known photographer Edward Steichen, and Gertrude Moulton, whose husband was a wealthy American-with-purchased-château, both suffered disintegrating marriages far away from home. In one case the dialogue/monologue with the lawyer turns around the loss of love; in the other it has to do with the loss of money. In both cases, the "free air" of France was perhaps an aggravating condition if not the proximate cause. Can it be blamed for Edward Steichen's presumed infidelities, perhaps Arthur Moulton's too? In any case it turned the women into willing or reticent European wanderers.

In the Steichens' case, France was the initial backdrop of a happy marriage. They hobnobbed with the Rodins and other French artists while enjoying the company of other Americans in Paris. But it ultimately became the stage for distance and separation, complicated by World War I, French servants, and curious neighbors. The aspiring artist Edward Steichen had gone to Paris in 1900 to visit Rodin's studio and to study painting. A dashing turtlenecked artistic type, Steichen spent two years in Paris, where he met another American living there, Clara E. Smith. They returned to the United States, wed there, and had two daughters. In 1906, after beginning the Photo-Secession movement with Alfred Stieglitz in New York, Steichen returned to France with his family in order to get back to his painting. Although at least one biographer claims that the marriage was haunted by a love triangle from the beginning—namely Edward, Clara, and his camera—the couple seems at first to have weathered Edward's rise to fame.[67] In his very first years in Paris, Steichen had already begun turning from painting to photography, cleverly realizing that it would help painters become better known if they were seen. His haunting photo of his friend Rodin facing Rodin's famous *Thinker* and his literally gripping photo of J. P. Morgan holding too tightly to the arm of a chair, like his photos of President Roosevelt, soon made Steichen "a celebrity photographer, in both senses of the phrase."[68]

With the declaration of war in 1914, Steichen evacuated his family to the United States, but by then the marriage was deeply troubled, and the couple spent the next few years crossing paths over the Atlantic. In 1915 they separated. Clara left with her younger daughter for France and contacted Samuel G. Archibald's law firm there. She returned to live in the farmhouse outside of Paris in Voulangis that the couple had leased ever since 1908. The neighbors viewed her reappearance alone with one child suspiciously. Three months after the United States entered the war in 1917, Steichen enrolled in the AEF, and he too returned to Europe, to take charge of aerial reconnaissance. In October of that year, Clara went back with daughter Kate to her parents in Missouri, and at the end of the war, the demobilized Steichen settled back alone into his beloved Voulangis. There he definitively redefined himself as a photographer, burning all of his paintings. He finally returned to the United States in 1923 and helped create a photographic aesthetic of glamour that also became a part of the "American Century."[69]

France was not merely the site of their discord. French *moeurs* and social relations in a small French town complicated Clara's cause. Edward Steichen's biographer stresses Clara's paranoid and tempestuous nature.[70] But in her lengthy correspondence with her lawyer, Clara is less paranoid than suspicious, unhappy, and hurt, convinced that her husband had had an affair with her former friend Marion Beckett.[71] In her poems, which she sent to friend Stieglitz hoping that, beyond the personal, they were publishable, she was biting yet forceful in her denunciation of her rival—"To A Petunia: M.H.B.," "You droop with all your lovely weight. / Empoisoned by your own perfume." She depicted herself as the pebble that would still support the edifice "Against the softer finer stones [of white marble/MKB] / Both men and time love to deface."[72] The problem, however, was that Clara had no proof. To Clara's despair, the French servants would not testify. Neither the gardener nor the maid would admit to what she said they said they had seen. Clara was particularly embittered about Francine, whom she had befriended and kept "from a wretched scandal."[73] Particularly in Clara's long correspondence with the understanding if paternalistic "Old Man" Stieglitz, however, it is clear that a gendered subtext to the story had to do with the proper role of the artist's wife. Stieglitz warned Clara about her consuming jealousy coming to no good for anyone and mused on the need of the artist's wife to bear up and provide the creator with a calm environment in which to work. In spite of her clear affection for Stieglitz, Clara later resentfully summarized to him her role in the Camera Group as "I swept and dusted and scrubbed."[74]

Clara filed an alienation of affection suit in New York State, with Beckett named as the culprit. It was against her Paris lawyer's advice. Sympathetic to her, Archibald nonetheless believed that it would be difficult to prove desertion (Edward had given her money) or adultery (given the lack of testimony), and that a suit for alienation of affection would simply create unnecessary scandal. It did. Clara ignored Archibald's advice, lost the suit, divorced without aggravating circumstances, and, years later, became the subject of a novel.[75]

The Steichen divorce may be a parable of the relative fates of the famous and the unknown Americans in Paris. Two Americans in France: one went home to fame and riches, as one more American-artist-who-had-been-in-Paris; the other ended up stuck in Missouri but then went in the 1930s to Mallorca, drawn there by the strong dollar, but increasingly hard on her luck as the dollar sank. Bitter that she had supported Edward when he was poor and unknown, Clara became an international traveler but an unhappy one. She hated Mallorca. "[With] all deference to its scenery I loathe [this hole], a very second-rate, pseudo-artistic colony of my own compatriots. . . . I am fed up on scenery and olive oil and such atmosphere."[76] She longed to be within reach of libraries and of streets that were passable in winter. Clara hoped that her alimony payment could be reevaluated, given Edward's fame and presumed fortune. This would allow her to return to France, the only place where this Ozarks-raised girl loved to live.

Gertrude Wood Bell and Arthur Moulton were already members of the American colony in Paris when they married in 1917, both for the second time. They ran in an international set replete with aristocratic French friends and the American elite. They shared their time between Arthur's Château de la Verrière near Rambouillet (purchased at auction in 1920) and their villa on the Côte d'Azur. In 1929, after "scenes," Mrs. Moulton moved out, to a suite at the Hôtel Princess in the 16th arrondissement. The divorce became final in 1932, and two years later Arthur Moulton married a Russian woman he had met while wintering in Florida. In Gertrude's typically spirited prose in her abundant correspondence with her lawyer, she described her replacement as "a very low character, diabolically clever, Russian—who has been the mistress of a rich Jew from Berlin, and God knows how many other men besides,"[77] and worse yet, "an ignoramus, and often befuddled from over indulgence in spiritus fermentae!"[78] After the separation, Gertrude Moulton remained a regular at the Hôtel

Princess for the next several years but then became a wanderer in the 1930s, "drifting about in hotels" around Europe, complaining about hotel food and life,[79] migrating between Vienna, Salzburg, and Paris. Wherever she roamed, Gertrude used the Chase Bank in Paris as her mailing address and kept in touch with her lawyer, Archibald, who was handling her divorce. Her letters are full of lively tirades about all sorts of things, but largely against her ex-husband.

For a good six years Gertrude Moulton focused on getting her things back from the château. Incredibly detailed inventories—testimony to the material culture of these Americans in Paris—went back and forth between the couple's lawyers, with disputed items identified room by numerous room, from the Louis XVI bedroom and bathroom to the bedroom named "Enfin seuls" (alone at last). Gertrude's "Belgian Shot Gun," a package of tiger skins, and her silver oyster forks were all there. She described the vases and statues, the furniture and silverware (four pages for the silver alone), with their motifs, monograms, and family crests, things Gertrude had inherited and wedding presents from her first marriage. She came from money and had married money. The most disputed items, however, were those she had purchased with money from Arthur. He claimed that items purchased by her with the money he had given her as birthday or Christmas gifts ($10,000) were rightfully his; he had given her the money "on the understanding that these sums would be used for aiding in the running and beautifying of our homes simply because she complained of everything being paid for by me," adding, "When a wife leaves her home and husband, she has absolutely no right to take with her anything but her personal wearing apparel."[80]

Gertrude was in tears over her porcelain collection. She had started it; she had added to it during their marriage; it belonged to her. Seeing a first list of items drawn up by Arthur's lawyer, Gertrude was filled with gloom: "I feel like setting [the list] to mournful dirge-like music! What really cuts me to the quick is having to renounce my Collection of Porcelains. It is like having part of my heart removed, the more so as Moulton has no knowledge nor reverance [sic] to guard and preserve these precious perishable things. I used to watch over them like a hawk, and tend them like delicate children. Well—sic transit glori mundi—accent on the sic !!!"[81] Arthur both contested her ownership of the later pieces and was indignant that she should want to claim even part of the collection, as it would ruin the ensemble, diminishing the beauty of his château. The Moultons' fight over the furniture and the furnishings was epic, although probably not unlike many other divorce settlements, except that the inventories were longer and more valuable. As one lawyer advised her: "don't risk money for furniture."[82]

Gertrude and Arthur fought for years over the lists, trading insults over honor. She insisted that ownership was "a question of honor and not of dispute."[83] He in turn was affronted that she impugned his honesty: "I have always taken her word that she would do nothing that would damage the beauty of La Verrière and I hope that she will live up to this, as I trust she has no desire to make me suffer further."[84]

As for his argument that he no longer knew where things were in the (rearranged) château, she countered, to her lawyer: "Like all misers he knows everything he owns, and counts even the lumps of sugar consumed per day by every servant or guest under his roof. This is one of the reasons I could not endure co-habiting with him!"[85] Gertrude and Arthur fought further, though not surprisingly, over who should pay the lawyers' bills. As she argued, in a huff, her first husband had paid all the fees without question.[86]

At the height of her ire and with characteristic high form, Mrs. Moulton wished to "crush the slimy Dragon under our heels!" She wrote of her own volcanic force to Archibald:

> Let them [Moulton and his lawyer] not try my forbearance and indulgence one whit further, for my righteous wrath and disgust is of such intensity and momentum that I am no longer a sober, balanced being. When a dynamic force like my unfortunate self is thwarted and outraged by foul treatment, chaos and destruction result, and I become a veritable Etna in cataclysmic eruption!! A famous French Statesman, recently dead, christened me 'Le Volcan'! and predicted the resurrection of the Unknown Soldier at the Arc de Triomphe due to the sheer vibrating force of my proximity in the Hotel Princess! ?? One can be a concentrated power for DESTRUCTION as potent as one can be a concentrated power for CONSTRUCTION, and my religion and will is to be solely CONSTRUCTIVE.[87]

Turning gender stereotypes around, Gertrude likened Arthur's arguments to those of "a weak feeble woman!!" "Hysterical women are obnoxious enough," she wrote, "but so called men with crise de nerfs, 'grab my goat' even more so!"[88]

For Gertrude, as for Clara Steichen, a peripatetic life and the relative impoverishment of divorce were set against the fluctuating politics and exchange rates of the interwar period. In 1936, with Roosevelt's upcoming election and dire predictions by some as to the dollar's fate, Arthur Moulton wanted to renegotiate the trust agreement that paid annuities to himself and to Gertrude as alimony. He wanted to shift the capital from American investments into British insurance annuities to be purchased in Canada. The problem had to do with second-guessing the political and economic future. Since the (ultimately temporary) abandonment of the gold standard in early 1933, bonds had been continually declining, and Moulton believed that things would greatly worsen if Roosevelt were reelected. A heated political-economic debate ensued with Moulton arguing that the long-term prospects of the British Empire were far better than those of the United States. Gertrude Moulton, however, like Archibald, still had greater faith in the dollar (describing all the talk about capital flight as so much "bunk and hysteria")[89]. Yet given that Arthur was so keen on his idea, she tried to negotiate to her advantage, agreeing to the change of investment only if he took the remarriage restriction out of the trust agreement. According to the initial settlement, payments to her would stop in the event of her remarriage. Gertrude seems to have coyly tried to spread a rumor that she might have met someone. She called Arthur a "King of misers," acting like Jews and poor white trash, and she again contrasted her own attitude—"calm as a clam over this possible devaluation of the Dollar"—to his state of nerves. "My opinion is that Roosevelt will not devaluate, should he be reelected, and even if he does (which, God forbid!)—in the end 'it will all come out in the wash'! . . . unless Roos. is a mad crashing lunatic. Of course I may be wrong. . . . In these days of world frenzy and chaos, *anything* can happen!"[90] In 1937, after Roosevelt's reelection, the trust was changed. Gertrude held out for American rather than British annuities, but she apparently lost on the remarriage clause. In order for Chase to send her the monthly payments, she had to send them a cable notification: "Alive. Unmarried."[91]

After Gertrude's divorce, she turned herself into a truly transnational European-roving woman, meeting the wealthy and the powerful, heads of church and of state, in order to promote a musical utopia for which she had drawn up detailed plans. As Archibald commented amusedly: "I imagine that before long you will be having the Hapsburgs back—perhaps they will revive the old days, and make the court a center of music, and put you in as musical director."[92] Her passport photo of 1915 shows an elegant young woman, Chihuahua in arms. A 1930s photo shows the pose of a more mature, stouter, dare I say Wagnerian, woman. As early as 1928, Gertrude had printed a proclamation in French, German, Spanish, and Italian to promote the idea of an international center of music near Paris. In it, the porcelain maven who negotiated asparagus tongs and oriental vases with her ex-husband showed a spiritual side as critical of commercial materialism as a Left Bank bohemian could be:

> The project for an International Center of Music is sponsored, upheld, and deemed an urgent spiritual, ethical and intellectual necessity by the Signers of this proclamation. . . .

In the present age, inspiration and the reverence for inspiration are shrouded and shackled by the forces of human envy and greed. The standard of all artistic endeavor and manifestation to-day is largely regulated and dominated by a materialism so crushing, and debased and dragged down by a commercialism so devouring and devastating, that in the near future the sacred fire will be well nigh quenched unless a counteracting, concerned, and desperate effort be made to save the world from the impending disaster.

And this Irishwoman who railed elsewhere against WASPs and miserly Jews pled for universal understanding: "[T]he disinterested encouragement of Art will be ever the most vital, potent and eternal bond between all races and creeds of the Earth; universal peace, mutual understanding and welfare, can only emanate from this divine spring." The printed brochure was somewhat toned down, but it still criticized the "world-wide commercialism which grinds to dust and decadence all who do not and cannot resist its nullifying influence." The International Musical Center would promote and nurture world peace and cosmic enlightenment "and instead of injustice and slothful routine, equity and vital spontaneity."[93]

Gertrude's initial project was to make France a center of music in the summer like Wagner's Bayreuth. Her detailed plans included a blueprint for a revolving outdoor auditorium where the stage set would be formed by the natural backdrop of lake and hill, and the auditorium would float and rotate silently on water, curing the technical problem of long and noisy scenery changes. The site would include studios, restaurants, and housing. The altruistic endeavor was noncommercial and nonpolitical. Its purpose was "to make music, not to make money." A mere four to six million dollars was needed. Combining a materialist critique of commercial society with a Bergsonian vision of élan vital yet also veering toward a 1930s language of the need for regeneration, Gertrude Moulton clearly survived her divorce with panache. As she wrote proudly to her favorite correspondent, Archibald, her husband would drop dead from shock if he saw her enviable position in Austria's capital.[94]

For Moulton had shifted her sights to Salzburg by force of circumstances— her divorce and the Depression. The French government had apparently been interested in her project in 1928 and had offered land in the Parc de St. Cloud. But after the world financial crisis hit, nothing had come of it. As she traveled around Europe, she took her project with her, and well into the 1930s she addressed and no doubt pestered the political and even religious elites of Austria. She was now arguing for the advantages of Salzburg over Paris and of the importance of bringing modern French and other music to Austria. Writing to

His Excellency Herr Bundeskanzler Dr. Dollfuss, she emphasized now that "a small provincial town for this Center" was in fact better than a great metropolis like Paris," for it must be a veritable *Mecca*, and therefore far removed from the vortex and confusion of a big commercial city."[95] She met the US ambassador of Austria and quoted Christ and Goethe to him in defense of her ideals. She had meetings with the cardinal and government officials. She hosted concerts, including one with Marian Anderson. And she gave a tea party to raise funds for new organs at the Salzburg Cathedral.

There was, however, an underside of naiveté at best to her enthusiasm. Gertrude realized that Salzburg might be asking her to run the summer Festspiel in order "to kick out Reinhardt and all the Jews who have the place completely throttled now. . . . I have had a very interesting interview here with Mussolini, and am to confer with him later in Rome—probably in January—on the subject of my plan for an International Center of Music. He is a man after my taste and heart! It has been an absorbingly exciting and interesting Spring and Summer for me."[96]

Europe was falling apart, but Gertrude Wood Bell Moulton was giddy with her newfound freedom and success: "My world used to be like yours," she wrote to Archibald, "and most other people's spheres, strictly confined to my own ego, my family and friends—(a couple of dogs and parrots, several servants and slaves, a few gasping gold fish in a bowl, an alledged [sic] husband, and—an army of Suckers!!) In other words I was bound but not gagged!—encumbered and overladen with possessions, parasites, and extra luggage." She now described herself as a free spirit, "in tune with the Infinite." God had whispered into her ear as she was making a round trip to Walhalla, about the importance of faith. "I even have faith in the DOLLAR!!" From the perspective of the sunlit Alpine slopes, Gertrude believed in the dawn of a new era. "I should love to haul you all out of the sordid depression, routine and dirty havoc of Paris. Here all is hale and healthy, beautiful and gemütlich, and amazingly calm despite the fact that we border on Bavaria and are a constant target for Nazi activities, and *Schrecklichkeit*."[97]

Stubbornly, Moulton remained conservatively optimistic in spite of the uncertainty of the political situation. In March 1935, she wrote: "Matters internationally certainly look stormy since the Germans intention to have things their own way. At least this coup will stir up munitions, give plenty of work to the unemployed, and it is easier to control men in uniform than out of it."[98] We lose trace of Gertrude Moulton after October 1937, but a letter after the war shows that her château furniture was still in storage.

Clara Steichen and Gertrude Moulton may be special cases. To what extent can the demise of their marriages and their lives abroad be attributed to France

itself, however defined? Arthur Moulton, like his wife, moved in a cosmopolitan crowd that led him to the next, Russian, Mrs. Moulton, while Gertrude
began wandering around MittelEuropa in the years before World War II in
her determination to create the perfect music festival. France was but the first
scene in her ultimately very transnational life. As for Clara Steichen, perhaps
France was to blame for her less sanguine rootlessness. In Emily Mitchell's
imagination, it is all Rodin's fault. It is he who, in Mitchell's novel, lays the
seeds of Edward Steichen's marital meanderings, impressing upon him that
artists need to be free from bourgeois convention. In Clara's letters to her
lawyer, it is rather the idea of the artist and the expectations incumbent upon
a creator's wife that are to blame, not to mention rumors of an affair with Isadora Duncan. Gertrude Moulton, at least, found her own freedom in Europe.
Ironically, prewar Austria became the epitome of liberty for her, compared to
Paris, which came to represent her confined married life. Clara Steichen, in
more straitened circumstances in Spain, remained committed to an idealized
version of her life in Paris.

Separation of American couples once they had seen Paris was not only the
province of the rich or well known. The consular records show the ways in
which the siren call of France may have abetted the ending of other American
marriages. For some it had to do with being far from home and leaving obligations—such as wives—at home. When L. Grace Mikell in New York City
stopped receiving alimony from her husband, jazz musician Otto Mikell, in
1929, she wrote to the State Department for help in finding him. He had left
New York to play with Lew Leslie's Blackbirds in Paris, and Grace, ill and
destitute, believed that her husband was now living with Nannie F. Branch in
Paris. The consulate answered that it was a private matter and sent her one of
its standard lists of American lawyers in Paris. When she wrote again four years
later, she complained that the lawyer had asked her for one hundred dollars up
front to try to recover the alimony and that if she had that kind of money she
would not have needed the consulate's help in the first place.[99]

More frequently, it was the war rather than the jazz world that led to amorous and geographic wanderings. One American woman in the United States
wrote to the State Department for help in finding her husband, a doctor who
had gone off to war and had not been heard from since. The State Department
tracked him down and found him alive and well, living in the 16th arrondissement, married to the daughter of a marquis whom he had met in a hospital in
the spring of 1919. He finally showed up at the consulate to advise them that
his attorney was handling the matter. And Dr. Charles F. Bove later became a
well-known surgeon at the American Hospital in Paris.[100]

French-American Divorces

As for Franco-American couples, *ça se complique*. It is impossible to know what role cultural differences played in breakups where other differences may have been the proximate causes. Franco-American divorces were the mirror image of Franco-American marriages, also divided sociologically into the upper crust and the rest. Among the super-wealthy, the extravagant marriages of American women to Frenchmen were sometimes followed by spectacular separations, giving proof of the mismatches to skeptics. Anna Gould and Boniface de Castellane's divorce, after twelve years of marriage, was as public as their marriage had been. Their progressive *désamour* was an incompatibility not just of *moeurs* or of spending habits but of national life views. And when she upped her title by marrying Boni's cousin the Duke of Talleyrand, aka Prince de Sagan, a nasty custody battle was commented upon in society columns. Boni accused the duke of being a "man of notoriously bad behavior" who would never do as father to Boni's children.[101] While Boni's entourage in the Faubourg Saint-Germain crowd mocked Gould's American accent and her lack of knowledge or respect for French aristocratic practices,[102] Boni's mother, Madame la Marquise, took a swipe at American women in general: "She was not raised like young French women; she does not know that if marriage is sometimes a pleasure, it is always a duty."[103]

Another high-class Franco-American marriage and divorce, that of Georges Clemenceau and Mary Plummer, was perhaps sui generis given the ultimate prominence of the French husband. But in many other ways it was perfectly banal. Plummer married Clemenceau in 1869 early in his political career, and, as Sylvie Brodziak has pointed out, there seem to be at least two versions of their story, a male (French) version and a female (American) version, each side defending its sex/compatriot. The first is sympathetic to Clemenceau, describing the young Frenchman who goes off to the United States, teaches riding and French at a girls' school in Connecticut, and meets a lovely young American woman, to whom he writes an impassioned love letter often cited subsequently as testimony to his feelings. The American female side of the story comes from Plummer's friends. They warned her that the dashing Frenchman and his romantic ways were too good to be true. Plummer apparently had trouble adapting to the Vendée, where the couple went to live. The American version emphasizes her courage in raising their children basically on her own. The couple divorced in 1877 according to some, in 1891 according to others. Afterward, while Clemenceau went on to political power, Plummer became a guide for American tourists in Paris and wrote articles for American magazines.[104]

American Men, French Wives: Desperately Seeking Lost Spouses

The divorces of American men and their French brides made *New York Times* headlines in 1925 under the title "Paths of French War Brides Are Rocky," with the subtitle "In American Men They Seldom Find Husbands Who Understand Their Racial Need."[105] In a couple of cases not mentioned in the article, African American soldiers and their white French sweethearts untied the knot several years down the line. Cabaret manager Eugene Bullard's flamboyant marriage to his wartime sweetheart, the daughter of a countess, in 1923, complete with a ten-taxi wedding party parading up Montmartre, ended in divorce seven years later.[106] Worse, black pianist Leon Crutcher's young French wife, the dancer Marie Boyard, shot him to death during a quarrel.[107] But the unhappy marriages that caught the attention of the *New York Times* were neither so explicitly black and white nor so spectacular either in start or finish. They had to do with the more frequent cases of wartime romances ending after the uniforms came off. The writer of the *New York Times* article, using a very pre–World War II language, had another sort of divide in mind when arguing that "racial differences promised incompatibility." They were those between the French "race" and the American one.

An estimated 30 percent of these marriages ended in divorce, according to the *New York Times* author, John R. Ellingston, who laid much of the blame on the American men. They included scheming husbands who suggested that their wives take a break by returning to France, then packed them off for good, subsequently claiming that the women were at fault for desertion. But more generally, in Ellingston's view, everything conspired for disappointment from the outset. Soldiers emerging from isolation in the trenches had been particularly "susceptible to the glamour of the mysterious and charming French women; while a sense of often hysterical national gratitude disposed the French maid to magnify to heroic proportions the virtues and attractions of the American trooper." "Il est si beau," they all gushed, until the reality of married life brought disenchantment for reasons often both material and moral. The relative wealth of the American doughboy in war-weary France might have misled the Frenchwoman, who found that in civilian life her hero was a two-dollar-a-day elevator boy. But beyond monetary difficulties, Ellingston seemed entirely sympathetic with the Frenchwomen who complained that life in the United States was one of money and speed rather than love and ritual. Adequate material comforts did not make a house into a home and were no substitute for what American men lacked, according to him: the art of love.

The consular archives are full of missing-persons complaints in which Frenchwomen turned to the US government for help in retrieving wayward American husbands who had returned to the United States and then, for a variety of reasons, ranging from lack of passage money to loss of love, were never heard from again. In 1922 Yvonne Scott, of Saint-Nazaire, filed a complaint for desertion against her husband, George C. Scott, but he was found alive and well and living with his mother in Brooklyn, simply unable to raise the money to bring his wife and child to the United States. The State Department turned the case over to the American Aid Society in Paris for help with funds for travel.[108] Other separations were more definitive. After Cecil M. Helm married his French girlfriend in the Sarthe in 1919 and they returned to Ohio, thirteen years later, as recounted by wife Marie, they decided that she and their son should return to France in order for him to learn French. But Marie Helm never heard from her husband again, and in 1938 she even wrote directly to the president of the United States to try to find him.[109] We don't know if he did, but the State Department considered that there was "a deep moral obligation underlying all this, irrespective of the international considerations involved."[110]

Not all Frenchwomen-turned-American-wives were eager to live in the United States. It is sometimes they who, after having followed their beau back to his native habitat, deserted their soldier hero in order to return to family and friends in France. For one thing, Frenchwomen in the United States were not always welcome in those 1920s anti-immigrant times. Seen as gold diggers by some and women of dubious virtue by others, Frenchwomen may have had their own reasons to flee home. Distraught American husbands thus also turned to the US government for help in finding French wives and children. G. A. Erickson, of Erickson Floral and Seed Company of Astoria, Oregon, officer in the AEF during the war, had married Yvonne Tabourier at the Hôtel de Ville of Versailles on December 24, 1918. He returned to the United States with her in August 1919, and on September 4, 1920, he became a father. However, when his wife's aunt came to live with them in Oregon, she "did everything to break our happiness." His wife, their baby, and the aunt returned to France for six months, and his wife then decided not to return to Oregon. Heartbroken, Mr. Erickson inquired: What rights do I, as an American citizen, have with regard to my baby girl? He assured the State Department that "we were always happy together. . . . I am in business here, we own our own home which is beautifully furnished, have a Reo car, in fact she has everything that any girl could ask for." The State Department said it was a private matter and sent him its standard list of American lawyers in Paris.[111]

"We are conquered and we like it," wrote ex-soldier and successful journalist Bernhard Ragner two decades after marrying and settling in France. Happy couples had no need for governmental or legal recourse; the consular and law firm archives may skew the story toward the lovelorn. Even the skeptical Ellingston had to admit that two-thirds of American soldier–French sweetheart marriages seem to have survived. Many of these couples settled in the United States, but many stayed in France. According to Ragner, some fifteen hundred of the couples were still in France when World War II broke out.[112]

Do the little-known tales of desertion and divorce nonetheless give the lie to the long-lived romantic vision of Paris and confirm the dangers of sex in the French city? At the very least, they remind us of a counternarrative that speaks to the difficult transition from wartime fling to marital bliss. Binational couples starting life in one country and then trying to live it in another had to navigate gaps between cultural expectations and quotidian realities. Money did not always solidify the Franco-American couples, if Anna Gould and even the florist Erickson are representative examples.

The perils of Paris may have been real, but the definition of freedom and danger was gendered and often class and age specific. Parents worried about their children, especially the females. Victorian Americans and clergymen worried about nude models in all of those art classes. Patriotic congressmen criticized swooning or scheming legatees who exported their inheritances abroad. And good midwestern families worried that they'd never be able to keep their sons down on the farm once they'd been to Paris. But then their sons had trouble keeping their wives in the Midwest once *they* had seen the farm. While the Left Bank of Paris has generated a literary image of a place of both great danger and great freedom, the more ho-hum Right Bank crowd had its own problems as well as its own forms of liberty. Laboring under greater constraints of middle- and upper-class norms, the American colony harbored the occasional bigamist and the American woman distressed by a philandering French husband. Being away from home and from the constraints of family and convention seems to have given added flight to fancy.

"International marriages" became miniature experiments in international relations, yet they varied greatly due less to love than to money. The wealthy American woman marrying a cash-poor French aristocrat lived a very different life from that of the American soldier married to his French girlfriend. The

former could become a bitter baroness or a contented countess. As for the latter, the footsoldier may have seemed more prosperous to a starry-eyed French
demoiselle than his bank account actually warranted. There too, the economics of coupledom would have to weather postwar settling down. For Ragner
and his legionnaire buddies, life in a bicultural environment was well worth
the skepticism of grandmas and of journalists back home. Many of the couples,
rich and poor, lived happily ever after, even if difficulties and disappointments
were also part of the story. The personal experiments in international relations
ultimately foundered or flourished like many marriages, while the romantic
image of French-American liaisons continues to prevail.

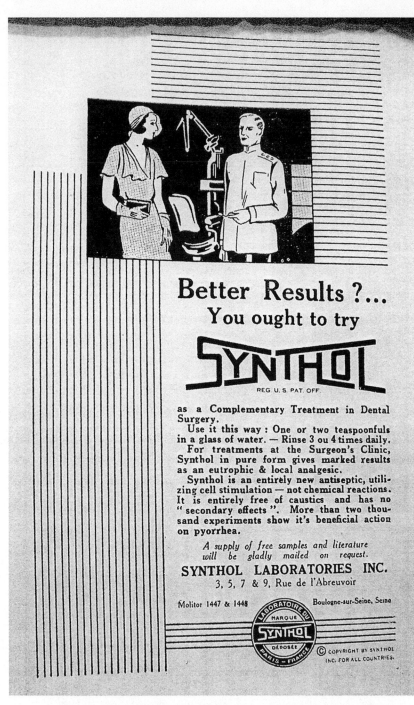

FIGURE 6. Dental ad (*Journal of the American Dental Club of Paris*, 1935).

CHAPTER 4

Americans at Work

Of Grocers, Fashion Writers,
Dentists, and Lawyers

A country wishing to export its products
must begin by exporting men.

AMERICAN CHAMBER OF COMMERCE IN PARIS[1]

The problem is that we do not usually think of Americans in Paris as Americans at work. We think of them as Americans in love or Americans at play, sitting in Left Bank cafés, gathering in salons, experimenting with avant-garde art, music, literature, sexuality. Or perhaps we think of the riches of the rentiers. To stretch a point, we could consider the ways in which the Right Bank rentiers "worked" at it. Conspicuous consumption takes a lot of effort, after all. The Right Bank wealthy men and especially women were assiduous big spenders and avid collectors of antiques, furnishing their vast apartments, choosing their porcelain pieces, holding balls, importing American-style bathrooms for their villas. And it was no easy task dealing with French dressmakers and caterers. However, the vast majority of Americans in the French capital were hard workers of another sort, notably involved in the dynamics of corporate business that we will see in the next chapter. But not everyone was a manufacturer's representative or industrialist. We can first look at the variety of jobs Americans did in Paris, from those servicing the American colony itself to those marketing American specialties to the French. Lawyers and the indefatigable organizers of the American Chamber of Commerce were important go-betweens with the French. Above all, jobs were gendered; men and women did different things. By the turn of the twentieth century, although some still settled in to spend, most Right Bank Americans were there to make money. The American colony was being transformed from a community of the idle rich into a busy group of the working rich. They were not your average immigrant workers.

CULTURAL WORKERS

Before turning to the dentists and jazzmen, I would suggest a rewriting of the Left Bank story as one of cultural work. While businessmen sold in Europe what they produced in the United States, cultural workers sold in the United States what they produced while in Europe. Writing is hard work, and the literal business of writing and publishing, a hot topic in today's changing technological climate, was no less tricky in the pen, paper, and printing-press era. Some, such as Gertrude Stein or Nancy Cunard, had family money sustaining them. Others had to hold day jobs: Henry Miller pursued commas and semicolons as financial page proofreader at the Paris edition of the *Chicago Tribune*, while Hemingway made ends meet, barely at times, as a journalist. Journalists were indeed an important group of American cultural workers in town who have too often been treated as accessories to the expatriate literary writers.[2] The wage workers of the word included foreign correspondents and the journalists of the Paris American papers. By 1926, there were sixty-two American magazines and newspapers published or represented in France, from the *Brooklyn Daily Eagle* to the *Dry Goods Economist*, not to mention the *Christian Science Monitor* and the *Wall Street Journal*. They and the Paris editions of the *Chicago Tribune* and the *New York Herald* furnished work for many "writers-in-waiting";[3] other newspaper workers were dedicated journalists also trying their hand at literature. In any case, journalism in Paris was not just adventure in the City of Light; it was hard work, even repetitive routine at first, as William Shirer admitted. Eric Sevareid wrote that if he was initially impressed by the beret-and-beard set hanging out on café terraces, he found it a certain embarrassment, and besides, he had no time for such things: "I was working."[4]

And so were bookshop owner Sylvia Beach and cabaret owner Bricktop, other American cultural workers making their living in Paris. Family money helped Sylvia Beach get started: "Opening bookshop in Paris. Please send money."[5] Decades ago Shari Benstock emphasized the importance of the women expatriates' involvement in publishing in Paris, with its financial risk and physical labor, from those setting up their own printing presses (as Cunard had been warned by Virginia Woolf, "Your hands will always be covered with ink!") to those, like Beach, who materially aided the publication of others. While Beach's claim to fame has most often centered on the fact that she was the woman who gave the world James Joyce's *Ulysses*, she was above all an enterprising, indefatigable businesswoman. Her memoirs reveal how shaky her finances were, both for the publication of *Ulysses* and for the bookshop. Beach had first thought she would open a French bookstore in New York, but she did not have enough capital to afford New York rents. Paris was cheaper, and Adrienne Monnier, one of the first women in France to open a bookstore and ultimately Beach's lifelong companion, encouraged Beach to open an American bookshop in Paris instead. Monnier taught her the ropes and helped her negotiate with the French landlord and get the required permits. They made a famous pair of Left Bank bookwomen.[6]

Shrewd businesswoman or softhearted pushover? "Sylvia's generosity of spirit refused commercial constraints," writes one biographer; her bookshop, like Monnier's, was an "intellectual rather than commercial success."[7] Beach used a rudimentary accounting and lending system: there were no catalogs or card index; she either remembered who had borrowed a book or had to look through all of the members' cards. Her great publishing venture of Joyce's masterpiece in 1922 may have made her fame, but it hurt her finances. Joyce, a demanding friend, was often low on cash, and Beach served not only as his publisher but also as his business agent and occasional banker. She fronted the money for the publication and helped Joyce out when he was in debt, taking out loans from her own family and friends to do so. And Joyce insisted that his works be sold at low prices. Furthermore, since the book was banned in the United States and thus not under copyright there, "the rape of *Ulysses*" by pirating there in 1926 meant that neither she nor Joyce benefited from the book's US initial distribution. Beach is too generous in her memoirs to do more than allude to her disappointment. But the Joyce archives show that she forthrightly demanded twenty-five thousand dollars from his literary agent when an American contract seemed impending. (No reply.) As Beach stoically commented: "People imagined, perhaps, that I was making a lot of money from *Ulysses*, [but while] the pleasure was mine—an infinite pleasure; the profits were for him." Beach never published another book, even though hopeful writers sent her all kinds of manuscripts, from long poems to pornography. On the verge of bankruptcy in the 1930s, as Americans went home and the dollar plunged, Shakespeare and Company nonetheless survived. Pride was stronger than profit, and it tickled Beach that her bookstore was one of the sights pointed out on American Express bus tours.[8]

Beach described her business talents in backhanded terms—"Imagine, too, the bookkeeping, besides the bookselling and lending! I had to run three bank accounts in three different currencies, American, French, and English, and calculating in tuppences and centimes and pennies was one of my most puzzling occupations."[9] But she need not have been dismissive of her business acumen. Although her dealings on behalf of Joyce sometimes leave her seeming the ultimately duped admirer, another story shows how Beach could outmaneuver the competition and play tough when needed. In the mid-1920s, Ford Madox Ford announced that he was going to open a bookshop in Paris that would sell books at better prices than the "notorious" prices expatriates had hitherto been paying. Beach took it personally. Overnight, Ford, his magazine, The *Transatlantic Review*, and its renowned authors disappeared from the window, tables, and bookshelves of Shakespeare and Company. Monthly sales of the magazine dropped from fifty to zero. The writers put pressure on Ford, who finally gave in. As Beach commented: "It taught them all a good lesson and me too."[10]

Just as Sylvia Beach was not simply James Joyce's publisher, Bricktop was not just a cabaret singer. Neither Bricktop nor the iconic but sui generis Josephine Baker could wire home for money like many of the white women in business in Paris. Josephine Baker's business talents are somewhat in dispute: was she manipulated by her husband-manager or did she make her own decisions as her recent biographer has stressed?[11] Bricktop, as well known in Montmartre as Josephine Baker was across town, ran not just her own career but also those of others. She reigned over the cash register at her famous Pigalle club in Montmartre and commented in her memoirs: "I wasn't worried about the money, but I was worried about not being taken seriously as a businesswoman." It was hardly an easy business. Throwing out ruffians when necessary, she improvised her own system of checking bills. "I had to keep my clients happy but make sure they didn't go too far with their antics, watch the waiters so they didn't cheat the customers, make change, tally the receipts, hire and fire the entertainers." As Kay Boyle described her, Bricktop could sing, stop for two lines to yell at the guys in the back to keep it down, and then continue, barely missing a beat. Bricktop made her cabaret into one of the most elegant and chic clubs in Paris—evening dress required; no ladies unescorted.[12]

In addition to her club, Bricktop did a good business entertaining at private parties, teaching the rudiments of jazz to the rhythm-impaired. When the Charleston became all the rage, Cole Porter organized a bash where Bricktop taught the dance to them all, including Aga Khan. She subsequently had an impressive list of "high-society dancing pupils," including the Prince of Wales—which explains how her address book was filled with the dukes and duchesses of Paris society—who hired her and her troop to perform. The stock market crash did not affect the Montmartre clubs at first, and Bricktop even decided to expand. In November 1931, with a new partner, the singer Mabel Mercer, she moved down the block to a new place three times the size of the old one.

French gangsters gave her trouble (they'd seen too many American gangster films, according to Bricktop), but with a little help from their Chinese cook, who threatened a mobster with a giant carving knife, Bricktop and Mercer held their own. They refused both protection and prostitutes at their club. However, as the Depression came to Montmartre and French labor laws restricted the number of foreign musicians, the African American musico-economic niche declined. By 1934, Bricktop moved the club to a smaller place and had to give up her country villa at Bougival. Her furs and sole diamond went in and out of the pawn shop, until she and Mercer finally closed the club in 1936. Mercer returned to New York, while Bricktop went to work for others and stayed stubbornly in Paris until October 1939.[13]

This focus on the cultural workers raises two important questions regarding all working Americans in Paris: for whom did the Americans toil? Was the journalists' work a largely intra-American affair, destined for a Brooklyn, Kansas, or San Francisco audience or aimed at the American readership in Paris? Could their work, like Beach's bookstore or Bricktop's cabaret, possibly be considered an "ethnic business," as migration scholars have called immigrant niche markets? We will return to the Americanness of the Americans' work, but first let us contemplate another fact of working life within the American colony: American women and men in the City of Light had largely different occupations.

WOMEN AT WORK

Gendered jobs were no less true for Americans than for other immigrants in the city or for the French labor market in general. But there was a division of labor among the American women themselves. While the legendary lesbians of the Left Bank and the heiresses of the Right Bank both "worked" at setting up salons or holding balls, and the bankers and lawyers' wives worked at laying wreaths and organizing their club activities, a good number of American women in Paris engaged in business activities. Some, like Beach and Bricktop, worked in otherwise "male" jobs, as bookstore or cabaret owners. But many others made their living in what were tenaciously considered "women's" jobs.

First of all, the women were more visible in the Professionals List of the *Americans in France* directories than in the much more voluminous and much more male Commercial List. In 1926, the top three professional categories for men and women combined were artists (178), writers (164) and musicians (61). Women were one-half of the writers although only one-quarter of the artists or musicians, but the male professionals were mostly engineers (61) and lawyers (42). Women were also teachers and lecturers (18) and librarians (8), importing the

Dewey decimal system and American library ideals to France.[14] There was one female osteopath and one female physician, who worked at the American Memorial Hospital in Reims.

The eighty-some women writers who listed themselves as professionals included Gertrude Stein and journalist May Birkhead. As Edith Wharton explained it, France was more accepting of women writers than the United States.[15] But not everyone was a successful novelist moving in elite French circles or an avant-garde American hobnobbing with Picasso like Stein. And neither Wharton nor Stein needed to write to make a living. It was journalism more than literary writing that provided a way for some American women (like men) to leave America behind while writing for it. Besides Janet Flanner, of *New Yorker* fame, who came to Paris in 1922, other well-known women journalists plied their pens in the interwar years, such as Dorothy Thompson and Mary Knight. Thompson at first eked out a living writing publicity copy for the American Red Cross at a penny a line, but she ultimately became a reporter, based in Berlin, covering nine European countries. Knight was a determined journalist who dressed as a man to sneak into a guillotining (still used for capital punishment in France until 1977). Florence Gilliam, theater critic and Latin Quarter gossip, and poet Pauline Avery Crawford also had regular newspaper columns.[16]

But May Birkhead, the American colony's well-known society columnist, had the kind of job more typically reserved for female reporters in Paris. Women covered "women's" topics: society gatherings or the fashion world. Society news was circulation-building; people loved to see themselves in the paper, whether on a ship's list or in coverage of gala balls. Birkhead had been a successful dressmaker in Missouri who had saved money for a European trip and just happened to be on one of the first ships that steamed over to help the sinking *Titanic* in 1912. Her on-the-spot interviews with survivors turned into a job at the Paris *Herald* before she moved to the *Tribune*. She would show up in the newsroom "in horn-rimmed glasses and a Lanvin evening gown covered by a Chanel velvet cloak, briskly pecking out on her typewriter that night's dinner list at the Ritz or the names of the guests at the Princess de Polignac's luncheon party."[17]

Fashion news by women and for women was aimed at American women both in Paris and at home. Bettina (Betty) Bedwell parlayed her reporting on Paris fashions into a job as Paris correspondent of the American Textile Color Card Association (TCCA). She frequented Montmartre artists while haunting Parisian streets for the latest color schemes. She reported excitedly on the appearance of almond green in all the store windows in May 1929 and on the colored glove fad in 1936. Whereas the TCCA had formerly relied on its members' trips to track French fashions, by 1923 it decided to hire its own representative in France. It hired a French consultant first but after a few years turned to Bedwell. She could cable in nuanced English, with full knowledge of both American and French styles—able to recognize those elements of Parisian elegance that would work for the more casually dressed American woman.[18]

Women were also professional shoppers. While many came to Paris to shop for themselves, several made it their business to help their sister shoppers who came to town. Tourists thus created jobs for residents. Expert shoppers working through travel bureaus or banks could get a 5–10 percent commission on purchases while helping visiting Americans make their way between dress shops and hatmakers. Over the six years she was in business, Helen Scott's Information Service for Americans offered help with everything from shopping advice to getting travel or theater tickets to hiring domestic servants or finding interpreters, lawyers, or chaperons. With her ten-person staff, she could help businesses hire twenty stenographers on a half-day's notice or help American tourists buy last-minute gifts. At the height of her activity, she was running her business out of a five-room suite on the fashionable rue du Faubourg Saint-Honoré. Other women shopped for department stores rather than for individuals. There were several women resident buyers for the major stores in the United States, but it wasn't easy. As Mrs. R. De V. Wodery, in Paris for over thirty years, pointed out, you needed to know both French and the city and go back to the United States regularly in order to mingle with women there.[19]

In their lighthearted but serious 1929 *Paris Is a Woman's Town*, Helen Josephy and Mary Margaret McBride proudly highlighted the American working women of Paris: "American women of energy, courage and ideas can always make their living in Paris." True, most American women went to Paris to spend and to enjoy, cashing traveler's checks recklessly until they ran out. "Unless there is somebody to whom she can cable for money, however, this phase is soon ended and the serious business of life begins." Even if they thought that women's work in Paris was more accidental than by design, Josephy and McBride theorized that women could be successful in the French capital because ingenuity counted more there than large amounts of capital and bewildered tourists were relieved to do business with Americans. The chief problems, they admitted, were the climate, the numerous holidays that slowed things down, and French taxes. But Josephy and McBride were convinced that another thing worked in favor of American woman: the fact that most middle-class French women stayed at home. "This attitude of French women is one of the reasons why Paris is a fertile field for the American business woman."[20]

Josephy and McBride advised their readers about jobs available to women, "women's jobs" all. The couturier Patou had started a small fad for American mannequins (models), but experience was required, and they warned that you needed to be twenty pounds underweight and keep off the French pastry and chocolates. The easiest jobs to find were as stenographers, for whom there was a demand within the American community itself. Banks, tourist bureaus, and American doctors and dentists all preferred American secretaries. The salaries were not New York scale, Josephy and McBride warned, and the secretarial chairs were antiques, but everyone got two hours for lunch and three weeks' paid vacation. Other women's jobs required more experience. Women taught at the American High School at 4bis rue d'Auteuil, and Mrs. Sanua-Seymour had founded and directed the Thursday School of the American Legion.[21] A graduate nurse could always register for private duty at the American Hospital, and the American Library had twenty women on staff.

Josephy and McBride were proud of the American women who had made careers for themselves in Paris and cheerfully gave several examples, beginning with Mary Bendelari, hailing from Missouri, McBride's home state. Bendelari had started the successful Sandarlari shoe business, which, true, had almost folded due to the dropping franc. But she had a trump card that French shoe companies did not: "Miss Bendelari cabled Dad." There was Rose White, an opera singer who had opened a deluxe shop on the ritzy rue de la Paix, selling bags she designed herself, and Agnes Anderson Butler, who had come to France with the Red Cross and now ran the Butler's Pantry in the Latin Quarter. The secret to her success? Going to the market hatless with a basket on her arm, just like French housewives, and getting bargains just like them.[22] Thus in some cases it was the specific American element (Dad's money) that was the key to success; in others it was doing like the French.

In the case of the more high-profile Thérèse Bonney, who embarked on a mission of exporting French modernity to the United States, success was a combination of a keen eye, determination, and excellent timing as French modern design took off. As Bonney put it, the United States might have skyscrapers, but its interior design was passé; France, on the other hand, had no skyscrapers, but its interior decorating incarnated ultramodernity. Bonney had moved to France, where she completed a doctorate at the Sorbonne on the theater of Alexandre Dumas *fils* (the fourth woman to get a doctorate at the Sorbonne and the tenth American to do so, as she proudly wrote her mother). While a student, she made her living translating captions for the first American movies shown in Paris, but by the early 1920s she had become a freelance journalist for French as well as American papers. Then she was offered a job as an assistant to the Paris photographer of Underwood and Underwood, the major US stereograph publisher. By 1924 she had set up her own agency, the Bonney Service, and within five years she was running the most important news photo service in Europe, with a staff of nine and clients in twenty countries. Bonney photographed famous French artists and acted as their New York agent. She captured in print the well-known Left Bank Americans in Paris, but she was a resolutely Right Bank woman herself, more interested in Helena Rubinstein's Right Bank art deco living room than in Sylvia Beach's Left Bank shop. Bonney stayed in France for sixty years, but she remained resolutely American, never considering herself an "expatriate." She continued to sell modernity to Americans while selling herself to the American press as a specialist in French art and modern life.[23]

Yet if the American working women of Paris were more often fashion writers than sportswriters and largely buyers rather than sellers, a small number of them seem to have broken into "men's" fields. If a sample of the American Chamber of Commerce's Commercial Lists is any indication, women represented only 2–3 percent of the American businesses in town, and most of them were resident department-store buyers or personal shoppers such as Helen Scott. There were a few exceptions to the gendered job rule, including Rosalind Wheeler, associated with Seaman and Pendergast, the successful female real estate operators in New York City, and Hortense McDonald, European publicity manager for the United States Steamship lines, the first woman member of the Neptune Association of Masters and Mates of Ocean and Coastwise Steam Vessels. Mrs. H. E. Seemuller, exporter of American machinery, is my favorite. A seller rather than a buyer, at the height of her career she represented six American machinery manufacturers from New York to Indiana, with offices at a fancy boulevard Malesherbes address.[24]

MEN AT WORK

While the women were taking steno or covering fashion shows and society events, most of the American men in France were, not surprisingly, engaged in "male" activities. There were the farming few and the hordes of manufacturers' representatives and company executives, but there was also boxing promoter Jeff Dickson, war veteran who renovated the Vel d'Hiv indoor sports stadium in 1931 and helped make ice hockey all the rage in Paris. The sales and corporate world was, as we will see, a decidedly man's world. But so were myriad other jobs that American men did. Some occupations seem to have been left over from the war. Truck repair undoubtedly prepared at least one ex-doughboy to become a mechanic, specializing in American cars, as he advertised (in French):

<blockquote>
REPARATIONS OF ALL AMERICAN AUTOMOBILES
Specialty: Fords and Dodges
Repairs done by an American Specialist
CAREFUL WORK, MODERATE PRICES[25]
</blockquote>

Some of the ex-soldiers in Paris made livings for themselves by transferring skills from home. Others married into the French in-laws' family farm, grocery, or garage.

By the interwar years, the sheer variety of men's jobs in France was impressive, from an American actually named Mr. Babbitt, running a garage in Besançon, to the prominent Seligmann art dealers. The embassy, the consulate, and, especially in the immediate postwar world, military organizations such as battle monument committees also provided a small number of government jobs. But the vast majority of Americans in Paris then and now were civilians. Some directed playgrounds and preparatory schools; others sold chicken feed or beer, managed news services, or ran brokerage firms. There were carpenters, dentists, lawyers, automobile dealers, machine and car repairmen, and restaurant owners, in addition to one man who was both armed guard and interpreter at the Chase Bank in Paris.[26]

Hitherto far from historians' gaze have been the admittedly few American "farmers" in France. Many of the soldiers may not have wanted to return to their American farms after they'd seen "Paree," but some of them did settle on French farms, presumably with their French sweethearts. The interwar French demographer Georges Mauco gave the Anglo-American *colons* or agricultural colonists their own subsection in his book on foreigners in France, only to dismiss them as an epiphenomenon.[27] The eighty-one Americans he counted in the 1926 census who owned or leased agricultural property in France were of three sorts, according to him: rich capitalists who had simply invested in land as the franc fell; absentee landlords who had bought themselves a vacation spot amidst picturesque French cows; and real American farmers, who worked the land. The latter were few in number, mostly former soldiers married to Frenchwomen; yet Stephen Jocelyn, the Harvard-trained poultry farmer in the Aisne, was not alone.

Already at the end of the nineteenth century, one Frank Gueydan had settled in the south of France, where he met and married a local woman, taking over the management of her father's eight-hundred-hectare vineyard and his name as well, becoming François Gueydan de Roussel. This Louisianan of French parentage arrived at a time when southern French vineyards were becoming more capital intensive and laborer-landowners less numerous. But in 1904 this outsider was accused by his local tenant farmer, with whom he had strained financial relations, of selling "artificial wine" made from lots of sugar and just a trace of grapes. Proclaiming vehemently his innocence and complaining just as loudly that an American could get no justice in France, Gueydan ultimately fled to Switzerland with his wife and five children.[28]

For the most part, however, American "farmers" in France were postwar veterans who transferred their farming skills to France or developed them there. The American Leghorn Farm in the Gironde imported and bred Holstein cattle and American breeds of poultry. Hjalmer Sagdahl, in the Maine-et-Loire, was successively throughout the 1920s a winegrower, farmer, and shipper of rabbits, eggs, chicken, and butter, finally listing himself as a purveyor of angora rabbit wool. Abram Hogewoning became the "Tulip King of France," and another American, Charles A. Van Riper, ran a model peach farm in the Lot-et-Garonne. Particular kudos, however, must go to Clifford De Ronde from New Orleans. He imported giant frogs from Louisiana to raise in France—bringing bigger (and better?) frogs' legs to the French.[29]

COMMUNITY JOBS

With the exception of the American frog-raiser and the American winemaker trying to beat the French at their own game, most Americans brought America to the French while still others brought America to Americans, servicing the community they had created. To what extent did any or all of these endeavors represent an early form of "Americanization"? From dentistry to sweet corn, Americans introduced certain techniques and products that were sometimes first and foremost for the colony itself. All immigrant communities secrete their own economic niches, but they may be of three sorts: those at first intended for the community itself (maple syrup); those aimed at promoting an exotic item to the locals (sweet corn); and those simply concentrated in a nonethnic market, from Jewish garment workers to Russian taxi drivers in interwar Paris. Americans largely fit the first two categories.

Many Americans in Paris set themselves up as purveyors to the community itself, catering to American needs with everything from travel bureaus to two detective agencies. Americans preferred to read their own newspapers, have their teeth cleaned to their own standards, and turn to lawyers in a language they felt they could better trust. And like all immigrant communities, even in the land of haute cuisine, Americans had their cravings. So there was Sam's place on the boulevard des Italiens, where you could get pork and beans or club sandwiches, or the Chicago-Texas Inn near the Eiffel Tower, run by a black Pullman-car chef, advertising authentic hot biscuits and corned beef hash. An American grocery store near the Madeleine advertised its "all American cereals" (Grape Nuts, Shredded Wheat, Puffed Wheat, Cream of Wheat), along with grape juice and popcorn. Milk mogul George R. Hull had a particularly successful business selling American-style, "sealed-up, no-hand-has-touched, done-with-triple precaution" certified milk and cream through his Necessary Luxuries Company. One man who could not find an American secretary in Paris opened his own soon-thriving secretarial service, employing one hundred Americans, mostly women. And a final, necessary service by Americans for Americans: the two American undertakers in Paris, one for each main church; they were not very rich, given the small number of Americans who died there, but they were "good reporters and invaluable tipsters," commented a Paris *Herald* reporter.[30]

While there were Americans producing American goods for Americans, there were also Americans producing American goods for the local market, or trying to, such as the appropriately named Lloyd Cornwall, who had, rather surprisingly, monopolized the sweet-corn market in France, in spite of the fact that "from the French viewpoint, nothing more asinine in undertaking could be imagined than persuading the public to eat corn on the cob."[31] Corn is for cows. He had an uphill battle, starting with a few restaurants catering to the American clientele, but by the end of the 1930s, the former Oregonian was selling 300,000 ears annually to Americans and other upscale foreigners in town. However, there were two other American specialties that spread well beyond the community and show how an "immigrant" niche can become a local fad. American dentistry and American jazz form an unlikely pair, but they both serve as reminders of the ways in which Americans "seduced the French" well before 1945.

OF DENTISTS AND JAZZ

As French philosopher Baudrillard once snidely put it: "What Americans lack in identity, they make up for with wonderful teeth."[32] Smile envy? According to the laudatory biographer of Thomas Evans, dentist, as we have seen, to Emperor Napoleon III, American supremacy in dental work dates to the nineteenth century; Evans's American expertise helped mark a turning point in the field in France. Yet according to historian Colin Jones, dentistry had already begun to make significant strides there in the eighteenth century, as a combination of coffee, chocolate, and syphilis increased cavities. The mouth shifted during the late eighteenth century, as Jones has cleverly analyzed it, from a Rabelaisian black hole, rarely visible in most portrait paintings—painters wisely kept their subjects' mouths shut—to "a new cultural construction of the body in general and the mouth in particular."[33] Everyone from royalty to commoners not only sought to escape the pain routinely connected with toothaches but also became sensitive to a new commercialism of the mouth. Paris became a leading producer of toothbrushes, and the French dentist known as the "Grand Thomas" pulled teeth before crowds on the Pont Neuf bridge from the 1720s to the 1750s. His critics argued for a more scientific approach to mouth care; however, the abolition of professional and workers' guilds before and during the French Revolution in any case seriously disorganized the dentists' trade.

Although French dentistry itself had had an influence on early American practices, the source of expertise shifted by the mid-nineteenth century. American dental methods brought innovation, even if historian René Rémond suggested that the appeal of American dentistry was perhaps as much due to snobbery as to its technical advances.[34] Evans himself was active in constructing professional standards, writing in dental magazines and keeping up with colleagues in the United States. The end of his life was made difficult by an ungrateful nephew whom he had brought over from the United States to join his practice and who, a decade later, was doing a brisk business on his own selling tooth powder and a mouthwash branded "Evans." (Uncle Thomas Evans sued and even tried to get him deported.) Nevertheless, from dental prowess to his whisking the empress to England, the nineteenth-century Thomas surpassed his eighteenth-century predecessor in economic, political, theatrical, and symbolic power. (Evans proudly wore the Legion of Honor rosette on his lapel—the first American to be so honored—to remind everyone.) Evans's "charm of manner" and "suave personality" were equaled by a "keen financial business sense."[35] By 1881 there were thirty American dentists attending to the teeth of the upper classes in Paris, and in 1890 Evans and Dr. John H. Spaulding, along with fourteen other founding members, created the American Dental Club of Paris. It was the very first American professional club in the city, and Evans was its first president. Early meetings were held in his palatial home, filled with souvenirs of Napoleon III, as the club sought to promote scientific dentistry and uphold the standards of American dentistry abroad.[36]

Brewster (Evans's predecessor), Evans, and Spaulding seem to have started a micro-migration stream, as William S. Davenport Sr., DDS, charted in his five-part 1935 article in the *Journal of the American Dental Club of Paris*, "Pioneer American Dentists in France and Their Successors."[37] The Davenports created their own dentist dynasty. William's brother Isaac had arrived first, in 1883; William had joined him in 1890; and Isaac's son subsequently joined the practice. The brothers became known for their face and jaw work after reconstructing mutilated faces during World War I. By the mid-1930s, monthly meetings of the American Dental Club brought American and French dentists together in impassioned discussions about extractions—"Would you take them out?"—root canals, the interpretation of x-rays, bridge work, improved gold castings, and tales from the dental chair. (Did you hear the one about the patient who gagged and swallowed the Novocain needle? It was finally eliminated three weeks later.) "We no longer see the tooth as a little object in the mouth but as an important part of the human being." With some ninety members by the mid-1930s, the American Dental Club of Paris continued to discuss the latest trends in smile repair and proudly accepted the snub—accolade?—of one French colleague who described it as "an aristocratic club." Yes, one member answered, insofar as it is incumbent upon us to raise professional ethics.[38]

For whom did the dentists drill? To what extent did American professionals service their own community, and to what extent were their practices—like other American goods—aimed at the locals? We can ask the same question of American jazz. One of the major imports that began to "Americanize" France during the interwar years, this African American specialty caught on among Left Bank Americans in Paris, but it became a craze among the French as well.

The cultural importance of jazz in Paris ever since World War I is well known, starting with James Reese Europe's enormously popular wartime band. Less well remembered is how jazz functioned as a labor market for African Americans in Paris and as a business for many of them. Certainly there were other occupations. There were black journalists in Paris, such as Edgar Wiggins, whose nom de plume was "the Street Wolf of Paris," and a certain number of blacks found work serving the white American associations in a racial division of labor. "Mammy Kitty" was the much-appreciated cook at the American Women's Club of Paris, described as "true to her race," making doughnuts and gingerbread and "the very best bread and hot rolls you ever did eat" while dispensing wise comments along the way. But it was the Montmartre music scene that provided the bulk of employment for African Americans in town.[39]

Many jazz musicians simply toured Europe in the interwar years, but others stayed on. Montmartre was seen as a haven from American racism; it was also a good place to find a job in an otherwise tight Parisian labor market. Claude

McKay and Langston Hughes both wrote of the difficulties of finding work, not because of racial discrimination but because the French labor market was already flooded with Italians and Poles. One skeptical black compatriot in a Montmartre café had told Hughes: "'Less you can play jazz or tap dance, you'd just as well go back home."[40] Just as the market for jazz jobs was becoming saturated in the United States, jazz became the rage in interwar France. Although most accounts attribute the arrival of jazz in France to Reese Europe, groups such as Louis Mitchell's Seven Spades Band ("the King of Noise," according to Jean Cocteau) had started coming to Paris before the war and stayed through much of the interwar period. Clubs opened, clubs closed; managers became owners; singers and dancers opened their own clubs. Florence Embry Jones was the flamboyant singer and star of Le Grand Duc until she left for another club, renamed Chez Florence in her honor. That was when Bullard, who had heard of Bricktop, induced her to come to Paris to replace Jones. (She broke into tears when she first saw the size of Le Grand Duc, compared to New York clubs.) Josephine Baker, first hired by the US embassy cultural attaché's wife to star in the Revue Nègre, stayed on to acclaim and fame and in 1926 opened her own club, Chez Joséphine, where she danced after her performances at the Folies Bergères. Bullard helped Bricktop; Bricktop helped Baker, who babysat for Bullard's daughter.[41] Although tiffs and jealousies would erupt there as elsewhere, Montmartre functioned both as a community and as a transatlantic labor market for black Americans in Paris.

Besides Bricktop and Baker, Eugene Bullard was perhaps the African American entrepreneur in Paris par excellence. He arrived in Paris before World War I via London, and he played in vaudeville and was a boxer before joining the French Foreign Legion to fight in the war. He was wounded near Verdun, earning the Croix de Guerre and, after a six-month recovery in Lyon, decided to train in French aviation schools. He became the first black combat pilot, but his career in the air was soon terminated; he was transferred back to the infantry, undoubtedly at US military request. After the war, Bullard realized there was work in jazz, and he learned the drums from Louis Mitchell and Seth Jones, although he admitted that he was not particularly talented. Bullard knew the clubs from before the war, and he became a performer, hiring agent, manager, and impresario in interwar Paris. In 1924 he became manager of Le Grand Duc at 52 rue Pigalle. He hired the unknown Langston Hughes as a dishwasher and the already-known Bricktop as singer. He later parted ways with Bricktop and went on to own an American-style bar L'Escadrille and Bullard's Athletic Club before trying to rejoin French forces in World War II, being wounded again, and finally leaving for New York in 1940.[42]

Montmartre's ultimate demise as a jazz center was due to a combination of the Depression, xenophobic French labor laws, and World War II. It was also due to the coming of records (the music without live musicians) and the development of indigenous French jazz talent. With unemployment rising in the 1930s, the French government passed a series of labor laws that restricted the number of foreign workers in a variety of fields. The Depression may have sent more white writers (dependent on American incomes) home than black musicians, who initially continued to find work in Montmartre clubs, but the French laws had their effect. The decrees of 1933 first limited the number of foreign musicians to 10 percent, and then, according to a quota system, clubs had to hire five French musicians for every foreign one. Some had American and French bands alternate sets, but at least one French club owner, who had eleven Americans at his place, hired fifty-five Frenchmen—to do nothing. The final blow to the Montmartre scene came with the war, however. The Germans simply canceled work permits for black performers.[43]

Dentistry and jazz were hardly uppermost in the minds of those who began to talk increasingly about Americanization in interwar France. But they were both examples of American specialties that took hold in Paris. At the same time, two other groups of Americans at work in Paris show even more clearly how American norms and goods settled into France by example and by intent. American lawyers and the American Chamber of Commerce represent the Right Bank colony at its most self-aware. They provided a service to the community while acting as middlemen with the French and US governments. Explicitly defending American firms and methods, they navigated between two systems. Ironically, if they were sometimes too American for the French, they could also be seen as too soft on the French for Americans at home.

LAWYERS AT WORK

When Emile Zola's heirs sought to bring suit again Goldwyn's 1934 film *Nana* for violation of Zola's moral rights, a North American law firm in Paris looked into the matter for Fox's French distribution arm.[44] The movie was a box-office flop anyway. American lawyers in Paris are consummate intermediaries. True, one member of the New York Bar, who had undoubtedly had a bad experience in Paris, railed against American lawyers there. He argued that they could not keep up with the law in the United States—"frequently he is in the position of not having learned much French law while having forgotten most of the American law he ever knew"—and that they had become vulgar traders and interpreters rather than professionals.[45] The ultimate insult. But the American lawyers practicing in Paris were proud of their skills, and they became noted experts on Franco-American issues. In 1885 Edmond Kelly wrote what was to be become a standard work in English, *The French Law of Marriage and the Conflict of Laws That Arises Therefrom*, republished a century later. The first edition was hailed from the *Manchester Guardian* to the *Gazette de Palais et du Notariat* and heartily recommended by the *American Register* for "the perusal of any of our fair countrywomen, inclined to bestow themselves and their belongings on citizens of the French Republic."[46] Henry Cachard of the Coudert law firm published the first English translation of the French Civil Code in 1895, and Charles Gerson Loeb published his five-hundred-page treatise *Legal Status of American Corporations in France* in 1922.[47]

The lawyers' work, by its very nature, aided and abetted the business community. Attorneys overseas, the ultimate translators of words, laws, and concepts, have always stressed their position as needed negotiators at the crossroads of two legal systems and two cultural and economic traditions. As one lawyer put it in the interwar period, commenting on the language limitations of one of his clients; "Mr. Hamilton, as you know, does not speak French. Mr. Culbert does speak French, but he only came into the picture late in the day. . . . That sort of negotiation could only be done by a man speaking French and English, with a knowledge of French law and a knowledge of the French people; in other words, a man speaking the same language both really and figuratively."[48] True, Samuel G. Archibald lauded his own pride of workmanship to justify questioned high legal fees. The language of billing needs to convince in order to be paid, but the explanation also speaks to the bilingual, bicultural, and literally *inter*national nature of these lawyers' work in France. They advised their American clients about French law and explained US law to the French administration.

Lawyers and accountants accompanied the American business movement overseas. Dun and Bradstreet opened an office in Paris in 1872, and Peat, Marwick, Mitchell did so in 1906. The first American law firm to set up an office in Paris (indeed in Europe) was Coudert Brothers, a firm with French origins. Charles Coudert (Sr.), a Bonapartist arrested during the Restoration, had escaped to England and then went to the United States in the early nineteenth century. Coudert's eldest son began practicing law in New York in 1853; by 1857 his two other brothers had joined him in what they named Coudert Brothers. In 1879 they set up a Paris office, Coudert Frères. There were scarcely a dozen American attorneys in Paris at the close of World War I. However, by the peak interwar year of 1929 there were sixty-seven attorneys-at-law listed in the American Chamber of Commerce's Professional List, more than twice the number of dental surgeons. Sullivan and Cromwell set up a permanent office in 1927; White and Case appeared in 1930.[49]

Throughout the interwar years, the two major firms and rivals in Paris were Coudert Frères and the Law Offices of S. G. Archibald. Edmond Kelly was a link between the two. Coudert Brothers had sent the twenty-eight-year-old Kelly to head up Coudert Frères, but the New York office became increasingly worried about Kelly's independence in Paris. They caught him signing papers with his individual stamp. Indeed, in 1883–84 Kelly set up his own practice, and Coudert replaced him with Henry Cachard, soon joined by Henry Peartree. Cachard is credited with bringing to Coudert the business of "all the important French society people, the wealthiest Americans, the best English families," while Peartree became one of the major figures of the early American Chamber of Commerce, which the two of them helped found. When Cachard and Peartree retired, John B. Robinson, an impressive six-foot figure bedecked with mustache, gloves, and walking stick, took over. He excelled at wills, estates, and trusts and "knew all the combinations of French and American law and how to make them work together." And everyone trusted him, even the adversary. In one telling Franco-American example, "some California movie people" came to Paris to negotiate a patent purchase, and all the paperwork had been completed by late Friday. But the Frenchman said he would not sign on Saturday: "Saturday he fishes. The Americans were appalled; they had to be in London on Monday. So, the Frenchman, not willing to give up his fishing, shrugged and asked John Robinson to take his power of attorney and sign for him." Even if Robinson seems to have preferred individual to corporate clients, explicitly wanting to keep the firm from too great a dependence on the latter, the 1920s were a golden age for the firm, and Robinson undoubtedly made more money in that period than did even the Coudert cousins then heading the New York office. If proof be needed, Robinson bought himself a château and furnished each room in the style of a different French *siècle*.[50]

In the meantime Kelly, a truly transatlantic figure—born near Toulouse of American parents in 1851, educated in England before moving with his parents to New York in 1868, then returning to England to study at Cambridge before ultimately graduating from Columbia Law School in 1877—had studied French law while working at Coudert's in Paris and in 1883 obtained a *licence en droit*, necessary in order to plead in French court.[51] From the mid-1880s on, he began publishing his legal briefs and commentaries, in both French and English. He notably defended the French baron Raymond Seillière, whose case became one of the most well-known contested psychiatric cases of the late

nineteenth century. Seillière had been committed to an insane asylum by his
family in 1887, apparently due to his largesse to people around him; squandering the family fortune was considered a sure sign of mental illness. Kelly drew
up a brief for the US Legation in which he pleaded eloquently that since Seillière had previously resided in the United States for about twelve months—he
had gone there in large part to avoid his contentious relatives—and had filed
papers of intent to become a citizen there, he should come under American
protection. Kelly added that, in any case, such a palpable case of injustice
should lead the US government to intervene. (It did, but to little avail.)[52] In another case, *Maxim contre Edison*, Kelly represented the American-born inventor Hiram Stevens Maxim, whose lamp exhibit was seized during the first Paris
Electricity Exhibition of 1881. Maxim had previously sued Thomas Edison for
patent infringement, and when Edison retaliated by having Maxim's exhibit
dismantled, Maxim sued again. As Kelly argued, it was not the first time that
Edison had tried to rely upon patents for inventions that were not properly his,
and it was not just Maxim who was hurt by Edison's aggressive patent practice:
"It's the entire French industry that needs to be freed [from Edison's meth-
ods]."[53] So the American lawyer in Paris defended French industry in general
and one American inventor against another, all in a French court.

In 1891 Kelly returned to New York, and for much of the next decade, he became even better known in the United States as a political and social reformer.
Sometime at the end of the 1890s, Kelly returned once again to Paris, where he
continued practicing law and lecturing and publishing in French and English
on various social issues. He was a member of the Cercle artistique et littéraire and of the American Chamber of Commerce, and he continued as legal
counsel to the US embassy. Kelly represented Anna Gould in her contentious
divorce from Boni de Castellane. But in 1907 Kelly had a heart attack. A friend
suggested that Samuel G. Archibald, a Canadian who knew French, English,
and international law, could take over Kelly's practice. Kelly returned to New
York, where he died in 1909. His last work, *Twentieth Century Socialism*, was
published posthumously.[54]

Archibald's firm, the successor to Kelly's practice, became, along with
Coudert's, one of the major legal representatives of American individuals and
companies in interwar France. In both firms, lawyers came and went, and
letterhead was constantly reprinted. We know more about the Law Offices of
S. G. Archibald because its archives survived until the end of the twentieth
century. The firm handled everything from personal problems of the famous
and the infamous to major corporate mergers. It dealt with Isadora Duncan's
creditors, advised with regard to Woolworth heiress Barbara Hutton's mar-

riages, and helped Teapot Dome Scandal figure Harry Blackmer, who was Archibald's personal friend, negotiate a settlement permitting him to return to the United States after years in exile in Paris. The firm looked into a matter concerning Shirley Temple and another relating to the right to use the "Toreador Song" in Carmen.[55] Archibald's office gave advice in connection with marriages, divorces, the occasional mistress, inheritances, and other property issues for its transatlantic clients. Following in Kelly's footsteps, an eighty-page memorandum detailed the property rights of American women, and another file examined the various citizenship laws concerning women who married foreigners.[56] The firm explained French law to couples about to tie the knot in Paris, and it clarified American marriage law to the French authorities and drew up the necessary certificates of law attesting to birth, citizenship, and the legal right to marry. The firm also drew up marriage contracts in order to exempt couples from the presumption of community property law in France, and at the other end of the demographic spectrum, it handled wills and estates and problems relating to the property of foreigners dying in France. The law firm also produced proofs of claim for the maid's or chauffeur's salary due at the time of an American boss's death.

Archibald's firm was multinational from the outset, including Canadian, American, French, British, and Swiss lawyers. The office expanded to seven lawyers by 1926, including two Americans: Charles Inman Barnard, a Harvard LLB who had been a newspaper correspondent in Paris since the 1880s; and Lindell T. Bates ("a roly-poly fellow with a perpetual smile on his face"), who became an expert on Franco-American divorces. In 1929 he published *The Divorce and Separation of Aliens in France*, which one reviewer said was even more thorough than Edmond Kelly's well-known treatise. Bates was later replaced by Gething J. Miller, another specialist of Franco-American affairs and author of a 129-page memorandum explaining how there was really nothing like a trust in France and suggesting alternate solutions.[57]

During the 1920s, the Archibald firm prospered and became a very successful commercial law practice. When Chrysler granted a license to Citroën in 1931 to manufacture and sell its "Floating Power" engine mountings and then, due to the Depression, Citroën went into receivership, Chrysler turned to Archibald's for help.[58] The firm advised major banks on corporate matters and helped negotiate the Chase-Equitable merger. It helped banks with claims concerning their clients and handled their personnel issues—the bank employee who countersigned fraudulent checks and then mysteriously disappeared. When an irate client who had lost money during the stock market crash of 1929 threatened to sue National City Bank, claiming that it was the bank's fault for having mismanaged his money, Archibald advised bank officials on how to respond: carefully but firmly.[59] The law firm checked out the viability of potential French partners for American clients wanting to invest in France, and it represented US creditors seeking to recoup royalties from bankrupt French companies. Not only did it assist when American companies encountered difficulties with French firms or French law, but it anticipated changes in the law and suggested preemptive remedies, explaining new French rules down to the correct size of paper needed to fill out a form. The firm could admonish clients about staying on the right side of French authorities as well as advise them as to whether the French administration was being lenient or strict in application of the laws and whether they should engage in "masterly inactivity," proactive compliance, or contestation in the French courts. Telling Palmolive when to speed up procedures and when to slow down—"nothing in the law obliges you to take the initiative"—was part of the job.[60] Above all, much legal advice concerned that consummate worry at the heart of so much corporate strategy, taxes: how to lessen the burden or how to structure business deals so as to minimize payments on future transactions. S. G. Archibald himself, along with Coudert's office, took part in drafting the 1936 French-American Double Taxation Treaty, working with both the French administration and the American embassy.

The bulk of overseas corporate law business then and now had less to do with litigation than with helping "Incs." become SAs (*sociétés anonymes*) and SARLs (*sociétés à responsabilité limitée*), forming French branches and subsidiaries for American corporations, or advising on the best form of distribution or licensing agreements. The firm innovated in the mid-1920s with the creation of a "Service des sociétés," a department that handled companies' corporate secretarial work: organizing board and shareholders' meetings, advising on share transfers, managing corporate documents, and filing the multitude of forms required for compliance with French administrative law, all with the abundant help of proxies.

Finally, the work of the lawyers, along with the consulate, also included helping Americans work legally in France—even if the number of undocumented Americans remained legion. With the Depression and increasingly xenophobic French labor laws in the 1930s, the number of legal job opportunities for foreigners shrank significantly. Americans were never the most stigmatized category. There were plenty of other immigrant workers—Italians, Poles, East European Jews—around for that. But 1930s legislation affected Americans as well, as the law and decrees progressively targeted foreign factory workers (1932), performing artists (1933), doctors (1933, 1935), artisans (1935), then foreign professionals and managers (1938). Americans who had worked off the books began turning to American lawyers and the consulate for help in getting or renewing their work permits. The American embassy had to intervene in 1935 to get clearance for the eight American doctors already practicing at the American Hospital in Neuilly to stay on. When one of them retired in 1938, the question of his replacement raised the issue anew. The hospital and embassy again intervened, proposing a tailor-made decree-law allowing the practice of medicine in France by foreign doctors attached to hospitals in the Seine Department founded before 1935 by citizens of the same nation and in principle serving citizens of the same nationality. Such doctors could practice outside the hospital only with patients of their own nationality, their number could not be higher than the number of foreign doctors already present in the hospital on July 26, 1935, and at least half of the staff had to consist of French doctors.[61] By the late 1930s, the French government was giving work permits only to foreigners who had resided in France for ten years or more. Musicians, actors, and dancers asked the consulate for help in providing proof of residence or explaining a particular situation in order to renew or get working papers.[62]

In 1938, the government also clamped down on foreign merchants by creating a new *carte d'identité d'étranger "commerçant"* (identity card for foreign "merchants") that affected foreign executives. The new card had no fiscal implications, but it served as a surveillance mechanism and had repercussions with regard to other regulations. It was necessary to have the card, for example, in order to register a subsidiary with the Registry of Commerce. Although not aimed specifically at them, the *carte de "commerçant"* affected American businessmen as well. Archibald's lawyers advised their clients' company directors and executives to turn in their French identity cards in exchange for the new *carte de "commerçant"*—and to do so promptly or else risk one hundred to two thounsand francs in fines, not to mention one to six months of imprisonment. The name of the card itself created much misunderstanding. Executives grumbled that they were not (lowly) merchants. But the decree that had defined the card had purposefully placed the word *commerçant* in quotation marks, acknowledging the cognitive dissonance between the usual use of the term and its application to high-level managers and manufacturers. It specified that managers, company directors, and their representatives were all included. One lawyer reassured her client that holding a *carte de "commerçant"* would not actually make him a *commerçant*. Problems arose for those who wore two hats: salaried employee (thus *travailleur*) in one (subsidiary) company and manager (*administrateur-délégué*, thus *commerçant*) in another. No one could have two ID cards. Uncertainty enveloped the business community. In March 1939, the American Chamber of Commerce in France advised that *administrateurs*—company directors without executive power—did not need the card. But Archibald's firm advised its clients to apply for it.[63]

"THE UNOFFICIAL HYPHEN": THE AMERICAN CHAMBER OF COMMERCE IN FRANCE

Markets are not abstract. Men make them. (And I use the masculine advisedly for the first half of the twentieth century.) The growing number of lawyers who lubricated the elite community's interactions with French law was in itself a powerful symbol of America's growing reach abroad. By the interwar years, various American professional organizations defended the colors of American business in Paris, wearing their American name and professional identities proudly. The American Automotive Club of Paris held monthly dinners bringing together sales reps of American vehicles, tires, spare parts, and accessories. There was also a Paris chapter of the National Aeronautic Association of the USA, the first chapter outside the country, unabashedly hoping to help "Make America First in the Air" while cultivating friendly relations between the American and French aeronautical worlds.[64]

But there is no better expression of the businessmen's own intent than their first overseas organization, the American Chamber of Commerce in Paris. The creation of the ACC in 1894 clearly marked a self-aware shift in the American colony in Paris from the idle rich to the working rich as "the requirements of business took precedence of the dispositions of pleasure."[65] The early chamber used strong language about the need for organizing in order to combat "the evils from which the Commercial Colony of Americans in France have so long suffered":[66] everything from differences of language and custom to iniquitous customs tariffs. Militating for everything from better mail service between France and the United States (successfully) to implementation of the metric system in the United States in order to simplify and thus increase international commerce (a rousing failure),[67] the ACC in France, still active today, has had a long career as a lobby well before the word expanded beyond theaters and hotels to become a political noun and verb.

Created four years after the precocious American Dental Club of Paris but eighteen years before the US Chamber of Commerce itself took form at home (1912), and twenty-five years before the International Chamber of Commerce (1919), the American Chamber of Commerce in Paris ("in France" after 1918) was the first such chamber outside the United States and staunchly proud of its resolutely international persona.[68] It joined other nations' chambers of commerce in the French capital—the British had set one up in 1872, the Italians in 1886. But the American initiative was a private one, not an official emanation of the state like the others. As the ACC itself pointed out, it was the French who had invented the chambers of commerce in the nineteenth century.[69] The most proximate cause of the ACC's creation was the passing of the protectionist Méline Tariffs in France in 1892. The American businessmen sought to counter the increased duties by petitioning both the French government and the US government for relief. They would tirelessly argue for the need of a commercial treaty to give American goods at least the same status as other imported goods in France.

Frédéric Bartholdi, the sculptor of the Statue of Liberty, along with the French foreign minister and the minister of commerce and industry, the US ambassador, the by now seventy-two-year-old dentist Evans, and a host of eminent American businessmen, some three hundred guests in all, attended the chamber's first banquet on July 4, 1895. The seven-course meal was replete with *petites croustades franco-américaines, filet de boeuf à la Richelieu, sorbets Chambre de Commerce*, and of course a *gâteau Lafayette mille-feuilles*. At the gala event, the chamber's cofounder and first president, Stephen H. Tyng, described the chamber's vocation as being "the unofficial hyphen, or '*trait d'union*,' between the public authorities and the private enterprises of these two nations," between the "land of our birth [and the] land of our adoption."[70]

Businessmen's club, mentor to newcomers, and important glue of the "American colony," the ACC created a virtual community through its wide-ranging directories while it offered a physical meeting place for American businessmen in the French capital. Its popularity went well beyond its membership figures (a thousand at its immediate post–World War I peak). The ACC acted then and now as an information clearinghouse. Some eighteen to twenty thousand people called in at its offices for information and advice in 1922 alone, from French exporters wanting information on American tariffs to Americans anxious to do business in France.[71] And ever since the beginning, the chamber has gathered the business community unto itself every Fourth of July for a gala banquet—accompanied in 2010 by two hundred Harley Davidsons!

A closer look at the chamber, however, shows both the challenges for Americans working abroad and the complexity of the ACC's own self-image. The chamber was clearly by Americans and for Americans, as the flags adorning its literature attest. Made up of self-described "American solid business men" whose "desire to make an honest penny" was "but natural," the chamber aimed to become not only the headquarters for American business in France but "the champion of Americanism in Europe."[72] Yet its hyphenating function meant that it also saw itself as a key Franco-American intermediary. References to those iconic go-betweens Lafayette and Rochambeau abundantly sprinkled the annual July Fourth banquet speeches, and the chamber repeatedly insisted that in defending free trade in general it was aiding commerce in both countries. In so doing, the ACC engaged tirelessly in two functions: meeting with French government officials to explain its needs and lobbying the US government on behalf of US interests overseas.

On the one hand, the ACC represented a patriotic, almost missionary view of American business setting out to expand if not regenerate the world. Its first president, Tyng, later portrayed fondly as a fanatic believer in the need for a chamber of commerce, had in fact previously been a popular New York Episcopalian rector. Found guilty by the church of preaching to Methodists, he later resigned from the church, became an insurance agent, and then moved to Paris to introduce American methods there. He opened the fourth annual meeting of the ACC in 1898 with an impassioned declaration about love of home and the chamber's patriotic purpose:

> We are voluntary exiles, but we still cherish the memories and are bound by the ties of our youth. The fairest land upon which the sun shines down is that from which we come! . . .
>
> Live as long as he may in France the American is an American still, and perhaps more American than others because distance for us, as in the study of the heavens, conceals the spots, and softens the light, which comes to him from that sun-land, of which every patriot must be a true worshipper.[73]

Religious motifs appear in many of the early proclamations, and not just because of Tyng. Another early president, Francis Kimbel, defined himself as "the disciple of a new religion, . . . namely, the peaceful expansion of American influence on commercial grounds, fostered by feelings of good will towards other nations and based on principles of reciprocity." A modern-day Pied Piper, he waxed enthusiastic in 1902:

> We preach the business gospel of the New World; we already have many converts, we shall have more and shall all the more be successful, as we use peaceful means. We are not fanatics. It is not our aim to conquer, to attack. We are like a military marching band, marching through a thoroughfare, that strikes a pleasant tune: the aged resist, but the young folk follow, and they will whistle

the air they retained and carry it into the sidestreets, across the town and the country.[74]

There was a growing sense of prerogative about America's place in the world.

On the other hand, American businessmen may have been gung-ho Americans, yet they never failed to express, via banquet, *Bulletin*, and *Year-Book*, their sympathy with France and with the French. In the early years the annual July Fourth banquets brought together anywhere from 250 to 450 major American and French political and business figures. The long speeches gave full vent to repeated odes of Franco-American friendship, and love of France became dithyrambic during World War I; members enthusiastically hailed the French ministers and war heroes who attended their wartime banquets. When, in 1931, for the first time in its history, the president of the French Republic, Paul Doumer, attended the chamber's yearly gathering, its leaders were thrilled—and added approvingly in the *Year-Book* account that he had been perfectly on time, "a striking example that might well be followed by other dignitaries of less exalted rank."[75]

At times the ACC even took the side of French purchasers or exporters, preaching to its compatriots about the need for greater flexibility in doing business abroad. The chamber chided those American businesses that tried to please the customer at home yet refused to make the slightest change or concessions for the foreign clientele. Modify your products to suit foreign requirements, print catalogs in foreign languages, and be sure to send capable representatives abroad, it exhorted. The ACC not only set up a Committee of Importation to promote American goods in France, but it also had a (smaller) Committee on Exportation to aid in the promotion of French goods in the United States. As President Kimbel had stressed: "We want our friends of France to feel that we have nothing to conceal, that we are not led by selfish motives, that while we are doing our utmost to increase American exports into France, we shall also be glad to notice an increase in the exports of French products of whatever kind they may be into our own country, and we shall gladly assist them in their own effort as best we can."[76]

The chamber even offered to help French cheeses go west. In 1938 the ACC approached the Comité national de propagande du lait to offer its aid in getting camembert, brie, port salut, and other not yet famous French cheeses up to the speed of roquefort. Roquefort had already been successful in marketing itself in the United States, and apparently the other cheeses were jealous. (Admittedly, they had shorter shelf lives and required more delicate handling.) A special cheese luncheon was organized to discuss the technical issues involved in packing, transporting, and warehousing different cheeses. A trial shipment was planned, although it is not clear whether it was able to sail before the war. Concomitantly, much attention was also given to the problem of French sardines.[77]

The ACC used a language of justice to buttress its belief in free trade, insisting frequently that its actions were unselfish, that it favored the extension of trade in both directions, but also that justice meant reciprocity. Foreigners in the United States benefited from freedom of trade; it should be accorded to Americans abroad. At the same time the ACC drew upon an age-old idea that trade furthers peace. Commercial interdependence would promote interdependence of all sorts, and the increased mobility of American businessmen to France as well as vice versa was seen as a solution for world peace. Even if the argument was often used for such practical purposes as criticizing double taxation (impeding the mutual exchange of American know-how and French artistry), the trade-equals-peace argument only increased as World War II loomed. Strengthening the ties of "commercial fraternity" would strengthen the ties of fraternity itself.[78]

To what extent was the language of fraternity and of free trade self-interested?—a "Janus-faced . . . principle of equal economic opportunity," as Joan Hoff-Wilson has described the US Open Door policy.[79] The chamber's literature was not shy in implying that helping France was also a way of helping itself. If the ACC's explicit purpose was one of free trade, this meant in particular "the opening of new outlets to the manufactured products of the United States in the markets of Europe."[80] Just as trade could help peace and peace could help trade, freer trade could help France while helping American interests.

To put their words into action, the ACC leaders spared no efforts in lobbying government officials both sides of the Atlantic. Hyphen between the public and private sectors, the chamber was also a hyphen between the two governments. Although its first task, trying to get a more flexible interpretation of the Méline Tariffs for American imports to France, ended in failure (the French market remained "one of the most restricted in the world for American manufacture"), the ACC protested to the French government about everything from sardine labeling to film restrictions to increased fees for French identity cards.[81] Energetically visiting French parliamentarians and French ministries, sending circulars to French chambers of commerce, the ACC leaders indefatigably defended free trade in general and American business interests and businessmen in particular to the French authorities.

But the American Chamber of Commerce in France clearly had to convince the American government as well. Patriotic representations of selling American goods abroad did not mean automatic backing at home. The ACC voted resolutions, cabled memorials to the president of the United States, and wrote to members of the Senate, the House, the US Chamber of Commerce, and leading US trade organizations arguing for the importance of developing American business abroad. Anything that interfered with commerce abroad and the men who made it was grist for the chamber's mill. The ACC excoriated US passport regulations and especially the "vexatious visa" and its fees as a serious handicap to American business travelers.[82] The chamber never lost an opportunity to encourage the signing of a general Franco-American trade treaty, but it was an uphill battle. The ACC had to defend American businessmen and their goods one tariff and one tax at a time, both against France and against a sometimes skeptical America.

One problem was that in many American eyes the chamber in Paris was something foreign, somewhat suspect for being located abroad. When delegates from the Paris ACC attended the National Consular Reform Convention of 1906, to which, after all, they brought real-life experience, they were put upon to explain themselves. Two years later, the ACC delegate to a US convention of the chambers of commerce, B. J. Shoninger, reported that "there still lurks an inexplicable suspicion on the part of the average American, that the American Chamber of Commerce in Paris is a foreign institution, whose main object is to further foreign interests." Shoninger had to take pains to explain that it was a "thoroughly American institution, duly incorporated at Washington," with only a limited percentage of foreign membership and with office-holding limited to American citizens.[83]

Last but hardly least, the ACC vigorously defended Americans abroad against the danger of double taxation, yet one more impediment to free trade. Although the idle rich were sometimes accused of having moved abroad to avoid taxes, the working rich potentially had the opposite problem, being taxed twice. Both the United States (1913) and France (1914), along with other major industrial countries, implemented modern income tax laws in the years preceding World War I. Alone among the major industrialized countries to do so, the United States still taxes its citizens wherever they live, to the groans of Americans abroad.[84] From the inception of the first Revenue Act of 1913, the ACC argued strenuously against its application to Americans abroad, worried that this would lead to double taxation and become a penalty for living and working overseas. According to the 1914 French tax law, modified in 1917, Americans residing in France, like other foreign residents, owed income tax there as well, not to mention a variety of other French taxes on pets, musical instruments, and domestic servants. The American Chamber of Commerce argued that tax relief for citizens abroad was important for foreign trade: to export US products, American businessmen had to reside overseas. Taxation should be based on where income is produced, irrespective of the domicile, residence, or nationality of the taxpayer. Deductions for foreign taxes (1918) and partial exclusion of foreign earned income (1926) ultimately eased the double burden, and the implementation of national income taxes led to a series of bilateral tax agreements in order to ease the pain for transnational individuals and companies.[85] The ACC remained vigilant.

Proud of its cordial relations with both US and French officials, the ACC vigorously defended its turf to them both. It pursued its own foreign trade agenda determinedly, defending American business and defending the importance of American businessmen abroad as a rampart against what one journalist called "the exasperating struggle of doing business with Europeans."[86] The name American Chamber of Commerce in France meant different things to different audiences. "American" defined the organization in France; "in France" gave them their specific and sometimes suspect identity in the United States. Feeling at times misunderstood back home and simultaneously browbeaten by French commercial rules, the chamber nonetheless persisted in repeated acclamations of both "Hurrah for the United States of America" and "Vive la France."

Many Americans came to Paris to play, but many more had to work to live there. They worked for each other, in typical intracommunity fashion (pasteurized milk; maple syrup). Or they worked for others. And in good American style, many went into business for themselves, from Sylvia's books to Sandarlari's shoes. Selling to each other, selling new and improved products to the French, from sweet corn to dental hygiene to jazz, Americans brought bits of America with them to the French capital, even when they were not explicit Americanizers.

Others, however, even more explicitly than the dentists or the musicians, set about expanding the American horizon. With at times boisterous boosterism accompanying their free-trading crusade, the American businessmen and lawyers in Paris keenly felt themselves to be on the frontier outpost of a new American expansion. Not everyone went over with such determination of purpose, and not everyone who did succeeded. But for many, opportunity or simply the French capital beckoned. Even in the late 1930s, after the worst of the Depression but before the war, Americans continued to seek work in

France. There was the mechanical engineer who had studied French for three years in high school and had heard that there were jobs for American engineers in France. He specified in a letter to the consulate that he would like something in Paris or any other French city of over 200,000 in population, and he carefully set out his qualifications—"I am neat, fairly fast & very accurate"—and his requirements: about $250 a month plus the difference between French and US income taxes. He added that he would want his fare to France paid and a guarantee of six months' work or his return fare paid. If there were several options, the consulate should please send him the list; he would know best what he could handle.[87] In another instance, a woman who complained of terrible economic conditions in Eureka, California, in 1938 wanted advice on opening a tap and ballroom dancing school in France. She had heard that there was hardly any unemployment there. The consul responded to her, as to the mechanical engineer, explaining that her information was incorrect: unemployment was high in France, and it was almost impossible to find salaried work. As for setting up a business in France, one needed to be very familiar with the French language and with French business customs.[88] Advice that was not lost on the corporate world, to which we now turn.

CHAPTER 5

Doing Business in France

The Formal and the Informal

We are the first empire of the world
to establish our sway without legions.
Our legions are dollars.

REINHOLD NIEBUHR[1]

We should give wings to our commerce.

AMERICAN CHAMBER OF COMMERCE IN PARIS[2]

Without design or intent, according to Reinhold Niebuhr in 1930, the United States had become an "awkward imperialist," forced to conquer foreign markets to prevent the glut of domestic ones. "We needed foreign investment opportunities to get rid of our surplus wealth, particularly since we had not learned to distribute it more equitably at home."[3] Economists may argue about the diagnosis, but two questions haunt any look at American businessmen abroad. Why did they go and what was their impact? Was/is business abroad a search for profits, for new markets, or for cheaper labor, or a way of avoiding import tariffs and customs hassles? Was American expansion due to surplus capital or thanks to the sheer force of innovation and a multiplication model, spreading outward from a single product or plant in a heroic tale of expanding empire and emporia, a serendipitous meeting of well-timed supply with newfound demand?[4] Economists left and right, abashed pessimists and proud optimists of American commercial success, have done battle over the causes.

One can mock the adventure stories of the moment when "plucky" company founders took the boat eastward and discovered the European market in the "gold-rush mindset of the 1920s."[5] But they had been coming since before the Great War, and as the twentieth century progressed, the salesmen overtook the rentiers. American businessmen became more ubiquitous and hit their stride after World War I. Selling products and setting up subsidiaries overseas were both cause and effect of the forward march of American expansion. Even the Depression only temporarily dampened their ardors; new entrepreneurs went overseas as domestic markets shrank. In multiple ways these early twentieth century entrepreneurs were the important precursors to the even-more-sure-of-themselves executives abroad who would head eastward after World War II. But their advance was not without difficulty.

There are at least three ways of thinking about American business abroad in the first half of the twentieth century. A first, now outdated, tale emphasized American isolation after World War I. But that legend, as William Appleman Williams has noted, was more political than economic, and it was a decidedly American viewpoint; many in Europe were already convinced of the opposite: America's growing world presence in the 1920s. If since Williams (1959), the isolationist theories have been largely discredited, this has led, however, to a second, perhaps overly optimistic story that draws a triumphant line of American expansion from the late nineteenth century through the post–World War II period and beyond. Victoria de Grazia has masterfully explored the irresistibility of America's commercial advance through Europe, examining how American mass consumer culture overcame European bourgeois commercial civilization thanks to Rotary Clubs, brand names, advertising, Hollywood, and the creation of a "Mrs. Consumer." Mira Wilkins, preeminent economic historian of American multinationals, has been the indefatigable analyst of the emergence, growth, and maturation of American ingenuity and technical know-how abroad. She has described the implacable march of the multinationals while arguing convincingly that they did not emerge suddenly full blown after World War II; their roots date well before World War I, after which expansion overseas bloomed.[6]

I would like to add a third reading of the first half of the twentieth century, one that lies between isolationism and conquering expansion. As America's commercial and industrial muscle grew, there was nothing inevitable or irresistible about the gains. Doing business abroad was not necessarily easy, as most observers have noted if in passing. This third vision looks more closely behind the scenes, noting the difficulties, the headaches, and the trials of setting up business abroad, as exemplified in France. The Americans may have been determined; the natives put up resistance. Many Europeans, and the French in particular, fought back against American peacetime incursions. The French government engaged in tough—nay exasperating, as seen from the State Department—tariff negotiations with the United States. It was also a day-to-day challenge to set up an American company.

How did the tractors or typewriters actually get licensed, sold, or produced abroad? While the general outline of business successes overseas is part of a teleological tale of the American Century, a look "from below" tells a less linear story. To be sure, American manufacturers did not have to reside abroad to invest there. Much direct foreign investment was made via telegraph and letter and surprisingly frequent (to our jaded jet-era eyes) steamer travel. But those who did settle overseas to oversee operations there, forming the backbone of the American colony and gathering in their select professional clubs to promote American cars and planes, laid the groundwork for the huge growth in American businesses abroad that would come after World War II. Many made fortunes and found the sailing smooth while appreciating life along the Seine. Yet thrusting and parrying with the French administration and French managers to secure a foothold in France was no easy task.

GO EAST, YOUNG MAN — EUROPE AS THE NEW FRONTIER

In spite of the glitz and glitter of a truly frenetic late twentieth-century activity that has been heralded as a new era, that of globalization, most historians agree that the American version of globalization began in the latter part of the nineteenth century. With different aims and economic goals in different parts of the world, the United States stretched beyond its sea-to-shining-sea self to search for supplies and expand its markets. The Pacific and the Americas were the initial focus of expansion, but by the end of the nineteenth century a decisive shift was under way. Even the Old World came to be seen as a lucrative trading post of a new frontier as the heyday of raw material exports (wheat, cotton, oil) gave way to the spectacular rise in sales of American semifinished and manufactured goods. US exports had already begun to exceed imports to the United States in the 1870s, with agricultural exports in the lead. From 1898 on, finished manufactured exports came to exceed manufactured imports, soon overturning a century of British dominance on world markets.[7] In 1902, banker and former assistant secretary of the treasury Frank Vanderlip attributed the arrival of "the American 'commercial invasion' of Europe" to the spread of instant communications, cheapening transportation, America's skilled workmen, the techniques of standardization, and the cheapest coal in the world. With an unabashed language of strength and superiority, Vanderlip was only worried about the rise of unions, and he made passing reference to French deftness and artistic touch and to the fact that standardized goods might need to be adapted for foreign practices.[8] By the early twentieth century, American innovations had begun to spread in the forms of machine tools, typewriting machines, and the factory-made shoe. Cash registers (National Cash Register), agricultural equipment (International Harvester), elevators (Otis), not to mention safety razors (Gillette), Kellogg's Corn Flakes, and Coca-Cola, all headed overseas.

By 1914, three indicators nonetheless relativized the impact of American economic expansion overseas. First, the United States was still a debtor nation, thanks to foreign investments that had helped construct the American railroads and mines. Second, US foreign interests overseas were still tiny compared to that major creditor nation, Great Britain. Third, most domestic firms could not care less about exporting. Yet US direct foreign investment, implying management involvement and not just portfolio investment, was on the rise, from Standard Oil to Singer. The largest investments before World War I went, by far, to America's closest neighbors, Canada ($618 million) and Mexico ($587 million), with Europe ($573) a close third, followed by South America ($323 million) and the Caribbean.[9] American expansion was accompanied by important variations across the globe.

Europe was both the economic and the symbolic prize. Forging into an already developed market, US manufactured exports gravitated toward the continent where increasing consumer demand already existed. The figures seem "to bear witness to relentless 'Americanization' and to validate both the contemporary American enthusiasm and the European apprehension." However, two important reminders are necessary for any understanding of the "American commercial invasion" of Europe. First, while American goods were flowing everywhere in a "worldwide onslaught," the US domestic market was still more important than foreign trade, while British, French, and German goods also continued to irrigate the world.[10]

Second, the successes of the American Century in Europe were also thanks, in no small part, to two world wars. As the French proverb sadly but lucidly comments on human nature—or capitalism, *le malheur des uns fait le bonheur des autres*: some people's misfortunes are others' opportunities. The United States' role in the wars was not just one of late entry and then military victory. The benefits of war in contributing to the ascendancy of America were threefold. The first success was symbolic, resulting in gratitude of all sorts, from French women falling for American soldiers to community thanks for help with the reconstruction of the cathedral in Reims. The second benefit was political, even if the rise of the United States as a political heavyweight in contrast to a weary Europe did not take place overnight. Finally, the economics of war played out in stark contrast on the two sides of the Atlantic. War brought desolation to Europe, while it led to prosperity in the United States. American war plants worked to full capacity, providing work for everyone from munitions merchants to those dealing in civilian goods and spare parts. World

War I changed the major European nations from creditors to debtors, while the "debt question," the repayment to the United States of the war loans it had made to France, became an ongoing economic, political, and symbolic struggle in the interwar period.

The importance of the first two decades of the twentieth century for a shift in American business practices was obvious to Frank A. Southard Jr. In his prescient and upbeat 1931 book *American Industry in Europe*, he hailed the newness of the times. Certainly Americans had been investing in Europe for the previous seventy-five years, but the United States had now shifted from being a borrower to being a lender, its banking system had become internationalized, and the domestic market was saturated. He detailed the ways and wiles of the "migration of American industry to Europe." Why not just export? Most American companies continued to sell directly to Europe, but since the 1870s American companies had been setting up European offices and plants in order to take advantage of lower wages (yes, in Europe, at the time), to reduce transportation costs, and to circumvent tariff barriers. They also helped produce goods to European specifications, from agricultural machines to office supplies. International Harvester's original tractors, for example, left high stubble that more large-scale American farmers perhaps did not mind but European farmers did. Not to mention the (continuing) nuisance of different-sized American and European paper. The only question was whether it made sense to set up submanufacturing units in the United States itself or produce the variations on a product abroad, closer to finicky consumers. Some of the European-based managers whom Southard interviewed mentioned other factors such as the fragility of their goods: Shredded Wheat, after all, would crumble if it had to make the long haul from the United States.[11]

The American pavilion at the 1900 World Exhibition in Paris proudly showed off fresh fruit from California, corn from Iowa, and locomotives, bicycles, automobiles, and other manufactured goods. By that year, twenty-eight American-owned manufacturing plants had located in Europe; in the next decade fifty more were added, and some companies became so familiar "as to almost lose their American origin." Increasingly high tariffs and intensification of national feeling after World War I only urged them on. While many of the American companies initially worked through local distributors ("the lazy man's route"), American firms found that European markets could be "more readily exploited" by branches (*succursales*) and subsidiaries (*filiales*) than by the simple export of goods. By 1929 there were over thirteen hundred companies in twenty-eight European countries that were owned or under the influence of American corporations. As Southard envisaged it, "the undeniable advantage of 'being on the ground'" would render this "new export technique" continuous. Of course, Southard's triumphant tone was possible because his research came right before the stock market crash, which sent some, but only some, scurrying home. But it is still a useful guide to the perceptions of the period. To each period its heralded globalization—although, as economic historian Charles Kindleberger wisely noted four decades later, we know more about the successes than the failures.[12]

AMERICAN PIONEERS IN FRANCE

By 1929, US direct investment in France ($145 million) ranked third in value after US investment in the United Kingdom ($485 million) and Germany ($217 million). However, there were more US firms in France than in Germany, albeit individually often smaller in value.[13] Even if France was third in terms of American dollar investment in Europe, Paris was the business capital of the Continent. American bankers had set up there since the early nineteenth century: Welles, Seligman, Harjes, Drexel, Morgan. At the end of the century, American Express opened its first foreign office there (1895), as its traveler's check business took off.

The city of course was its own draw, while the American colony, with its clubs and community life, was both cause and effect of the growing American presence there. American businesses came to France in the first half of the twentieth century to sell everything from chewing gum (Adams, Chicle, Wrigley) to reducing girdles and corsets to Stetson hats and BVD athletic underwear. The early corporate members of the American Chamber of Commerce (ACC) in Paris included National Cash Register—what better symbol of the rise of the American emporium?—and the Singer Manufacturing Company, that ur-multinational whose first foreign outpost was in Paris and which was a symbol of America abroad well before Coca-Cola. The economic activities of Americans in France only grew after World War I, although not all were immediately successful in the context of Europe's difficult postwar reconstruction. Coca-Cola's new French bottling plant lost so much money that it shifted to licensing. Westinghouse Electric sold off its French subsidiary and turned to licensing rather than direct manufacturing investment. But as the war loans were renegotiated, any major bank not already present came to Paris. American car and film companies and Chicago meat and oats purveyors (Swift and Company and Quaker Oats) all came to France along with the Dry Milk Company and Sorbo's Rubber Sponge Products.[14]

The mirage of desire worked in both directions. Before Americans sold to Europe, they came to buy. Marshall Field himself first went to France to purchase goods for his Chicago store in 1865. Then he started sending a trusted employee, and by 1872 he set up a Paris purchasing office. Other major department stores followed suit. John Wanamaker sent his son to Paris, where Rodman Wanamaker lived for some ten years (1888–98), becoming a cosmopolitan man about town, studying art and collecting it. He sent catalogues to his (amazed, and worried?) father and silk underwear to (delighted) female relatives back home. After Rodman returned to the United States and took over the New York store, Wanamaker's ultimately created a special room to display French lingerie. French phrases came to sprinkle magic dust on department stores' special events: "vente de blanc" sounded better than "white sale" for the winter linen specials.[15] By the interwar period, Macy's, Bonwit Teller, and Sears also had resident buyers in Paris, and Roditi and Sons was buying for thirty-one US dry goods and department stores, including Abercrombie & Fitch.

But the sellers outnumbered the buyers, and it is they who are taxed with "Americanizing" the world. The Haviland story provides the perfect transition from buying to selling and settling in France. The Havilands first came to buy, then started manufacturing in France, and in the end undoubtedly became more French than American. David Haviland, a New York importer of china, was so impressed with Limoges quality porcelain that he moved there in 1842 to buy goods made to order. He soon set up his own plant in Limoges, the first American direct manufacturing investment venture in France. The company's success was considered to be due to its inimitable combination of French workmanship and American marketing. It used its dual identity accordingly. While Charles-Edouard Haviland could describe himself as a modest French porcelain manufacturer as he vociferously defended the industry against the Sèvres state monopoly, his brother Théodore could write to the American ambassador hoping for help against irate strikers. In 1935 (rather belatedly?), the company was listed as an (American) member of the American Chamber of Commerce.[16] The other early American sales company in France was Tiffany's. It represents a different but more classic and long-lasting model: marketing a known American brand to Americans abroad. In the early 1850s, Tiffany opened a diamond store in Paris in order to offer luxury merchandise to traveling Americans who trusted its name.[17]

World War I was the beginning of the American Century for many. By World War I many American companies were already well situated in the French capital, but the war and pent-up postwar demand would create a veritable take-off, as the American Chamber of Commerce predicted as early as October

1914.[18] Six months into the war, Sidney B. Veit, an importer of French hats to New York, made a spirited appeal to American manufacturers and exporters, arguing that the conflict offered vast opportunities to make American manufactured products better known. He provided practical advice about sending neat and tastefully packaged merchandising and labeling goods and catalogs in French and in the metric system. The Chamber of Commerce served as a clearinghouse for information, providing thousands of names of American businesses to the French, but it also warned: Paris hotels were flooded with all sorts of characters hoping for military contracts, some of whom might give a bad name to American manufacturers.[19]

In January 1916, the ACC predicted that the end of the war would bring unparalleled changes in the world's commerce. "The struggle for military and political supremacy will be succeeded by an economic conflict no less intense. All the weapons of commercial rivalry will be enlisted in this new warfare." American interests needed to be proactive, and the ACC in Paris saw its job as providing the guidance and enlightenment necessary. It admitted honestly that "[i]t would be unbusinesslike to pretend that the United States, in seeking to broaden her commercial and financial relations with France, is inspired solely by motives of altruism." The new commercial order would help both countries.[20]

Sales would never have taken off without increasing consumer demand, even if that meant, as one president of Colgate-Palmolive later put it, "overcoming housewife resistance through advertising."[21] The soap bars, the tins of asparagus, and the typewriters would not have made a dent without supply's counterpart, increasing consumer—and business—demand in a modernizing France. "But challenging European manufacturers in their own backyards was risky business."[22] By 1930, American manufacturers were selling everything on the French market from machinery and machine tools to automobiles and auto parts, electrical apparatuses, office equipment, food products (including Shredded Wheat and Sun-Maid Raisins), leather and hides, and petroleum products. In some cases a single firm represented an entire swath of American manufactured products. Fenwick SA, probably the most active American sales agent in Paris, worked on behalf of almost one hundred American machine and machine tool companies, selling everything from sandslinger machines to drill sharpeners to jacks, hammers, and chisels.[23]

GOVERNMENT HELP?

Before looking at how they did it, we need to ask to what extent the businessmen braved it on their own. Many American businessmen abroad made a virtue if not a religion of private enterprise, proud of their self-reliance: "[W]e do not require official help to found and develop great things, and private enterprise has done more in our country than has been accomplished elsewhere with the aid of governments."[24] Others, however, were disappointed that the government did not help more. As Upton Sinclair's fictional World War I arms merchant, Robbie Budd, complained, American business was getting no help whatsoever from its pacifist president, whereas other countries had their diplomats backing them.[25] Real life Willard Bartlett, the American Chicle Company's distributor of chewing gum in Paris, was equally disappointed. He wrote to the company's export manager in Long Island in 1933, complaining that the Department of Commerce was not doing its job and chiding the company as well for not being more forceful in the matter: "[A]n energetic protest on your part will perhaps make our dormant government in Washington wake up to the fact that the world over American made goods are disappearing from the markets due to the 'isolation policy' adopted by our representatives abroad. . . . A corporation such as yours should worry the Department of Commerce until action and results are obtained."[26]

To what extent did the US government aid and abet American investment in France in the first half of the twentieth century, during war and during peace? American historians have debated the influence of business interests on American foreign policy and of US government policy as an aid to business ventures. While traditional historians downplayed government help, revisionist historians from the 1960s on have given credit to the notion that the US government was an important ally to American business abroad. As the consulates expanded their functions after World War I to include trade promotion, they began helping businessmen more directly. The Bureau of Foreign and Domestic Commerce was active, writing reports and counseling consulates as part of the "promotional state," as Emily Rosenberg has called it.[27]

The American Chamber of Commerce in France, as we have seen, frequently petitioned the US government on behalf of commerce abroad, and it seems to have constituted a mutual admiration society with the consulate. They complemented and complimented each other, the ACC thanking the consulate for its help, the consuls general exhorting the ACC to keep up the good work. But was the US government simply the executive committee of the bourgeoisie, to use Marx's pithy phrase? Some businesses clearly hoped so, especially in wartime. During World War I, worried company executives wrote directly to the government for aid. The New York Life Insurance Company contacted the secretary of state for help in protecting its valuable property at the corner of boulevard des Italiens and rue Le Peletier. An artificial limb company during the war and a tire company after the war hoped for help in procuring French government contracts.[28] Beyond these protective and proactive requests, other companies turned to the government for help in defending them against accusations of complicity with the enemy. The fur firm of Joseph Ullmann pleaded for aid to get back its Russian Colinsky furs and Russian squirrel backs, which had been confiscated by the French government, mistaking the firm for German. Ullmann protested that his grandfather, the firm's founder, had been an Alsatian who became a naturalized US citizen. After checking credentials, the State Department agreed to afford all possible protection to the firm's furs in France.[29]

Even during peacetime the government could give a helping hand. Wanting to open offices in France dealing directly with the public but turned down by the French government, which had instituted a state monopoly on certain cable company activities, Western Union turned to the US government. The secretary of state wrote to the French ambassador to the United States on behalf of all American cable companies, arguing for reciprocity with a not-so-veiled threat with regard to the seven French cable offices in New York City: American cable companies in France should be treated as French companies are in the United States.[30]

Manufacturers of everything from chewing gum to canned asparagus, machine tools to tomato juice, increasingly turned to the State Department, writing from the United States or from France. It could be a specific matter, such as preventing a shipment of tobacco from rotting: the American and Reynolds Tobacco Companies needed help to release a load from Turkey that had been held up in customs in Algiers on its way to Gibraltar.[31] But companies mostly asked the US government for relief from French tariff increases—outraged, for example, when due to a special agreement French import tariffs were lowered for Italian goods but not for American ones.

The consulate served US firms doing business abroad largely as a fact-finding agency. Consular reports investigated everything from the French codfish catch of 1903 to alcoholism in France to the French market for toys in 1936.[32] And the consulate handled requests from everyone from plumbers to birch log exporters. When the Flushometer Company, a high-end plumbing manufacturer in New York, wrote to the US Commercial Attaché asking for help in contacting appropriate counterparts in France who could help mount its Dome Jet Siphon Water Closet and Urinal stand at the Paris International Exhibition of 1937, the consulate responded with the addresses of five recommended firms. It added the caveat that it took no responsibility for the list while suggesting, as it did to others, that the company should give careful attention to the question of import duties and quota restrictions and should write in the French language if possible; this would improve chances for reply.[33] Companies also turned to the consulate, as we have seen, for help with working papers. Three years after setting up a new plant in Paris in 1933, Coca-Cola wanted to hire an American expert "in order to reach the maximum perfection in our manufacturing methods." The company laid out Steele Powers's qualifications, especially those that could hopefully impress the French authorities: his father had fought in France during the war, and the young Powers, although born in Atlanta, had attended the prestigious Lycée Janson de Sailly; he currently lived with his parents outside Paris in their château in Ville d'Avray.[34]

The question of US government intervention is thus not just a theoretical debate among historians. Many American businessmen explicitly expected help. In 1906, as consular reform was being debated in Congress, a national convention of business organizations met in Washington to discuss the issue. It passed a resolution arguing that "we require a much larger share of the world's trade than that which we control to-day," and that consular reform and efficient, professional officers were needed. as a necessary impetus to American economic expansion abroad, not the least because other countries' consulates were helping *their* businessmen work abroad. When the 1918 Webb-Pomerene law was passed, exempting certain exporters' associations from various aspects of antitrust law, members of the American Chamber of Commerce in Paris were thrilled, even if they felt the law did not go far enough: "Legislation of this kind by Congress is so rare that the opportunity to encourage it ought never to be lost."[35]

Yet by the interwar period, government and businessmen could also exchange disgruntled barbs concerning reciprocal disappointments. Although the government took on an even more explicit role both at home and abroad after the stock market crash, George S. Messersmith, assistant secretary of state, apparently still felt it necessary to defend his department's record in 1937. Stressing that the State Department was the oldest and least costly of the government departments and that the total reversal in American trade over the previous thirty years (from importing to exporting) meant that its importance for economic affairs was invaluable, he lamented—more hurt than peeved?— that the government's role in business overseas had not been given due recognition. This was undoubtedly "due to the fact that it is not only a tradition but a necessity that this Department not blow its own horn."[36] But he emphasized "how baseless is the criticism . . . that [the Department of State] does not concern itself with matters of business and is not deeply enough interested in the problems of the American businessman." And he was particularly miffed that "even well-informed businessmen who have for many years been using information originally provided by our Foreign Service and who prize it very highly have occasionally been among the most vocal critics of this Department and its agents." [37] True, the embassy had to choose its battles, and at times it had to refuse to intervene for a special cause—however worthy, such as tax relief for the American Church in Paris—that might "use up a bargaining advantage when there are so many general American interests claiming our Government's good offices." [38] But by and large, the consular archives strike a blow at the notion of either the complete autonomy of business overseas or of US isolationism in the 1920s. The State Department's expertise was an invaluable aid to trade, as seen by the State Department itself but also by the companies that sought its help. The consulate and embassy served as an important hub in the American businessmen's network.

OF SARDINES, TRADE, AND TARIFFS

From Taft's "Dollar Diplomacy" to post–World War II Marshall Plan agreements, there can be little question that the US government often gave a helping hand to businessmen overseas in one particular realm: tariff and trade negotiations. Reading the laments of the Parisian ACC in the mid-1930s, one would think that American goods would have never surmounted the obstacle course of French quotas, duties, license taxes, special import taxes, and sanitary regulations that blocked American goods. The ACC worked constantly with the embassy in trying to reduce border barriers to free, that is, American, trade. Battles over wheat and wine and tariff tussles of many other sorts preoccupied American businessmen and diplomats then as now.

Franco-American negotiations over tariffs and double taxation from the late nineteenth to the mid-twentieth century were never solely economic issues. They were also political. The initial salvo for our period was the French Méline Tariffs of 1892 and then the US Dingley Tariff bill of 1897. The Franco-American Treaty of Reciprocity was signed in 1899, giving each country minimum tariff status for a specific list of products ranging from French opera glasses, cement, chessmen, and woolen hats entering the United States to American stallions, clover seed, top boots, and electric dynamo machines going to France. Another reciprocity agreement on trade was signed in 1908. Certain US tariffs were lowered via the Payne-Aldrich Act of 1909, although they were to be increased by 25 percent on products of any country that discriminated against the United States. The French took note, and the revised

French tariff law of 1910 made concessions for certain American manufactured articles.

World War I exacerbated export problems just as more and more American businessmen were poised for the great leap overseas. ACC businessmen blamed the Germans for having imposed minimum rates on France after the war of 1870, already wanting "to injure" Franco-American commerce.[39] The situation only worsened after World War I, when France agreed to reparations in kind from Germany. Political exasperation added to economic ire as US businessmen and diplomats observed the ultimate irony of the war's aftermath: German goods were being favored over American ones, while French war debts to the United States were left unpaid![40] Although the United States initially moved toward lower tariffs in the 1920s, by the 1930s tariff wars had again become generalized. In France, with continuing acrimony over the war debt and increasing xenophobia, there were nonetheless continued but slow efforts to come to an agreement on a more general commercial treaty between the two countries. But the United States continued to raise its rates, culminating in the protectionist Smoot-Hawley duties imposed in 1930. France responded with quotas on American agricultural and industrial goods. A reciprocal quota agreement went into effect on May 31, 1932, and it was just as quickly contested.

Throughout the period, while the French pouted that their (mostly luxury) goods suffered under higher taxes in the United States, American manufacturers groused increasingly loudly themselves. Alternating protestations of friendship with outrage, American businessmen clamored that the French were discriminating against American products and demanded reciprocity. They appealed to themes of equality and justice when the language of free trade did not suffice. The crux of the matter, from the American Chamber of Commerce's point of view, was that the United States and France had different principles concerning import duties.[41] France had two tariff schedules, a minimum rate generally applied to favored nations and a maximum rate for everyone else, including the United States. Needed American raw materials were allowed in under the minimum rate, but American finished and semi-finished manufactured goods came under the maximum rates. By contrast, as one American ambassador patiently tried to explain to the French Foreign Office, the theory behind the US tariff was "equal treatment to all."[42] The United States had just one tariff for all countries; differences were based on the nature of the item, not its provenance. Tariffs were low to nil on items deemed necessary for the country, high on luxury goods. Thus, contrary to French opinion, tariffs on champagne and Roquefort cheese were not aimed against French goods per se but were simply applied to luxury goods no matter where they hailed from. The basic problem, as seen from the United States, was simply that Americans were paying maximum rates of import duties into France, while most of the European countries exporting to France benefited from minimum rates.

In the continued absence of a general commercial treaty between the two countries, negotiations over specific goods in the 1930s sometimes sound like a wildly disparate laundry list as each country bartered over its prize possessions. The United States worried about patent-leather quotas, apples, and whether copper could be classified as a raw material—if so, it would get advantageous import tax treatment in France, and the United States would be kinder to French dress samples in exchange. During Prohibition, France complained that the United States was importing some spirits for medicinal purposes; could not cognac be put on the medicinal list? Erroneous information, countered the US government. Once Prohibition was lifted in 1933, greatly increased quotas for French wine were granted in exchange for more bushels of American pears and apples. With the US rice surplus of 1934, the government-as-salesman tried to exchange trade concessions of wine for rice, all the while insisting that it preferred a general agreement to these item-by-item negotiations. When France passed a new 1934 law on wine names, reinforcing its AOC—*appellation d'origine contrôlée*—system, American officials at first thought that this could be used as a bargaining chip, offering to protect French wine names in the United States in exchange for a lower tariff on rice. But they had to recognize that *champagne* and *burgundy* had already become generic names in the United States. And just when the United States thought that France might be ready to negotiate a more general agreement, new tariff increases were threatened on canned asparagus and dried prunes. Then the French dug in their heels on wine and champagne, of course, but also on cigarette papers and Calais lace. In internal documents, the State Department made reference to pressure from "our fruit people," while, similarly, the French minister of agriculture waited for crop estimates before bargaining.[43]

The early 1930s were especially gloomy for American businessmen in France, as the ACC summed it up in a cable to US senator Hiram Bingham: "Present time most critical and discouraging of history for American business men abroad, who are fighting with backs to wall to maintain trade in American products against overwhelming handicaps of quotas, embargoes, tariffs, monetary troubles, restrictions and high local taxation." It was not just the "veritable rain of quotas" that irked. An embargo was placed on American apples in 1933, when too many San Jose scales—tiny but highly destructive insects—were found sneaking into France along with the fruit. New quotas were instituted in 1933, on automobiles and gramophones for example, along with asbestos goods and canned asparagus. The latter was considered a typical instance of an American specialty being hit with a 500 percent tariff increase, which, even if it was intended to be temporary, quickly disrupted the asparagus trade. Woe too to the American patent-leather business in France. The ACC lamented that an "[unnecessary and stupid] economic war almost as devastating as real war now exists between friendly nations." And it repeated the need for a regular commercial treaty between the nations. "The paralyzation [sic] of the international exchange of goods is the outstanding cause of the prolongation of the world's economic crisis."[44]

"U.S. Gets Roquefort, France Teeth by Pact."[45] The Reciprocal Trade Agreement was finally signed in 1936. In it, among other things, American false teeth ("an indirect gastronomical benefit") were negotiated against bona fide French cheese. The agreement was negotiated one step ahead of the French Popular Front and published one week after the socialist coalition came to power. But the agreement did not end the quarreling and quibbling, as each side believed that the other had the better deal. While the American headlines were triumphant, the French ones were more measured, and the Calais lace manufacturers were furious that the champagne and cigarette manufacturers seemed to have gotten a better deal than they had.[46]

HOLLYWOOD: A TALE OF TWO GOVERNMENTS

Hollywood! No industry has been more identified with Americanization than the film industry, and perhaps no consumer industry has raised more questions concerning the governmental boost behind it. Not to mention that Hollywood has been at the symbolic epicenter of twentieth-century Franco-American culture and economic wars. Most of the resentment from the French side has been focused on the Motion Picture Export Association (1945) and the 1946 Blum-Byrnes agreement that, even before the implementation of the Marshall Plan, cut a deal between France and the United States. The United States forgave French war debts in exchange, among other things, for opening wide French movie theaters to American movies and hence the American way of life. These agreements have come to symbolize the epitome of an American state-industrial complex, while the government's role in US cultural exportation has been castigated as a major villain in the Americanization of the world.[47] Yet it started well before World War II.

The French firms Gaumont (1896) and especially Pathé (1897) were the first film-industry multinationals. Leaders in both production and distribution, they set up studios and distribution companies in the United States. Before World War I, it was France who exported films and expertise to the United States.[48] Little by little, however, with the help of a new movie genre, the western, American cowboys began to compete successfully with the wildly popular French chase movies. And Pathé Frères could not keep up with growing demand for films at the American nickelodeons. So movie theater moguls in the United States, such as Wilhelm Fuchs–turned–William Fox, began producing films themselves. New York became the corporate headquarters of the industry, while the sunny slopes of Hollywood, where good weather and cheap land were abundant, became the favored site for production studios. Already before World War I, the "Hollywood" (New York) companies began to outrun French domination of the film industry, first within the United States and soon by exporting to Europe and elsewhere.

World War I made the trend into a long-term reality. Production in France and elsewhere on the Continent was halted during the hostilities, although the growth of French movie theaters continued apace, creating a demand that French films, even as production resumed, could not fill. Postwar recovery would take time, affecting this industry as others. This alone gave the Hollywood studios an important edge while they were distributing their already largely amortized films in Europe. The movie industry was the major beneficiary of the Webb-Pomerene Act of 1918, and in 1922 American film producers and distributors (one and the same, unlike the situation in France) created the Motion Picture Producers and Distributors of America (MPPDA), with Will H. Hays at its head. Film industry historian Kristin Thompson has forcefully argued that it was the new distribution practices rather than production overseas that explains the American takeover of the film industry. The MPPDA became the vigorous export arm of the industry, and after World War I, the flow of films thus changed direction.[49]

Pathé and Gaumont retrenched to concentrate on lucrative distribution rather than production. By the 1920s one-quarter of US movie revenue came from European sales, and the US film companies became some of the earliest successful vertically integrated multinationals.[50] By 1924 well over three-quarters of the films shown in France were American westerns and musicals, although that figure dropped to under half by the early 1930s, largely thanks to the "Film Europe" movement in which Germany, Britain, and France banded together to promote their own films. The shift away from silent films initially did more than weed out actors with squeaky voices. It seemed to threaten Hollywood's overseas expansion. And a secondary struggle ensued over dubbing: into what language, with what actors, where to be done. The talkies, however, ultimately had less of an impact on the industry than the Depression.[51]

If, from the 1920s on, American hegemony in world film markets became clear, the golden years of the Studio Era (1930–48) were not, as the Hollywood success story would have it, devoid of struggle. Business was difficult for Hollywood in France in the 1930s. Fox, for one, was losing money in France in the mid- to late 1930s. The European quotas along with the Depression decreased the American studios' film revenues abroad during the early part of the decade.[52] Some of Fox's problems were worldwide. The novelty of the talkies was wearing off, and radio was still a cheaper form of entertainment. But even more so than some of the other studios, Fox's general production costs, including increasingly exorbitant stars' fees that were the ransom of the Hollywood system itself, had risen far above revenues, and the Depression reversed the profits of 1930. Furthermore, Fox seemed to be losing its talent edge and increasingly specialized in B-category films. In France, a "drastic drop" in business over the period 1926–34 led to such an accumulated loss for Fox Film SA that by the beginning of 1935 it was decided to halt production there. By November 1936, the shares of Fox Film SA were "not worth the paper they are written on from the balance sheet point of view"; the company had lost three-quarters of its capital. Another subsidiary, Les Productions Fox Europa SA, shifted from production to distribution, which helped somewhat (if rendering its name a misnomer). At the end of 1935, losses roughly equaled capital for Fox Europa. But 1937 was a bad year, and 1938 not much better, even though the quality of the pictures released was better, with bigger turnover. But the expenses of expanding the business had increased as much as turnover, so there were still losses. Paramount, too, closed down its production activities in France in March 1933. Hollywood was still trying out different business models abroad in the interwar years.[53]

And in the meantime France fought back, with anger and with quotas, like other European countries. Writer/actor René Jeanne, in a well-known 1930 article titled "The American Cinematic Invasion," accused Hollywood of "a deliberate plan carefully nurtured and patiently put into practice" to use film as political and way-of-life propaganda. He accused Hollywood not just of colonizing France but of colonizing all of Europe with its industrial practices. Through block booking, French distributors and film theaters had to rent bad films along with the good ones.[54]

Both the US and French governments got involved in the culture war. In this case, the battle was over quotas rather than tariffs. As early as 1921, Germany, with its well-structured film production industry (especially before so many filmmakers fled Nazism to the United States), was the first country to implement a quota restricting American films. Italy, Hungary, Austria, Britain, Portugal, and France followed suit over the next decade. Hays, not surprisingly, countered with calls for open markets, echoed forcefully by Harold L. Smith, a vice consul at the US Consulate from 1925 to 1928 who became head of MPPDA's Paris office in April 1928. In the receiving countries, producers and distributors had in any case different interests. In France, the producers remained independent—and poorly organized—while the French distributors wanted films at any price.

In 1928, the Herriot decree instituted the first film quotas in France, allowing for seven American films to be imported to France for every French film sent to the United States. This was better from the American perspective than a 4:1 ratio initially contemplated. In 1929, however, the French proposed a ratio of 3:1, and Hays organized a boycott in retaliation. For six months that year, the American film offices in France closed their doors, while the embassy tried to calm the reportedly aggressive attitude of Hays and Smith, stressing the need for cordiality and united action. From the government's perspective, import-export issues were never solely about films. France and the United States were simultaneously negotiating tariffs and quotas on everything from asparagus to copper. In the meantime, the French tried to link the film issue to the war debt issue: they would be more generous to American films if the US government eased the terms of debt repayment. In the end, an agreement of 4:1 was initially negotiated, but then the quota was again increased to 7:1. The quotas were abolished in 1931, but tensions remained. And one industry specialist grumbled, "The difference in language and psychology of the people of our two Republics is already the most formidable quota that could be devised."[55]

The intrepid Harold L. Smith was smack in the middle of the industry and governments' tug of war, and he managed to irritate French and US government officials alike. He wrote regularly to the American embassy, forwarding studies, rumors, and reports on the perfidious plots of the French government against the American film industry. In 1930 the French espied him photographing a French poster titled "La France colonisée par le film américain" (France colonized by American films) that protested the quota negotiations. Smith complained about the poster to the US chargé d'affaires, and the embassy in turn protested to the French Ministry of Foreign Affairs. This led to telegrams being sent to the prefects of France and Algeria asking them to remove the posters discreetly, which in turn raised a storm when the text of the confidential telegram was published in the right-wing *Action Française*.[56]

Smith's constant complaints about discrimination, censorship, and "the enemies of our films in France"—"a small clique of functionnaires" and a group of failed movie men, a "dictatorial control of the entire industry"—were considered too heavy-handed, and the embassy at times had to put a brake on his recriminations. When Smith implored the embassy's help in early 1936, it responded that its hands were tied while it was finalizing the Franco-American trade agreement.[57]

Three different story lines usually share top billing in explaining Hollywood's successes around the world: culture, economics, and politics. There are those who emphasize quality and intrinsic customer preference to account for strong demand. Others insist that the economic power of an amortized vast domestic market is the real key to Hollywood's success. Still others stress the US government's help. Thus American business methods and government help rather than the story line or an animated mouse may explain US film success. In spite of Smith's grousing or because of it, the American film industry made considerable strides in France in the interwar period as Hollywood's rise coincided with that of the United States itself. But the advances made during the crucial interwar period were not without a struggle. The pre–World War II period had nothing like the 1946 Blum-Byrnes agreement to flex US muscle, but it would be disingenuous to argue that the US government had nothing to do with the industry's success. If at moments the US government supported its apples and rice instead of its films, the US ambassador, for one, was keenly aware of the importance of the US film industry. He compared it to France's wine industry. Let in our films, he argued just before Prohibition was abolished, and we'll look favorably on your wine—once we can drink again.[58]

DOUBLE TAXATION

Taxes were another issue fraught with Franco-American tensions. Avoiding taxes, that national sport, is even more challenging when citizens go abroad. At best certain Americans abroad might duck home obligations. At worst they could be taxed twice. Americans in France were vigilant about the latter, and they complained vociferously to the embassy when they were discriminated against as foreigners in France, or, more precisely, as foreigners whose country did not have a fiscal reciprocity agreement with France. If double taxation was a risk for individuals, as we have seen, it was also a decidedly unpleasant liability for companies. Indeed, it was deemed the "bugbear of foreign business in France."[59] This was not a concern in France alone. The issue led to animated discussions at the International Chamber of Commerce and the

League of Nations in the 1920s, as leaders worried that double taxation was impeding trade.[60] Ultimately a series of double taxation treaties were signed. But in the meantime, American companies in France sought to keep one step ahead of French tax law.

An 1872 French tax law had initially affected foreign companies that set up branches but not subsidiaries incorporated under French law. When France reformulated its tax law in 1913, it began to tax foreign companies doing business in France more rigorously. As Southard noted, one of the reasons for transforming an American branch into a French subsidiary was to redefine it as a domestic corporation for French tax purposes.[61] In the aftermath of World War I, France needed foreign investment to rebuild just as American companies were eager to go abroad. Lawyer Charles Gordon Loeb discussed the openness of the French system toward foreign investment in his 1921 book *Legal Status of American Corporations in France*, and his praise of France was reciprocated in a laudatory preface by none other than René Viviani, former French premier: "You have brought out clearly the liberalism of French Legislation towards Foreign Corporations and have shown that under all circumstances France rises above the narrow furrows of Egotism."[62] Yet as more and more foreign companies moved into France in the 1920s and 1930s, the French government, torn between opening up to foreign investors and being vigilant about taxing their profits in France, successively redefined the contours of foreign businesses in France. In early 1929 it changed the definition of the nationality of a corporation so that subsidiaries' dividends were now to be taxed like those of any French company. In addition, any dividends paid out to individuals or companies in foreign countries were liable to a further tax. American business interests, with the help of their lawyers, engaged in creative transformations of their business identities in response.

The issue of double taxation came to a head over shoe polish. The Boston Blacking Company had set up a branch in France to manufacture its shoe polish in 1921. Two years later it turned the American concern over to its French company in exchange for 1,788 shares of the new company's 2,000 shares. When, in the mid-1920s, the French government attempted to apply the 1872 law to companies that had controlling interests in French subsidiaries, many American companies refused and withheld payment. When Blacking insisted that it had sold its assets to a French company, the French government countered that Blacking's new legal structure still constituted foreign control. The French government thus wanted to tax Blacking in the United States (as well as the French subsidiary), while Boston Blacking argued that this constituted double taxation and furthermore contravened the 1853 Franco-American

Consular Convention that guaranteed American citizens in France the same rights as French citizens. In the first instance judgment was favorable to the American company, but the French government appealed in 1931, and the case dragged on.[63] In the meantime, the dispute led to a movement in favor of bilateral treaties to deal with such problems. A treaty between the United States and France—the first such bilateral treaty on double taxation for the United States—was finally signed in 1932, although it took another three years for the French government to ratify it. It finally went into effect on January 1, 1936. "This treaty will not, of course, solve all our difficulties, by any means," warned one lawyer.[64] But for the most part, Americans were relieved that some clarity had been reached.

SETTING UP IN FRANCE, DOING BUSINESS FROM A HOTEL

How then best to set up a company in France? How to exercise American corporate power from across the sea? The question is hardly new, but time and again American companies and their lawyers mused as to whether the French bureaucratic hassles were worth it. As one company put it, "[M]ore may be lost through French complications arising than we can safely anticipate saving in American taxation." When executives had to decide whether the American or the French end was more important, "it was agreed that the American end was the one to be considered."[65]

Doing business in France ultimately included a combination of formal and informal practices. "The question as to whether a foreign company is doing business in France has always been a very delicate one. Companies have always wanted to do business here but they never wanted to be considered doing business here."[66] Businessmen who came to France regularly, often for months on end, overstaying their two-month tourist visa, did not necessarily qualify or want to be qualified as setting up a permanent establishment in France, due to the tax consequences. But this could create as many personal and corporate problems as it solved. Thus, in June 1939, the great Pennsylvania cork merchant, Mr. Armstrong, was unable to register his company at the Registre de Commerce since he did not have a *carte de commerçant*. But as his lawyer pointed out to the French authorities, he was not eligible for an identity card of any sort, since he came to France for only several weeks per year. Being turned down at the Registre de Commerce was not only personally humiliating for Mr. Armstrong, an eminent citizen in his own country, but also most prejudicial to the French subsidiary involved and to the French economy as a whole, his lawyer argued. After all, the Pennsylvania cork company purchased almost the entire cork production of North Africa for foreign export.[67]

The difficulties of doing business in France had to do with everything from registration laws to thorny tax issues to personnel problems—hire locals or stick to Americans? But first of all, what exactly did "doing business" in France mean? The definition itself was often in dispute between American firms and the French tax authorities.

An episode in the tax wars could be titled "The Businessman, the Hotel, and the Secretary" were it not for the fact that this might imply something even more than what was actually involved, at least as far as the historian can tell.[68] The 1930s found the pioneering aviator Thomas F. Hamilton in Europe as representative for the United Aircraft Export Company, which represented Hamilton's own Hamilton Standard Company along with Sikorsky Aviation, Chance Vought Aircraft, and Pratt & Whitney. By 1936 Hamilton, known as the "Yankee Peddler," was president of the export company. He set up his headquarters at the fancy Hôtel George V, where he and his second in command, F. P. Culbert, spent long months negotiating to sell and license airplanes and airplane engines to the French Air Ministry. There was no question of setting up a French subsidiary, or even a formal office or place of business that might be construed as a "stable establishment." That would have made the company liable to French taxation on commercial profits and revenue. The company's lawyer's offices served as its place of domicile for the purpose of signing the agreements—a common legal practice.

Two separate participant-observers questioned this arrangement: the French tax authorities and Hamilton's former secretary Miss Timper. In 1939 Hamilton received a formal inquiry from his local French tax office addressed to him at 31 avenue George V wanting to know why a tax return for 1938 had not been received. He replied that his usual place of residence was the United States, that he had no principal residence in France (his address was the hotel), and that he had left the hotel on the previous December 10 and had returned only in March. In the meantime, we do know, from the law firm files, that Hamilton had a yacht in Cannes as well as the lease on a property in Tours, while Culbert rented an apartment in 1939 in the 16th arrondissement, where he lived with his French wife, their four children, and his mother.[69]

Elisabeth Timper also lived in the 16th arrondissement. However, she was a secretary and would not have corroborated Hamilton's I-don't-work-here tax defense. She had apparently worked a good nine to ten months for United Aircraft during 1938, and she needed an official income statement for that year. A draft employment certificate dated October 3, 1938, was in the file, but it had never been finalized; it would have been proof of the company's establishment in France. Timper was furious that she had no proof of her employment. She kept close tabs on Hamilton's and Culbert's movements in Paris and kept calling their lawyer's office to try to arrange a meeting with them. She employed veiled threats about sending a report to the company's US headquarters and wrote directly to Culbert complaining that she had once before lost her working permit and almost got thrown out of France after it had been discovered that she had worked for ten years for the American Radiator Company without being properly declared. She was not about to risk that again: "You must understand," she wrote to Culbert, "that, between getting you into trouble or getting myself into trouble, I have not the slightest hesitation, for reasons you know." She then advised Culbert as to French administrative procedure and the best way for him to file an income declaration form for her. Culbert turned the matter over to his lawyer. The latter's memorandum to the file admits that "Monsieur X, ingénieur" (Hamilton) had been in Paris "for most of 1938, if not the entire year, for business reasons" but that his company had not been registered at the Commercial Registry and that Monsieur X had been working out of the apartment of a hotel "due to the transitory nature of their type of business."[70]

One way of doing business in France was thus by doing it under the radar of the French administration. How many Americans were working there illegally, either as secretary or executive sales representative? The latter could stay for months on end in hotel apartments in order to avoid setting up a business as defined by French tax law. Admittedly, this may not have been too difficult when the address was the luxurious Hôtel George V. Ultimately, however, "doing business in France" was practically an existential issue. When French tax authorities considered the exclusive contracts that two American typewriter companies, Smith Corona and the Lanston Monotype Machine Company, had with a French distributor, Mamet et Cie., they determined that this meant that the American companies were established in France and thus taxable. Smith Corona's lawyer contended, however, that the French authorities were deliberately misconstruing the notion of a permanent establishment. The embassy intervened to try to get the French authorities to reconsider, the commercial attaché making the fine distinction that the American companies were doing business with France but not within France: "regular liaisons" and exclusive sales contracts were simple business relations. The French government conceded that neither of the companies had a permanent establishment in France, but in the end argued that the exclusive sales agreements nonetheless rendered them taxable.[71]

By the mid-1930s, the taxable definition of doing business in France had thus been expanded—unfairly in US eyes—to exclusive sales arrangements. And this had worrisome consequences for all Americans with business relations of this nature in France. American companies abroad defined or redefined themselves as French or American, as distributors or producers, in order to minimize taxes. The question was how to capitalize, in all senses of the term, on the best of two worlds. To be or not to be an *établissement stable* (permanent establishment) meant choosing to be present without being visible as such. Clearly Hamilton was not the only businessman hiding out in a hotel.

BRANCHES AND SUBSIDIARIES: OF KINSHIP, CONTROL, AND CAMOUFLAGE

If informal or simple contractual business arrangements risked unfavorable scrutiny, setting up more formal entities abroad came with its own headaches. Historical accounts of the triumph of the American multinational have suggested an evolutionary vision of industrial expansion from exporting to licensing to setting up fully controlled branches or more independent but still controlled subsidiaries abroad. Companies tended first to work through independent overseas agents before appointing their own dedicated export manager or setting up their own sales office. From sales alone, overseas activities could then shift into various means of manufacturing abroad, by first signing patent and licensing agreements with overseas manufacturers, then buying or setting up finishing, assembly, or manufacturing plants of their own.[72]

There were many ways for Americans to set up a more formal business in early twentieth-century France. One way was first to set up business in Great Britain. By the 1920s, almost 40 percent of American manufacturing plants (but only 27 percent of American direct investment) in Europe were in (supposedly) language-friendly Great Britain.[73] The British subsidiaries in turn often worked with continental branches or even set them up. The British byway, however, often gave way to direct control of continental branches by the US parent.

For Southard, analyzing American industries in Europe, the "much talked-of" novelty of the 1920s was the increase in the fully controlled yet more independent subsidiary.[74] A truly French company would not be liable to double taxation, but it had to be careful about proving its identity. Making an SA (*société anonyme*) from an Inc. was no easy matter. American companies could purchase stock in an already-existing company, as Sweets Laboratories of New York did when it created Le Chewing Gum Français out of a former French candy company. Or they could incorporate a new French entity. American Express operated in Paris simply through a vice president and general manager for half a century. Then, just when it decided to form a separate French company, American Express (France) SA, its timing was poor. Initial papers were drawn up and signed in the early months of 1940. When the Germans invaded France on May 10, the AMEX plans were scuttled, to be resumed only after the war.[75]

Swift and Company, in Chicago, had been present in France since at least 1909, and the war years were lucrative for this Chicago meat packer that supplied European armies.[76] By the interwar years, Swift had two French companies distributing its products, Swift et Cie. and Villette & Cie. Their controlling shares were held respectively by two subsidiaries in the United States: Swift and Company, West Virginia, and the anodyne-sounding Foreign Securities Company. While Swift et Cie. was not particularly profitable, Villette was doing well. The question presented to the lawyers was this: when the French tax authorities sought to identify the owners of Villette & Cie., would they necessarily think that it was related to Swift and Company, Chicago, and accuse it of avoiding French taxation? Indeed, from the Chicago perspective, as one lawyer put it, Villette was a domestic French company. Yet in a confidential letter Villette was described as a French firm whose (American) stock holding was "camouflaged." The lawyers stressed that Swift Chicago, Swift et Cie., and Villette & Cie. had to be run as though they were independent concerns. After all, "you are always at the mercy of some discharged employee who knows the facts, and you are constantly, and all the time, sitting, so to speak, on a keg of dynamite." This was no idle speculation; a personnel file included distraught letters from an employee who had been dismissed after nineteen years of service, and the lawyers knew that given the economic climate and xenophobic times, a mid-1930s French circular had instructed the authorities henceforth to take denunciation letters more seriously.[77]

Overseas businesses thus raised questions of open or hidden "family" relationships and the eventual danger of discovery. Family metaphors are rife in the legal files, and as in many families, the relationship between members was often one of power and control. Given that this was a man's world, it is perhaps surprising (or not) that the "parent" companies are at times called "mother" companies, with their *filiales* (literally referring to a child's relation to its parent) sometimes dubbed "daughter" companies. In other cases they are the "alter ego of the parent." By extension, one lawyer suggested calling a holding company the "grandparent" or perhaps "great grandparent" of the French company.[78] While within the United States American companies could be proud of their overseas progeny, the same companies abroad might want to hide their parentage for tax reasons even more than due to fear of xenophobia. The files are full of concern about fear of disclosure, especially in the early 1930s. As the number of American subsidiaries in France had grown and the Double Taxation Agreement had not yet been signed, there was worry that American companies could be attacked by energetic French fiscal agents.

So how best to hide kinship relationships? A new name, that of a French company or a local representative, was one obvious tactic. Bulova in France operated under the name of Francis Guinand, the "alter ego" of the company. But even then its lawyers warned that the authorities could claim that he was just a facade.[79] Setting up a French subsidiary rather than a mere American branch was a logical ploy, "provided all appearance, direction and control by American parent is avoided" and that "they were willing to put up the necessary camouflage."[80] Camouflage included letterhead. As Charles Loeb wrote in his 1921 opus, the font and who was highlighted on the stationery, the corporation or its French agent, could determine the legal status of an American corporation in France.[81] After the Chase-Equitable merger occurred, Samuel G. Archibald could not have been more adamant in his lawyerly disapproval of one version of the new stationery. It was bad enough, he wrote to the head of the new Paris office, that your salary and expenses are paid from New York, itself a dangerous practice vis-à-vis the French tax authorities, but the letterhead is a dead giveaway. "I do not want to stand up so straight that I fall over backward," he avowed, but he warned that the new office had to be more careful with the paper on which it wrote.[82]

The key issue was nonetheless maintaining control, that which distinguishes direct foreign investment from other forms of capital investment. American companies were often reticent to lose any modicum of control, even when their lawyers in France explained that it was in their best interest. Thus Archibald's firm advised the Twentieth Century Fox Film Corporation in 1936 that it should not hold the entirety of the shares of its French company, Les Productions Fox Europa SA. Forty-five percent of the shares would be optimal, and there had to be at least seven real or bona fide shareholders in the French company under French law. "Real" shareholders meant ones who had actually paid for their shares with their own funds and therefore ran the risk of loss or gain; they should not be simple nominees. Furthermore, the company name and nationality of the real shareholders should be varied to complete the appearance of independence from US control. The lawyers also advised that presigned share transfer forms, which allowed ultimate control to revert to America if needed, should not be physically held by the French company itself, although they should be kept in Europe, at the lawyers' office, for example, "so as to be rapidly at our disposal if any urgent steps ever become necessary." In the Fox case, the parent and daughter had separate accounts, separate officers and directors, and a distribution agreement between the two, and the parent company did not manage the details of the subsidiary's business. The lawyer was furthermore adamant that the New York company should never state to any professional publications or in any American tax returns that it controlled the whole of the shares in the French company. He urged that the Frenchifying of Fox Europa be taken care of immediately—although years later S. G. Archibald sighed, "It would be a miracle if any such documents existed between a parent and a subsidiary anywhere" that would "prove the absolute and complete independence of the French company of its parent organization."[83]

Having control but not showing it was a fine line to walk. American companies in France needed to emphasize the French structure of their subsidiaries. The lawyers repeated their advice: hold French board meetings regularly; make sure that company minutes are substantial and careful in their wording, although they need not be too precise. Yet at the same time, be sure that "nothing can happen which would be contrary to the parent Company's wishes or protection."[84] Although Dun's or Bradstreet's might have published statements that the American company wholly owned its French company, Palmolive was strongly advised that the parent company needed to be able to show that it did not own more than a certain percentage of the shares of its French company. "I know that generally speaking American companies do not like to sell out any of their shares, but I repeat it is essential."[85]

Some American companies, however, were adamant in wanting total control. John Michel of Fox Corporation in New York insisted that he preferred nominee shareholders on the grounds that this was what other American parents had for their foreign subsidiaries; he objected to the idea of giving the French authorities "a sort of club over the parent's head."[86] To which Arthur Vanson, the lawyer in Paris, replied that it looked as if French authorities were beginning to look into such matters, and that the hundred or so companies he advised were in the process of heeding his recommendation. Vanson concluded reassuringly, however, that these real purchasers would provide just as many documents for the protection of the parent company as at present, "so that in effect it [the parent] will always have a 100% control of the shares, but not through direct ownership as at present." Furthermore, if at least three members of the law firm itself held shares, "if necessity arose, we could, on instructions from America and with the necessary proxies, hold Meetings irrespective of what anyone in the European organization might wish to do."[87]

Questions of control and camouflage fluctuated over the interwar years due to economics and politics. Whereas the French attitude toward foreign companies immediately after World War I had been rather open, both the growth of foreign companies in the 1920s and the rise of xenophobia in the 1930s meant that French rules about foreign investment increasingly tightened. Thus before the Double Taxation Agreement was implemented in 1936, many American companies were generally more interested in shielding their "children" from French scrutiny. After the agreement went into effect, many companies came out of the closet, filing the declaration to prevent double taxation. However, the declaration in itself meant admitting that the companies were controlled from America, and not everyone was convinced of the advisability of filing it. Many businesses continued to use a variety of subterfuges to mask ownership abroad: bearer shares, shares held by French-domiciled American executives or by holding companies. And Archibald's had devised a certain number of measures such as blank stock option forms, which would allow American companies to repurchase their shares as needed. The French-American Treaty did away with some of the necessity of pretending to be a French company, but lawyers continued to advise their clients to take measures to ensure that their French companies would be regarded as distinct legal entities, leading their corporate life according to the laws of France.[88] With the coming to power of the left Popular Front government in 1936, American businessmen and lawyers were also wary of nationalization. One lawyer thus advised Kodak confidentially that future patents should not be taken out in the name of the French company; they should remain the property of the American company and simply licensed to the French company for a royalty.[89] But even without fears of nationalization, transatlantic kinship relations left American companies fluctuating between pride of ownership and shrouded control.

HIRING THE FRENCH — MAX FACTOR'S ROUGE

Yet another problem confronting American companies setting up abroad was (and is), whom could they trust? Running business at a distance means having trusted intermediaries who can act on the spot without necessarily waiting for instructions coming by the next boat or cablegram. The doyen of American business historians, Alfred Chandler, has elevated managers to the pinnacle of capitalism's key workers, the trusted, visible hands of American managerial capitalism. But what happens when a company goes overseas and distance, language, and foreign customs are added to the bargain? It is commonplace today that global firms need to be attentive to local conditions, and Southard himself spoke of "national temperament" and "national preferences" when emphasizing that Americans must adapt to foreign business climes.[90] This meant being attentive to native knowledge and—why not?—hiring a local manager. One of the hardest strategic choices for American companies then and now has to do with who is to manage it, an American or not. Export one's own executive or hire one of two types of "locals": native informants eager to participate in American expansion or Americans already abroad, with hard-earned experience with the locals.

For the day-to-day management of an overseas firm, local help was neces-sary. There are trends in hiring and perhaps oscillating periods of trusting locals or swearing by one's own. During the first half of the twentieth century, American companies attempted a variety of schemes. Max Factor tried them all in an endeavor that may seem like taking coal to Newcastle: selling beauty products to the French.[91] Factor was certainly not the first American who tried. Eternal rivals, America-based but Canada-born Elizabeth Arden and Jewish, Poland-born, Australia-raised, and America-wed Helena Rubinstein were ultimately among the most successful. A host of other beauty methods, chinstraps, lotions and potions began to cross the Atlantic from west to east in the interwar years. Max Factor got a foothold in France in stages common to many American enterprises abroad. The company first set up a London subsidiary, where the language was sure(r), even if local customs were not necessarily so. The cosmetics company then traversed the channel via the London office, which first hired a sales representative in France and then or-chestrated the setting up of a French company. In both instances, Max Factor hired French locals. In both cases, the company was disappointed.

Rouge is rouge is rouge is rouge, Gertrude Stein might have said. But as any woman knows, cheek powder is a very personal thing. And, it turns out, there are national preferences regarding face colors. Polish-Jewish-born, Los Angeles–adopted Maximilian Faktorowicz himself was happy enough just to sell his cosmetic inventions locally to Hollywood starlets and to find the per-fect makeup to let too-blonde Americans blend in with the Italian extras on the *Ben Hur* set. But with his sons urging him to expand beyond the film crowd, first nationally and then overseas, the Max Factor Company eventually went to France in the late 1930s. There, as in England, it stressed its very Ameri-canness, capitalizing on its Hollywood image, "Les cosmétiques des stars." The French manager even made a dream-team list of stars whose photographs and autographs he wanted for advertising purposes: French-born Claudette Colbert, of course, but also Ginger Rogers, Jean Harlow, Joan Crawford, and Myrna Loy.

However, the company (via London) was unhappy with its French collaborators. First it parted ways with Madame Erdman, its initial sales representative in France. She was later described as having had a bad business reputation, requesting cash advances from clients and not coming through on time with deliveries. Furthermore, she had given an exclusive agreement to the Galeries Lafayette department store which had only served to alienate other department stores. Her replacement, André Joussein, was hired to expand the French operation. Forty-four years old, Joussein had been president and general director of sales at Parfums d'Orsay since 1917, but he had recently resigned after an organizational shake-up there. Hired by Max Factor in November 1936, he got to work, among other things, by giving a talk at the Salon des Arts Ménagers in Paris in February 1937 to some six to seven hundred people, "Make-Up through the Ages, from the Egyptians to Max Factor." Max Factor Hollywood & France, SA, was created in April 1937 with Joussein having 50 shares, Davis Factor (Max's son and now company president) having 5,050, and A. J. Klein (the London managing director) having 4,800. Joussein headed the French company, but Klein and other London executives were his immediate supervisors, with the Hollywood office giving its views from time to time. Joussein proceeded to hire traveling salesmen and demonstrators to call on the most important hairdressers and best perfume shops throughout France. He kept the big department store clients for himself, although Galeries Lafayette was now unhappy that it no longer had exclusive rights. And Joussein found a good location for a factory just twenty minutes outside Paris. Croissy-sur-Seine had three advantages: it was close to Paris, yet salaries were lower, and it was far enough away from the turbulent metallurgy factories that had been in the forefront of strikes during the Popular Front period.

Joussein signed the company's bylaws on April 15, 1937. By November of that year he was fired. The falling out seems to have been a classic example of tensions between American standardization and local markets. From language to advertising to accounting methods to makeup colors, the American company and its British henchmen seemed to differ from French practices. Joussein was patient in explaining the problems. It was not just that they had got the translations wrong—"Le Maquillage des Stars" was better than the more literal "Cosmétiques des Stars"—but "fabrique en Amérique" needed an *accent aigu* (*fabriqué*) to mean "made in" instead of "factory." Packaging and advertising also had to be adapted for the French market. While Joussein politely agreed to follow British advertising copy, he just as politely asked Mr. Factor "to consider the fact that certain texts or presentations can not be copied exactly but must be adapted to the French taste, which obliges us, besides London cooperation, to do some artistic work here." Finally, Joussein had to keep insisting that darker shades of rouge and eye makeup were preferred in France.[92] Max Factor's standardized color chart was not universal for all cheeks and eyelids after all.

Tensions were apparent by late July. Joussein was chastised: sales to date had been ridiculously low; demonstrations were being run in the wrong stores; traveling salesmen were spending too much time in small towns and needed to redeploy to larger ones. Joussein was reminded that *no* store should be given any exclusivity. Furthermore, the preparation and use of French Color Harmony Charts had to be speeded up, and sales representatives had to make sure shop assistants knew how to use the charts. The London overseers emphasized that accounting had to be done in exact accordance with English methods. (Bookkeeping, too, has its national variants.) The accounting department had to be simplified, and a copy of all the books had to be mailed to London monthly without delay. All in all, Joussein had to provide better oversight. Although the August minutes, two weeks later, were more conciliatory, congratulating Joussein on having turned certain things around, in November his one-year contract was not renewed.[93]

Was it a question of personalities, of strategies, of national difference, of a triangular power problem? Klein from the London office had initially preferred setting up a French branch of the London company, whereas Joussein had successfully argued for setting up the French subsidiary. Perhaps Klein continued to want greater control and was never happy with the modicum of independence that the French SA represented. Joussein had also stressed that the goods should come from the United States rather than England, given client expectations of the Hollywood image. And perhaps the French color preferences were just one sign of larger national differences. In September, Klein took Joussein to task, holding forth on the hazards of doing business overseas and on the superiority of American products and methods:

> I quite realize that the launching of any new business presents difficulties, and that each country has its separate problems, but every time we go to a new country we meet with similar arguments—"We cannot do this in England, Holland, Germany etc." according to the country being dealt with. However, our experience has proved that this is absolutely wrong, and that Max Factor products can be sold in every country in the world, and can only be sold by Max Factor methods. When you say that French girls know how to make up and therefore it is difficult to sell merchandise, I entirely disagree with you.

Max Factor is primarily selling a service. We are the people who made the most glamorous creatures on this earth more beautiful; having that in mind, surely to goodness the French girl realizes that she can be made more beautiful. In order to be made more beautiful she must have knowledge, and this knowledge can come to her from the Arch Priest of make-up—MAX FACTOR.[94]

Joussein defended himself by politely criticizing the company's "lack of assimilation to the French market," its imperviousness to national character, and its insensitive managerial methods. The company needed to adapt to French norms: "All American concerns which have made a name in France have been subjected to a similar evolution." Even the Hollywood references were not working well: "Hollywood—the stars—is a considerable strength, but we express this badly, very often with photographs of stars unknown to the general public, and especially with texts which are too long, badly worded, because you absolutely wish to give all that there is in American publicity. The spirit must be maintained, but we must not simply translate the text."[95]

Max Factor's first foray into the French market had been a flop. The company parted ways with Joussein and replaced him with Sidney Smith, an American who had been in the London office.

Language, personality, nationality? American investment overseas in the interwar period proceeded slowly, testing the waters. Some tried French personnel; many set up London offices first and wove a web from there. Others sent over their own managers or hired Americans already abroad.

THE NATIONALITY OF COMPANIES

Les Productions Fox Europa SA, for example, hired an American already in Europe—a good example of the formation of a transatlantic labor pool of American executives abroad. But they got into a dispute over management practices, and Ralph Knapp took Fox to French court over his dismissal. Part of the issue turned on the question whether Les Productions Fox Europa SA was French or American. In the first instance, the French court doubted that the French company was truly independent. Knapp's contract had made no reference either to French law or to the French company, and Productions Fox Europa was entirely dependent for all of its films on the New York / Hollywood firm. Although the judgment was otherwise favorable to Fox, it considered the American corporation and the French subsidiary to be one and the same company (as Knapp had argued), and Fox USA appealed the verdict in order to stress the independence of its French company.[96]

Another existential and, more prosaically, tax problem thus had to do with how to define a company's nationality: by its name, its headquarters, its place of business, or a list of shareholders? Some American organizations in France remained resolutely American organizations, although the legal options were numerous. The American Hospital was set up under French law in 1906 and was then chartered as a private nonprofit Delaware corporation in 1913, as was the American Library in Paris in 1920. The title to the property of the Church of the Holy Trinity (the American Cathedral) was held by the Board of Trustees of Foreign Parishes of the American Protestant Episcopal Church, a New York corporation. Being a New York corporation in Paris explicitly gave the church more latitude, freeing it from the obligations of the French 1905 law separating church and state, which would have brought its property under the aegis of the French state. As one dean commented, the church paid heavy taxes as a foreign church corporation, but it was more independent than it would have been otherwise.[97] Other American organizations in France chose to be French. The Fondation des États-Unis college dorms were a gift from private American citizens to the Université de Paris.

From the late nineteenth century on, the French government had become increasingly worried about foreign companies' nationality and their activities in France. Before World War I, French law was silent on the matter; jurisprudence considered, however, that companies had a nationality, based on the domicile of the head office. During World War I, this issue came to the fore in defining enemy companies. It thus behooved American companies to prove their identity. The French sequestered enemy property during the war, and some American companies whose name, managers, or shareholders had German-sounding names, like the Alsatian-turned-American Ullmanns discussed above, risked expulsion of their executives or confiscation of their plants if they were suspected of being German. Even the French subsidiary of the Singer Manufacturing Company had to prove during the war that La Compagnie Singer was owned by the American company. It was attacked in an anonymous leaflet campaign and in the French Senate by an overly zealous senator, Gaudin de Villaine, who showed photos of the Singer manufacturing plant on the Elbe as proof that the company was German. Aristide Briand, minister of justice, replied, however, that "[i]t is American; it is notoriously, indisputably American," and defended its multinational nature.[98] Whether buying or selling in France, coffee brokers, lace and handkerchief importers, or commission agents with names such as Baruch, Metzger, and Mautner came under suspicion.[99] American lead pencils too. One of the traveling salesmen of the American Lead Pencil Company, Leon Dreyfus (no relation to the more famous Alfred), pleaded to the head office in the United States that it write to the State Department to transmit proof that the company was indeed producing all-American pencils, defined by virtue of the company's shareholders and the fact that its products were all manufactured in Hoboken.[100]

After World War I, given the growth of direct foreign investment, French and American lawyers began studying the issue in greater detail. French law had considered but rejected different criteria for determining the nationality of a company: place of incorporation did not work because of possible fraud, nor did the nationality of the majority of stockholders because they were continually subject to change. The place of principal business interests was not sufficient either since a company could be active in several countries—including semicivilized or barbaric ones, added Charles Loeb in his analysis of the issue. The best criterion was deemed to be the corporation's domicile, that is, where general management was situated, general stockholders' meetings were held, and books were kept.[101]

If nationality issues could have dire consequences of confiscation or expulsion in times of war, they could also have dolorous consequences in times of peace. Tariffs, quotas, and taxes were based on nationality and could reflect popular opprobrium. By the late 1920s and particularly in the 1930s, there were increasingly strident xenophobic calls to limit the "foreign economic invasion." Otis Elevator was attacked for having replaced a French manager with an American director who had a French name, all the better to mask the maneuver.[102] In 1935 the American Chamber of Commerce took worried note of a "buy French" campaign calling for a boycott of articles made in France by French workmen if foreign capital was invested in the factories. The ACC called the drastic proposal an "extreme economic nationalism" far beyond any previously expressed.[103]

A FRANCO-AMERICAN SOAP OPERA: PALMOLIVE AND CADUM

Even soap has been subject to the nationality question. Along with Hollywood, Cadum soap, that most French of soap bars, with its ubiquitous baby face mascot, was castigated in the interwar period as a sign of Americanization. In this case, Cadum, a "French" product, was seen as succumbing to American advertising techniques and heavily criticized as an egregious example of the American-billboardization of the City of Light in the 1930s. But what if Cadum had been simply American all along, from its first promoter to its subsequent integration into the Palmolive empire? Was the new soap craze in

interwar France American or French? Could Palmolive and its French manufacturer, Cadum, merge without revealing that Cadum was already American,
which flies in the face of debates over the Americanization of this very French
product?

"Bébé Cadum," that archetypical rosy-cheeked baby in a demographi-
cally challenged France, became the symbol for new French hygiene practices thanks to an American businessman, a French pharmacist, and a French
painter. Michael Winburn, head of a New York lotion company, had his eu-
reka moment while on vacation in Paris. Staying at a hotel and itching wildly
with eczema, Winburn realized that his own company's Omega liniment ("For
What Ails You") was not sufficient. He went to a nearby pharmacy for relief,
and happily he found it, thanks to Louis Nathan's special cream formula. In
1907 the American businessman and the French pharmacist joined forces to
develop the cream and, soon thereafter, a new soap based on prickly juniper
(or cade) oil. Winburn realized that there was an untapped market for soap; he
wanted to democratize it from a perfumed luxury for a few to a democratic necessity for all, a "symbol of the radiant future of industrial society."[104] But what
made Winburn the Singer of the soap business was his marketing technique.

As French industry modernized in the interwar period, some companies
such as Michelin looked to American methods, and a debate has ensued about
the spread of American advertising methods in general and the Americanization of French soap in particular.[105] In 1912 "Bébé Cadum," a baby face
drawn by the French artist Arsène-Marie Le Feuvre, was born. After the war,
Winburn and his commercial director, Herbert Michaëlis, would engineer an
advertising campaign such as Paris had never seen. The Bébé Cadum image
was soon everywhere, on large, larger, and extra-large billboards plastered up
and down the boulevards on scaffolding, covering whole sides of buildings,
or perched on building tops. By the 1930s Bébé Cadum became the butt of
satire and derision as advertising itself came under attack in a prickly Europe
in crisis; there were those who considered Le Feuvre's drawing sickeningly
cutesy. But in 1928 a new factory had opened in Courbevoie, where 130 workers produced forty million bars of soap per year, and, little known to the general public, the Cadum factory was producing Palmolive products as well.[106]
Were the Cadum and Palmolive soaps a sign of Franco-American competition,
or were they already partners in soap suds?

Palmolive had set out to expand. In 1919 it began exporting its palm- and
olive-oil-based soaps manufactured in its Canadian subsidiary to France via its
English subsidiary. But then R. B. Foster, the managing director of Palmolive
Company of England, set up a subsidiary of the English subsidiary in Paris,

although apparently without the US company's authorization. He incorporated SA Palmolive on January 1, 1923, but two years later the US company bought out Foster and spent the next decade pursuing several trademark infringement suits in France against "Lanolinolive," "Palme e Olive," and the like.[107] Henceforth Palmolive would have its own, American, representatives overseeing French operations. And it began producing soap in France.

Palmolive soap was manufactured in Cadum's factory, while Cadum continued to manufacture its own, still better-known, soap there. Palmolive considered Cadum to be its subcontractor (*façonnier*): Palmolive provided the raw materials and the specifications and then took over the finished product, packaged and ready for sale. However, when on April 7, 1932, the French government implemented a new 7 percent production tax on *corps gras* (itself a sign of new hygienic times?), Palmolive decided to change its persona in France. It notified the government that it was ceasing all manufacturing operations as of July 1, 1932, and thus was a distributor but not a producer of soap and therefore not subject to the 7 percent tax rate. Since the French state defined the producer as those persons or companies that furnished all or part of the raw materials, with a flick of a pen Palmolive decided to stop providing the raw materials to Cadum. It simply bought from Cadum the entirely produced, finished, and packaged "Palmolive" soaps. Palmolive appealed the production tax law, leading to a ten-year legal case that went all the way to France's highest administrative jurisdiction. In 1943, in the middle of the war, the Conseil d'État found against Palmolive, reaffirmed the close links between Palmolive and Cadum, and maintained that Palmolive was indeed a producer, not simply a seller, of soap. In the meantime, the government prepared a new law, broadening the definition of producer to include any entity that even had another entity manufacture for it, regardless of who owned the raw materials; it was the use of the trademark that henceforth counted.[108]

At what point did Cadum SA become a part rather than just a partner of Palmolive? Secret talks between Cadum and the Colgate-Palmolive-Peet Company began in the late 1930s to merge the two companies, but an internal memorandum had already admitted the common parentage: "in our production tax case, our position would be jeopardized if it could be shown that there was one parent Company at the back of the two French ones."[109] One draft legal document seems to indicate, contrary to official Cadum firm history, that Cadum was already a French subsidiary of the American soap manufacturers, apparently since 1920.[110] The idea of the merger in the 1930s was to simplify corporate structure and eliminate the double sales force in France. Thus while Palmolive SA was trying to pretend it was French, the very French Bébé

Cadum, started by an American, had really been American all along. At any rate, as of April 1938, the option of merging "our two French companies" was considered.[111] Confidential epistolary discussions were exchanged among the London, US, and Paris offices, discussing the barely masked "P" and "C" or "Pee" and "Cee" Companies to determine whether it was more advantageous to have P absorb C or vice versa or to create a third new company. The directors, accountants, and lawyers debated the pros and cons of a merger from an economic and fiscal point of view, as well as more intangible identity issues of image and sales.[112] As war loomed, the uncertainties on the horizon argued for putting off the merger—although in a postscript one lawyer commented that "a merger at this time will attract less attention than in normal times."[113] By February, the lawyer advised the US company to wait, and three months later, after the Germans invaded France, he himself left for the Unoccupied Zone. Business continued, but the merger was put on hold until after the war. When it finally occurred in 1952, Cadum alone of all Palmolive mergers was allowed to maintain a separate existence.[114] In 2003, the Société Cadum became once again *independent* and *French*, as its website stresses in bold letters—without mentioning that one of its founders and long-time directors was American or noting when it had become part of Colgate-Palmolive.[115] The Americanization of Cadum or the ultimate Frenchification of Winburn?

HARD WORK

Southard's 1931 optimism about American industry in Europe was not unfounded. From the beginning of the twentieth century and accelerating in the 1920s, American supply and European demand were linked. American businesses and American businessmen came to France to test the waters (and presumably the wine). Many made money and stayed. Others left, only to return after World War II. Many had grandiose ideas. In 1904 the president of the American Chamber of Commerce in Paris and a former French minister jointly called upon the president of France to suggest transforming the old Palais Royal into a grand new American trade showroom.[116] Nothing seems to have come of it. (Phew.) After World War I, there was a big influx of American businessmen, as ACC membership attested, although the chamber had to chide those who got cold feet and returned home without giving France (or the ACC's proffered help) a sufficient try. But many stayed on, creating a vigorous chamber, a vibrant community, and a good deal of profit.

Yet doing business in France was (is) hard work. "I hope the revolutionists have not bothered you," Sidney Kent, president of Twentieth Century–Fox

Film, wrote worriedly to his executive assistant in Paris in 1934.[117] Against the backdrop of a radicalized French political scene, from the far right riot at the place de la Concorde on February 6, 1934, through the Popular Front left government of 1936–37, rising xenophobia, and worries about war in the late 1930s, American businesses in France had more than their share of worries. Certainly Hollywood was becoming more and more prevalent as French film-goers and distributors urged on the cowboys and femmes fatales. However, if Max Factor and Fox are any indication, as a business venture alone Hollywood was not an unqualified triumph in France before the war. Cheek blush colors and adaptation to local market and tax laws all made doing business in France a challenge for everyone from filmmakers to soap producers. At worst, perhaps the companies could have folded altogether. At best, the interwar years were uneven stepping-stones on the way to postwar persistence.

Post–World War II triumphs of American multinationals have made the project(s) seem irresistible and have masked the day-to-day uncertainties of doing business in general, of doing it abroad, and of setting up foreign outlets in the first half of the "American Century" in particular. In the twenty years of its presence in Paris, before it merged with Chase, the Equitable Trust Company's branch there had lost fifty-five million francs.[118] Some companies that would later be great post-1945 successes had only paltry business abroad in the interwar period. J. Walter Thompson opened a branch office in Paris in 1927, just as the French advertising business was expanding, but it was too late to get off the ground before the Depression undercut business. It may have been the world's largest advertising agency by the 1930s, but its Paris branch was still losing money in 1933. Thompson depended on American clients from Coca-Cola to Sun-Maid Raisins, but they did not have significant French market shares at the time. Although it later became the Continental office for the French colonies, boosting business, it was not until after World War II that J. Walter Thompson became profitable in France, when it finally garnered French clients.[119]

Were the members of the American colony colonizers or missionaries bringing their money, means, mores, and especially goods and techniques to the natives? "Americanization" in Europe before the Marshall Plan was, if anything, a more subtle affair, subject to quotation marks during the first half of the century. There were those companies who wanted to show off Americanness with pride—the "intent and desire of the Company being to spread abroad the knowledge that Yale [locks and other] products are American goods"[120]—and others who took cover. Is *colonization* too strong a word? Americans in France were not Americans in Mexico or in China, in more explicitly colonial-type situations or extraterritorial enclaves. And the European countries themselves remained strong in both fact and fiction and were of course colonial powers in their own right. Yet they worried about growing American strength. And while many consumer products would become Frenchified, just as immigrants become assimilated, France resisted the American economic invasion with tariffs and treaties, quotas, digging in its heels on makeup colors, and scrutinizing contracts. It all made doing business in France a challenge—and a lucrative business for lawyers. The first half of the twentieth century set the stage for the Americanization-without-quotation-marks that followed World War II and was vigorously contested in turn. The American business workers in Paris participated in the process—some without any intent other than making money, others with greater designs of spreading American ways and means abroad. All while dealing with often cantankerous partners.

FIGURE 7. Life in a garret. From Helen Josephy and Mary Margaret McBride, *Paris Is a Woman's Town* (Paris: Coward-McCann, 1929).

CHAPTER 6

Down and Out in Paris

The Tailed, the Arrested, and the Poor

[Drifters, bartenders, pimps, shunned the Left Bank and]
formed a motley colony of their own, along with . . .
tourist guides, gamblers, confidence men, and
vendors of pornographic pictures who had swarmed over to France
during the years immediately following the war.
They all constituted a demimonde that was half French, half American,
a sort of weird amalgam of Brooklyn and Montmartre.

SAMUEL PUTNAM[1]

To the amused incredulity of the audience, a penniless American appeared in
a 1928 play in Paris. Of course he turned out to be a millionaire.[2] The idea of
poor Americans just seemed (and seems) ludicrous to most French. And this
in spite of all of those starving art students and "the legend of good-humored
poverty, of mutual accommodation fairly raised to the romantic," as Henry
James put it.[3] The poor American art student or destitute writer may be a
fairly well-known figure to an American audience at least. The down-at-heel
ex-soldier, the struggling English teacher, or the jailed American in Paris is
not. Yet from the late nineteenth century into the twentieth, stereotypes (and
the two previous chapters) notwithstanding, not all Americans in Paris were
rich. Nor were they all upstanding, hardworking lawyers, dentists, or manufacturers' representatives on the go. The City of Light also attracted—and produced—underfunded, overspending Americans who had to turn to the American Aid Society for help. And the French capital was riddled with a small but
lively assortment of wayward souls. Some were troubled, others made trouble
on purpose. Some ended up in French jails, in spite of themselves or as will-
ful crooks. Altogether this mixed lot of the financially "down" and the legally
"out" were a frequent enough if frequently ignored phenomenon. We can start
with the troublemakers, suspected or real, many of whom added prison to
their Paris itinerary.

SUSPECTS AND TROUBLEMAKERS

The archivist at the Paris Police Archives arched a quizzical Gallic eyebrow when I asked about finding records of arrested Americans. Yet just as there were those Americans in trouble whose traces can be found in the consular and law firm records, others left their mark in the Paris police archives. Sometimes the Americans whose files are extant were simply under surveillance; sometimes they were victims who had filed a complaint, like the embassy attaché who had been belted by an offended *garçon de café* after he had complained about the drinks at the café.[4] For the most part, however, the Americans in trouble, whether turning up at the consulate, their lawyer's office, or the police station, were perpetrators rather than victims. The voluntary and sometimes involuntary miscreants had committed "crimes" ranging from "forgetting" to pay their hotel bill to shoplifting to disorderly behavior to outright wheeling and dealing. There were drunken soldiers and other irate and inebriated citizens. White Americans got into fights with black Americans who were hanging out with white women in Paris cafés. There were jazzmen who got into scuffles among themselves, and there were fisticuffs among the café set of Montparnasse. Americans were arrested for everything from stealing a bicycle to passing Confederate money(!) to trafficking in cigarettes or cocaine. (Your honor, I did not know what was in the suitcase; I was simply helping my countryman, Mr. Green.[5]) And there was the grandmother who, as has been seen, kidnapped her granddaughter. There were professional small-time crooks, including a few fugitives from justice, "those who beat a sheriff to the gangplank,"[6] and famous fugitives who used Paris as their place of refuge. Notably the celebrated interwar fugitive from the Teapot Dome Scandal, Harry Blackmer, who spent twenty-five years in exile overseas, "lightened by a second marriage and some high living in France."[7]

It is not as though transgressive Americans had been unknown to the Paris police in an earlier period. In the late nineteenth century, Mrs. Blackford, née Ely Fanny, but later known as Miss Phoenix or Fanny Lear (after the heroine of a popular French play), a New York native, stabbed her husband (unless it was he who shot at her—the French police reports are contradictory—or perhaps both) and headed off first for London and then for Russia, where she became the mistress of a grand duke—to the great displeasure of his uncle the Russian emperor. So she moved on to the French capital, where she became a well-known courtesan, followed by the police, who noted the comings and goings of her visitors. When her memoirs, *Le roman d'une Américaine en Russie* (The novel of an American woman in Russia), appeared in 1875, they caused such a scandal in Paris that they nearly provoked a diplomatic incident between France and Russia. She was expelled from France, and the contents of her luxurious lodgings were sold off at the Drouot auction house.[8]

The vast majority of Americans who came to the attention of the Paris police or the US consulate in the first half of the twentieth century, however, were mostly drunks, small-time thieves, or unscrupulous businessmen rather than high-class prostitutes. The Paris police found that the American colony included a certain number of ne'er-do-wells who followed their wealthy compatriots. They picked up a number of American pickpockets at the racetrack, and according to one report, in 1910 seventy-nine Americans were arrested in the Seine Department, nineteen of whom were expelled from France.[9]

The World War I "invasion" of soldiers and relief workers brought in its wake a wide variety of petty and not so petty crimes and misdeeds. Indeed, when embassy officials worried about how best to keep track of Americans in France during the war, it was because, as one report stated in August 1918, "the problem of eliminating the useless relief worker is the most difficult question of the moment." Some thirty-four Red Cross and YMCA workers were repatriated to the United States for reasons ranging from inefficiency and unwillingness to disorderly conduct and disobedience, vile language and destruction of Red Cross property, petty thievery, intoxication, and "indiscreet misconduct" on the part of one woman.[10] After the November 1918 armistice, demobilized soldiers were left with time on their hands before the government could arrange enough transportation back to the United States. Some went to classes. Others got into trouble.[11] Men, alcohol, guns. *Le Matin* reported that 34 murders, 220 assaults, and 500 serious fights by American soldiers had taken place in December 1918 alone, although the American authorities questioned those figures.[12] The American press ultimately took pity on those boys who ended up penniless or, worse yet, in jail in France. In 1921 a press and petition campaign led in part by the Churches Prison Commission of Atlanta, Georgia, raised alarm about those in French jails—with one- to five-year sentences for having stolen or received stolen goods, sometimes with violence. The secretary treasurer of the Churches Prison Commission blamed the US government: "Speaking at right angles, we feel that the French Government is not so much to blame for the ill-treatment of American patriots in French civil jails as is our own State Department."[13] Bring our boys home.

The fact that Americans who got into trouble with French law often knew no French and had trouble defending themselves did not help. Many of them were outraged at the way they were "repaid" for having come to help France:

"Three years as a token of 'gratitude' for my sacrifices to 'poor, bleeding France'!" wrote one interned former soldier: "'Les Miserables.' I am one." The *misérable* was Stevens Lewis Tyler, a former soldier who was sentenced to three years in jail for trafficking in postwar materiel. He had acted as "commissioner" to find buyers for two American automobiles and ended up in prison when it turned out that the seller, a Frenchman who got a six-month sentence, did not have proper authorization for the cars, which had originally belonged to the US Army. In a letter to his parents, Tyler moaned, "Why did the American Gov't permit me to be demobilized in France? If I had not been permitted to be demobilized in France, I certainly would not be in prison." He blamed the government for his situation, and he begged his parents to write to their congressman to find a high government official to intervene on his behalf.[14]

Who was to blame? The US government? The young men? The dangers of the city, corrupting wholesome American fellows? One newspaper reported the sad tale of a young boy who spoke no French, was openly ridiculed by the judge in court, and was sentenced to ten years in prison for attacking the clerk at a rue St. Honoré jewelry store. "The boy fainted and was carried back to his cell. He was one more of the seemingly endless train of ex-soldiers, the lotus eaters, who cannot resist the allurement of Paris, who spend all they have, borrow until their credit is gone, and at last do something like this."[15]

Sympathy for Americans languishing in French jails competed with criticism of their having caroused in Paris in the first place. Life in Paris was dangerous for young American men. The American consular officer in Cherbourg related the story of a Brooklynite and newly naturalized citizen. After being honorably discharged from the US military, Louis Cibulsky had returned to France, where he claimed "he got intoxicated by the Parisian life and the so-called pleasure, and step by step degraded himself so low as to commit a high robbery in the true style of movies burglaries."[16] He was sentenced on June 9, 1920, to ten years in prison and was still there in 1927.

The soldiers were not alone. Men and women, whether tourists or residents, largely got into different types of trouble. Women mostly had shoplifting (including Sylvia Beach's mother) and unpaid bills to their discredit.[17] One mother and daughter who were arrested for shoplifting at the Bon Marché department store in 1926 eventually got off with a fine and a one-month suspended sentence after they submitted affidavits from the governor, a judge, a senator, and a House representative from Oklahoma, all attesting to the honesty, integrity, and moral qualities of the family. There was a Miss Louisa Gates, who described herself as the daughter of a judge and the sister of a well-known

New York lawyer, who was arrested in Paris on July 28, 1926, for stealing a pair of gloves. As the *Chicago Tribune European Edition* noted, at the time she had $300 in cash on her and a ring valued at $1,100. She was released on bail.[18]

Unpaid bills may be a female or a male "crime," given that purchase and payment most often involved them both. Literary accounts mocked the American husband in Paris who followed his wife resignedly as she gaily made the rounds at the dressmakers.[19] More often the husband was merely consigned to the payment function. A hefty post-crash document file at the Law Offices of S. G. Archibald showed the firm corresponding with New York lawyers in attempts to collect numerous unpaid bills on behalf of the well-known French dressmaker Jeanne Lanvin. The lawyers first had to track down the wealthy but delinquent—either distracted or dishonest—American clients who had fled after the stock market debacle. When they could be found, from New York to Palm Beach to San Francisco to a sanatorium near Baltimore, they or their lawyers tendered a variety of sob stories, from having no recollection of the purchase to poverty after the crash to, more frequently, the plunging exchange rate after 1933. (The dollar dropped from twenty-five francs to the dollar in November 1931 to fifteen francs to the dollar in April 1935.) Everyone from Gloria Vanderbilt to a variety of American countesses pleaded poverty in the face of bills ranging from one thousand to ninety thousand francs. And since orders between top-notch couturiers and their high-society clients were customarily oral, some claims were difficult to prove. Language differences were no excuse, however; one of Lanvin's top saleswomen remembered that the discussions about Vanderbilt's order took place in English, while Vanderbilt spoke French during the fitting. More than one client argued that she would not be able to pay until the exchange rate improved in her favor, and one woman offered to give Lanvin her Lassalle motorcar in payment of her ten-thousand-franc debt, even though the car was currently in Pennsylvania. (Refused.)[20]

Sometimes the woman had divorced, making collection more complicated. Or there were newlyweds whose fathers turned the matter over to recalcitrant husbands. When the Comtesse Giovanni Gardelli defaulted on paying for the ninety thousand francs' worth of clothing that she had purchased during 1929 and 1930, the lawyers found the situation rather hopeless. The countess, née Miss Stewart, had been a minor at the time of purchase. Her parents were divorced, and her father, who had paid earlier dressmaker bills, reneged this time. Her mother, the former Mrs. Stewart, had no fortune of her own and had subsequently married Count Raoul de Roussy de Sales. He was described by one admirer as being the evident product of two old aristocratic French families, having "the face, fine-boned and chiseled to the point of emaciation, the extraordinarily long fingers, sensitive and mobile, the dignified reserve, coupled with a power of quiet but always trenchant conversations." Fine features perhaps, but little fortune. (He became a journalist and writer in the United States in the 1930s.) Miss Stewart herself had recently married an Italian count, but he too was apparently of little means, and in any case a husband was not legally responsible for his wife's prenuptial debts. The lawyers concluded that recovery of the debt seemed hopeless, regardless of the fact that the poor countess was living in the posh 16th arrondissement in Paris.[21] In the end, one of the lawyers involved in these cases commented on "these somewhat uninteresting matters," presumably in contrast to everything else going on in the 1930s.[22]

It is difficult to know whether American misdeeds in Paris were the results of specific circumstances (demobilization; the stock market crash), the legendary dangers of the city, or the recidivism of bad habits taken abroad. There was the American student who tried to smuggle a thousand American cigarettes into France and pleaded ignorance of the law; the consulate helped him get off with a reduced fine. Then there was a twenty-four-year-old(!) student from Madison, Wis., who was arrested for stealing a book, and not just any book: *Lady Chatterley's Lover*. After a night in prison, he claimed it was a mistake—and offered to pay for the book.[23] There were American writers, jazz musicians, and dancers who had run-ins with the Paris police due to hot and inebriated tempers, disputes with the French or with their own—imported quarrels that were exacerbated in the French capital. Fists, revolvers, and even veils all figured as more or less dangerous props, as we will see.

Some of the more famous Left Bank scrapes made their way into literary history, if not always the police, consular, or law firm archives. Laurence Vail, the bohemian and hot-tempered first husband of Peggy Guggenheim, was arrested several times for violent behavior and spent time in French prisons according to her memoirs, although there is no extant file on him at the police archives.[24] (The perpetrator of the crime had to have become sufficiently renowned for the file to have later escaped archival triage.) As Beach put it: "This was the sort of thing that happened to some of our friends with too many drinks in them and too few French words."[25] However, Vail probably and Malcolm Cowley surely could swear like the locals in their native idiom. And that, in part, is what got Cowley into trouble. "The Battle of Montparnasse," as the *New York Times* wryly depicted a serious scuffle in 1923, was apparently due to the café La Rotonde's refusal to extend unlimited credit to Malcolm Cowley, John Dos Passos, E. E. Cummings, and other serious drinking Americans. They protested in two ways: first by moving their business across the street to the rival Le Dôme café, then by provoking a fight at La Rotonde. As Cowley wrote somewhat proudly in his memoirs, he had punched the owner of La Rotonde in the jaw for reasons more serious than credit. The French and American surrealists suspected the café owner of being a police informer, and they furthermore disliked the way he often treated American girls like prostitutes. So on that hot July 14, 1923 (the French daily *Le Matin* reported that it hit 90°F in the shade), amidst debates over the future of Dadaism, a slightly inebriated group of American and French writers crossed the boulevard Montparnasse, awash with a festive Bastille Day throng, to teach the Rotonde owner a lesson. Cowley says he surprised himself for doing the deed, but he punched the man and then was swept out with the crowd. Walking back in front of the café later that evening, he then literally added insult to injury by shouting "Quel salaud [you bastard]! Ah, quel petit mouchard! [you little snitch]!" at the proprietor in his perfectly colloquial French. That was when he was caught and hauled into jail. He was released, as he recounts it, only after bribing a policeman to retract a false charge of resisting an officer and after nine American girls, dressed in their finest (but who had not even been present at the incident), came to court to testify on his behalf. In halting French, they confirmed that the café owner was mean to American women. Their gender, class, and nationality apparently trumped the prosecution's arguments. The judge took the young women's words over those of the waiters on behalf of their boss and released Cowley.[26]

A more serious altercation on Montmartre, where cabaret life was a constant source of concern to the Paris police, led the not-yet-famous African American jazz musician Sidney Bechet to spend a year in jail for pulling a gun on a friend and injuring three passersby in the process.[27] In late December 1928, tension had been mounting between Bechet and Mike McKendrick, both of whom had been in Paris for several months working in Montmartre clubs. Bechet was playing saxophone at Chez Florence (either the police reporter could not tell a clarinet from a saxophone or, more likely, the famous clarinetist was still in his early saxophone phase); McKendrick was playing banjo at Le Capitole. Bechet had previously come to Paris as part of the initial Revue Nègre show with Josephine Baker before he moved on. In 1928 he had duly registered at the police station for an ID card; McKendrick had not. As the police reported after they snooped around the culprits' respective domiciles, the men's neighbors had no complaints. However, the "two Negroes" had gotten into an increasingly acrimonious running argument, "like two little kids," as to who was the better musician.

After work, at 6:00 a.m. on December 22, Bechet and McKendrick met up as usual for drinks at Le Grand Duc, where many musicians went after their own shows. By 8:00 a.m., Bechet had finally had enough of McKendrick's sarcastic boasting and stormed out. McKendrick followed Bechet outside, kept up the taunting, and punched him. Then they both pulled out their revolvers and shot. With bad aim. Neither of them was hurt, except for a little graze on McKendrick's forehead, but three passersby were hit. One bullet ricocheted off a gas lamp and hit a sixty-year old French cook who had gone out to get the morning milk. She was taken to the Lariboisière hospital for a slight head injury, as was a twenty-one-year old Australian dancer who had been shot in the thorax and was initially listed in serious condition. Glover Compton, a jazz pianist who was with the dancer, was hit in the knee and was taken to the American Hospital. According to the police report, Compton was not directly involved in the dispute, although according to Bechet's memoirs Compton had been egging on McKendrick for days. One legend has it that McKendrick criticized Bechet for playing the wrong chord; Bechet says that McKendrick, who was drunk, was yelling, "You'll see what we Northerners do with Southerners like you." Bechet also explained in his memoirs that everyone on Montmartre had a gun, given the racketeering atmosphere of the neighborhood. But he claimed he just didn't know what came over him to actually use his. And he also claimed that McKendrick shot first. But Bechet's volatile temperament was legendary, and he had previously been imprisoned and expelled from England for assaulting a woman. This time he spent one year in jail before being expelled from France. It took several pleas in the postwar period, including support from the famous Le Hot Club de France, to rescind the expulsion order. While a 1948 police report considered that his profession was of no interest to the French economy, by 1951 the police recognized that he was a world-renowned jazz artist who, furthermore, had considerable means. He was allowed to settle and marry in France. He became the darling of the Saint-Germain set. And his police file was saved for posterity.

Another American in Paris who made headlines and the police archives did so due to a run-in with the French rather than with a compatriot.[28] Joan Warner, a twenty-two-year-old white American artiste who had come to France in 1934 was not quite as celebrated as Josephine Baker, but she certainly made a distinctive name for herself in 1935 when her "nu integral" (completely nude) show at the elegant Bagdad tea-dancing restaurant near the Champs-Élysées was cited for "gross indecency" (*outrage à la pudeur*). The trial brought her fame and apparently some jealousy from other dancers, along with compassionate snickers from (male) French journalists reporting on the case. Warner was described as a beautiful blonde with a charming accent. The French press largely took her side, suggesting with a penned wink that the judge should insist on reconstructing the "crime" and commenting ironically on the largely plunging necklines of the magistrates' wives who attended the proceedings—due to a summer heat wave, *n'est-ce pas*. Even the American press in Paris was clement, describing Warner as a "long-limbed acrobatic star" and noting that the same dances had been performed in Chicago without police restraint.

The charges against Warner had been brought by one Fernand Boverat, apparently as a test case. He claimed that, in all innocence, he had taken his eleven-year old daughter to the Bagdad for a drink one Sunday afternoon. ("There is certainly other entertainment for children on Sunday afternoons," noted one of the defense lawyers wryly.) Thinking his daughter would be bored by the dancing, Boverat sent her and her friends home early. He himself was described as a severe-looking man with spectacles and mocked as "Professor Virtue." Boverat pressed charges under article 330 of an old 1863 law that the French press deemed austere and outdated, like Boverat himself. But Boverat was head of the Alliance nationale contre la dépopulation, and with a logic that made at least one journalist (and historian) chuckle in disbelief, he argued that Warner was causing depopulation by distracting husbands from their wives' charms. Furthermore, during the trial, Boverat approvingly cited the fact that national-socialist Germany had, after all, "struggled successfully against immorality." The judge then asked the defense lawyer if he had anything to add, and he just said, with dripping irony, that they could leave it at that, with this praise for Hitler. (Laughter from the audience.)

Warner's defense was that her show was artistic and that she had been completely covered in thick white greasepaint and performed behind a veil (a sheer lavender silk veil, to be sure). Debate turned on the effectiveness of the veil. The deputy public prosecutor had to admit that there was nothing obscene or lecherous in her act, as "she knew how to put chastity in her nudity." Various writers and artists (all male) got up to defend Warner and to plead for a certain form of art against a certain form of bourgeois morality (Francis Carco) or to declare that the nudity of a pretty woman was "a hymn to life" (Maurice de Vlaminck). In the end Warner was condemned, albeit lightly. The judges admitted that "in fact, it is impossible to define precisely just how far art extends and where lubricity begins." She was sentenced to a fifty-franc fine—the cost of a day's greasepaint, she said.

However, besides Warner's stance against French prudery—a noteworthy inversion of the usual stereotypes—the police were even more interested, a couple of years later, in her no-good "manager," another American in Paris who seemed to be leading her, as one who had lived a "regular life" until then, down a slippery path of debt and bounced checks. In France since childhood, Alfred Lesser had initially attended the prestigious Lycée Janson de Sailly, only to become the despair of his parents, "honorable hosiery shopkeepers" according to the police report. While still a minor, he had falsified the age on his passport in order to get into gambling clubs. He had married a Frenchwoman in 1932 and had had a child with her in 1937, only to leave them sometime in early 1938. By November 1938, not only was Lesser leading Warner to ruin, but his other victims included his landlord, the maid, the butcher, and the baker, all holding unpaid bills. The fact that Lesser had abandoned his French wife and child was clearly an aggravating factor in police eyes.[29]

When not adjudicating between American hotheads or resolving Franco-American disputes between café patrons and owners, or with a self-appointed morality squad, the Paris police kept an eye out on Americans who could be suspect for a variety of reasons. Henry Miller ("Henri Miller," as one police inventory would have it) was never arrested, but he was tailed. Frequenting prostitutes or doing "research" with same for novels was not a crime. But while he was in Paris in the early 1930s, unaccompanied by his wife (second of five), very responsibly notifying the police department of his changes of address as demanded by the law, Miller was under surveillance. A September 1934 report noted that he was often absent from his apartment in Clichy, that his wife came to visit only once, and that his mail, like his visitors, was sparse. The police determined that his morals and his integrity were fine and that he had not made any untoward political remarks. But he was kept under observation nonetheless. In May 1939, when he requested a visa to leave France for "~~Greece~~ All countries," he stated that his purpose (as always?) was *pour le plaisir*.[30]

The Paris police could also undertake discreet investigations of upstanding American residents if, at best, they were nominated for a Legion of Honor ribbon or, at worst, they were objects of a denunciation letter. Both happened to Clarence Bertrand Thompson, grandson of a slave, former Unitarian minister, and brilliant Harvard graduate and later professor there (or at "Harward," as the police report put it). Vigorous proponent of Taylor's scientific management, introducing the Taylor gospel in both English and French, Thompson had become a pioneer international management consultant. He had settled in France and counseled the Galeries Lafayette and La Samaritaine department stores on management methods. But in 1934 a former military officer overheard him talking while on a trip to Prague and denounced Thompson's attitude as ambiguous. The officer suspected that Thompson was spying for both the Italians and the Germans. The police investigation found no complaints about him at his well-heeled 16th arrondissement Paris address. And the denunciation did not prevent Thompson from being awarded the Legion of Honor that year.[31]

The police were worried not only about dangerous political liaisons but about industrial espionage as well. "This foreigner who calls himself an engineer" is how they described one Henry Brownback. Born in 1891 in Morristown, he had arrived in France in 1927 and two years later had married (in Morristown) a Frenchwoman thirteen years his junior. By May 1935 he was living alone in Neuilly (Lucie was in Philadelphia) and engaging in behavior that was seen as both suspect and perfectly normal. From the point of view of the concierge (the presumed informant), he led a very regular life, leaving every morning at around 8:00 a.m., returning every evening; he received a couple of letters per week from the United States and occasionally had visitors who came around—nationality unknown. However, particularly suspicious, in the police view, was that his daily destination was the Maison Chauvière, a manufacturer of boat and airplane propellers. He was not salaried by it and was, according to the company, there for an internship "whose reason has not been disclosed." He had been there a year and was supposedly going to leave France shortly. He merited at least a police report if nothing else.[32]

Finally, one last very real if somewhat surprising American crook must be mentioned. As the *New York Herald Tribune* headlined its June 25, 1938, article: "Brooklyn Rabbi Held in Paris with Drug-Filled Prayer Books." The article was accompanied by a photo from *Paris-Soir* of a man in Hasidic garb, complete with beard and glasses. The poorly reproduced Wide World Photo used on the first page of the *Milwaukee Journal* was even more ominous. Isak Leifer, his accomplice, and a taxiload of narcotics were all seized near the boulevard Saint-Michel on their way to the post office. Leifer was about to ship Hebrew prayer books concealing packets of heroin to a New York drug dealer. He was a forty-five-year-old Polish-born, naturalized American described by the police as a rabbi from Brooklyn, although the French Jewish authorities wrote in with a disclaimer: Leifer's name did not appear in their registry of rabbis in the United States. The police had been trailing him for some time on his frequent trips to a Jewish bookbinder on the Left Bank. The bookbinder, held briefly for questioning, swore that he thought that the prayer books contained "holy sand" from Jerusalem destined for unfortunate Jews living in exile. Almost forty pounds of heroin, estimated to be worth 600,000 francs, was found in the hollow of the books.[33]

A "motley colony," as Putnam described it, indeed.[34]

HARD TIMES: POVERTY IN PARIS

Some of the American crooks seem almost comical, but they handily prove that not all Americans in Paris were Left Bank writers or successful Right Bank specimens of American industry and wealth. So do those Americans who ran out of funds in the City of Light. Poor Americans of Paris have existed for as long as US citizens have been going to the French capital, but they have remained practically invisible in most accounts of Americans in Paris. For some the poverty was relative. In her 1880 novel *Under the Tricolor*, Lucy Hooper, keen participant-observer of the American colony scene, depicted déclassé Americans in Paris, some of whom simply did not have a proper dress to wear to an official reception. And, well before the current spam scams, Hooper's characters even included a family that were veritable "licensed mendicants," known for asking fellow Americans for money on the pretext that they were just about to receive a large fortune and needed a loan to hold them over.[35]

For many Americans, however, there was serious need that both belied the French (and American) image of the rich American abroad and was sufficient for the American colony to do something about it. The ubiquitous dentist Thomas Evans organized perhaps the first American relief aid for Americans in Paris, the American Charitable Association, whose purpose was to provide temporary relief for needy Americans in France or to help finance their trip home.[36] Both American churches helped out their poor compatriots. The (Episcopalian) Church of the Holy Trinity's work began with the Dorcas Society, set up during the Franco-Prussian War mainly to aid the French poor. But over the next couple of decades it found that it increasingly had to provide aid to Americans. In 1882–83 it added a Fund for Americans in Need, and the 1891–92 annual report again referred to the increasing distress "among our own country people." In 1883 the American Church set up its own Relief Society of the US, which the following year helped 110 Americans return home or go elsewhere in Europe where they thought they could earn a living. The two groups sometimes worked together, as when the Church of the Holy Trinity topped off the Relief Society's contribution in order to help some Americans "of too great refinement" go home "comfortably" rather than via third class. A perhaps typical case was that of a Mr. Phillips, who, drawn by the 1900 World's Fair, had sold his decorating business in New York in order to set up shop in Paris. But when his Paris business failed, he had to return home to start anew, leaving Mrs. Phillips and their child behind until he could send them passage money. Time dragged on, and it was the Episcopalian church that ultimately helped the remaining Phillipses return to New York.[37]

Americans in transit and American residents were no more impervious to illness, destitution, unemployment, or family disintegration than the French. And there were more and more Americans who could not make ends meet, especially after World War I left many hopeful but soon impecunious ex-servicemen in its wake. The American poor of Paris caught the attention of newspapers back home. The *St. Petersburg Times* reported in 1926 on three thousand Americans stranded in Paris without enough money to come home, ranging from professional bums to disconsolate heiresses. For the folks back home, poor Americans in Paris were a novelty and to be pitied. However, as the reporter added, there was one consolation: they were, after all, in Paris.[38]

According to Hemingway, two people could live comfortably on five dollars a day in Europe in the 1920s.[39] The writers' memoirs of the Lost Generation regale us with their (temporary) poverty. "Naked, soaped, and shivering" is how the young Waverly Root described himself in the bathroom of the primitive apartment in which he lived and where he had "never been happier with a home. While my new address was short on creature comforts, it was long on everything needed to nourish the soul."[40] While wealthy Americans in Paris renovated their apartments with bathrooms *à l'américaine*, others suffered through the more "French" experience of cold water flats. Those who did have bathrooms could be quite popular: "[A]ll your bathroomless friends will rush in to use your tub. We know American girls whose apartments are filled with bathing artists and writers from morning to night."[41] But being cold and shivering was not always so romantic. Claude McKay almost died of pneumonia while modeling in chilly artists' studios in Montparnasse.[42] And Alex Small, caustic columnist for the *Chicago Tribune European Edition*, commented on the poorer fixed-income female expatriates who undoubtedly felt that they could get by with less in France or Florence, while getting an aesthetic or spiritual experience, than they could in Peoria: "but almost all are bewildered and uncomfortable."[43]

The traces of American poverty in Paris thus range from tragicomic literary accounts to US journalistic surprise and a smidgeon of envy, to tales from the aid societies—to postmortem inventories. While lawyers' archives hold elaborate wills of the rich, consular archives have death certificates and reports that testify to the down-and-out whose days ended in Paris. When the American professional cyclist Philip Reese (originally Philip A. S. Blair), died in 1916 in Paris, where he had been living on the rue Pergolèse in the 16th arrondissement, the consular file shows that even life in that well-to-do neighborhood could be tough. Reese owed money to his butcher, his chauffeur, the baker, and the clockmaker. All of them made claims against his estate, for meat and bread supplied, repairs made, and money loaned. When the thirty-one-year-old Addison A. Armstrong, a war veteran, died of anthrax septicemia in Paris in late December 1929, survivors included his divorced French wife and daughter, living in Tours, and his mother, of New Jersey. The consular inventory showed that the furniture at his residence in Boulogne-sur-Seine was limited to a wardrobe, a divan, a filing cabinet, a kitchen table, and a typewriter table. The itemized contents of an old brown leather suitcase and a damaged steamer trunk included such items as: rulers (three, one broken), dictionaries (two), a tin box of old screws, eight packages of razor blades, thirteen neckties, stiff collars (eleven) and soft ones (five), eleven pairs of socks, drafting instruments perhaps indicative of his trade, a gas mask ("no value"), and one pair of khaki-colored army breeches. The most valuable item of clothing was a three-piece tuxedo, valued at two dollars. The total effects came to $51.15.[44]

In the worst cases, poverty in Paris combined with despair and resulted in suicide. In his 1913 report "American Young Women Art Students in Paris," Consul General Frank H. Mason had had to counter rumors of frequent suicide among young American women in Paris. According to him, the suicides that had occurred had been due to hunger or destitution. But he warned girls (and boys) and their families of the eventual danger of dashed expectations, demoralization, and weakened morality when the art prodigy of home is confronted with "a rude and often dispairing [*sic*] consciousness of his or her limitations." In 1916 when Clara Elizabeth Lord, thirty-two-year-old newspaper reporter for a New York paper, died after falling from the window of her fourth-story apartment, her death was considered an apparent suicide. The inventory of her personal effects at 218 blvd Raspail showed her modest belongings: a writing table, a bed that consisted of a mattress mounted on wood blocks, several wooden chairs, kitchenware, two trunks, one sweater, three dresses, six skirts, nine jackets, two cloaks, four hats, and five pairs of boots. No estimate of value.[45]

AMERICANS HELPING AMERICANS:
THE AMERICAN AID SOCIETY OF PARIS

After World War I, as the demographic composition of Americans in Paris changed, down-on-their-luck former soldiers largely replaced neurasthenic female art students as the most prevalent species of poor Americans in Paris. But the veterans were not alone. As a 1926 *New York Times* article described an arriving boatload of some six to eight hundred hard-up returning Americans, almost every stratum of life was represented: "tourists who have spent more money than they possessed . . . aged American expatriates who have outlived their fortunes"; deserted wives and children of American servicemen ("weddings gone wrong"); vaudeville artists; and a college professor or two. There were professional criminals, from panhandlers to those who, "prosperous appearing and happy," waylaid other Americans "with offers to act as guides on visits to unnamable places, or to try to sell indescribable post cards." The journalist left no literary allusion unused in describing these "innocents abroad," who formed a crowd as varied as Noah's Ark and faced "hard times." The cases ranged from truly pathetic to tragic to funny to disgusting in his eyes. Some had been stupid, some had been disowned by their families, some were drinkers who "found the freedom of Paris too alluring after dry America." The problem, the author concluded, was that by shipping this lot home, the decks were merely cleared for new cases of need that would arise "as long as Americans respond to the lure of Paris."[46]

New welfare organizations were created to help the postwar deserving poor in Paris, starting with a welfare committee of the American Legion Paris Post no. 1. It served ex-servicemen and their wives, widows, and orphans, and especially helped the disabled file their claims with the Veterans Bureau and fill out other forms. The post also helped deserving veterans and their families return home, as far as means permitted. At the same time, a Red Cross Fund was established for the relief of stranded American civilians, and in 1922 the American Aid Society of Paris (AAS) was created.

The AAS became the major organization helping poor Americans in the City of Light and is still active today. It was incorporated in Delaware, but it was apparently never properly registered in France until World War II. When it finally did request authorization from the Paris prefecture in 1941, the magnanimous police reporter bore no grudge, since he noted with satisfaction that all of the board members were Francophiles.[47] The society's initial purpose was to aid demobilized ex-servicemen (while referring others to the Legion Post), but its focus on veterans quickly expanded to helping everyone: stranded students, deserted wives and widows, the elderly, the ill, the unemployed, and the destitute. The society prided itself on helping people help themselves. At the same time, it sought to verify credentials and weed out the deserving poor from downright crooks. They were not always successful, as one man's disgruntled mother-in-law wrote after the AAS helped send him home: according to her, he was a crook and a procurer, and he had obtained his naturalization papers by fraud. But, typical of most charitable organizations, the society also wanted to centralize help ("change spasmodic giving into systematic constructive relief") and protect donors "from fraudulent appeals and . . . prevent them from duplicating the help they give." Funds came from private donations from the American colony in France, although fundraising appeals had to repeatedly remind the rich of their poor compatriots in need.[48]

If 1926 was the high point of American presence in interwar Paris, it was also the busiest year for the Aid Society. Applications for relief came from 2,842 people: some 1,091 wanted help with transportation, another 754 turned to the society due to unemployment (positions were found for 53 people); stranded students (423), deserted wives (340), and stranded seamen (181) made up the bulk of the rest of the requests. Help was given to 1,877: families were cabled, hospitals or homes found, but most of all meals (823), beds (411), and cash relief (159) were provided. The society was often able to secure half-price steamer tickets for returnees. Of the monies disbursed, 38 percent was reimbursed by the beneficiaries. From 1922 through 1936, the society handled 2,780 repatriation cases. A 1929 *New York Times* article gave as examples a female English teacher who had been in Paris twenty-five years but was now ill and out of work; a seamstress who had been there for fifty years but now suffered from failing eyesight; and a doctor who had spent too much time at the Deauville casino.[49]

After the Roaring Twenties, when life in Paris was cheap and well lubricated, the stock market crash in the United States and the ultimately deepening depression in France meant that new populations of Americans in distress turned to the AAS. The rentiers saw their savings melt, and the AAS had to help some of the newly poor return home. The new xenophobic laws that tightened restrictions on immigrant workers in France also affected those Americans who worked for a living. They could have trouble finding or keeping work, especially if their working papers were not in order. African American musicians were among the first affected, as we have seen, when a new labor law instituted a quota on foreign musicians. They too turned to the AAS.[50]

The impoverishment of Americans in Paris was thus linked to specific moments—post–World War I demobilization and the 1930s Great Depression—while also reflecting more structural difficulties of those who thought they could make a living or a career in Paris, often with little knowledge of the language. The files show a certain exasperation on the part of some consular officers and Aid Society leaders as to the tenacious nature of American poverty in Paris. In 1923 the society reported that in spite of helping five hundred (mostly ex-servicemen) return home the previous year, it still received daily requests for aid.[51] And some Americans crisscrossed Europe looking for help, to the irked officials' dismay. In one instance, an American couple from Germany who had fallen on bad times (after the wife had fallen ill, incurring hospital bills) had been "shipped on to Paris" by the American consul in Stuttgart, as the American Aid Society complained to the State Department: "and we now have them on our hands." The Paris AAS had explicitly told the Stuttgart consul that it could not help indigent Americans outside France. And apparently the American Aid Society of Berlin had similarly responded that it could not help anyone living outside Berlin. The Stuttgart consul had taken up a collection among Americans in Stuttgart, but there was not enough money to send the family to the United States. At that point the American man, French by birth, requested to be sent to Paris, which seemed "perfectly natural" to the Stuttgart consul, especially given that "on account of their French descent they were subjected to very harsh treatment in Germany" (during the French occupation of the Ruhr). The couple had been given train tickets to Paris and twenty-five dollars and sent along—to the Paris Aid Society's frustration.[52]

One solution was to curb emigration and thus thwart the American poor at the source. Already in 1924 one American consul suggested that passports be restricted. In the same consular file noting funds granted to help repatriate a worthy Mr. Bennett—his past war record (gassed, wounded, decorated with the French Croix de Guerre), current ill health (tuberculosis), and honest, hardworking demeanor all argued in his favor, according to Consul General A. M. Thackara—there is a four-page memo from Thackara's replacement, John Farr Simons, to the secretary of state respectfully asking the State Department to seriously consider refusing to issue passports to stranded Americans who had already been helped. Indeed, he wrote that he intended henceforth to refuse relief for all recidivists, suggesting that a sort of confidential blacklist be created so that consular officers would know if aid had already been given.[53] Major Cotchett, former assistant military attaché in Paris and current president of the AAS, concurred. In a 1925 letter to the embassy pointing to the difficulties of recipients and donors alike, he wrote that "the American colony in Paris should [not] continue indefinitely to annually take care of several hundred improvident American citizens who become stranded here." Two years later, he went further in his reasoning. Proud of the value of the society's work in maintaining cordial relations between France and the United States, notably by making good on unpaid bills to the smaller hotels and thus preventing impecunious Americans from being jailed by the French authorities, Cotchett nonetheless despaired that his work was increasing rather than decreasing. He therefore suggested that the State Department refuse passports to those who could not show the means to purchase at least a third-class return ticket. The Passport Division refused, however. An unsigned memo responded that this would mean "unduly interfer[ing] with the movements of the general traveling public and would react unfavorably upon the [State] Department," adding, somewhat philosophically, that "relief will no doubt be necessary as long as Paris is 'Paris.' The bees will gravitate towards the honey (even though it is synthetic)"![54]

With the deepening of the economic crisis during the Depression (somewhat later in France than in the United States), the AAS helped with the repatriation of eight-eight destitute Americans (including children) in the first half of 1932 alone. But it was in increasingly difficult straits itself as the colony dwindled; many of its usual donors among the rich Americans in Paris had returned home or were limiting expenditures. Still frustrated by some repeat customers, the AAS thus again appealed to the US government to tighten passport regulations: at the least, the State Department should refuse to issue new passports to those people whom the AAS had already helped return to the United States until they had reimbursed the society for previous costs. By November 1934 the society was even more insistent and inclusive in its request, hoping that the State Department could discourage emigration to France entirely. Persons and families with insufficient funds "should not be permitted, or at least not encouraged, to leave the United States," since only French citizens could obtain work in France, and the relief society was having difficulty obtaining funds under the present circumstances. The situation was leading "to hardships and danger of starvation."[55]

Ambassador (from 1933 to 1936) Jesse Isidor Straus, recognizing the increasingly difficult situation in France, asked the State Department to consider appropriating a small portion of the New Deal's Federal Emergency Relief Administration (FERA) allocation for repatriation purposes. "It would appear to me that as a nation we cannot afford to let American citizens starve or even suffer."[56] After due consideration, the Relief Administration said that, already hard pressed to help Americans in the United States, it had no funds available for aid in France. The assistant secretary of state opined to the American consul general that the problems of the American colony in Paris were "apparently no more pressing than that presented at many other places throughout the world where numbers of destitute Americans are consistently seeking maintenance and repatriation in circumstances equally appealing [*sic*]."[57] The government had already concluded that it had no funds available, but the State Department had offered to continue its "whereabouts" services, this time in the reverse direction: if the names and addresses of individual cases were furnished, it would help stranded Americans locate relatives or friends in the United States who might help them.[58] Whereabouts aid, yes; financial help, no. Herman C. Huffer Jr., now president of the AAS, increasingly insistent, wrote directly to the president of the United States, feeling that he might not have been sufficiently informed, only to have his letter bounced back to the State Department, which reiterated its inability to help.[59]

However, these appeals to the State Department also led to a minidebate about the actual extent of difficulties in France and who the American poor actually were. Huffer estimated that there were some one thousand people in need of aid in the mid-1930s, 90 percent of whom were former AEF men and their families. Was he exaggerating the proportion of veterans in order to convince the government of its moral obligation to help poor Americans? A year earlier Ambassador Straus had quoted figures that would give a rather different image of the American poor in Paris: from 1922 to 1934, the AAS had paid repatriation fares, in whole or part, in 2,674 cases; it was assisted by the American Legion, which had contributed a proportion of funds for 1,527 of these cases. Does this mean that some 57 percent were veterans and 43 percent were other poor? In any case, the consul general confidentially advised the State Department that Huffer, although "entirely sincere and honest," was also "a gentleman of determined views" with an "argumentative attitude" who was perhaps exaggerating his case; according to the chairman of the American Legion in Paris's Unemployment Committee, only about one hundred ex-servicemen in France should return to the United States due to their economic situation, of whom approximately fifty were unemployed *and* belonged to the Paris Post. But even of those fifty, the chairman felt only about ten were really destitute and sincerely wished to return to the United States; most had French wives and preferred to find employment in France.[60] If Huffer had exaggerated both the composition (ex-servicemen) and their numbers in an effort for the AAS to get aid from the US government, it had backfired. In any case, by the mid-1930s the Depression was affecting everyone. It seems that it was the American Aid Society that now needed aid.

Guns and drugs and poverty, oh my. American misdeeds and lack of funds in the French capital were perhaps no greater than for any other group. The circumstances of place (letting it all hang out, from morals to money) and of period (the Depression), combined with bad habits, led some Americans directly to jail, perhaps with a stop at the consulate or their lawyer's office on the way. Crime or meager resources could be imported from home. Or they could be discovered in the big city.

Some had come to Paris because it was cheaper and they could live better. Others came because it was cheaper and they could live even more cheaply, even if they had to compromise on comfort—"the cult of poor plumbing," as the Paris *Tribune* put it.[61] Some who got in trouble could not wait to go home. Stevens Lewis Tyler, the ex-serviceman who ended up in prison for facilitating the sale of army automobiles, concluded: "It has made me realize what a good country my own country is. Oh, if some kind fairy would touch me with her wand, so that I may awake tomorrow morning at home 'chez moi.'"[62] But others, even in straitened circumstances, just could not bring themselves to return. When the American Aid Society tried to help one seventy-five-year-old man return home, he ultimately refused. He had lived in Paris for twenty-seven years and had repeatedly turned to the society for aid. Its staff finally said they could no longer continue to help him in Paris. They bought him a new suit and secured transportation for him. But when he got to the train station for the trip to the Cherbourg seaport, "courage failed him," and he canceled passage.[63]

CHAPTER 7

French Connections, Reciprocal Visions

Love, Hate, Awe, Disdain

He discovered slowly,
and always with a little astonishment,
that the French were human,
even according to the standard
of the United States of America.

SINCLAIR LEWIS, *Dodsworth*[1]

July 4, 1900. The American flag flies from the top of the Eiffel Tower, and "Paris burst[s] into an eruption of American flags." With the World's Fair in full bloom, Americans fêted and were fêted by Paris in what was hailed as the largest gathering of Americans beyond US shores (five to ten thousand, depending on the estimate) and the first time, according to American accounts, that the great capital had so entirely given itself up to guests. The day began with the unveiling of Lafayette's statue in the Caroussel du Louvre: Ambassador Horace Porter warmly praised the bonds of friendship between the two countries, and the ceremony concluded, like all good Franco-American ceremonies, with the singing of both "La Marseillaise" and "The Star Spangled Banner." The day ended for the in-crowd with supping at Maxim's, where Maxim himself "was hospitable to a degree." For the hoi polloi, the place de l'Opéra was closed to traffic from 9:00 p.m. to 1:00 a.m. as Sousa and his band entertained the crowd.[2]

The statue, the speeches, the songs: they were all part of a long repertoire of official Franco-American friendship. For the next four decades, whatever the diplomatic issues, whatever the tariff tiffs, even through the acrimony over war debts and wildly fluctuating exchange rates, Americans and French gathered regularly to invoke Lafayette and profess their long friendship. Diplomatic

Chapter Seven

discourse intersected with social and economic encounters. Official functions, like business banquets, were full of enthusiasm.

July 13, 1926. An "anti-American riot" almost broke out in Paris. A mob of several hundred angry Parisians surrounded six "Paris by Night" sightseeing buses on the Grands Boulevards. Hooting and hissing, while several thousand onlookers encouraged them from the sidewalk, the disgruntled locals shouted insults and catcalls until the frightened tourists disembarked and dispersed. Not your everyday tourist experience. As Edwin L. James, the *New York Times* eyewitness bureau chief, himself a "dapper boulevardier," reported it, a full-blown riot had only just been averted, thanks to prompt police action that quelled the crowd. In the end, no really serious harm was done, but the booing continued until the empty buses had pulled away.[3]

The immediate cause was not just the 200,000 American tourists roaming France as usual that summer, but the fact that some of the more insensitive of them flagrantly flaunted their dollars and used francs to decorate their trunks, while asking that eternally insensitive question "How much is that in real money?"[4] That summer the dollar hit its apex. Americans were getting fifty francs for every dollar, and they went on spending sprees, eating and drinking themselves silly with fifty-cent dinners, ten-cent cocktails, and two-dollar bottles of champagne. The emergency was largely calmed thanks to President Raymond Poincaré, who devalued the franc, which returned the dollar to a "mere" twenty-five francs. The crisis was over. The tourists could return to their buses. Ocean liners continued to debark great hordes of Americans who descended on the French capital, while the Parisians themselves packed up for their annual August exodus to the countryside.[5] And American residents stuck it out, in Paris or at their own country getaways.

The 1900 World's Fair toasts to friendship forever and the 1926 anti-American almost-riot are not just simple contrasts in French-American relations. They are, after all, fundamentally different types of events, from highly choreographed political protocol to spontaneous social and economic outrage. They are separated by a quarter of a century during which wartime friendship followed by postwar bitterness over the debt issue prevailed. They are also activities that once again highlight differences between the American resident business community and the Paris-by-night short-term crowd. But above all, these two very opposite scenarios serve as a powerful reminder of the complexities involved in understanding intercultural relations.

From the ooh-là-làing of Louvre-struck Americans to the tsk-tsk-tsking of skeptical French, the story of Franco-American reciprocal visions has too often been written from single points of view. There are the endearing tales of American Francophiles, from David McCullough's nineteenth-century cast of characters through the 1920s Lost Generation to Woody Allen's *Moveable Feast*-clutching protagonist in *Midnight in Paris*. But there are also the American Francophobes, disdainful of French tradition, hailing democracy and modernity as specifically American traits to be emulated. As for the French, their anti-Americanism has often been portrayed as a seamless thread of seething angst and anger over creeping Americanization. Yet there were also the French Americanophiles, admiring everything from the independence of American women to new and improved appliances. Franco-American perceptions of each other are more complicated than the usually separate studies of American Francophilia or French Americanophobia let on.

Let us take a more comprehensive view that extends from actual social mixers and club events to the cross-eyed literature of the period as each viewed the other. On the one hand, the French and Americans rubbed shoulders with each other. There could be misunderstandings or better understandings as a result. Proximity can trump stereotypes. Or not. On the other hand, literary and "scientific" accounts of each other permeated stage and book during the first half of the twentieth century, ranging from laudatory encomia to dismissive disdain. We need to confront the actual points of contact and the plays and pamphlets in order to explore the constants and the contradictions, the permeability of encounters and impressions, and underscore the kaleidoscope of attitudes.

MIXERS

Americans of Paris, an island unto themselves? To show how they created a vibrant community is not to say that they were oblivious to their hosts. Americans clustered in Paris, created their own institutions, married and divorced each other, ran to the consulate for help, and laid wreaths on American statues and tombs. But the very Americanness of the American colony, defined through its clubs and societies, is only part of the story. As we have seen, their amorous and business activities brought them cheek by jowl with the French, for better or for worse. While trying to recreate and hang on to a parcel of "home," they were also living and breathing in a foreign city, enjoying its sights and sounds and shopping and above all engaging with the natives—with all of the exhilaration and exasperation that entails.

If the church- and chamber-of-commerce attendees of the Right Bank that I have described seem more resolutely insular than either the cosmopolitan *salonnières* or the Left Bank bohemian crowd, it is time to rewind and turn the "community" paradigm on its head. The writing of history emerges not only from the sources but from the eye of the beholder: ask different questions, get different answers. Looking at the archives and club records in another way makes Franco-American connections perceptible even within the most American of American organizations. Theirs was not just an ingathering of compatriots. French friends, business associates, and local notables attended the balls, the banquets, and the wreath layings. They even became members of the American clubs.

Whitelaw Reid's 1892 farewell banquet recounted in this book's opening was both a symbol of the heralded American colony itself and a sign of its growing economic power. The event was also clearly a social mixer. The table of honor included the prefect of the Seine, Eugène Poubelle (whose last name would go down in history as the term for a garbage container), the deputy Félix Faure, and a marquis and a count who were great-grandsons of Lafayette. Three French ministers were present. Glass after glass was raised to the "two great Republics of the World." One could argue that diplomatic internationalism is part of the job description, but this was neither the first nor the last time that the French and American elite supped together. Washington's Birthday and Thanksgiving banquets, but also ceremonies to honor Lafayette and Rochambeau, became staples of the American colony's activities, occasions for speeches by prominent Americans and Frenchmen—even at the risk of boring the locals, as one snide American observer claimed.[6]

Even the most resolutely American of Americans had their French friends. There were always plenty of "natives" around: French husbands, French wives, French friends and business partners. Sex, friendship, art, music, books, philanthropic endeavors, and business brought the French and Americans together. There were well-known pairs of friends and lovers: Winnaretta Singer and Edmond de Polignac, joined by their appreciation of music; Adrienne Monnier and Sylvia Beach, the plump and thin booksellers on the rue de l'Odéon, bound by their love of books. About half of the customers of Shakespeare and Company were French, eager to read the new American writers, and when the bookstore almost had to close during the Depression, André Gide helped it stay open by organizing Les Amis de Shakespeare and Company.[7] Other Americans boasted of their close acquaintanceship with prominent Frenchmen. One dentist loved to tell a story about being at a dinner party with Pasteur, who exhorted all the guests to wash their grapes before eating them. But when he then blithely drank from the glass of rinsing water by mistake, no one dared tell him.[8] The American men may have been more discreet about their close acquaintances with Frenchwomen (Thomas

Evans's *demi-mondaine* paramour, Méry Laurent). Or not (Henry Miller's prostitutes).

Beyond individual encounters, what is noteworthy, however, is how many proudly, defiantly "American" clubs and organizations, set up by Americans for Americans, quintessential "immigrant institutions," were in fact meeting halls for mixed crowds. Americans and French met to exchange ideas or business and calling cards. But mixing takes many forms, from the banquets and balls of the business elites to the more asymmetrical relations undertaken by earnest postwar American philanthropists. Americans were friends, sellers, and donors to the French. Relations could be collegial, hierarchical, or paternalistic.

American clubs were thus not just by and for Americans. While also linked to larger movements in the United States or other international American organizations abroad, all of them explicitly carved out their own roles abroad and firmly expressed Franco-American friendship and cooperation as part of their purpose. The American Women's Club of Paris hosted literary and artistic events featuring French authors and artists. As the head of the art committee reported in 1931, "I am so often asked, as this Club is an American one, if our artists must be Americans; I feel very decidedly that art has no nationality."[9] The AWCP was explicit in expanding its purpose from cultivating relations among American residents of Paris to developing Franco-American social intercourse. The American Library in Paris aimed at acquainting French men of letters and journalists with American literature, institutions, and thought in order to correct misconceptions about the United States.[10] The American Hospital and American doctors, renowned for their World War I work, served increasing numbers of French patients. American organizations thus linked expatriate togetherness with American expertise, philanthropy, and culture directed toward French society. Some of the outreach was self-interested, to be sure. In other cases encounters were more purely social. In either case, the trope of Franco-American friendship was widespread.

Even the most patriotic of American organizations, the Daughters of the American Revolution, took great pleasure and pride in its French connections. After having chosen for their chapter the name of a French army general, co-hero of the Battle of Yorktown, the Rochambeau women eagerly opened their socials to their aristocratic and politically high-placed French friends. Business meetings began by saluting the American flag and reciting the American Creed, but the lectures that followed were sometimes presented in French by prominent French figures. The chapter's activities included studying the lives of French patriots who had aided the American cause. The compliments were returned. At one chapter meeting, French diplomat and author Paul Morand gave a talk in which he praised "the energy and enterprise of American women in all walks of life, but particularly in the work of the patriotic societies in America."[11]

Both the American Dental Club in Paris and the American Chamber of Commerce in Paris also heartily welcomed the French not only as visitors but also ultimately as members. Interacting with their French counterparts was a way for the professional clubs to promote American expertise while encouraging emulation, if not clients. Both their integration into French society and, more concretely, the Depression led these for-and-by-American clubs to open up their membership. The first foreign member of the American Dental Club of Paris was none other than the "natural" (i.e., out of wedlock) son of the emperor, Arthur Hugenschmidt, whom Dr. Evans had taken on as protégé at the emperor's request. He was sent to Evans's hometown, where he took his DDS degree at the University of Pennsylvania in the early 1880s, and then he went into practice with Evans in Paris. By the mid-1930s, as American-born dentists in Paris became a declining breed, membership rules changed. At first the non-American members of the club had at least to have been trained in the United States, but ultimately, as dental training in France itself made great strides, this requirement was dropped. By February 1935, there were sixty-five foreign members out of a total of ninety active members, and only forty of them had their degrees from US institutions.[12]

Similarly, the American Chamber of Commerce in Paris's changing membership rules show how the chamber included French members while debating its own identity. From the beginning, the ACC had both non-American (mostly French) and nonresident American members (American manufacturers and individuals in the United States whom the chamber encouraged to join in order to help make their goods better known in France). At first the non-American members had equal voting rights. But in 1908 the chamber decided to reinforce its purely American voice vis-à-vis both governments and limited voting membership to American individuals and firms only. As the war and the perspective of a lucrative postwar French market brought hundreds of eager Americans and American firms to France, overall membership increased to over five hundred by 1919 and double that a year later. The tone of reports and minutes from these years is triumphant. However, as many of the post–World War I newcomers got cold feet and went home, to the ACC's disappointment and admonishment, membership declined slightly in 1923, to 960. The chamber worried, and it again changed its membership policy in order to increase the number of non-US associate members. As American companies increasingly set up *sociétés anonymes* that were also "French" for membership purposes, this too spurred the ACC in 1927 to revise its rules to include more associate members. Two years later, the stock market crashed, leaving the American business community in Paris reeling. Thus, after having initially embraced French members, then worried about losing its American identity, as membership declined the chamber rewelcomed French members. By December 1936, membership totaled 539: 264 American firms and individuals in France, 88 American members in the United States, and 187 French firms and individuals. All devoted to the chamber's slogan of *Pax Labor Liberta*.[13]

PHILANTHROPIC ENDEAVORS

Philanthropy, it is too often forgotten, is also one of the great social "mixers"—of class and of culture, albeit in a very structured manner. Philanthropic gestures of Americans in Paris on behalf of the French could be small or large, from furnishing handwork to the needy to spectacularly rebuilding the Reims cathedral's roof. Almost all of the American organizations in town seemed to take part, from fundraising to bandage-making during the war to other hands-on social work afterward. Some of the American organizations *for Americans* attracted the French to their information and help desks. But there were also American organizations set up by Americans *for the French*, continuing a long tradition of help in which ambulances play an important role.

Through three wars, American ambulances stood as the first gesture and symbol of Franco-American friendship. During the Franco-Prussian War, the dentist Evans paved the way, as we have seen, with his American ambulance project. Even if the US government sat out that war entirely (leading to some French accusations of American ingratitude), American charitable organizations helped out in various ways then and at the turn of the century. The American Cathedral Mission aided French, American, and British women who came for needlework, clothing, or coal. In 1910, when the Seine dramatically overflowed, the American Chamber of Commerce organized a special relief fund to help the homeless. For as its president, B. J. Shoninger, said, "The very name of France makes the heart of every American throb faster."[14]

With World War I, there was an explosion of aid-in-kind, from the college men who volunteered for that war's ambulance corps to the fearless women who joined the armed services or the Red Cross to the myriad organizations set up during and after the war for relief and reconstruction. Edith Wharton threw herself into relief work, raising money and traveling to the front to write about conditions there. Her two wartime books, *Fighting France* (1916) and

French Ways and Their Meaning (1919), were both paeans to the French civilization she loved and attempts to help the war effort by explaining the French to Americans. Wharton did not just fight with her pen. She set up sewing workrooms that eventually employed over eight hundred women, and she was the active president of the American Hostels for Refugees. She distributed medical supplies at the front and created convalescent homes and the Children of Flanders Rescue Committee. It is ungenerous of literary scholars to pan her political writings during this period. She was busy, and she had a cause.[15]

Wealthy and determined professionals brought their dollars and expertise to France à la Anne Morgan, who, with her friend Anne Murray Dike, ran the Comité Américain pour les Régions Dévastées, a civilian relief organization near the northern front during the war. The CARD set up health services, aided in agricultural reconstruction, trained medical and social services personnel, and helped set up public libraries in the devastated areas. After the war Morgan stayed on until 1924 and purchased the CARD's temporary headquarters, the Château de Blérancourt, to create a memorial museum of Franco-American cooperation that still exists today. And, well into her sixties, she returned in 1939 to repeat her efforts.[16] The other great friend of France, who, unlike Anne Morgan, never lived there, was John D. Rockefeller Jr. His foundation set up tuberculosis dispensaries in France during the war, and he was a major donor to the Committee of Fatherless Children of France. Rockefeller was fêted at Versailles in 1936 in thanks for the millions of dollars he had given since the 1920s for the restoration of Louis XIV's palace, the Château de Fontainebleau, and the famous vaulted ceiling of the Notre-Dame Cathedral of Reims. Philanthropic rival Andrew Carnegie also pitched in. He built a new municipal library and the American Memorial Hospital in Reims, aiding in the reconstruction of a city seen as the symbol of both the war's devastation and of French national soul.[17]

American philanthropy after World War I did not come from only the super-wealthy, and it addressed a wide variety of domains. African American soldiers gave 300,000 francs to a fund for French war orphans in thanks for the welcome they had received during the war. An American artists' committee extended aid to needy French artists. The American Chamber of Commerce set up a farm rehabilitation center for disabled soldiers, while in 1915 American directors of the Lighthouse in New York started a rehabilitation school in France for those blinded in battle. The organization established workshops for caning chairs, knitting and weaving rugs, making card cases, and the like, and its building also housed a modern gym and even a model candy kitchen, where American peanut brittle was made and sold. (To give the American dentists some extra work?) About forty to fifty men lived on the premises, and there was dancing every Tuesday afternoon, to the strains of a jazz band of course.[18]

Several American women started a settlement house in the poor Belleville district, hoping that it, like its American counterparts, would help children stay off the streets after school and become law-abiding citizens. Following the American Red Cross's work in the neighborhood, the Franco-American Social Settlement of Belleville also tried to prevent epidemics and reduce infant mortality by offering prenatal care for pregnant mothers. The city of Winchester, Massachusetts, provided a model dispensary, the city of Paris installed an up-to-date clinic, and the Junior Red Cross fitted out a playground with a particularly "thrilling innovation," American hot and cold shower baths, in a district where there were few baths of any kind. Even its dental clinic was a success, "having overcome the prejudice and fear of children not brought up to the toothbrush."[19]

From baths to books, American women in particular "worked" in philanthropy, spending their husband's or inherited money while bringing their brand of social service to postwar France. This too fed into the image of the energetic, efficient, and independent American female. Anne Morgan also helped to set up open-access libraries in France after the war—and, to the surprise of some French skeptics, they were quite popular. Some felt that the more rigid class structure in France would prevent "people of every condition [from] rub[bing] shoulders without embarrassment." Others did not quite believe in the virtues of open stacks, a literal eye-opener that was quite a change from the more directed reading habits counseled by librarians in most French libraries. After setting up the libraries, the CARD and the American Library Association worked together to set up a school to train French librarians in American methods. The Paris Library School, housed at the American Library in Paris, helped propagate new post–World War I libraries *à l'américaine*. The American women worked closely with progressive French library leaders, helping both to import the Dewey decimal system and to feminize library work in France. Eighty-nine of the 103 French students who completed the PLS program were women at a time when the profession was 80 percent male in France.[20]

Rare, however, is the good deed that escapes criticism. Foot-in-the-door for foreign trade or altruistic mode of bringing new methods and expertise to the world? There is a long, unresolved debate over American philanthropy. It too could be a conduit for the American way of life, from hot showers to toothbrushes to basketball (thanks to the YMCA). American philanthropy was also a place where businessmen, like the female philanthropists, imported American models. By the early 1920s, the numerous American aid organizations in France constituted a sort of early Marshall Plan of American philanthropy, as Nicole Fouché has called it.[21] However, although neither state-backed nor explicitly ideologically oriented or economically driven like the later Marshall Plan, post–World War I aid already raised some hackles.

Like many recipients of aid, the French were both grateful and wary. Two groups in particular worried about the effects of American aid in France: the Catholic Church and the *chartistes*, the elite of French professional librarians and curators. While American leaders protested (too much?) that they were not out to Americanize or proselytize, the YMCA's Foyers du Soldat and their centers that remained after the war furrowed French brows. Cardinal Luçon, the archbishop of Reims, worried that the YMCA, like the Rockefeller money, the Carnegie Foundation, and the Red Cross, could be a threat to the Catholic Church. What ideas might be lurking in the two thousand books brought to the Reims Foyer franco-américain? He ultimately welcomed the wartime aid in spite of his doubts, convinced that it was better to work with American Prot-estants than against them; and he undoubtedly had great personal satisfaction when Henry du Bellet, the former American consul in Reims and head of the American Red Cross there during the war, converted to Catholicism in 1924. As for the (largely male) *chartistes*, they were initially exasperated with the new library methods. Fundamentally suspicious of undirected public reading, they were relieved when the Paris Library School closed in 1929 for lack of funds.[22]

All in all, the philanthropic endeavors—another form of importing Ameri-can dollars and methods rather than by dowry or branch companies—show how even the best intentions with multiple aims and sometimes mixed results raise conflicting issues of Franco-American togetherness. The American do-gooders were pleased with themselves and proud to show off their efficient philanthropic traditions. For the most part, the helpers were hailed as exem-plars of dynamic efficiency. But what did they really think of each other? In any case, American aid reinforced at least one long-standing French stereotype of Americans: that they are rich.

Diplomatic functions, social events, business clubs, and philanthropic aid were all occasions for French and Americans to mingle. At times the Franco-American interactions took place among peers, but they could also be hierarchically inscribed, and the *rapports de force* shifted subtly but decisively after World War I. Philanthropy entailed encounters between the wealthy and the poor; technologically savvy dentists sought to spread their knowledge; businessmen were ultimately trying to make a sale. Relations were never forged on a perfectly even playing field. Let us turn, then, from the club membership and philanthropic interventions, however condescending, however generous, to the mélange of views of each other expressed through business bulletins but also on stage and in print, from erudite tomes to the occasional comic book and murder mystery.

Five possibilities may describe the range of Franco-American reciprocal visions, and they all existed, sometimes simultaneously. First, the banal: people may just get along. At teas and in clubs, the Americans and the French could laud each other's qualities in a mutual admiration society. The language could verge on the formulaic or the hyperbolic, but there is no reason to question the basic sincerity of the moment. Yet four other types of distinct attitudes may be identified, two on each side. First, there were those Americans who adored all things French (why else were they there?) and sought to emulate them, as in the neo-Gothic architecture of the two majestic American churches in Paris. But second, there were also those Americans who chafed at every fractious contact. The vast majority fell somewhere in between. From the other side, French views of Americans could range from heartfelt gratitude and eager acceptance of American models to wary if not hostile resentment of encroaching "Americanization," with the persistent critics increasingly audible in testy interwar Paris. After the euphoria of being allies in winning the war, tensions set in, fueled by the debt debate. But literary and journalistic barbs did not prevent hobnobbing. *Au contraire.*

THE CLASSIC CONTRASTS

> Henriette: Replace our memories!
> Smith: Yes.
> Henriette: With what?
> Smith: Projects.
>
> B R I E U X , *Les Américains chez nous*[23]

On January 9, 1920, *Les Américains chez nous* (the Americans in our midst), a play by the French academician Eugène Brieux, opened at the Théâtre national de l'Odéon, presenting, via Henri and Henriette Charvet, French brother and sister, and Nellie Brown and Mr. Smith, respectively American Red Cross volunteer and US veteran, a compact comedy of Franco-American misunderstandings and reconciliation. Brieux had a keen eye for some of the classic differences of style as seen by the French: the boorish American, evident in both the overly vigorous American handshake and the friendly tap on the shoulder that Smith gives the *notaire*—after having yelled at him. The refined Frenchman responds, "Ouch, that hurts . . ." to which the clueless Smith replies, "Oh, don't be silly." Smith, acting on behalf of the American army, is there to buy a parcel of Monsieur Charvet's land for development, while Nellie Brown is out to convince Henri, her fiancé, to return to Chicago with her. Everyone stays in France in the end, even Mr. Smith, who, after razing Henriette's favorite oak, agrees that the new factory is ugly and promises to replant trees to hide the electric plant—before asking her to marry him. In the process some of the basic Franco-American stereotypes of difference are depicted: American money and grandiose projects versus French tradition and memory. The factory whistle? "The cry of the beast," exclaims Henriette; Smith counters that dowries and inheritances are monstrosities bound to disappear, like "living off of rent, that energy-killer!" Nellie gets into a dispute with Henriette and shouts exasperatedly that she can't stand the "ancestral amulets": "I'm suffocating here." But in the end, after a dispute at the factory is resolved by her adored Henri, even she gives in and gives up Chicago for France.[24]

The classic themes of Franco-American difference are well known: old versus new, art versus industry, quality versus quantity, genius versus energy, theory versus practicality. Each category may, however, be either positive or negative, depending on the beholder. Wharton and James heralded old Europe, while Thérèse Bonney preferred and promoted Parisian modernity. Some French businessmen became partners in the selling of new and improved gadgets or soap, while French critics despised the crass commercialism of American culture. One of the most enduring Franco-American differences, played out from stage to business dealings, has to do with differing perceptions of time and tradition. In Brieux's play, when the French landowners object that every corner of their estate that Smith wants to tear down holds a memory, the American responds: "But, instead of thinking of your ancestors, think of your children! You should respect the past, but you should create for the future." Brieux's depiction was not far from that of the American businessmen themselves: "We have no hereditary nobility, we also have no idlers. . . . [T]he American nation has become the richest of the world, owing to the untiring activity of its people."[25] For the businessmen, the energetic present trumps the tired past.

Yet others sought to temper the theme of young America versus old France. James Hyde, businessman, lecturer, and man-about-town, pithily summarized a different premise: Americans envied the French past while the French envied the American present. Similarly, Baron d'Estournelles de Constant, deputy of the Sarthe and minister plenipotentiary, called for better mutual understanding by arguing that "France is not so aged as some people imagine, but that she is in reality the European country which starts a-going the newest of things, not only in the way of fashions and arts, but automobiles and balloons too," while Americans, after all, were old faithfuls of political liberty.[26] He may have been playing to his audience at the ACC annual banquet, but some pragmatic American businessmen also sought to mitigate the dichotomies of art versus industry. Were they merely being polite when they hailed the Panama Canal as an example of French ingenuity at its inception and American energetic engineering skills at its completion? The men of the ACC in Paris often stressed the interdependence of US-French commercial relations. France was acclaimed as the artistic producer for which the United States offered the best and largest market; the United States, at the same time, was seen as having the raw materials and machinery that France would need for reconstruction after the war. The US "go-ahead systems of business" and French artistic tastes based on centuries-old traditions could go hand in hand. The viewpoints were perhaps self-interested, imbued with wartime allied friendship or embedded in arguments to encourage favorable tariff rates or to bemoan double taxation. But they drew on old dichotomies of understanding while arguing for mutual interests.[27]

Declarations of complementarity were perhaps more easily made before World War I. Afterward the hierarchies of encounter between the two nations began to shift. Face-to-face meetings, when predicated on unequal *rapports de force*, could sharpen rather than weaken national or cultural differences.[28] Nonetheless, all types of Franco-American encounters persisted from the nineteenth to the twentieth century: American Francophilia and Francophobia, French Americanophilia and Americanophobia.

AMERICANS IN FRANCE—LOVING IT

So there are the two sides to a Frenchman, logic and fashion, and that is the reason why French people are exciting and peaceful.

GERTRUDE STEIN, *Paris France*[29]

Ah, the wine, ah "the pleasant coarse texture of the napkin and the crunch of the thick-crusted bread." And, ah, the transformative powers of Paris, where Henry James's hero Chad Newsome was made over from rough to smooth, from shapeless into a fine mold, an elegant self-assured, wonderful young man, largely, of course, thanks to Mme de Vionnet's tutelage.[30] Freed from the conventions of home, Boston Brahmins found the Paris experience new and liberating, as it would be for African Americans, white youth, young women, heterosexuals, and homosexuals alike. Perhaps there is little need to describe Americans' love affair with France since so much has been written about the gushing of American Francophiles. Ever since Americans started crossing the Atlantic eastward, from the early nineteenth-century visitors on, they seem to have been wowed by many of the same things. (Of course it is the early twenty-first-century observer of nineteenth-century visitors who giggles at how some stereotypes have traversed the centuries.) The early Americans were already ecstatic about the coffee (but they warned their compatriots about eating sauce dishes that could mask the dubious quality of the meat). They already noted how small the portions were in contrast to American abundance, visible on the dinner plate. And they all commented on the wine: lots of it, but fewer drunks. And if you see one, he's often an American.[31]

Views of France also depend on which Americans. African Americans, as we have seen, had good reason to appreciate a city where race relations seemed more relaxed than at home and where the occasional café owner took their side against racist white American patrons. Well before James Baldwin, Richard Wright, and the post–World War II crowd, Frederick Douglass imagined he saw the lines of liberty on every French face (he was also delighted to find his *Narrative* at the Bibliothèque nationale), although France was a bit too feminine and frivolous for Booker T. Washington's taste.[32] But not only African American writers and musicians and Left Bank lesbians enjoyed the greater freedom of being in France. American violinist Alexander Zukovsky moved there with his children and sent them to French schools because "I like the French character; we don't know it well enough in the U.S."[33]

Even the businessmen chose Paris for a reason. Beyond the oft-recounted awe of travelers and writers, appreciation of French art and manners affected American countesses and industrious businessmen alike. The "title envy" of American countesses was often accompanied by a passion for the art and artifacts of the eras of the Louis monarchs (XIV–XVI) and the Napoleons (I and III). But you did not have to be married to a French nobleman to inhabit and furnish a château. That thrill extended, as we have seen, to wealthy American women married to wealthy American men, proud of their porcelain collections and fancy French friends. The businessmen too had art envy, industrial-art envy. They prided themselves on their practical labor-saving devices, but they nonetheless admitted somewhat ruefully that the French excelled in tasteful and artistic industrial exhibits. A 1906 consular report on French industrial art was a paean to French aesthetic taste that exhorted the United States to learn from French industrial education. Wartime fervor raised the American Chamber of

Commerce's Fourth of July banquets to new heights of admiration of the heroic Frenchman and Frenchwoman sacrificing their sons for the country. But, above all, World War I gave the American businessmen opportunities to express their love of France, place of their "happy exile": "France is a second homeland for us. . . . And we savor the qualities of the French: charm, grace, gaiety, finesse, *esprit*, uprightness (*droiture*), the sense of duty, and relentless work."[34]

AMERICANS IN FRANCE—INVETERATE COMPLAINERS

What scoundrels these Frenchmen are, especially in the matter of candles.

JOHN RUSSELL YOUNG (1877)[35]

Yet the emotional effusions of praise for French art and courage seem to disappear from the ACC *Bulletin* as the twentieth century progressed. Is it just that the *Bulletin* itself became drier? The long, lyrical, but soon repetitive (to the historian reading yearly banquet accounts in compressed fashion) accolades of Franco-American cooperation disappeared. References to Lafayette, Rochambeau, and the sister republics seem to decline after World War I, replaced by occasional references to Foch and Pershing. As the interwar period advanced, however, with America's military might a fait accompli and its economic exuberance asserting itself ever more, to the wary displeasure of its former allies, the process of doing business in France became increasingly fraught with tensions. Tariff and debt debates dampened the enthusiastic rhetoric of Franco-American cooperation.

Of course some complaints, like some praise, seem to traverse the ages. Being overcharged for candles by hotel proprietors certainly may have become less of an issue as the twentieth century wore on, but at least one late twentieth-century American student was reproached by her landlady for keeping the lights on too late at night. Americans have complained, from the early nineteenth century to the twenty-first, about everything from dirty streets (mud then, dog droppings more recently) to lack of comfort to French driving habits to slow service in French restaurants (countered by the French view that Americans are always in a hurry). And Americans have often fretted about unsanitary conditions. There was indeed the occasional flea in the bedclothes.[36]

It was not just the insufferable suffering tourists who complained. The more settled had even more occasion for observation. In 1877, keen eyewitness John Russell Young distinguished between the satisfied and dissatisfied American "colonists." The first loved Paris and the Parisians, although even after twenty years they knew that it was not home ("you never take root"). The dissatisfied colonist, however, was always out of sorts. Following New York events closely, he was more often than not always angry with the French, quarreling with his concierge, bootmaker, and florist. One such grumbler considered the French cowards, hypocrites, and worse: they were poor hosts for serving thin little cakes and liquors at their parties rather than boned turkey and champagne, like civilized people.[37] Such complaints, like most cross-cultural comparisons, say as much about the complainers as it does about the objects of their disdain. The constant cry "Why can't they do it like us?" extended to all walks of life and business and endured through the decades. A late 1920s visitor spoke of the frustrations of trying to cash a check: standing in line for an hour only to be told to go to the Contrôle desk and then being sent back to the first line.[38]

Even food could come in for a measure of dissatisfaction. Breakfast, for example. As one US ambassador to France wryly commented: "A wider gulf than language separates the French from the Anglo-Saxon, and that is—what to eat for breakfast"; "no buckwheat cakes, no hot biscuits, sausages that were only such in name, oatmeal that was glue, bacon and eggs dishonored as only a great French chef [the embassy chef] could dishonor them."[39] And Americans perennially complained (and still do) about the lack of ice water, great symbol of American freezers and prosperity. Horror could even extend to that sacred food object, bread. As one woman wrote to her girlfriend back home: Just imagine! The ubiquitous baguette was delivered unwrapped: "I've seen it riding in open carts in the streets, unprotected from dust and all those unhygienic horrors we good Americans fear. I've seen it tucked under grimy, small arms, trailing its heedless length along the street."[40]

The litany of complaints may ultimately be as humorous or tiresome as any stream of ooh-ing and ah-ing. By the interwar period, American residents of Paris were also dealing with other problems of settling in, not the least of which had to do with the differential legal status of women. Those wishing to marry there were shocked at the strictures surrounding matrimony. As the same woman confided to her girlfriend, love in the City of Light was a study in contrasts. At first she recounted gleefully that she was able to hold hands shamelessly in public with her American boyfriend Ted. But when they decided to tie the knot there, the lawyer explained that she would need her husband's permission to leave the country or to have a separate bank account. So she said she would rather get married under the *séparation de biens* regime, at which Ted looked so hurt that she then burst into tears: "I'm not going to be married in this damn, suspicious, cold-blooded old country." Then Ted got mad. Then she capitulated. And she signed her letter to her girlfriend, "Pray for your erstwhile carefree friend."[41]

As for American blacks, they were not all immediately enamored with the place. Although he later changed his mind, three weeks after his arrival in Paris Langston Hughes advised Countee Cullen to stay home: "Kid, stay in Harlem! The French are the most franc-loving, sou-clutching, hard-faced, hard-worked, cold and half-starved set of people I've ever seen in my life. Heat unknown. Hot water, what is it? You even pay for a smile here. You even pay for water in a restaurant or the use of the toilette. And do they like Americans *of any color*? They do not!!"[42]

Difficulties with the law, difficulties with French neighbors or acquaintances, could sour the most ardent Francophiles. Mary Bromfield made clear the contrast between just visiting Paris and living there: the former was exhilarating, the latter an exhausting experience. She complained of distressingly skimpy French breakfasts and interminably long lunches and dinners. In her despairing search for a suitable long-term apartment (ideally four bedrooms plus two servants' rooms for $150–$400/month!), she found fault with French interior decorating: inherited chairs were lined up against a wall as though no one ever pulled up a chair for a little chat. No wonder she and her husband, agricultural novelist Louis Bromfield, moved out to the countryside.[43]

A successful American businesswoman, Georgia Blackman Pratt, who had come to France with the Red Cross during the war and stayed on for seventeen years, got into a legal dispute over her Paris apartment when her French subletter pressured her to negotiate its renewal for him at a favorable rate or return the 100,000 francs he had paid her for the improvements (modern bathroom, parquet floors, and more). She refused. He sued her for fraud and won. (The sublease had never been properly registered.) In the end, Pratt interpreted the entire affair as one of French trickery versus American naiveté. This "fantastic series of slimy evasions, intrigues and trickeries, backed by French political 'pull' and collusion," had occurred through "no fault of hers except over-trustfulness in French character and inexpertness in the French language." (That the subletter's fiancée had been both his and his father's mistress only added to Pratt's moral outrage as she told the tale.) She concluded: "Foreigners, especially Americans, have small chance in court against the chicaneries of the French." By 1935 Mrs. Pratt, now Mrs. Mullaney, had left Paris for Chicago.[44]

How many disappointed Americans went home? As with any immigrant group, it is hard to know.[45] There were those who never planned to stay and didn't. There were those who wanted to stay but whose money ran out. And there were the Mrs. Pratts who met their Mr. Mullaneys and followed them home. Like most immigrant stories of return, these may be triumphant, they may represent defeat, or they may reflect a simple change of circumstances. The disappointed have left far fewer traces than those who went home in the halo of having been "Americans in Paris." They remind us that migration is a process, full of trial and error and emotional and physical roundtrips. American Francophobia made-in-France, in any case, merits its historical footnote.

ON FRENCH ANTI-AMERICANISM

We hear of the rising tide of resentment against us with a mingled feeling of incredulity and injured innocence.

REINHOLD NIEBUHR[46]

Georges Simenon depicted both Left Bank and Right Bank Americans in Paris in two of his numerous Maigret murder mysteries. Two are cadavers. As for those who are suspects, the portraits are not flattering. There is the indebted Left Bank hanger-on William Crosby, a fixture at La Coupole who wishes his rich aunt dead and pays an evil Czech to do the deed in *La tête d'un homme*. In *Les caves du Majestic*, set in a posh Right Bank hotel, the wife of Oswald Clark, an American ball-bearings businessman from Detroit, is murdered in the hotel basement. She may have been a former French prostitute, and Mr. Clark may have been cheating on her with his son's American teacher, but more to the point here is that Mr. Clark is always described as accompanied by his lawyer, and he punches Maigret in the nose. For the most part, however, Clark and Maigret spend much of the novel saying exasperatedly about each other: "Qu'est-ce qu'il dit?"—What'd he say?[47]

French ideas about the Americans in their midst were no less complex than those of the Americans vis-à-vis their French hosts. French opinion could range from the enthusiastic crowds and expansive press coverage of Lindbergh's landing at Le Bourget airport in May 1927 to outraged protests over Sacco and Vanzetti's execution three months later.[48] Brooke Blower has called anti-Americanism in Paris "a flexible framework used to evoke a cluster of grievances," from the leftist protests concerning Sacco and Vanzetti to conservative antimodernist anxiety, angry at too many neon signs.[49] Yet the French both admired and disapproved of the Americans they met. One American journalist remarked, "No Frenchman is indifferent to an American. He either looks down upon him as a boisterous, uneducated, mercenary individual, or he admires him as an enterprising, ingenious, energetic soul," concluding that the first were a hundred times more numerous than the latter.[50] Praise was sometimes peppered with caution, and criticism could be leavened with measured appreciation. French views of America have been judiciously described as a complex melange of "reticent fascination," "ambiguous passion," and simple misgivings.[51]

It is above all French anti-Americanism that has captured the imagination and the pen of literary critics and historians alike. Philippe Roger has impressively and exhaustively argued for an imperturbable *longue durée* of French anti-Americanism, from Buffon through Baudelaire to Bernanos and Baudrillard: the eighteenth-century naturalists' vision of a physically degenerate continent and the nineteenth-century view of the United States as an agricultural backwater were only slowly replaced by reluctant admiration for American agricultural and industrial prowess until the 1898 Spanish-American War shockingly revealed the United States' political ambitions. Anti-Americanism thenceforth went beyond a simple critique of Americans as boorish and greedy for gain. Literary and political pundits alike increasingly joined their concern over America's lack of culture and civilization with alarmed accounts of the nation's growing political and industrial power and images of machinery and standardization ruining the French countryside and city alike. In Roger's long view of "the American enemy," friend Lafayette and even the allied cooperation during World War I are but epiphenomena.[52]

The problem is that the idea of America, the image of Americans, and views about Americans in Paris often coincide, sometimes collide, but in most cases are difficult to separate from each other. Many "observers" wrote about the United States without having crossed the Atlantic; they extrapolated from books or films or from the few Americans they knew. Certainly rowdy American soldiers, flirting and drinking, and thirsty Americans who sought relief in Paris during Prohibition disabused more than one French person of the vision of Americans as abstemious Puritans. Yet ideas about America could be made in the absence of contact with actual Americans in France, while the latter, in turn, could become the metonymy for the United States that most French never visited. It is hard to keep these different constructions of images apart. Expressions of fast friendship and economic admiration alternate with worries, fears, and the great snub.

The French image of Americans themselves changed over time. Although in the early part of the nineteenth century, many French viewed Americans as a chaste, honest, strong, and virtuous lot, by the end of the century they added heartless American industrialists and scheming adventuresses to the repertoire. In the 1898 play *Les transatlantiques,* Abel Hermant painted a withering depiction of a rich American father out to purchase a genealogy for his family through his daughter's marriage to a French marquis.[53] The French nobility who participated in these exchanges of money for titles were not duped.

Before World War I, French aristocratic scorn for the great contradiction of American republicans' fascination with nobility was a frequent theme in the literature. And it could surge in the salons. The former friend of the Princesse de Polignac, the count Robert de Montesquiou, apparently furious at some slight, claimed that Winnaretta Singer was cruel; he "dreamed of seeing her victims stitched up by sewing machines."[54] (But he was mean to everyone.) One could become a princess without losing the stigma of origin. This was as much a critique of the nouveau riche Americans as it was an expression of an embattled French aristocracy on the wane.

Take Count Boniface de Castellane. First husband of the wealthiest legatee of them all, Anna Gould, he benefited extravagantly from her riches before they divorced. He then licked his wounded pride in a successful memoir titled *L'art d'être pauvre* (The art of being poor) in which he makes snide comments about rich Americans' poor taste. As an impoverished divorcé, he was forced to start working for a living, went into the antique business (what else?), and ultimately appreciated at least those Americans who appreciated *his* good taste and bought his wares at good prices. He actually continued to spend time with young American women after his divorce, but he complained that even if they were indeed more independent and lively than Frenchwomen, their intellectual and practical ignorance rendered them comical. Above all, they lacked the refinement of *la Parisienne*. And, as he realized at his own expense, the American woman "tires rather quickly of her husband."[55]

By the turn of the twentieth century, changing power relations between aristocrats and commoners and between French and Americans alike would change French preoccupations and at the least shove French aristocratic snobbery under the tasteful tapestry. American imperialism and Americanization in general became more immediate matters of concern than aristocrats' sensitivities. The Spanish-American War, for one, led to a spate of anti-American screeds. The "brutal aggression" of the United States showed at the very least that it was "still too close to the state of nature" and had not yet learned the art of chivalry. Henri Hauser concluded his *L'impérialisme américain* in 1905 by admitting that fears of "the American peril" and an upcoming Americanization of the planet were undoubtedly exaggerated, but he conceded that Europe was no longer the queen of the world.[56]

After the outpouring of mutual admiration between the Allies during World War I (not exempt from certain outbursts of bad humor, to be sure), an antimodernist critique against America coalesced in the 1920s, as both David Strauss and Philippe Roger have emphasized.[57] Anti-American sentiment formed part of an intra-French debate over France's future as much as it was a discussion about the United States or about Americans in France. Certainly, worries about modernization and industrial standardization were not new. Ever since Comte Laborde's anxious mid-nineteenth-century plea for a reasonable union of art and industry, the relationship between the two had been fraught with angst. By the end of the nineteenth century, as the United States began to rival Britain and Germany as an object of French competitive concern, the art-industry debate came to distill the French-American dichotomy. Emile Levasseur's 1898 study *L'ouvrier américain* admired the American worker impressively turning out products faster, cheaper, and in greater quantities than his French counterpart. Yet in Levasseur's discerning opinion, the products lacked taste, finish, and artistic sense.[58] The 1920s and 1930s saw a profusion of books revising Tocqueville's century-old admiration of the young republic, generally shifting the terms of debate from politics to economics and its feared cultural corollary.

Three interwar texts in particular are most often cited as examples of the French intellectuals' interwar ire. They range from the critical to the very critical to the hypercritical. Political scientist André Siegfried was the most moderate of the three, although his understanding of the United States was rooted in an old racial notion of national character. He had been visiting the United States for a quarter of a century before he finally decided to write his "dispassionate analysis" of "a great people in-process." Like others before and after him, Siegfried worried about America's fundamentally materialistic conception of society. For Siegfried, the French mentality was not compatible with serial production, and he noted, somewhat ominously, that "Americans would like to be everywhere, while not being there officially."[59]

After a critical *Voyage à Moscou*, well-known writer Georges Duhamel set his sardonic sights on the United States. His 1930 *Scènes de la vie future*, a vivid account of his US travels, was a bestseller. Full of lively dialogue with his somewhat unsuspecting American hosts (impervious, it seems, to the dripping irony of his courteous tone), the book went through 150 editions in its first year of publication. Duhamel prefaced his account with an age-old disclaimer: some of his best friends were Americans, and it was not Americans but American civilization that he was describing. His easy-to-read rant describes a trip from hell. He hated everything, from the fake leather car seats to the drunks to racism to the lack of originality in the museums and modern advertising that he described as "visual masturbation." Even if he did eat the best beef of his life in Chicago, the smell of the slaughterhouses stayed with him, and so did the sound: he thought he heard the squeals of pigs while riding the "L" (the elevated metro). He won a special prize from the Académie française for his book, and five years after its publication he was inducted into that noble assembly. Not to mention that his book helped inspire Hergé's successful comic-book *Tintin en Amérique*, where Indians' land is plundered when oil is found on it and blacks are lynched while the real bank robber escapes.[60]

Robert Aron and Arnaud Dandieu's extended 1931 metaphor *Le cancer américain* was published the same year as their *Décadence de la nation française*. Founders of the Ordre Nouveau, an anticapitalist, anticommunist, antiparliamentarian variant on personalism, the authors likened American capitalism, the triumph of rationality over sentiment, to mortal cells eating away at the individual and the group. Aron and Dandieu criticized French Americanophiles as well as other Americanophobes: the former were but traveling salesmen returning from trips to the United States and wanting to enroll everyone in their camp; the latter, including Duhamel, had not fundamentally understood the nature of the disease. The authors protested (too much?) that their indictment was not against America or Americans but against that which the United States currently represented. And like other critics of America, they ended with a plea for a stronger Europe to counter the American menace.[61]

French anti-Americanism was mostly but not entirely an emanation of the Right before World War II. On the Left, Gustave Le Rouge and Gustave Guitton had published at the turn of the century a popular science-fiction potboiler *La conspiration des milliardaires* (The billionnaires' conspiracy) that was as heartily anticapitalist as it was anti-American.[62] The book begins with a European-US tariff war and a hardhearted Chicago industrialist, the "King of Canned Goods," who is determined to crush Europe so as better to export his goods there. He and his allies, who range from an evil engineer to a medium, first bankroll two vast, futuristic laboratories to build a secret army and then resort to hypnosis. The plot sets up a stark contrast between the insufferable hubris of the American industrialists and a small band of humanist French scientists and their loyal domestic sidekicks. A French scientist saves the day, and the book ends with all of the Americans converted to the utopian cause of peace. However, Le Rouge and Guitton notwithstanding, the Left's critique of Americanization would come more fully to the fore after World War II, as French communist hatred of all things American reached its heyday during the Cold War. True, between the wars the French secret services trailed Americans they suspected of espousing either of their most feared ideologies: communism or Germanophilia. However, the interwar Ministry of Interior files on surveillance of Americans are slim.[63]

The most spectacular popular expression of interwar French anti-American sentiment was the mini-riot described above that pitted angry Parisians against befuddled tourists. Underlying anxieties about US economic power and about the state of interwar France led the French rioters to castigate the Americans as "destructive grasshoppers."[64] In the end, while the Far Right disparaged "les gens du dollar" as "métèques," the Left deplored the xenophobic nature of the event, and the Catholic *La Croix* implied that those on the prurient night bus tours had it coming to them, by and large the general French press took a fairly even-handed approach. One article in the *Paris-Midi* made the distinction between rich and poor(er) Americans, arguing that even if American financiers were exploiting Europe in general and France in particular, there was no reason to take it out on the middle-class tourists who came to see the city at a low price. The French paper made a clear distinction between obsequiousness toward the US government, which should hold no sway, and politeness toward those "who come here as friends" and could return to their country as advocates for France against German propaganda.[65]

Anti-American sentiment in France, then as now, remained more verbal than physical and played itself out against an ever-changing political and economic environment. The war debt dispute loomed large. When France insisted on linking its repayment of wartime debt to the United States to German reparations to France, the two countries incarnated different ideas of justice: economic and legal in the United States, moral and political in France.[66] In late 1932, as the Chamber of Deputies again held debates on the issue, the communist paper *L'Humanité* denounced "Yankee imperialism," and several far-right wing groups held protest rallies against repayment. Although they told their demonstrators to leave their canes and clubs at home, several windows were broken, and some 556 people were arrested. The demonstration had not, however, been the show of force the organizers had expected and the police had feared.[67] Yet the meaning of the United States' initials had changed for some. The occasional European caricature depicted Uncle Sam as a usurious Uncle Shylock with anti-Semitic overtones. More generally, the critique turned on American economic culture. "America's role as debt collector helped to feed the image of American materialism."[68]

Thus, as the fraternity of the allied wartime experience receded into memory, for many the feared American corporation replaced the friendly doughboy in their image of America. Americans were no longer brave knights who had helped save France from the hated Huns. They were now seen as benighted slaves, subjugated to profits, standardized production, and consumption. The assembly line, which had previously benefited from an indulgent interpretation of its efficiency, became the central symbol of everything that was wrong with America's standardized mass society. If Fox, Max Factor, and others ran

into snags while peddling their products in France, it was not just due to tariff battles or war debt disputes. The American industrialists and merchants
abroad were working in an environment that by many accounts was overtly
hostile to the very basis of their endeavors.

Attacks on American business were not necessarily direct attacks on American businessmen in Paris. However, the anti-American rhetoric of a good-
natured Duhamel or an unsmiling Robert Aron formed part of the climate in
which these businessmen lived and worked. Besides the occasional outburst
against tourists—from whom the residents in any case firmly separated themselves—anti-American sentiment could include a Latin Quarter youth boycott
of American cigarettes, food, clothing, razors, and movies.[69] But more ominous
for Right Bank businessmen were things such as the large posters, along with
pamphlets and magazine articles, that appeared in Paris in June 1938 castigat-
ing past and prospective purchasers of foreign cars. American brands were
clearly targeted by the call for a boycott, and the American Chamber of Commerce contacted French ministers and trade organizations in order to try to
get the posters removed.[70] Hardly life-threatening in a period of increasingly
muscular xenophobia, such manifestations of anti-Americanism nonetheless
unnerved American businessmen, who felt targeted and understandably worried for their very raison d'être.

Economic nationalism was perhaps one of the most concrete expressions of French fury over creeping Americanization. The great boycott
of Hollywood films has already been described. We have seen how tariff
and quota disputes were fought out in legal and diplomatic channels during the 1920s. Specific business practices could even be targeted in Parliament. In the 1930s, French deputy Taudière twice proposed legislation
to denounce "chain" contracts that bound French shoe manufacturers to
the United Shoe Machinery Company. He likened the "tithe" relationship
to serfdom or slavery rather than the free competition necessary for good
economic relations, and he appealed to the honor of the French Parliament
to do its duty in making the American company rewrite its contracts.[71] At
the same time that Frank Southard was hailing American direct investment
overseas, Jean Bonnefon-Craponne published a law thesis on the same topic
with a strikingly different perspective. Like Southard, he spoke of "invasion" and "penetration," but they were worrisome, not heralded, categories
for Bonnefon-Craponne. The electrical, automobile, and film industries in
particular had been affected by American investments (often hidden under
very French-sounding labels). He did not believe that an "américanisation à
outrance" of the European economy was about to take place, but the "danger

américain" was named—along with the hope that naming it would galvanize French energy to ward it off.[72]

FRENCH ADMIRERS

Through it all the Americanization of Paris went steadily forward. Young Frenchmen made a fetish of everything American.

AL LANEY, *Paris "Herald"*[73]

In spite of intellectuals' fears of economic competition and cultural dissolution and Parisians' anger over invasive tourists, there were others who embraced Americans and even Americanization. If warily. In an article titled "Contre l'anti-Américanisme," a French psychiatrist both acknowledged the phenomenon and criticized it. He argued that the French needed to avoid anti-Americanism while nonetheless warding off Americanization: "While taking that which is good from America, let us not become its plagiarizers."[74] Admiration, like disdain, could cut across political, cultural, and economic categories. French Americanophiles could range from a baron to a socialist. In 1912 Baron d'Estournelles de Constant explicitly sought to contradict the legend that "America is a country of dollars, of unscrupulous businessmen and loveless heiresses destined to restore Europe's worm-eaten coats of armor." Rather, he emphasized that Americans were good republicans and needed friends. Jean Jaurès agreed with him. On the occasion of a reception for the American ambassador in late 1911, Jaurès had spoken before the Chamber of Deputies lauding "the pacifying force of American idealism." "Puritans in their soul," he said, Americans were on the side of liberty and justice. It was not just a formal speech for a formal occasion. It was punctuated by enthusiastic applause from the left wing of the Chamber.[75]

The debate over Taylorism epitomizes the mixed feelings over "Americanization." Taylor's time-efficiency experts and Ford's assembly line crossed the Atlantic eastward, for better or for worse. "Terrorism" is what one irate factory worker calls Taylorism in Brieux's 1920 play.[76] In the years just preceding the war, French workers had repeatedly gone on strike to protest employers' efforts to implement the new methods. Historians have debated not so much whether Taylorism took hold in France as when and under whose aegis: engineers, industrialists, ergonomists (themselves divided over the issue), academics, the state.[77] The war was a turning point. Its emergencies and exigencies led French industrialists and even some workers to rationalize methods and embrace Taylorism. Only four years after the major anti-Taylorist strike of 1913 at the Renault car factory, during which one labor leader described scientific management as "the organization of exhaustion," in the middle of the war a CGT (Confédération générale du travail; General Confederation of Labor) union leader proclaimed: "We ask that, in the future, the new American methods be used."[78] By the interwar period, André Citroën was called "the Henry Ford of Europe" for having introduced the assembly line and installment selling while putting his name in lights on the Eiffel Tower. Michelin itself—what better symbol of Frenchness than the Michelin Man helping sell tires and gastronomy guides?—explicitly encouraged scientific management and mass production. The point was not to imitate the Americans slavishly but to better compete with them.[79]

One of the most cited French pro-Taylor boosters was the machine operator-journalist-sociologist Hyacinthe Dubreuil. He spent fifteen months working his way across the United States, ending up in Ford's own Detroit factory. In his 1931 book *Standards*, Dubreuil peppered his account with pungent but also constructive criticism of the United States. The spirit of cooperation between American workers and their employers particularly impressed him. Admitting that he had selected his examples in order to counter the naysayers such as Duhamel, Dubreuil nonetheless noted some misgivings. He had been mystified that his untalkative coworkers ate lunch in just ten minutes, until he realized that they were going outside to play baseball; he was amazed at the profound American ignorance of things French (just imagine, they thought Jeanne d'Arc was in the Panthéon); and it irked him that his coworkers believed that everything had been invented in the United States. But Dubreuil argued that Taylorism itself had been softened in practice, and that thanks to it the world was on the eve of a revolution as important as the French Revolution.[80]

There were other high-profile defenders of the United States in the interwar period, such as André Tardieu, who had been to the United States and had worked closely with Americans in France during and after the war. Prime minister three times between November 1929 and May 1932, he implemented an American-like policy of economic modernization paradoxically just as the United States itself was entering the Depression. And over the span of three decades he wrote as many books about the United States. In his prewar *Notes sur les États-Unis* (1908), Tardieu explicitly countered his compatriots' facile imagery of the United States as a giant factory. He described the bad and the good in American society: skyscrapers yet home life; frequent poor taste yet masterpieces hanging in the museums; politics and American diplomacy that combined natural egotism with true friendship. In 1919 he published his wartime talks, a paean to Franco-American cooperation. By 1927 his enthusiasm had become more cautious, however. In *Devant l'obstacle: L'Amérique et nous* (1927), he noted with gratitude the contribution to the war by Americans in Paris and the numerous charities set up in its aftermath. But Tardieu tempered his own appreciation with advice against official optimism, reminding his readers of the fundamentally different temperaments of one civilization brought up on Greece and Rome and another brought up on the Bible. He lamented the complete misunderstanding of the debt problem. His advice: know the other, in order to measure the obstacles necessary to working together.[81]

Americans in Paris, as distinct from "America," came in for their own evolving imagery among French admirers. In the early nineteenth century, Americans had first of all been seen as fascinating "exotics." It was not just that Parisians flocked to Catlin's American Indian paintings in his 1839 exhibit and then to the "real thing" when Buffalo Bill's Wild West Show came to Paris in 1889 and again in 1905 (three million spectators amassed under the Eiffel Tower).[82] As the number of American residents in Paris grew, the minister of commerce raised his glass to the growing American colony "which brings smiles and grace to our capital." The American social set was itself described as having its own "exotic and novel allure." Before De Castellane and others became disenchanted, the open gaiety of the American salons was seen (albeit "at times with rough edges") as generally refreshing, particularly when compared to the "twisted mentalities [*les tortillages d'esprit*] to which we are accustomed." Young American women were particularly appreciated, with a special nod to "the charming American girls of Reid Hall, tall, svelte, and smiling with their splendid teeth at the flower sellers."[83]

By 1920 the Americans were no longer exotics of the upper crust. They were heroes of the masses. On May 30, 1923, when the War Memorial Battle Cloister at the American Cathedral was unveiled in solemn tribute to the American war dead in France, "throngs of French folks . . . piously took part" in the ceremony.[84] Four years later, as the mayor of the city got ready to greet the Legionnaires at their 1927 convention in Paris, he declared that he could not imagine Paris without Americans. Perhaps he was overcompensating for the anti-American Sacco and Vanzetti rioting a month earlier.[85] But the postwar thank you parties continued through the 1936 celebration of John D. Rockefeller Jr. at Versailles, whose war wounds he had helped to heal.

Official French recognition of Americans in France came in various forms, the most highly prized being the Legion of Honor. Indeed Consuelo Vanderbilt Balsan commented wryly that her compatriots were adept at maneuvering to get it.[86] Like the French. Although you do not have to live in France to be so honored (American recipients have ranged from Thomas Edison to Walt

Disney), the award was given to many of the Americans of Paris, starting of course with the dentist Thomas Evans in 1853. Lawyers, church clerics, philanthropists, artists, and war heroes all received the honorific badge: Edmond Kelly (1906), Mrs. Whitelaw Reid (1922), Dean (1924) and Mrs. (1937) Beekman of the American Cathedral. Anne Morgan was first honored in 1919 and was promoted to officer in 1924, the medal pinned on her by none other than the war hero Marshal Philippe Pétain; in 1932 she became one of the rare women elevated to the rank of commander. The first female American artist to receive the honor was Cecilia de Wentworth (1901), although there were snide comments that her talent in public relations outstripped her flair with a paintbrush. Mary Cassatt, the second female American artist (1904), went on to much greater fame (including a French postage stamp in 2006). Edith Wharton received the honor in 1916 for her war relief work. Josephine Baker was also inducted, although not until after World War II, for her activity in the Resistance rather than her banana skirt. World War I African American flying ace Eugene Bullard received the honor for his efforts in both wars, albeit not until 1959. Other forms of recognition include street naming. Myron Herrick, twice ambassador to France, became a *rue* in the 8th arrondissement. And the United States got its own square, the place des États-Unis, after the American Legation relocated there in 1881 and its previous name, place de Bitche (named after a city in the Moselle), was deemed inappropriate for visiting Americans.[87]

Beyond the subtle politics of the French state's gratitude, did Americanophiles admire all Americans in their midst equally? The French adored Josephine Baker, who was probably the most beloved American in interwar Paris, although her fans were caught up in a more general fascination with primitivism. There were also the French jazz lovers who welcomed the new music and its performers. But the French defense of American blacks could in fact be a critique of American racism rather than a sign of love for all things American.[88]

Finally, one element of the American stereotype that was often a source of envious scorn could also be turned into a virtue: their wealth. Some French welcomed Americans not just for their efficient methods but for their profligate spending habits. The belief that Americans were rich dates to those who were: those who made the Grand Tour in the nineteenth century and those who married into the aristocracy. Even modest American doughboys were well off compared to French farmers. The image of American wealth, regardless of the down-at-heel or downright deadbeat who also populated Paris, differentiated Americans from other immigrants in town. American money was good for France, and some worried observers feared that Americans, whether tourists or residents, could leave and take it home. After the tourist bus incident in 1926, *Le Temps*, while pointing out that foreigners should refrain from ostentatious behavior, admonished Parisians that instead of rioting against American tourists they should smile—"if only from tact." The worry over losing American dollars only increased as the Depression hit France. In 1934 the journalist and soon-to-be diplomat Wladimir D'Ormesson made a vibrant plea on the front page of *Le Temps* on behalf of rich foreigners living in France. They brought in money, hired domestics, and shopped. Inveighing particularly against various forms of "double taxation" as "simplement imbécile," D'Ormesson argued that the French should be more hospitable and leave foreigners in fiscal peace.[89]

AMERICANS ON FRENCH VIEWS OF AMERICA AND AMERICANS ON EACH OTHER

While the French were agonizing over the importation of American methods of modernity, the Americans in Paris were anxiously scrutinizing some of the French views about them. To be sure, the Right Bank colony cringed at the 1926 bus attack, but it distanced itself from the troublesome tourists and largely downplayed the incident.[90] As for keeping up with French writings on Americanization, it is doubtful that many if any of them read Bonnefon-Craponne's law thesis on American financial penetration mentioned above, but Siegfried's and Tardieu's treatises both came to the worried attention of the American residents of Paris. Businessmen in particular were fully aware of the criticisms lobbed at American standardization. Book reviews in the American Women's Club of Paris's well-respected *Bulletin* analyzed the French critique of America while insisting that constructive criticism and more information about the other could lead to better Franco-American understanding.

André Siegfried's critical book, published but a year after the rebound of fierce debt-restructuring talks and the antitourist melee in Montmartre, had quickly been translated into English. American readers in France considered his book to be the work of an honest observer. However, its criticism of American conformity clearly bothered William Leon Smyser, who reviewed both Siegfried's and Tardieu's books in the *Bulletin*. Smyser laid the blame for French attitudes on American rebels. It was the Theodore Dreisers, Sinclair Lewises, and Harold Stearnses, he surmised, who had inspired the French critics with their disdain of Rotary Club vocabulary and American standardization. A firm believer in the inevitability of Taylorism, Smyser put the French and American opponents of New World methods in the same basket.[91] Tardieu's more moderate critique garnered thanks rather than skepticism from another reviewer in the same issue. Arthur K. Griggs emphasized Tardieu's main point: that, in spite of all the differences between the two countries, there was no reason they should not work together. Griggs indeed heartily endorsed this position as the veritable raison d'être of all good Americans living in France. Not surprisingly, he gave Dubreuil's *Standards* the heartiest praise of all and considered that it deserved the subtitle "Apologia of Civilization in the United States." Not since Tardieu had any Frenchman been so outspoken in condemning "certain racial tendencies towards pettiness of vision" among his own countrymen. The success of the book, to Griggs's clear relief, was itself a sign of the decline of French anti-Americanism.[92]

Yet while Americans could worry about French opinions of themselves, they could also be their own severest critics. Albert Sutliffe, in his otherwise resolutely upbeat 1887 guide *Americans in Paris*, had felt the need to include a forty-page (out of 208) section on good manners that undoubtedly would not have been necessary if he felt that American etiquette was up to European snuff. Why would he write, "Hanging around church doors and staring at the ladies, making remarks, is very ill-bred," if he were not cringing in the wings? Twice he insisted that "[a]ll egotism must be banished from the drawing-room"; "self should never except in case of absolute necessity be the subject of conversation." And, above all, speak softly.[93]

American residents belittled tourists and complained of being solicited by mere acquaintances visiting from home who wanted advice on everything.[94] But the residents also mocked each other. Whole books, chapters, and articles written by Americans abroad were devoted to disparaging their compatriots' airs. The American countesses were one of the earliest objects of outright scorn. But more generally, American critics contrasted their compatriots' Europeanized dissolution to homegrown manners, drawing stark distinctions between the unnatural and the genuine types. In an 1893 book titled *Americans in Europe, by One of Them*, published anonymously (due to the arrows slung at his compatriots?), George Monroe Royce, otherwise known as an American parson in Europe, exuded his disdain for Europe, with the possible exception of England. It was "American soil, and under the influences of the New-World thought and feeling and aspiration, and not in the wholly sensual atmosphere of Paris, or in the graveyards of Rome," that American artists could create a truly indigenous American art form. If Americans abroad were not already a lower form of life ("[t]here are people in society in Paris who would be in prison in America"), they would certainly lose their good American character there, and furthermore they would never successfully assimilate anyway. In his wide-ranging critique, Royce even scoffed at those Americans who thought that the American minister plenipotentiary should necessarily know French: that "would be to surrender the post entirely into the hands of the snobocracy of America." "Home-bred culture, be it never [*sic*] so homely, is infinitely better than European paste and varnish." Royce was adamant: "I have come to the conclusion that Europe is the asylum for American fools."[95]

Richard Harding Davis was an equally harsh early critic of his compatriots, mocking everyone from the summer tourists who never ventured beyond the Champs-Élysées and their bankers' offices to the women who wore themselves out in that endless ceremony of trying on clothes at the dressmakers to the pseudo-artist "struggling and fluttering and biting his nails and eating his heart out in private" while waiting to be discovered. Davis even ridiculed the Lafayette cult of the Right Bank crowd:

> When it so happens that no one of prominence has died for some time, and there seems to be no other way of getting themselves noticed, the American Colony rises in its strength and remembers Lafayette. . . . [A few descendants of Lafayette] are brought into the suburbs many times a year in the rain and storm to watch different American Colonists place a wreath on the tomb of their distinguished ancestor, and make speeches about a man who left his country only to fight for the independence of another country, and not to live in it after it was free. Some day the descendants of Lafayette and the secretaries of the American embassy will rise up and rebel, and refuse to lend themselves longer to the uses of these gentlemen.[96]

Americans abroad could admonish one another all the better to keep up good American appearances or to mock the failings of their compatriots. And wish them to click their slippers Dorothy-in-Oz-like and return home.

Americanization? Frenchification? With all of these cross-eyed glances— Americans on the French, French on America and on Americans, and Americans on Americans—we seem to be faced with double angst: the French worried about Americanization, and some Americans worried about their own Frenchification. Close encounters and the literary imagination combined to provide a cornucopia of Franco-American reciprocal visions. By the turn of the twentieth century Americanization in France was defined as the arrival of American plumbing and elevators, not to mention huge signs advertising American dentistry. As the century progressed, French pundits increasingly denounced (already) the English words that had crept into the language: *whiskey, cocktail, bacon, pull-over, tennis.* "One gloomy French scribe even went so far the other day as to maintain that we were not merely 'Americanizing' France but 'colonizing' her."[97] Americanization was not just *les mots* but also *les choses*. Traffic lights, neon signs, and revolving doors added to the definition. As the *New York Times* correspondent in Paris, T. B. Ybarra, reported the complaints of creeping Americanization, it was the urban planning demolishing the Paris ramparts, the car companies transforming the Champs-Élysées into a shopping street with no residents, English spoken everywhere (well, around the place Vendôme, where many Americans gathered), soda fountains, and, worst of all, the shortening of the two-hour lunch. As one Parisian told him: If I took a shorter lunch I could earn more money, but what could I buy with more money that would give me greater pleasure than a two-hour lunch?[98]

"Americanization" pained visitors and natives alike. Ybarra mocked the French pessimists (as he had mocked American "Paris-Maniacs," sipping their aperitifs on the Left Bank, ready to march forward to "chase those traitors, the Parisians, out of Paris in order to save the City of Light from Americanization"). After all, weren't signs of "English Spoken Here" just signs of friendliness rather than a boding of linguistic doom? And weren't the "sinister symptoms of the spread of the American 'quick lunch'" overstated?[99] Similarly, a year later journalist Golda Goldman stressed that whiskey had not trounced fine wines, and light lunches had not replaced rabbit stew and mussels in wine. If French friends worried about an invasion of corned beef hash and Shredded Wheat, she insisted that no American at the Folies Bergères "look[ing] his fill upon woman as nature made her" could imagine he was back in the United States. Goldman admitted to a certain Americanization of Paris, while arguing that whatever Americanization there was had in fact been Frenchified in turn. "No, Paris is not America," she resolutely concluded.[100]

But had the Americans of Paris become Frenchified? The vast majority of Americans in France, for all of their grumbling, were Francophiles. Right Bank Americans, like Left Bank ones, thus objected to the accusation of causing Americanization. The AWCP *Bulletin* ran a testy article in 1927 titled "The American Business 'Invasion'" by journalist Henry Tosti Russell, emphasizing the quotation marks. He dismissed reports of French complaints that dollars were buying up important French industries and buildings by quoting a prominent French financier: "France is still French and no American impresarios or capitalists have tried to purchase the Opéra, Opéra-Comique or Comédie Française." Even if some Americans had bought châteaus while the franc was low, the restored buildings had been "saved from ruin by American dollars," and the purchase of business buildings in Paris meant that the Americans paid heavy taxes. As Georges Jacquet, the well-known French architect who had helped rebuild the devastated regions with American money had told him: "I have never feared the so-called American Business Invasion of France. I will, however, and gladly so, admit that there has been a serious invasion of France by American Philanthropy." French national honor was safe.[101]

American men and women of the Right Bank often stressed their love of France, certainly to their French audiences. They were nonetheless on the defensive, not just against French accusations of their Americanizing France but vis-à-vis American audiences, about their own Frenchification. The American Legionnaires living abroad were "hypersensitive" about their American identity, as veteran and journalist Bernhard Ragner explained in his long *Saturday Evening Post* article of November 11, 1939, arguing for US entry into World War II. A US congressman who had once addressed the post members abroad as "you foreigners" nearly caused a small riot. Ragner's article is both proud and defensive: defensive about staying on in France, defensive about living in a totally French environment with children whose English was sometimes shaky. Battling the handicap of language (and sometimes in-laws), Ragner admitted that "much that is Gallic" had entered the lifestyles of Americans-in-France: two-hour lunches, tipping theater ushers, shaking hands "indiscriminately," putting a dash through the figure 7. Worse, only 35 percent of their children were fully Anglophone, according to him; another 35 percent read it well enough "to grasp grandma's letters from America"; but another 30 percent neither read nor spoke English and probably never would, an issue of some embarrassment to the expatriates. But if the American grandmothers complained about the lack of American traits in their grandchildren, the French grandmothers complained just as often that the kids were too American. Indeed, Ragner insisted, the Americans abroad were "incorrigibly American." "We represent America to the French, and we do so with pride. . . . Symbolically, we carry the flag every waking minute and we are fully aware of the responsibility," without being sanctimonious about it. Noting the waves of homesickness that could hit at any time, Ragner stressed the Americanness of waffle-loving citizens abroad, calling up images of front porches and skating ponds to define home. The American Legion Post in Paris was, after all, a place where American slang and sarcasm were understood and where buddies could bond. But he concluded, "We are not men without a country. . . . We are men with two countries."[102]

FIGURE 8. Expatriates, their dressmakers, and their bartenders alike cried over the Americans' return home. From Eleanor Kinsella McDonnell, "The American Expatriate Intones a Dirge," *Saturday Evening Post* 60, no. 17 (October 21, 1933).

CHAPTER 8

Heading Home

War, Again

Where to?

TRYPHOSA BATES-BATCHELLER[1]

By the fall of 1938, the DAR women noted in their minutes that the American colony was shrinking. They attributed it to fear of war. In fact, although Americans kept coming to visit and even to settle in Paris through the 1930s, larger numbers of Americans residents, businessmen, socialites, and writers alike left Paris massively in two waves. A first group left after the stock market crash melted fortunes. A second wave left with the outbreak of World War II. They left reluctantly, ending—temporarily for some, permanently for others—the world they had known for years or for decades. For those who had made their home in Paris, the return to the United States was wrenching, leaving jobs, French friends, antiques, and other possessions behind. However, the very leaving process also left in its wake compelling evidence of what the lives of this elite migration had been like for many.

"For sale, cheap. Nice old château. . . . Will sacrifice."[2] When the stock market crashed, the Left Bank and Right Bank bartenders lost their habitués, and the Parisian couturiers wept as *les Américaines*—tourists as well as many residents—went home, leaving dress orders uncollected and bills unpaid. After days of alarming headlines about what was happening in the United States, on October 29, 1929, the *Chicago Tribune European Edition* turned the spotlight on Americans in Paris. The paper compared the panic to the first days of World War I, when Americans scurried to go home. Travel agencies were besieged. Brokerage offices were jammed with men in evening dress and women in décolleté gowns and fur wraps who, given the time difference, had come directly from the opera for news and were "helplessly watching the ticker whittling away [their] fortunes." Desperate speculators tried to get on the first boat available, "even second class."[3] A few months later, however, the irreverent *Paris Comet* mocked the headlines of gloom: "One heard that a prominent New York broker vacationing in France was not able to pay for his dry Martini."[4] But the paper itself closed a few months later. The *Chicago Tribune*'s Paris edition also closed a few years later (merged into the Paris *Herald*); journalists lost jobs, and writers went home. "By the end of the 1920s the American Colony looked more like a gigantic garage sale what with automobiles, mink coats, and antiques on the auction block."[5]

Yet the flight home for many did not occur until a few years later. The Depression was slower to come to France. It took until May 1931 for it to be mentioned in the American Women's Club monthly *Bulletin* and another year before the *Bulletin* lost its color cover and reverted to a slimmer, all black-and-white format. Over the next couple of years, as its membership declined, the club continually reduced expenses, although it refused to consider, as other clubs had, extending membership to gentlemen.[6]

Not everyone left after the crash. There were notable exceptions among the literary set: Edith Wharton and Gertrude Stein, who both had come earlier, stayed longer, and ultimately died in their adopted country. Josephine Baker and Bricktop stayed. And a new DAR chapter was founded in 1934, the same year that the American Students' and Artists' Center expanded to its new home on the boulevard Raspail. The National City Bank moved to its 60 avenue des Champs-Élysées office in 1931 ("in spite of the current crisis, there is an increase in business"), a "most modern installation" that included private safety deposit boxes.[7]

Businessmen too hung on in the 1930s. There were those too far invested in France to leave. And new entrepreneurs showed up. Some came to France during the early days of the Depression in the United States, looking for work when things still looked better in France. Others would come to sell arms or airplane parts as the military buildup began in the late 1930s. The number of pages in the Commercial List of the American Chamber of Commerce's *Directory* stayed pretty much the same.

THE WAR, THE FLAG, AND PROTECTION

Yet in 1938, as international tensions heated up in Europe, Americans there became increasingly nervous. First the German *Anschluss* annexing Austria in March and then Hitler's coveting of Czechoslovakia made many feel that it was only a matter of time before a second war occurred. On September 26, 1938, Ambassador William C. Bullitt sent letters to all Americans registered at consulates in France, advising them to return to the United States. Distraught parents encouraged their sons and daughters to come home immediately, but even before some of them had been contacted, the crisis abated with the false reassurance of the Munich Agreement. The embassy canceled its warning.[8] At the same time, the French secret services noted with satisfaction that prominent members of the American colony were speaking out in favor of France and Great Britain and that at a veterans' meeting in 1939, one speaker assured that, if necessary, "veritable legions of volunteers will arrive once more to serve immortal France."[9]

On September 1, 1939, Germany invaded Poland. Two days later, France and Britain declared war on Germany. Then nothing happened. For months, during what was known as the "phony war" (*drôle de guerre*), people got used to carrying around gas masks, and as one of the Archibald lawyers told me years later, they ultimately began to use them as lunch pails for thankful want of any more serious purpose. But on May 10, 1940, German troops invaded the north of France and headed toward Paris. Within six weeks it was over. Paris was occupied on June 14, and France capitulated and signed an armistice on June 25.

According to the American consul, there were still thirty thousand Americans in and around Paris at the declaration of World War II.[10] During the phony war, the American men and women in the city zoomed into action. By January 25, 1940, the American Cathedral's Junior Guild and the Women's Auxiliary had made 175,000 surgical dressings and knitted and purchased socks, winter caps, gloves, and pajamas for men at the front.[11] As for the men, the Legionnaires bucked their national organization's official policy of neutrality by readying to fight again: they organized a battalion and an ambulance service, even if they could not use the American Legion's name to do so. As Bernhard Ragner wrote, "[W]e ['the Permanent AEF'] are violently pro-French," yet "[w]e of Uncle Sam's Never-Go-Home Battalion are not any the less American." Not a single member had forfeited his US citizenship. "Our spiritual home is across the Atlantic," he emphasized, all the while arguing that it was once again time for the United States to defend France.[12]

The US embassy had drawn up secret memoranda concerning relief, protection, and evacuation of American citizens as early as August 1936 and did so again in November 1938. In April 1939, gas masks were shipped to the embassy for its personnel and their dependents, although no provisions were made for private citizens. When Ragner inquired on behalf of the legionnaires, the embassy simply sent him a list of French supply houses—even though the French government had said that no foreigners were to receive gas masks.[13]

At the same time, a personal and confidential memo was sent to Max Shoop, lawyer at Sullivan and Cromwell, asking him to chair a committee that would be "representative of our Paris colony" to cooperate with the embassy in the event of an emergency. By July 1, 1939, the American consul in Bordeaux had reserved 500 rooms in hotels in Royan and another 145 in Bordeaux in the event of an evacuation of the American colony in Paris.[14]

On August 24, 1939, a week before Germany invaded Poland, the American embassy in Paris had given notice to American citizens abroad that those who had no compelling reason to stay in Europe should arrange to return to the United States.[15] At the same time, diplomatic and consular officers started telegraphing the State Department to request extra large flags for display in case of war. But the department answered that: it did not have them; the cost would be prohibitive; and experience had shown that they were not very effective. It suggested instead that large-sized letters such as "U.S.A." seven feet high, one foot wide, should be painted on horizontal surfaces in chrome yellow on a black background, to be more clearly visible from the air.[16]

The consulates once again became hubs of activity to which worried citizens flocked. From August 20 to November 15, the Paris, Bordeaux, and Nice consulates assisted over twenty thousand Americans, giving them advice, assistance, and even money. Citizens had to pay for their own transportation, but the government helped them get in touch with family or friends back home who could provide funds. Thirty-one cases were refused help because citizenship was not established.[17] Protection was not always a simple matter. During the phony war, the United States sent five special ships ("at great expense") to retrieve American citizens, but many residents balked at leaving, while some who took up the offer complained about the less than luxurious conditions. As one State Department official retorted, "[T]hey were not dispatched on a pleasure cruise."[18] The government was also getting exasperated at those who insisted on staying on, unnecessarily risking danger.

When the Germans invaded France and reached Paris on June 14, Americans who had called upon their government during the interwar years for intercession with the French now hoped that the American flag could protect them from the Germans. American neutrality was a theoretical shield for as long as the United States was not at war. Some people were unsure about the best strategy. One man at first thought it prudent not to publicize the fact that his property was American but then thought better of it in September 1940 as he prepared to leave.[19] As in 1870 and in 1914, American organizations and individuals, from countesses to ordinary citizens, applied for protection certificates that would, it was hoped, prevent the occupiers from occupying their premises or confiscating their contents. Once people proved their citizenship and their ownership of the property, the certificates were drawn up in three languages (English, French, German). What better hex signs on lintels to ward off danger? Just asking for them affirmed belief in the strength of the United States; one grateful woman wrote in thanks, "I feel much safer with my big red seals."[20]

The Applications for the Protection of Property Certificates are a goldmine revealing the extent of Americans' moorings in France. Sylvia Beach, "proprietress," wrote in, worried about her bookstore, her apartment, and her Savoie chalet, specifying that the first two were rented but that their contents, like the chalet, were her property. Henri Weill, Gertrude Stein's landlord, came in to request a certificate for the contents of the seven-room apartment she leased from him at 5 rue Christine, where she and Alice B. Toklas had moved from the rue de Fleurus in 1938. As is now well known, they sat out the war in a small town in the French Alps, thanks in part to the protection of an old French friend-turned-collaborator, Bernard Fäy. "Dear Sirs," wrote Natalie Barney on August 24, 1940: "I wish to call your powerful and kind attention to two places in which I have all my belongings in France." Although the two-story pavilion where she had held salon for thirty years at 20 rue Jacob remained unharmed, the villa she owned in the country and shared with Romaine Brooks was bombed during the war.[21]

The material innards of lives abroad were revealed in this moment of crisis as citizens attached to the Application detailed descriptions of their possessions down to the last oyster fork. Some sent their concierge, maid, or landlord to the embassy, or they wrote from the South of France, New York, or elsewhere inquiring as to the safety of their safe deposit boxes, châteaus, or Chevrolets. They asked for help in getting goods into storage or out of storage in order to ship them to the United States. In addition to his Parisian villa, his Normandy château, and his car, one man wanted certificates for his two horses, Ketty and Perdrix. Helena Rubinstein, aka Princess Helena Gourielli, wrote from New York on May 17, 1940, asking for twenty-eight certificates for her Paris apartments and shops along with her house, laboratories, and sheds in the Paris suburbs. People submitted long, sometimes notarized, lists of their possessions. For some that meant Louis XVI tables, Victor Hugo–style armchairs, pianos, oriental rugs. For others, the applications reveal more modest contents of rented apartments, specifying a large woolen American flag and every electric fixture, number of light bulbs included. One man attached a drawing of the layout of his rental house in Brittany along with a six-page handwritten description of its contents room by room, listing everything from his framed Harvard diploma to the leather-bound diary of his famous ancestor John Bertram and an oil portrait of same, not to mention the recently uphol-stered couch, two family Bibles, Junior's violin and train set, down to sewing materials, kerosene and alcohol drums, one year's supply of eggs "preserved in a reliable solution" in the basement, and a bottle of Listerine on the bedside table.[22]

Some longtime residents of France turned to the embassy for the first time, emphasizing their American credentials: "In the 22 years I have lived in Paris I have never before had to ask the embassy for help of any kind, and I implore you to do all you can for me now," wrote George Balkema. He specified that he had served in the American army in France in 1918 and had been a lieutenant in the American Volunteer Ambulance Corps from September 1939 to Octo-ber 1940. He was an antique dealer who had already lost one shipment to the United States, and he hoped that the embassy could intervene on his behalf at German military headquarters in order to get one last shipment across. "This merchandise is all I have left in the world, and I cannot return to America until I get it on its way. For on its arrival there now it can be sold at an excellent profit and will put me on my feet again." The embassy secretary regretted that the embassy could not officially help him, but he assured Balkema, in a letter that he could use with the Germans, that the embassy supported his plea.[23]

Even French companies asked for protection to the extent that they repre-sented American interests. The Société des Auteurs, Compositeurs et Éditeurs de Musique (SACEM), having always represented in France the American Society of Composers, Authors and Publishers, used its best formal language to beseech help: "Your Excellency, I would like to ask you if our company could benefit from the moral protection of the United States by flying, with your eminent authorization, the American flag and by posting a protection certificate . . . with the seal of the U.S. Embassy."[24] After visiting its premises, confirming the contract linking the SACEM to the ASCAP, and seeing the list of amounts paid to American authors for the years 1936–39, Consul Tyler Thompson signed a form on June 17, 1940, certifying that the SACEM "has certain assets which belong to the American Society of Composers, Authors and Publishers, an American organization." Similarly, Les Artistes associés, French subsidiary for United Artists, asked for certificates like those posted for the Twentieth Century Fox Film and MGM agencies, listing the contents of its offices, down to the twelve freestanding ashtrays.[25]

But how useful were the embassy certificates as protective talismans? A memo dated August 20, 1940, shows that some 2,230 property protection certificates had been issued to 1,066 individuals, companies, and organizations, and another 168 certificates had been made out for automobile protection alone. The embassy itself was nonetheless dubious about their efficacy and warned their recipients: "The issuance of protection certificates by the embassy does not entitle property to any more or any less protection than if such certificates were not issued. They might however deter [variant: act as a psychological deterrent in the event] unauthorized persons from breaking into or damaging property covered by them. [variant: The protection of property of foreigners is the duty of the central government and of the local authorities]."[26] A disclaimer on the bottom of the application forms stated: "In the event of loss or damage to the property mentioned in the embassy's certificate, no recourse can be had against the United States government or the embassy because of the issuance of such a certificate."

Over the course of the first year of the war, German policy shifted. In a confidential telegram of October 22, 1940, the embassy informed the State Department that although in the early days of the Occupation it had received informal official and private assurances that American property would not be harmed, it was now becoming clear that this was not the case. The embassy had been pursuing redress for confiscation and had been successful in approximately a quarter of the cases, and therefore the ambassador believed that the German government still wanted to conciliate American opinion. So it seemed best not to press the point for the moment. However, over the next two months the US embassy reported that the Germans were still refusing to evacuate American property, even at the embassy's request, and apparently the French police authorities had been preparing special lists of Americans for use by the German authorities.[27] On December 6, the Germans officially declared that they could requisition the property of citizens from neutral countries. As the Germans disregarded the certificates, they seized cars (and painted one gray! its owner complained) and confiscated wine cellars, not to mention "1 ping-pong table, 4 rackets, 1 box of balls (10 or 12),"[28] of particular value because they had been imported from the United States. American citizens were outraged about this violation of property. Margaret DeWitt Benedict complained on September 11, 1940, that in spite of US embassy seals on her doors, German soldiers had occupied her place in the Seine-et-Oise and she could not get her vegetables, which she needed to put up for the coming winter.[29] All the embassy could do was to instruct people on how to file a claim.

On December 8, 1941, the United States entered the war, and on December 22 the *Militärbefehlshaber* (military governor) ordered that all American goods in France, from shares held to buildings owned and occupied, had to be declared before February 10, 1942. Anyone connected with American property was supposed to fill out the forms, in quadruplicate, be they Americans living in France or French directors of American companies, American landlords or their French tenants, and of course all lawyers and notaries involved with American businesses.[30] By the following year, the Germans had sequestered the accounts of the American Chamber of Commerce, and it was seeking donations from its French friends, with checks payable to the order of the Comité français de la Chambre de commerce américaine en France.[31]

If citizenship is a form of protection, timing is everything. Once the United States entered the war, US citizenship became a millstone. Protective certificates and flags were hastily removed from doorposts. It was time for many who had not yet done so to flee.

THE GETAWAY

"The Exodus," as the Parisians called the vast movement south in June 1940 as the Germans headed toward the city, was frightful by all accounts. Etta Shiber describes the traffic jam out of Paris on June 13 as backed up from the Porte d'Orléans's southern exit from the city all the way to the intersection of boulevard Saint-German and the boulevard Raspail. She and her British friend Kitty Beaurepos inched their way through the honking and frayed nerves with their dogs on their laps. In eight hours they advanced twelve miles. After German bombs strafed the road to clear the way for the Germany army rushing southward, she and Kitty eventually turned back to Paris—and resistance work. Dr. Charles Bove also edged his way south amidst the chaos, helping wounded refugees along the way. He spent the next four weeks operating on hundreds of wounded at the Bellevue Casino–turned-makeshift-hospital in Biarritz. After returning to Paris to find that the Nazis had confiscated his hospital and home office equipment, he dismantled his twenty-two-room house with its valuable antiques and Napoleon-era clock and headed back to the United States.[32]

Yet it turns out that not all the tales of departure are told with tragic effect. An alternate, more humorous if still dramatic description of leavetaking was given by Russell H. Porter in a long letter addressed to his friends once he was safely back in New York.[33] American counselor at law in Paris in the first half of the twentieth century, Porter told of his adventuresome "escape from the Huns" in the best Hollywood tradition. He had been an admiralty lawyer who had come to France during World War I to deal with sinking ships. In 1922 he opened a law practice that initially specialized in "lives, wills and wrecks," as his son later put it with a twinkle in his eye (personal law, estates, and maritime law).[34] With the outbreak of World War II, as Porter *père* explained in his letter, he did not join the initial 1940 Exodus but stayed on in Paris after the American embassy had moved to Vichy and the American banks had "folded their tents and disappeared from the scene." Using his contacts and clients throughout France and putting his legal skills to use, Porter began helping people get out of France. He helped more than one American woman who had become British through marriage to escape from the early internment camps by "proving" that they were Irish.

By the fall of 1941, as Porter related rather proudly, he was living a life of crime. He had organized a bootleg bank through which he helped Americans who could not take their francs out of the country: he took their francs and doled them out to those who had no cash in France but had dollars in the United States. Even more dangerously, he and some friends raised three pigs illegally in a backyard hideout at the country place of one of his British clients. They gleefully named the succession of domestic swine Adolph, Herman, and Goebbels and, as each came to maturity, assassinated them in the dead of night, salting them away with the help of the village gold-medal sausage maker. After Pearl Harbor, Porter realized that it behooved him to find somewhere else to sleep. Indeed, several days later the Gestapo came looking for him at home. Since he had decamped, he avoided the fate of some 340 others in Paris who were arrested in the first roundup of American men to be interned as hostages by the Germans to ensure good treatment of Germans in the United States.[35]

On Saturday, December 13, 1941, Porter began his getaway. His French secretary had reconnoitered the movements of the Germans at the Gare de Lyon train station and bought a ticket for the Unoccupied Zone in southern France while Porter bought a ticket for the suburbs. They exchanged tickets and quais. It worked. Porter had no baggage, and, as he added for the benefit of his readers (friends, family, and belatedly a historian, who all clearly still imagined him a suited-up lawyer), he "was dressed as much like a third class passenger as was possible." Porter debarked near the demarcation zone, hoping to make contact with a gamekeeper who had been helping his friends cross the line, only to learn that his contact had been arrested two days earlier. He then proceeded on foot in the general direction of the line, camping out one night on the remains of a bed in a looted château, then continuing along narrow country lanes. At one point he ended up in a backyard with Germans in the front; "[I] cocked my hat over my right eye, put my hands in my raincoat pockets and strolled through the courtyard. . . . Believe me it's hard to stroll when you want to run." Through woods and thorny hedges, in muddy fields with melting snow and water up to his ankles, he got lost. But Porter finally ended up in the Free Zone, with bloody feet and torn toenails, "looking like a tramp and worn to a frazzle": "55 kilometers, 13 hours and no food, not so moldy for an old boy of 57." He stayed the next night "with a joyous band of poachers, smugglers, gendarmes and others" and then headed to Lyon, ever the lawyer, seeing three or four clients along the way.

Porter then went to Avignon, where he turned his attention to getting his wife Anne "out of pawn." This entailed getting her fake papers and thus a new name and identity. The transformed Madame Marie Claudine Portero, "farmeress," set off from Paris on January 23, and although she forgot her new name at a crucial moment, the German that she swore was 7 feet 6 inches tall never asked her for it. The Porters set up house at the priory near Avignon. There was very little heat and no hot water, and they subsisted mostly on cabbage, turnips, and leeks but also those hearty vitamins in the Château Neuf du Pape still in the wine cellar, to which Porter attributed their survival. They had plenty of friends and clients in the Unoccupied Zone, and Porter continued to help people leave the country. This brought him a certain amount of fame but also ultimately unease and danger. The US government kindly invited them to scoot home on the SS *Drottningholm* (Swedish American Line) as paying guests. (It had been commissioned to drop off Axis officials who had been in the United States. in exchange for picking up American diplomats, newspapermen and others who had got stuck in Europe.)[36] This time they both traveled by train, from Avignon to Nîmes to Montpellier to Toulouse to Pau to Canfranc in Spain, past beautiful country and the Lourdes grotto alit at night. Porter still had the fortitude to take in the Prado in Madrid, while his wife sat it out on a bench, more dead than alive. Then on to "the incredible cleanliness of Portugal," real coffee, and then a month in Lisbon waiting for the ship. Mostly everyone they had befriended along the way, except the hardy Porter himself, was soon laid up with "Lisbon belly"—the result of too much good food after months of near starvation. Never at a loss for activity, Porter decided to take Portuguese lessons: "Written it looks like Spanish, but the pronunciation is half way between Chinese and Yiddish." At last the SS *Drottningholm* arrived. Porter described the savior ship as a modern-day Noah's Ark due to the 950 international passengers aboard, along with eleven dogs, five cats, five canaries, and one parrot.

"The sea was smooth, the food was good," but the seven days at sea were then followed by almost as many in the New Jersey harbor. First the ship was visited by a medical inspection team, then the "immigration troop," with cigars and stout bellies. ("In a way, it did one's heart good to see so many cigars at one time and to know there was plenty to eat in the good old U.S.A.") The immigration officials were protected by some "hard-boiled young men [with outsize revolvers], whom we christened the Hitler youth," who were followed in turn by double-breasted-dark-blue-and-brass-button-garbed customs officials accompanied by more men with guns and others in overalls, who all "did a sort of ballet on the ship, looking under the carpets and in all the corners." The next visitors were neatly suited handsome lads, who looked just like the G-men in the movies and, given their piercing glances, left no doubt that they were FBI agents. The naval intelligence officers, with the nicest uniforms of all, were a great hit with the ladies. And last but not least, the Jersey City police came on board and closed the bar; the ship had no New Jersey license to sell liquor. All in all, this succession of "so many fine specimens of American manhood" amused the passengers, as they were still "full of hope and joy at being back in the land of the free and the home of the brave."

But that was just day 1. It was another five days before the Porters were allowed to disembark. They were told that the boat was undoubtedly full of spies and that they must be good Americans and be patient. Female soldiers in becoming costumes suggestive of the Civil War offered them doughnuts and coffee, but as the days stretched out, life without pajamas, toothbrushes, clean shirts, or baths began to take its toll. Their luggage had already been taken ashore. July Fourth came and went, the summer heat got hotter, the ship and its sewerage dirtier and smellier. On day 6, Porter was finally able to talk his way to release "by an avowedly disgraceful combination of menaces and hot air." Three months later the Porters received a bill for seventeen days on board, ten of which had been in port in Lisbon and Jersey City.

Porter's story of escape reminds us vividly of the material conditions of travel. The waiting, the ships, the trains or immobilized cars are the understudied moments and spaces in the history of migration and mobility.[37] The urgency of war only crystallized the matter, so that the tales of departure reveal as much about the events themselves as about the former lives of Americans of Paris. Privileged migrants with greater means to leave, they also had more possessions to worry about. Even the intrepid Etta Shiber was initially paralyzed by the traveler's dilemma: what to take? As for Peggy Guggenheim, the day Hitler invaded Norway she was at Fernand Léger's atelier buying a marvelous 1919 painting of his for one thousand dollars. But as the Germans approached Paris, she finally packed up her art collection (sent mostly to Geneva) and headed home. She ultimately crossed the Atlantic with tickets for ten: herself, her ex-husband Laurence Vail, his second but already former wife the writer Kay Boyle, six children, and Max Ernst, Guggenheim's current lover and future (brief) husband.[38]

Having the means to leave "in style" helped, whether with a numerous extended family or alone. The widowed DAR socialite Tryphosa Bates-Batcheller needed a ticket for only herself and her longtime Italian *dame de compagnie*. Stoic, she was at first determined to stay on, albeit outraged by the German occupation. She gave the flag and the DAR papers to the Comtesse de Pange for safekeeping, a foresightful move given that her villa, where so many of their meetings and teas had been convened, was looted, and the commanding officer, finding some DAR papers still there, considered her a dangerous revolutionary, to be shot before sunset. But as Bates-Batcheller put it in her memoirs, when friends urged her to leave France she answered in a bit of a huff: "Where to?" She stayed on, frightened by the noise of the airplanes and cannons, worrying about the monuments and about her friend the Duc de Broglie's autographed letter collection. She continued singing in spite of the cold—in gloves, galoshes, and a fur coat. She braved the metro for the first time in her life, in order to buy a heater, and was pleasantly surprised by the "kindly peasant" who did not doff his hat for a lady but did help her get through the crowd. When, resignedly, she finally decided to leave France, she prepared sixteen Louis Vuitton trunks. En route, when a German officer criticized her excessive luggage, she looked him straight in the eye and answered, in very good German:

> "But, Mr. Officer, I do not think that I have too much baggage. I am a woman of the world and I go out a great deal in fashionable society. I am going to my own country for two, three, four, five years. I don't know . . ." (hoping he would understand that we meant to lick them eventually, and I fancy he did). And I continued, "You would hardly expect me to wear a furcoat in July or an organdy in winter, would you?"[39]

But as we have seen, not all Americans in Paris were doctors, lawyers, or legatees. The African Americans in Paris were divided first about whether war would really come and then what to do once it was declared. Opal Cooper, who had not been back to the United States for twenty years, went "home." Some entertainers who stayed, such as Charlie Lewis and Arthur Briggs, were imprisoned along with other Americans. As for Bricktop, many people encouraged her to leave, but she considered Paris her home. She was now forty-five years old and loath to return to a country she had not seen for sixteen years. At first she helped the Duchess of Windsor set up a soup kitchen for artists, but the duchess insisted that she leave and booked passage for her. Bricktop sailed on October 26, 1939, as seasick on the return voyage as she had been on her initial trip over. After the war she opened clubs in Mexico City and Rome; she died in New York City in 1984.[40] During the phony war, Eugene Bullard reopened Le Grand Duc, which attracted an international crowd, including Germans, which allowed him to keep his eyes and ears open and inform the French. But as the fighting approached Paris, the forty-six-year old World War I veteran set off to go back into service. He found his old commanding officer and was wounded in the Loire Valley, hospitalized, and urged to leave France. He did so only reluctantly, on July 9, 1940, leaving his two French children behind. The first black military pilot, a boxer, and a club manager in Paris, Bullard ended up an elevator operator at Rockefeller Center in New York City, where he died in 1961.[41]

Dean Frederick Beekman of the American Cathedral, who had come to France with the AEF and had been dean of the cathedral since 1918, also went home, entrusting the cathedral to its organist, Lawrence K. Whipp. Beekman's diary too describes the chaos of the Exodus. He made it to Spain, to Lisbon, and across the Atlantic. According to one account, Beekman started lecturing while on the ship heading back home, shoring up morale in spite of the German American stewards "mit smiles on deir faces" every time the radio told of German successes. At age seventy-two, he undertook a "preaching mission," traveling around the United States. By September 1944, he had given 509 sermons and addresses alerting Americans to the danger to democracy, Christianity, and civilization.[42] As for Whipp, his story was both heroic and tragic. Organist at the cathedral since 1922 but also lay reader, he continued to hold services there after Beekman left. But after Pearl Harbor he was arrested along with the first group of American men who were interned at Compiègne. He was put in charge of some of the Americans (in effect becoming a *Kapo*). By the time Whipp was released (in August or October 1942, depending on the account), the German military authorities had requisitioned the cathedral for Lutheran services. Whipp returned to his post and worked with the German pastor there—whom he described after the war as having anti-Nazi sympathies. Finally, in October 1944 he was able to write exultantly to Beekman that the cathedral was now packed every Sunday with loudly singing American soldiers and officers as American troops moved through liberated Paris. "I am thin, old, tired, but so happy! . . . Come as soon as you can." Beekman returned. But in a mystery never resolved, five months later Whipp was found dead in the Seine. Murder related to wartime activities? Suicide? In any case, a plaque in his memory still exists in the cathedral.[43]

So some Americans stayed on, carrying on as usual, more or less. Clara Longworth de Chambrun and her husband Aldebert went to Vichy, their usual summer vacation, and hobnobbed there with Pétain and other old friends, while also helping to keep the American Hospital and the American Library open in Paris. Some Americans collaborated with the occupying forces, others resisted, as Charles Glass has forcefully described. Josephine Baker, as is well known, joined the Resistance. Etta Shiber and Kitty Beaurepos helped British aviators escape from France, as did Dr. Sumner Jackson of the American Hospital and his wife. They and their son took part in the Goélette resistance group until the three of them were arrested just ten days before the Allied landing in Normandy. Athough they were all decorated after the war, the honor was posthumous for Jackson. He died tragically when the Allies bombed the German prison ships in the Baltic Sea, thinking the Nazis were amassing for a counterattack there.[44]

AMERICAN BUSINESSES STICKING IT OUT

For the most part, individuals left, but companies and institutions stayed on. While wealthy Americans packed up their ball gowns and asparagus holders, American companies and their representatives had more complicated problems. As the Germans moved toward Paris, some companies, like the French government, headed to Bordeaux. Others wrapped up business, left their affairs in the safekeeping of others, or transferred funds to the South of France in hopes that the Germans would not reach it there. Even before the outbreak of war, Archibald's lawyers had started advising American clients to do some preventive paperwork, notably setting up proxies "with the indication that the power is being issued for use in case of war or eminence [sic] of war." As the Palmolive people were advised, they should have cash available, and they should think of a place to which the directors could retreat. They should prepare one or more old cars—not fit enough to be requisitioned—along with a supply of gas, oil, and food. And they should draw up plans for removing their vital records (but not a too cumbersome amount) to some one hundred miles away from Paris.[45]

Law firm letters shifted from double space to single space, undoubtedly to save paper. The lawyers themselves scattered, and they sent many of their files to the country for safekeeping. The Archibald firm's files went to Châteauroux, to the country estate of one of its French lawyers. In the absence of its British, Canadian, and American lawyers, the firm stayed open during the war under the vigilant custody of a French lawyer, Auguste Lechanteur. The Coudert Frères' files went first to Robinson's château on the Rhône and later to a convent. After the Exodus, he reopened the office in Paris and stayed throughout the war. He was never interned because he was over sixty-five years of age, but he did get regular visits (as did Archibald's firm) from the German *administrateur-provisoire*. As the German troops paraded daily up the Champs-Élysées, the Coudert lawyers and secretaries responded by going to the window and ostentatiously turning their backs on the occupiers.[46]

During the phony war, business remained good for at least one industry. People continued to go to the movies. From January through April 1940, Fox's sales in France were better than they had been for that period in 1939. But when the Germans entered France on May 10 and the Exodus began, business halted. Fox's films were evacuated for safekeeping to Rambouillet (50 km outside of Paris), but the facility was burned down, and five thousand kilograms of films were destroyed. True, they were films that had already been amortized, but it was a blow nonetheless. With the economy collapsing, Fox Europa, like other American companies and individuals, sought to renegotiate its rent. A French government decree passed on September 26, 1939, allowed renters to request reduced rents, given the circumstances, and the American embassy had submitted a specific request to the Ministry of Foreign Affairs that American citizens be able to benefit as well. (Under an earlier French rent law of 1933, the ministry had confirmed that Americans should be equal to French citizens before their landlords.) However, in January 1940, the ministry responded that war rent reductions only applied to those French citizens who were enrolled in the army; only those Americans who did likewise would be eligible. Nonetheless, Fox Europa requested a 75 percent rent decrease for a building it occupied in Lille, arguing that its economic situation had changed. The building manager could hardly contain his disdain. Surely, he wrote, such an American company, undoubtedly with "immense resources," could not be considered to be in difficult circumstances, as the law intended: "qui peut payer doit payer" (who can pay must pay). The lawyer handling Fox's affairs replied that the company was entirely cut off from the United States, its films now seized and unusable, but the managing company dug in its heels.[47]

Fox Europa also asked for a rent reduction on its Champs-Élysées premises, went to court over it, and eventually settled for a 50 percent decrease. But that was before the Germans requisitioned the premises, hauled off the files, and proposed a sublease, which Fox tried to object to on the grounds that its lease prohibited it from subleasing. In May 1941 the Germans took over part of the Fox premises until May 1942, when they took over all of the space, as they would soon do for all of France. At that point Fox Europa had to move, meaning a series of legal hassles: effecting a transfer of headquarters; determining how much rent was due the building owner (on the requisitioned and the non-requisitioned space, prorated over the number of days occupied by the Germans); figuring out how to take an option on renewing the Champs-Élysées lease that came due in 1943. In any case, at the Liberation it was the American army that occupied the premises.[48]

The definition of companies' nationality that was tricky for tax and image reasons during peacetime became a question of survival during the war. And the definition of enemy property shifted over time. When war was declared, Monsieur Guillo, the French manager of Scholl France, apparently thought it prudent to disassociate the company from the American embassy. He advised the embassy that Scholl Manufacturing Company (France) was French and not American. Mr. Scholl in Chicago, however, took umbrage and wrote directly to the State Department to insist that although Guillo was a sound practical businessman who had worked for the firm for a number of years, his analysis was flawed. All of the shares, with the exception of a few employees' shares, belonged to American citizens, and Scholl was eager to have the company come under the embassy's protection. By December, Guillo came around. He still insisted that as far as the public was concerned "our Company was and is still carrying out its transactions in a normal way like all the French firms." But, recognizing that the German authorities were starting to look into enemy shareholding, he admitted, "I think that now the protection of the U.S.A. Embassy would be useful."[49] That was probably true, but only until late 1941.

When the United States entered the war, subsidiaries had a renewed interest in proving how French they were. Lawyers helped Frenchify and "Aryanize" American companies, as they had British and Jewish ones since the beginning of the war. Presigned, undated share transfer forms proved invaluable for the process of retroactively eliminating traces of American nationals from boards of directors, reappointing directors, and transferring shares from "enemies" to French lawyers, their relatives, or even trusted concierges, who all became the new board members of this legal fiction. As early as June 1941, one lawyer had advised his client that Americans should not be appointed as administrators of their French companies in case the United States entered the war or communications became impossible. A year later, after the United States had entered the war, he had to chastise the same client: "[I]t does not suffice that the Président Directeur Général be French for the company to be French, but at least two-thirds of the Board of Directors must be French. That is not your case, because you believed you had to re-elect American directors."[50] A subsequent meeting in October reelected only one of the Americans to the board.

After 1942, the lawyers had to advise their American clients on how to fill out German forms, including the *déclaration des biens ennemis*, declaration of enemy goods.

So the Porters, the Bates-Batchellers, and the Bricktops eventually went "home." The businesses stayed on. The American Chamber of Commerce in France kept a low profile, and the churches remained standing albeit empty of their usual parishioners. Companies turned their affairs over to their French managers or to straw men. They were obliged in any case to adapt to German strictures. From late 1941 to 1944, the Americans and their companies that stayed in France were not just eventual harbingers of a decried Americanization. They were downright alien enemies. But for the most part, the Americans of Paris were luckier than other immigrants. They had a place to go and the means to get there. And they returned to being Americans of New York or Americans of Kansas.

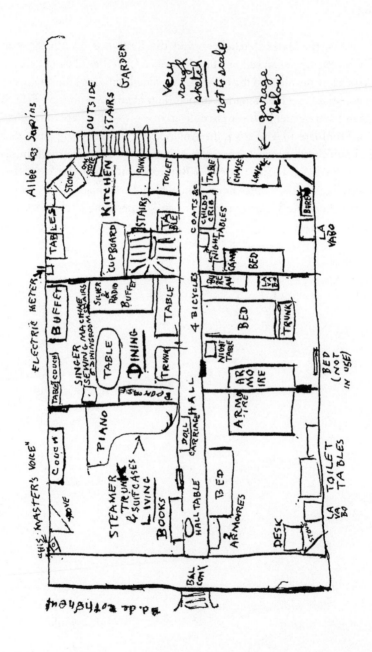

FIGURE 9 · John B. Sanders's sketch of his house and belongings accompanying his request for a US Protection Certificate (1940).

CONCLUSION

Dear Sir [to the US consulate in Paris],

. . . I wish to visit France this summer and have only enough money to get there and back, and that in the cheapest possible way. Since I have no available financial resources except passage money, unless you are kind enough and in a position to provide me with some job, any kind, by which I can earn my board and room, I shall be forced to forego the realization of my fondest dream, to use a cliché, since it best expresses the sentiments with which I have looked forward to a trip to that country où on parle "La Plus Belle Langue du Monde."

I am a pre-medical student at the University of Chicago and have studied French, both in high school and at the university, and can both read and speak it slightly. At the end of the present quarter I shall have finished my second year. I am 20 years old, about five foot seven, and weigh about 125 pounds. Without boasting, and purely in order that you may know more about me, I may say that I have not done badly there, having received at the end of my first year a $200 scholarship on the basis of the comprehensive examinations (and need, I presume).

If I have bored you by this much overlong letter ascribe it to my enthusiasm and forgive me. If my cause is not hopeless tell me quickly and let me feel light with joy; but if there is no hope, tell me that as quickly, too, so that I may recover from the blow in time to enjoy what is left of the hollow pleasure you will have made my summer with your sad words.

Amen,

Elliott A. Kaplan[1]

It was June 1938, and young Kaplan wanted to start out just as many Americans were about to head home. But Kaplan's letter attests to an enthusiasm that would never wane. The war signaled the end of an era, but it was an era that was an important preview of more to come. Eager students and hopeful writers would pick up the "continual pilgrimage," as Christopher Sawyer-Lauçanno has called it, and continue to arrive after World War II.[2] And so would, in even greater numbers, more businessmen.

BEING AMERICANS OF PARIS

From 1880 to 1940 the cosmopolitan Americans à la Mrs. Mackay and Win-naretta Singer had given way before a more heterogeneous "elite" consisting of bankers and lawyers, manufacturers' representatives, their wives, and former soldiers turned jazzmen, spare parts salesmen, or sports entrepreneurs. Parallel to the individual expatriate writers and artists, the Right Bank Americans of the early twentieth century created a fulsome community, complete with impressive edifices and bowling alleys for the spiritual and social needs of their members. True, they did not perhaps have the panache of the raging heterosexuals like Hemingway and Miller or the lively lesbians such as Stein and Barney. The Right Bank women nonetheless represented in their own way one of the images of American women: independent in action and spirit. The Right Bank bankers fulfilled another French stereotype: that all Americans are rich. All in all, the Right Bank men and women represented a more familial, less bohemian Americanism, a harbinger of many Americans to come.

If the Americans of Paris were transnationals who nonetheless banded together and created a community stable in its institutions if more fluctuating in its actual members, how "American" were they? For the most part the Americans of Paris—or at least those who did not melt into the French wood-work—were identified and self-identified as such. Edith Wharton, Gertrude Stein, and others thought and wrote about America, signed in to the American Chamber of Commerce's Residential List, and lived their lives in France. Few Americans sought (or were able) to "pass," even when they attracted French honors or even if they were considered "a Frenchman of American origin," as Proust praised Walter Berry, lawyer, banker, close friend of Edith Wharton, francophone and francophile president of the American Chamber of Commerce.[3] From the women of the DAR to the men of the American Legion and the American Chamber of Commerce, "America" was defined by Americans abroad as the front porch or waffles but also as hardworking businessmen or wreath-laying philanthropists providing a model of feminine cooperation. These "American" characteristics took on sharper relief in the context of being abroad. Coming together to create community and ward off bouts of home-sickness, the Americans in Paris re-created an image of America for themselves but also clearly with two other audiences in mind: the French and the skeptical Americans back home. With the former they often wore their Americanness up front, sometimes sanctimoniously, bringing new models to the natives. With the latter, whether American grandmothers of barely bilingual grandchildren or Uncle Sam, their tone was more defensive than defiant.

Did the Americanness of the Americans of Paris affect the decried Americanization of Paris? Philanthropists or librarians could be missionaries of a secular sort. Many of the businessmen exuded unabashed economic patriotism, using the flag as a form of identity. The America of the American businessmen in France was both a prideful patriotism and a marketing mechanism. Home was the up-and-coming economic power of the century flexing its muscle in its early decades. But the America of the American Chamber of Commerce was more or less salient depending on the audience. The ACC represented American businessmen to the French government, but they were expatriates in the eyes of many at home. Perhaps their business clubs embody the relative autonomy of the economic sphere. They maneuvered between French and American laws, customs, and practices and fought off protectionists on both sides of the Atlantic. In many ways they formed their own committee for the ruling of their affairs. Their culture and their capitalism were at times in tension in the context of incipient twentieth-century globalization.

In salon settings, in lawyers' offices, or whining at the consulate, Americans abroad have moved among conflicting loyalties. To use Albert Hirschmann's famous triad: exit, voice, and loyalty have been combined in different ways by different Americans overseas. If the literary expatriates combined exit and protest (voice), the businessmen combined exit and loyalty, even if that loyalty—to American goods or simply to their own goods—could exasperate the French and sometimes lead to a complicated relationship with their own government. Some interacted with the locals as unremitting "Americanizers" bringing their own vision of modernity to the world, trying to "seduce the French" or take part in "spreading the American dream," consciously carrying their capital and their culture with them.[4] Others may have represented their Americanness abroad in spite of themselves.

PLUS ÇA CHANGE—POSTWAR EPILOGUE

As the *New York Times* announced it on September 2, 1944, "Gertrude Stein Found; Just Finishing a Book." Eric Sevareid reported that Stein and Toklas, both a little thinner, had been found safe at her "château" in southeastern France. He quoted her as saying that "this war is far more logical than the last war and much more interesting."[5]

By the fall of 1944, the State Department began encouraging and helping organize the return of American businessmen to France. It issued new guidelines for obtaining passports. In July of the following year the American Chamber of Commerce in France pitched in with its own Special Committee on Post-war

Problems to help resolve some of the issues still apparent a year after the end of the Occupation.[6] By 1962, there were once again more Americans in France than in any other country overseas: over sixty-nine thousand.[7]

Neither the Depression nor World War II put a halt to the eastward migration. People came back after the war, some to get their belongings, others to resume where they had left off. Possessions were scattered or in a pitiful state. Carpets had disappeared, furniture had been damaged or lost; warehouse owners were sued, and they in turn pressed charges against certain indelicate employees. Journalist Arthur K. Train, who had written to the embassy from New York in July 1940 asking for protection of his property, had entrusted his charming ivy-covered French country house in Dannemois, outside of Paris, to a real estate agency and to the colorful Russian caretaker, Mr. Nazaroff. When Train later returned, he finally sold the property to the Zubers and then they to the Bouviers. By the time I visited, Nazaroff was but a vivid memory. The real estate agency had, in the meantime, done a lucrative business during the war looking after people's property.[8]

The war postscripts were varied. Thanks to the combined talents of George Gershwin and Gene Kelly, the image of a former soldier falling in love with a French girl was popularized in the 1951 film *An American in Paris* (Gershwin's score dated to 1928). In the end Jerry Mulligan gets his French girlfriend, Lise Bouvier, and he presumably settles with her in the French capital. True, he is a poor aspiring painter rather than an American businessman at work—the latter being rarely depicted in guidebooks or fiction. In real postwar Paris, Sylvia Beach never reopened Shakespeare and Company; she donated her collection to the American Library in Paris and later let George Whitman take over the bookshop's name. After the war Arthur Moulton married for a third time, and his château was sold in 1951 to the French national teachers' insurance group (MGEN); to this day it serves as a psychiatric rehabilitation center for education professionals. In 1986, Welles Bosworth's by now run-down building of the American Students' and Artists' Center closed and was replaced by the Fondation Cartier for contemporary art. The institution that had become the American Center for Students and Artists (shedding the apostrophes that had undoubtedly mystified the French) had become more popular with French than American students after the war, and it moved into a fancy new Frank Gehry building across the Seine in 1994. However, shortly thereafter, beset by financial and other difficulties, the center closed.[9] And after almost a century of setting up *sociétés anonymes* and doing so many mergers and acquisitions, Archibald's and then Coudert's law firms were merged out of existence by the turn of the twenty-first century.

Other organizations were transformed in different ways, some with *Sturm und Drang*, others with lulls and spurts. Pershing Hall is no longer (the building has become a luxury boutique hotel), although the American Legion Paris Post no. 1 was rejuvenated by World War II war veterans. The interwar American Women's Club of Paris metamorphosed after World War II into the American Women's Group (founded in 1949), joined over a decade later by the Association of American Wives of Europeans, catering especially to bicultural couples. FAWCO is still present, as is the Rochambeau DAR chapter. American university alumni clubs in France abound; at last count there were 145 of them.[10] And the old stalwarts are still going strong: the American Church, the American Cathedral Church of the Holy Trinity, the American Chamber of Commerce in France, the American Club, the American Hospital, and the American Library in Paris. And they all have French members, readers, doctors, or patients. Last but hardly least, the American Dental Club of Paris still exists, bringing better smiles to all.

The early American colony in Paris set the stage for the post–World War II expansion. With the Normandy landings and the arrival of the GIs, there were more love stories (and divorces) to follow.[11] When Phyllis Michaux was told in 1946 by a US counselor officer that if she married her French fiancé as intended she would lose her US citizenship, it only spurred her to spend the next half-century in France fighting for the rights of overseas Americans.[12] When she was fêted in 2011 at the fiftieth anniversary of the Association of American Wives of Europeans, women of all ages came up to her to thank her for all she had done for them and their children. Above all, the Marshall Plan encouraged the next wave of American businessmen to seek out the European frontier. By the end of the twentieth century, brochures for expats abounded, with titles such as *Expatriates Employment Handbook: Seeing the World and Getting Paid for It!* and *The Complete Guide to International Jobs and Careers: Your Passport to a World of Exciting and Exotic Employment.*[13]

The paradoxes are many. The early Americans of Paris were what we now call transnationals. They were highly mobile. Yet they created a community, like other immigrant groups. At the same time, there were many individuals who undoubtedly never set foot in any of the American institutions in town— like many other immigrants and *their* organizations. The "other" Americans in Paris had money and means, although there were those with limited income if not downright poor scattered among the businessmen and lawyers. The bankers, lawyers, socialites, and dentists created "American" institutions—all of which eventually had French members. Above all, while many came to live out their own French *rêve*, others came explicitly to spread the American dream.

It would be hard to argue that their presence did not leave an impact on the French capital. Is this perhaps the last lesson of elite migration? It can partake in a reverse assimilation, although everyone continues to argue about who is Americanizing or Frenchifying whom.

The legend of the café-poets has serious competition from the pinstriped salesmen. The early twentieth-century Americans of Paris set the stage for the variegated lot of post-1945 economic, cultural, and social crossings that were to follow. There are surely fewer American countesses in the twenty-first century than in the first half of the twentieth, but there are plenty of businessmen and still the occasional lost soul. When *Le Monde* featured an article in 2009 about a forty-three-year-old American woman sleeping on the streets for lack of funds to return home, French eyebrows were once again raised in amazement at the notion of a penniless American. The American Aid Society, founded in 1922, just sighed and assured everyone that it was still, alas, in business, catering to wayward youth and improvident tourists.[14]

A C K N O W L E D G M E N T S

This book was conceived between a boat ride on the Seine and a plunge into the archives. In 1982 the Law Offices of S. G. Archibald celebrated its seventy-fifth anniversary with a Seine glide on a bateau-mouche, *Ma Normandie.* I was working there part time as a secretary and bill-writer while finishing my dissertation and first book. (In good time-sheet mode, one lawyer asked how many hours it took me to write that book . . .) The recognition of the firm's long history prompted it to commission me to write its history. Like much public history, the first version ended up in a drawer. Not celebratory enough? Too interested in everything from the clients to the lawyers to the modernization of the secretarial pool? But the project led me to the firm's old client registers and the realization that the history of "Americanization" is a long one, if one looks at the ways in which American firms had been setting up in France since the beginning of the twentieth century.

Over a decade later, I had long left Archibald to become a practicing historian, and Archibald had by then left its Haussmanian headquarters on the avenue de Messine after merging with Arthur Anderson. I approached my old friend Ruth Darnaud, Archibald archivist, about getting back into the archives, and the law firm in turn asked me to prepare a more complete version of its history. No time like a merger to try to shore up the troops with a look at the past. Shortly after that version was complete, with a final chapter on the synergies of the law and accounting fields, Anderson got caught in the Enron scandal. And the synergies of internationalism brought the entire worldwide structure down like a house of cards. The Archibald gang—and alas, the archives—have long since dispersed, but secretaries and lawyers still meet for the occasional retirement party, and I have my boxfuls of notes telling the tale of American expansion into France from the unique vantage point of the lawyers who helped individuals and companies settle in.

Many thanks, then, to Ruth and to Sandrine Karauc, who patiently called up box after box of files for me, as thrilled as I to find a letter from Edith Wharton lurking in the cache. Other American institutions in Paris also generously let me sit for days in their offices, with photocopying privileges to boot: the American Cathedral (special thanks to Joanne Dauphin), the American Chamber of Commerce (thanks to Oliver Griffith, Michelle Barton, and Philippe Rochefort). Special thanks also go to Ellen Hampton for lending me the old DAR minutes.

But this was a project happily transnational in itself. No history of the "other" Americans in Paris would have been complete without the invaluable State Department records at the National Archives and Records Administration facility in College Park, Maryland. The consular records and protection of citizen files had me glued to the center's comfortable chairs between bouts of laughter at some of the Americans' shenanigans in Paris and the occasional emotional tear (when I discovered my husband's family's country house among the files). My thanks to the staff, who always impressed me with their "ma'am" politeness, reminding me that Maryland is not the Midwest.

After research, writing: lonelier and more anxiety producing. How to thank my two most faithful and encouraging readers, Phyllis Michaux, doyenne of *Américaines* in Paris, ever urging me on, and Alice Kaplan, regaling me with her own stories of Jackie, Angela, and Susan, not to mention Pierre Bouvier, stoic over my stubborn research into "Americanization." John Merriman and Rosemary Wakeman, the no-longer-anonymous "Reader 1" and "Reader 2," gave thoughtful and encouraging suggestions, while Donna Gabaccia gave me a perceptive US immigration historian's view. Thanks too to Emily Rosenberg, who encouraged me with my overly long but key chapter 5. More diffuse but ongoing intellectual support has come from long-running conversations with other immigration historians, including Dorothee Schneider, Leslie Page Moch, and the much-missed Nora Faires. Carrie Landfried—thanks again!—spent hours counting data from my archaic 3×5 note cards, and Cynthia Cardona and Susan Perlman helped out just when I needed it.

Last but not least, I have been sustained in my endeavors by lunches with my Archibald friends Salli Swartz and Kathie Claret. They agreed to read a historian's take on their trade, but as the classic disclaimer goes, any possible errors of fact or judgment remain mine and mine alone.

A longer version of chapter 2 was published as "Americans Abroad and the Uses of Citizenship: Paris, 1914–1940," *Journal of American Ethnic History* 31, no. 3 (Spring 2012): 5–32. It won the Immigration and Ethnic History Society's Carlton C. Qualey Memorial Article Award.

NOTES

A full bibliography may be accessed at http://press.uchicago.edu/green/green_bibliography.pdf.

INTRODUCTION

1. Theodore Stanton, ed., *Mr. Whitelaw Reid in France, 1889–1892: The Farewell Dinner to the United States Minister, Paris, March 24, 1892* (Paris: Brentano's, n.d. [1892]), 22.

2. For two recent overviews, see Adam Gopnik, ed., *Americans in Paris: A Literary Anthology* (New York: Library of America, 2004); David McCullough, *The Greater Journey: Americans in Paris* (New York: Simon and Schuster, 2011).

3. Warren Susman estimated that (only) about one-tenth of the permanent Americans in interwar Paris were intellectuals, writers, and artists. Warren Irving Susman, "Pilgrimage to Paris: The Backgrounds of American Expatriation, 1920–1934," PhD thesis, University of Wisconsin, 1957, 205, 180. On the recent interest in internationalizing American history, see, e.g., Thomas Bender, ed., *Rethinking American History in a Global Age* (Berkeley: University of California Press, 2002); Akira Iriye, *Cultural Internationalism and World Order* (Baltimore: Johns Hopkins University Press, 1997); "The Nation and Beyond," special issue of *Journal of American History*, 86, no. 3 (December 1999); Daniel Rodgers, *Atlantic Crossings: Social Politics in a Progressive Age* (Cambridge, MA: Harvard University Press, 1998); Ian Tyrrell, *Transnational Nation: U.S. History in Global Perspective since 1789* (Houndmills, Basingstoke, UK: Palgrave Macmillan, 2007). Cf. Walter LaFeber's critique "The United States and Europe in an Age of American Unilateralism," in R. Laurence Moore and Maurizio Vaudagna, eds., *The American Century in Europe* (Ithaca, NY: Cornell University Press, 2003), 25–46, 45n4.

4. William Schell Jr., *Integral Outsiders: The American Colony in Mexico City, 1876–1911* (Wilmington, DE: SR Books, 2001); Eileen Scully, *Bargaining with the State from Afar: American Citizenship in Treaty Port China, 1844–1942* (New York: Columbia University Press, 2001); cf. Erik Cohen, "Expatriate Communities," special issue of *Current Sociology* 24, no. 3 (1977).

5. See, however, Brooke Blower's evocative *Becoming Americans in Paris: Transatlantic Politics and Culture between the World Wars* (New York: Oxford University Press, 2011).

6. Susman, "Pilgrimage to Paris," 180; Frank Costigliola, *Awkward Dominion: American Political, Economic, and Cultural Relations with Europe, 1919-1933* (Ithaca, NY: Cornell University Press, 1984), 169, 174-76.

7. Eric Sevareid, *Not So Wild a Dream* (orig. 1940; New York: Atheneum, 1976), 11; Susman, "Pilgrimage to Paris," 178, 187. See also Rodgers, *Atlantic Crossings,* chap. 9.

8. Edmond Goncourt and Jules Goncourt, January 16, 1867, entry, in *Journal*, vol. 2 (Paris: Robert Laffont Bouquins, 1956), 64; Charles Baudelaire, "Méthode de critique de l'idée moderne du progrès appliquée aux Beaux-Arts, Déplacement de la vitalité," *Le Pays*, May 26, 1855, reprinted in Baudelaire, *Curiosités esthétiques* (Paris: Classiques Garnier, 1999), 218.

9. *Times*, quoted in the *Oxford English Dictionary*, 2nd ed., 1989.

10. Matthew 16:26. William Thomas Stead, *The Americanization of the World* (New York: H. Markley, 1901), 164.

11. Gertrude Stein, *Paris France* (orig. 1940; New York: Liveright, 1970), 52, 114.

12. Costigliola, *Awkward Dominion*, 167, 141; Jacqueline Tavernier-Courbin, "E. Hemingway et le clan des expatriés américains à Paris," *Canadian Review of American Studies* 8, no. 2 (Fall 1977): 129.

13. Malcolm Cowley, *Exile's Return: A Literary Odyssey of the 1920s* (orig. 1934; New York: Viking Compass, 1956), 62; Henry R. Luce, "The American Century," *Life Magazine*, February 17, 1941, reprinted in *Diplomatic History* 23, no. 2 (Spring 1999): 159-71; Gertrude Stein, *The Autobiography of Alice B. Toklas* (orig. 1933; New York: Vintage Books, 1990), 78.

14. The debate over Americanization—when it happened, and how, through American push or receptors' pull, through supply or demand—has been the object of a vigorous literature from LaFeber on. Walter LaFeber, *The New Empire: An Interpretation of American Expansion, 1860-1898* (orig. 1963; Ithaca, NY: Cornell University Press, 1988); "The American Century: A Roundtable," part 1, *Diplomatic History* 23, no. 2 (Spring 1999): 157-370; part 2, *Diplomatic History* 23, no. 3 (Summer 1999): 391-537; Costigliola, *Awkward Dominion*; Alfred E. Eckes Jr. and Thomas W. Zeiler, *Globalization and the American Century* (New York: Cambridge University Press, 2003); Heide Fehrenbach and Uta G. Poiger, eds., *Transactions, Transgressions, Transformations: American Culture in Western Europe and Japan* (New York: Berghahn Books, 2000); Victoria de Grazia, *Irresistible Empire: America's Advance through 20th-Century Europe* (Cambridge, MA: Harvard University Press, 2005); Joan Hoff-Wilson, *American Business and Foreign Policy, 1920-1933* (Lexington: University Press of Kentucky, 1971); Rob Kroes, *If You've Seen One, You've Seen the Mall: Europeans and American Mass Culture* (Urbana: University of Illinois Press, 1996); Richard Kuisel, *Seducing the French: The Dilemma of Americanization* (Berkeley: University of California Press, 1993); Ernest R. May, *Imperial Democracy: The Emergence of America as a Great Power* (New York: Harper Torchbooks, 1961); Mary Nolan, *Visions of Modernity: American Business and the Modernization of Germany* (New York: Oxford University Press, 1994); Richard Pells, *Not Like Us: How Europeans Have Loved, Hated, and Transformed American Culture since World War II* (New York: Basic Books, 1997); Philippe Roger, *The American Enemy: A Story of French Anti-Americanism* (Chicago: University of Chicago Press, 2005); Emily Rosenberg, *Spreading the American Dream: American Economic and*

Cultural Expansion, 1890–1945 (New York: Hill and Wang, 1982); Donald White, *The American Century* (New Haven, CT: Yale University Press, 1996); Jonathan Zeitlin and Gary Herrigel, eds., *Americanization and Its Limits: Reworking US Technology and Management in Post-war Europe and Japan* (Oxford: Oxford University Press, 2000); Olivier Zunz, *Why the American Century?* (Chicago: University of Chicago Press, 1998).

15. Kuisel, *Seducing the French*; Brian A. McKenzie, *Remaking France: Americanization, Public Diplomacy, and the Marshall Plan* (New York: Berghahn Books, 2005); Irwin M. Wall, *The United States and the Making of Postwar France, 1945–1954* (New York: Cambridge University Press, 1991).

16. Rosenberg, *Spreading the American Dream*; Paul A. Kramer, "Power and Connection: Imperial Histories of the United States in the World," *American Historical Review* 116, no. 5 (December 2011): 1348–91.

17. Denise Artaud, "La question des dettes interalliées et la reconstruction de l'Europe," 2 vols., doctoral diss., Lille, 1978; André Kaspi, *Le temps des Américains: Le concours américain à la France en 1917–1918* (Paris: Université de Paris I, 1976); Dominique Barjot, Isabelle Lescent-Giles, and Marc de Ferrière Le Vayer, eds., *L'Américanisation en Europe au XXe siècle: Economie, culture, politique*, vol. 1 (Lille: Centre de Recherche sur l'Histoire de l'Europe du Nord-Ouest, Université de Lille 3, 2002).

18. Eckes and Zeiler, *Globalization and the American Century*, chaps. 1–3; Jacques Portes, *Buffalo Bill* (Paris: Fayard, 2002), chap. 7; Robert W. Rydell and Rob Kroes, *Buffalo Bill in Bologna: The Americanization of the World, 1869–1922* (Chicago: University of Chicago Press, 2005).

19. Costigliola, *Awkward Dominion*; De Grazia, *Irresistible Empire*.

20. Hoff-Wilson, *American Business*.

21. Cf. Mira Wilkins, *The Maturing of Multinational Enterprise: American Business Abroad from 1914 to 1970* (Cambridge, MA: Harvard University Press, 1974).

22. Kramer, "Power and Connection," esp. 1374–78. Costigliola, *Awkward Dominion*, 167, 141, suggested three decades ago that the origin of America's "informal economic empire" could be found with the early economic and cultural sojourners. William H. Sewell Jr. has called for a "social and cultural history of capitalism," cited in "Reports and Correspondence," *International Labor and Working-Class History* 51 (Spring 1997): 165. Besides C. Wright Mills's classic *Power Elite*, see, e.g., Sven Beckert, *The Monied Metropolis: New York City and the Consolidation of the American Bourgeoisie, 1850–1896* (Cambridge: Cambridge University Press, 2001); Steve Fraser and Gary Gerstle, eds., *Ruling America: A History of Wealth and Power in a Democracy* (Cambridge, MA: Harvard University Press, 2005); Frederic C. Jaher, *The Urban Establishment: Upper Strata in Boston, New York, Charleston, Chicago and Los Angeles* (Urbana: University of Illinois Press, 1982).

23. Alain Tarrius with Lamia Missaoui, *Les nouveaux cosmopolitains: Mobilités, identités, territoires* (La Tour-d'Aigues, France: Éd. de l'Aube, 2000), 253.

24. Jacqueline Lindenfeld and Gabrielle Varro use the term "Fortunate Immigrants" in "Language Maintenance among 'Fortunate Immigrants': The French in the United States and Americans in France," *International Journal of the Sociology of Language*, no. 189 (2008): 115–31.

25. Cohen, "Expatriate Communities"; Sheila Croucher, *The Other Side of the Fence: American Migrants in Mexico* (Austin: University of Texas Press, 2009); Anne-Meike Fechter and

Katie Walsh, eds., special issue "Examining 'Expatriate' Continuities: Postcolonial Approaches to Mobile Professionals," *Journal of Ethnic and Migration Studies* 36, no. 8 (September 2010); Allan M. Findlay, "Skilled Transients: The Invisible Phenomenon?" in *The Cambridge Survey of World Migration*, ed. Robin Cohen (Cambridge: Cambridge University Press, 1995), 515–22; Aihwa Ong, *Flexible Citizenship: The Cultural Logics of Transnationality* (Durham, NC: Duke University Press, 1999); Saskia Sassen, *Globalization and Its Discontents: Essays on the New Mobility of People and Money* (New York: New Press, 1999); Tarrius, *Les nouveaux cosmopolitains*; Alain Tarrius, *Les fourmis d'Europe: Migrants riches, migrants pauvres et nouvelles villes internationales* (Paris: L'Harmattan, 1992); Anne-Catherine Wagner, *Les nouvelles élites de la mondialisation: Une immigration dorée en France* (Paris: Presses Universitaires de France, 1998).

26. Donna R. Gabaccia, *Foreign Relations: American Immigration in Global Perspective* (Princeton, NJ: Princeton University Press, 2012), 77–92; Elihu Root, "The Basis of Protection to Citizens Residing Abroad," *American Journal of International Law* 4 (1910): 517, 518.

27. Yet see Nicole Fouché, "L'American Chamber of Commerce of Paris (1894–1919), est-elle aussi une institution ethnique?" *Bulletin du CENA-EHESS*, no. 5 (February 1999): 51–78.

28. Nancy L. Green, "Tocqueville, Comparative History and Immigration in Two Democracies," *French Politics, Culture and Society* 26, no. 2 (Summer 2008): 1–12.

29. *Résultats statistiques du recensement général de la population*, 1931, vol. 2, 1; 1936, vol. 2, 1; Costigliola, *Awkward Dominion*, 173; article on Hull in *Chicago Tribune European Edition*. Americans abroad are notoriously difficult to count. The State Department estimates that over six million citizens live abroad today, first and foremost in the Western Hemisphere (2.5 million, mostly Mexico and Canada), with over 1.5 million in Europe. www.aaro.org/about-aaro/6m-americans-abroad (accessed August 18, 2012). See also Karen M. Mills, *Americans Overseas in U.S. Censuses*, Technical Paper 62 (Washington, DC: US Department of Commerce, Bureau of the Census, 1993), 3–4, 43, 45; Robert Warren and Ellen Percy Kraly, "The Elusive Exodus: Emigration from the United States," *Population Trends and Public Policy, Occasional Papers*, no. 8 (March 1985): 5.

30. "South American Colony Is Richest in Paris," *Chicago Tribune European Edition*, February 3, 1925, 3. Joanne Vajda, "Paris: Rendez-vous Cosmopolite; Du voyage élitaire à l'industrie touristique, 1855–1937," doctoral thesis, EHESS, 2005.

31. Harvey Levenstein, *Seductive Journey: American Tourists in France from Jefferson to the Jazz Age* (Chicago: University of Chicago Press, 1998), and *We'll Always Have Paris: American Tourists in France since 1930* (Chicago: University of Chicago Press, 2004); Christopher Endy, *Cold War Holidays: American Tourism in France* (Chapel Hill: University of North Carolina Press, 2004); Blower, *Becoming Americans*.

32. Henry James, "Americans Abroad," *The Nation*, October 3, 1878, in James, *Collected Travel Writings: Great Britain and America* (New York: Library of America, 1993), 786–92.

33. Albert Sutliffe, *The Americans in Paris* (Paris: Author, 1887), 53.

34. Alex Small, "Why Americans Leave Home and Settle Down Permanently in Europe," *Chicago Tribune European Edition*, July 10, 1930; Frank Ward O'Malley, cited in William G. Bailey, ed., *Americans in Paris, 1900–1930: A Selected, Annotated Bibliography* (Westport, CT: Greenwood, 1989), xiii.

35. Tryphosa Bates-Batcheller, *France in Sunshine and Shadow* (New York: Brentano's, 1944), 18.

36. "32,000 Paris Bars Listed," *New York Times*, November 25, 1927.

37. Colonel T. Bentley Mott, *Myron T. Herrick, Friend of France: An Autobiographical Biography* (Garden City, NY: Doubleday, Doran, 1929), 289–91; Blower, *Becoming Americans*, chaps. 3 (Sacco-Vanzetti) and 5 (Legionnaires), esp. 98, 106, 120–21; http://www.legion.org/library/3409/1927-national-convention-paris (accessed July 27, 2012); Moshik Temkin, *The Sacco-Vanzetti Affair: America on Trial* (New Haven, CT: Yale University Press, 2009), esp. chap. 3, 101–40.

38. Samuel Putnam, *Paris Was Our Mistress: Memoirs of a Lost and Found Generation* (New York: Viking, 1947), 17, 18.

39. Michael de Cossart, *Une Américaine à Paris: La Princesse Edmond de Polignac et son salon, 1865–1943* (Paris: Plon, 1979), 111; Sylvia Kahan, *Music's Modern Muse: A Life of Winnaretta Singer, Princesse de Polignac* (Rochester, NY: University of Rochester Press, 2003). She created the Fondation Singer-Polignac to support the arts in 1928.

40. *Journal of the American Dental Club of Paris* 3, no. 5 (March 1935): 7.

41. Letter, S .G. Archibald to John G. Archibald, April 30, 1945, VD39, Archives 631, Mr. S. G. Archibald (June 1945), Law Offices of S. G. Archibald Archives, Paris.

42. E-mail to author, April 1, 2006. See Nora Faires, "'Talented and Charming Strangers from Across the Line': Gendered Nationalism, Class Privilege, and the American Women's Club of Calgary," in *One Step over the Line: Toward a History of Women in the North American Wests*, ed. Elizabeth Jameson and Sheila McManus (Edmonton: University of Alberta Press, 2008), 261–92.

CHAPTER 1

1. Alexis de Tocqueville, *Democracy in America*, trans. Arthur Goldhammer (orig. 1835, 1840; New York: Penguin, Library of America, 2004), vol. 2, part 2, chap. 7, 604.

2. See chapter 7 below.

3. Guillaume de Bertier de Sauvigny, *La France et les Français vus par les voyageurs américains, 1814–1848*, 2 vols. (Paris: Flammarion, 1982); Robert C. L. Scott, "American Travellers in France, 1830–1860: A Study of Some American Ideas against a European Background," PhD diss., Yale University, 1940; Philip Katz, *From Appomattox to Montmartre: Americans and the Paris Commune* (Cambridge, MA: Harvard University Press, 1998)—for a lively view of Americans in Paris at the time of the Paris Commune, see esp. chaps. 2 and 3.

4. 1814–48: Bertier de Sauvigny, *France et les Français*, 1:11, 17, 19, 21; ca. 1853: Scott, "American Travellers in France," 3. See also René Rémond, *Les États-Unis devant l'opinion française, 1815–1852*, 2 vols. (Paris: Armand Colin, 1962), 1:214–31.

5. Gerald Carson, *The Dentist and the Empress: The Adventures of Dr. Tom Evans in Gas-Lit Paris* (Boston: Houghton Mifflin, 1983), 174; Edward A. Crane, ed., *The Memoirs of Dr. Thomas W. Evans: Recollections of the Second French Empire* (London: T. Fisher Unwin, 1905).

6. Carson, *The Dentist and the Empress*, 110; Thomas W. Evans [US commissioner and member of the jury, Class XI], *Report on Ambulance and Sanitary Materiel, Class XI, Group II,*

Paris Exposition, 1867 (Paris: E. Brière, 1867), and "An Account of the Formation of the American International Sanitary Committee of Paris, Together with the History of the American Ambulance," in Evans, *History of the American Ambulance Established in Paris during the Siege of 1870–1871* (London: Sampson Low, Marston, Low and Searle, 1873).

7. *St. Paul Pioneer Press*, September 28, 1897, cited in Carson, *The Dentist and the Empress*, 174 (whiskers). On Laurent: Carson, 151–59, 175; Gabrielle Houbre, *Le livre des courtisanes: Archives secrètes de la police des mœurs, 1861–1876* (Paris: Tallandier, 2006), 121, 540; cf. Rosemary Lloyd, *Mallarmé: The Poet and His Circle* (Ithaca, NY: Cornell University Press, 2005), 157.

8. Katz, *From Appomattox to Montmartre*, 35.

9. Ibid., 26 (5,000); *American Register*, January 9 through April 30, 1904 (after which the masthead changed) (30,000).

10. Richard Harding Davis, *About Paris* (New York: Harper and Brothers, 1895), 190.

11. Ellin Berlin, *Silver Platter* (Garden City, NY: Doubleday, 1957); my telephone interviews with her great-granddaughter Linda Berlin Emmett, June 30, July 1, September 30, 2003.

12. Cited in Foster Rhea Dulles, "A Historical View of Americans Abroad," *Annals of the American Academy of Political and Social Science* 368 (1966): 11–20, 14.

13. Harvey Levenstein, *Seductive Journey: American Tourists in France from Jefferson to the Jazz Age* (Chicago: University of Chicago Press, 1998), part 4. Cf. Mark Meigs, *Optimism at Armageddon: Voices of American Participants in the First World War* (Houndmills, Basingstoke, UK: Macmillan, 1997).

14. 100,000, 1906: *American Hospital of Paris, 1906–2006: A Century of Adventure* (Paris: Le Cherche Midi, [2006]), 17, 36; and Nicole Fouché, *Le mouvement perpétuel: Histoire de l'Hôpital Américain de Paris des origines à nos jours* (Toulouse: Érès, 1991), 18. 300,000, interwar: Warren Irving Susman, "Pilgrimage to Paris: The Backgrounds of American Expatriation, 1920–1934," PhD thesis, University of Wisconsin, 1957, 26n71.

15. Belgians (85,000), Italians (81,000), Russians (42,000), Swiss (42,000), and British (38,000). *Chicago Tribune European Edition* (hereafter *CTEE*), November 16, 1923, 2, reporting on the city's figures; Americans thus composed 6.7% of the total of 478,000 foreigners in the city. National figure: *Résultats statistiques du recensement générale de la population, 1926*, vol. 1, pt. 5, p. 39, and *1946*, vol. 2, p. 348.

16. Candice Lewis Bredbenner, *A Nationality of Her Own: Women, Marriage, and the Law of Citizenship* (Berkeley: University of California Press, 1998), 225n75, citing "Americans Living Abroad," US Department of State press release 209 (September 26, 1933), 186–89. The French statistic was reported in Annex, American Consul in Paris to Secretary of State, February 19, 1934, 349.111, General Records of the Department of State, Decimal Files, Record Group 59 (hereafter RG59), 1930–1939, National Archives at College Park, MD (hereafter NACP).

17. Susman, "Pilgrimage to Paris," 165, citing the *CTEE*. The American Women's Club of Paris (hereafter AWCP) estimated that there were 30,000–40,000 Americans in Paris for a "short time" or "many years." AWCP, *Bulletin* 4, no. 2 (February 1926): 119. A *New York Times* article estimated 50,000: "American Divorces Not Numerous in Paris," February 4, 1926.

18. Berlin, *Silver Platter*, 393 (a week away); Albert Sutliffe, *The Americans in Paris, 1887* (Paris: Author, 1887), 14.

19. Susman, "Pilgrimage to Paris," 175; Jennifer D. Keene, *Doughboys, the Great War, and the Remaking of America* (Baltimore: Johns Hopkins University Press, 2001).

20. Susan Zeiger, *In Uncle Sam's Service: Women Workers with the American Expeditionary Force, 1917–1919* (Ithaca, NY: Cornell University Press, 1999), esp. chap. 3; Adriane Lentz-Smith, *Freedom Struggles: African Americans and World War I* (Cambridge, MA: Harvard University Press, 2009).

21. Mark Meigs, *Optimism at Armageddon: Voices of American Participants in the First World War* (Houndmills, Basingstoke, UK: Macmillan, 1997), 30, 33–34, 69, 86; Elihu Root, "The Basis of Protection to Citizens Residing Abroad," *American Journal of International Law* 4 (1910): 517–18 (vast armies).

22. Waverley Lewis Root, *The Paris Edition, 1927–1934* (orig. 1987; San Francisco: North Point, 1989), 161.

23. John Russell Young, *Around the World with General Grant*, 2 vols. (New York: American News, 1879), 1:136 (floating population); Sutliffe, *Americans in Paris*. On elite guidebooks, see Joanne Vajda, "Paris: Rendez-vous cosmopolite; Du voyage élitaire à l'industrie touristique, 1855–1937," doctoral thesis, École des Hautes Études en Sciences Sociales, 2005, 131–41.

24. Sutliffe, *Americans in Paris*, 62.

25. *Americans in France: A Directory* (Paris: American Chamber of Commerce, 1925–40) (hereafter ACC *Directory*).

26. Even though he told a French journalist that his one regret was that French musicians knew too little about American composers and conductors. "M. Alexandre Joukowski," *Paris-Presse*, May 6, 1930, 1; interview, Olga Gow, Paris.

27. Sutliffe, *Americans in Paris*, 56; cf. Erik Cohen, "Expatriate Communities," *Current Sociology* 24, no. 3 (1977): 47–54.

28. Young, *Around the World*, 1:142.

29. Sutliffe, *Americans in Paris*, 56–57 (gregarious), 58 (abuse), 57 (unity).

30. Bernhard Ragner, "The Permanent A.E.F.," *Saturday Evening Post*, November 11, 1939, 31.

31. Ernest Earnest, *Expatriates and Patriots: American Artists, Scholars, and Writers in Europe* (Durham, NC: Duke University Press, 1968), 269.

32. Gertrude Stein, *The Autobiography of Alice B. Toklas* (orig. 1933; New York: Vintage Books, 1990), 184 (so much better), 180 (americans).

33. Sheri Benstock, *Women of the Left Bank: Paris, 1900–1940* (Austin: University of Texas Press, 1986); Brassaï, *Henry Miller: The Paris Years*, trans. Timothy Bent (orig. 1975; New York: Arcade, 1995), 201–3; Claude McKay, *A Long Way from Home* (New York: Lee Furman, 1937), 249.

34. Harry Crosby, *Shadows of the Sun: The Diaries of Harry Crosby*, ed. Edward Germain (Santa Barbara, CA: Black Sparrow, 1977), 14–16, 106–7.

35. Peggy Guggenheim, *Out of This Century: Confessions of an Art Addict* (orig. 1946; New York: Universe Books, 1979), 49 (mother), 48 (Lysol).

36. Lisa Schlansker Kolosek, *The Invention of Chic* (New York: Thomas and Hudson, 2002), 89. Thanks to Mary Lynn Stewart for pointing out this book to me.

37. Al Laney, *Paris "Herald": The Incredible Newspaper* (New York: Appleton-Century, 1947), 152.

38. Charles F. Bove with Dana Lee Thomas, *A Paris Surgeon's Story* (Boston: Little, Brown, 1956), 41.

39. See especially Tyler Stovall, *Paris Noir: African Americans in the City of Light* (Boston: Houghton Mifflin, 1996); Michel Fabre, *From Harlem to Paris: Black American Writers in France, 1840–1980* (Urbana: University of Illinois Press, 1991); William A. Shack, *Harlem in Montmartre: A Paris Jazz Story between the Great Wars* (Berkeley: University of California Press, 2001).

40. Brooke Blower, *Becoming Americans in Paris: Transatlantic Politics and Culture between the World Wars* (New York: Oxford University Press, 2011), chap. 4.

41. Craig Lloyd, *Eugene Bullard: Black Expatriate in Jazz-Age Paris* (Athens: University of Georgia Press, 2000), 65–86; Stovall, *Paris Noir*, 14–15, 18; Fabre, *From Harlem to Paris*, 51; Lentz-Smith, *Freedom Struggles*, 103.

42. E.g., Levenstein, *Seductive Journey*, 263–66; Harvey Levenstein, *We'll Always Have Paris: American Tourists in France since 1930* (Chicago: University of Chicago Press, 2004), 50–53.

43. *CTEE*, January 2 and May 24 (Bullard's response), 1923; Lloyd, *Eugene Bullard*, 81–84.

44. Josephine Baker, in interview with Baker and James Baldwin by Henry Louis Gates Jr., *Southern Review* 21, no. 3 (July 1985): 597. The interview took place in 1973.

45. McKay, *Long Way from Home*, 272.

46. Keene, *Doughboys*, 126–31, 129. Also in Stovall, *Paris Noir*, 18; and Fabre, *From Harlem to Paris*, 52.

47. Lloyd, *Eugene Bullard*, 66, 86 (memo); Walter White, "The Color Line in Europe," *Annals of the American Academy of Political and Social Science* 140, no. 229 (November 1928): 331–36 (official statement).

48. Lloyd, *Eugene Bullard*, 69.

49. René Maran, "L'américanisation de la France," *Monde*, July 6, 1929, 11.

50. Tyler Stovall, "Colour-Blind France? Colonial Workers during the First World War," *Race and Class* 35, no. 2 (October–December 1993): 35–55; Stovall, *Paris Noir*, xiii (complex), 80; Fabre, *From Harlem to Paris*, 7, on the "multiple images" of France among American blacks; Lentz-Smith, *Freedom Struggles*, 108, 130.

51. William H. Ingram, ed., *Who's Who in Paris, Anglo-American Colony: A Biographical Dictionary of the Leading Members of the Anglo-American Colony of Paris* (Paris: American Register, 1905); Stovall, *Paris Noir*; Fabre, *From Harlem to Paris*.

52. Philippe Dewitte, *Les mouvements nègres en France, 1919–1939* (Paris: L'Harmattan, 1985).

53. Cited in Lloyd, *Eugene Bullard*, 39.

54. Stovall, *Paris Noir*, 151.

55. Fabre, *From Harlem to Paris*, 64–65 (Hughes); McKay, *Long Way from Home*, 277.

56. McKay, *Long Way from Home*, 243; see also Stovall, *Paris Noir*, 59; Fabre, *From Harlem to Paris*, 106.

57. Bennetta Jules-Rosette, *Josephine Baker in Art and Life: The Icon and the Image* (Urbana: University of Illinois Press, 2007).

58. McKay, *Long Way from Home*, 311, 314.

59. Stovall, *Paris Noir*, 46, 26.

60. Shack, *Harlem in Montmartre*, 79 (dandies); Ludovic Tournès, *New Orleans sur Seine: Histoire du Jazz en France* (Paris: Fayard, 1999); Bricktop with James Haskins, *Bricktop* (New York: Atheneum, 1983).

61. Minutes, Daughters of the American Revolution, Rochambeau chapter, Paris, February 22, 1937.

62. Erik Cohen, "Expatriate Communities," 15.

63. With the sole exception of Pamela Harriman, 1993–97.

64. GA R6—Rotary Club, Préfecture de Police Archives, Paris. For an incisive analysis of the Rotary Club's activities in France and elsewhere in Europe, see Victoria de Grazia, *Irresistible Empire: America's Advance through 20th-Century Europe* (Cambridge, MA: Harvard University Press, 2005), esp. 38, 42, 55, 60, 62, 74 on the Rotary in France. The YMCA of course also took in errant Americans. Ian Tyrrell, *Reforming the World: The Creation of America's Moral Empire* (Princeton, NJ: Princeton University Press, 2010). On philanthropic work in France, see chap. 7 below.

65. Reverend E. N. Kirk, in Joseph Wilson Cochran, *Friendly Adventurers: A Chronicle of the American Church of Paris* (Paris: Brentano's, 1931), 61.

66. There were apparently never enough interested American Jews in Paris to create a congregation until the late twentieth century. Meanwhile. American Catholics gravitated to St. Joseph's Anglophone church.

67. Cochran, *Friendly Adventurers*, 79–80 (undignified); ACC *Directory*, 1926, 12–13 (irrespective); Laney, *Paris "Herald,"* 146 (tony).

68. Hugh D. Ford, *The Left Bank Revisited: Selections from the Paris Tribune, 1917–1934* (University Park: Pennsylvania State University Press, 1972), 19–20.

69. Anna Julia Cooper, *L'attitude de la France à l'égard de l'esclavage pendant la Révolution* (Paris: L. Maretheux, 1925), translated with an introduction by Frances Richardson Keller as *Slavery and the French Revolutionists (1788–1805)* (Lewiston, NY: Edwin Mellen, 1988).

70. Louvella B. Mendenhall [pseud. Laura Mac Proud], *American Students' Census, Paris, 1903* (n.p., 1903), 22–25 (my calculations).

71. Martha Hannah, "French Women and American Men: 'Foreign' Students at the University of Paris, 1915–1925," *French Historical Studies* 22, no. 1 (Winter 1999): 93, 95 (re Durkheim), 104, 111.

72. Whitney Walton, *Internationalism, National Identities, and Study Abroad: France and the United States, 1890–1970* (Stanford, CA: Stanford University Press, 2010); cf. *For the 5,000 American Students in the Latin Quarter of Paris*, File "American Students' and Artists' Center," Box "Altar and Processional Crosses (1922–27) . . . Funeral and Memorial Services," American Pro-Cathedral of the Holy Trinity Archives, Paris; Fondation des États-Unis Archives, Paris, vol. 1, 1927–1930.

73. Carson, *Dentist and the Empress*, 170–71; [William W. Davenport], *The Story of Reid Hall: An Old House in Paris* (Paris: Reid Hall, n.d.), 13 (charm).

74. Report of the Work among Students to the Women's Auxiliary, May 9, 1928, Box "Women's Auxiliary—Misc. Reports 1927–1940," 6–11, American Pro-Cathedral of the Holy Trinity Archives, Paris.

75. W. S. Scott, *A Crusading Dean: An Era in the Life of the American Colony in Paris* (Langham, UK: Herald, 1967), 63, 74; Nelcya Delanoë, *Le Raspail Vert: L'American Center à Paris, 1934–1994* (Paris: Seghers, 1994), 41 (citing Jack Egle on refuge), 34, 44, 73, 210 (members).

76. Cochran, *Friendly Adventurers*, 179.

77. Correspondence, 1928, file "Bernard J. Lane," box "Gold Star Mother Pilgrimages, 1930–1931 . . . Mission Work," American Pro-Cathedral of the Holy Trinity Archives, Paris.

78. Memo, Hugh G. Grant to Mr. Moffat, June 13, 1935, 351.116 AM 31/14, RG59, 1930–1939, NACP; American Hospital of Paris, *Annual Report, 1925* (Paris and Neuilly-sur-Seine, 1925), 5 (common rooms).

79. American Hospital, *Annual Report, 1925*, 6 (beds), 82 (consultations); *American Hospital of Paris, 1906–2006*, 36 (suites), 38 (Hemingway), 43 (fur); Fouché, *Le Mouvement perpétuel*, 43; Bricktop with Haskins, *Bricktop*, 139.

80. "History: In 1777 . . . ," http://www.americanclubparis.org/history.html (accessed August 28, 2013).

81. ACC *Directory*, 1926, 19 (nonpartisan); American Chamber of Commerce in Paris, *Bulletin*, no. 119 (November 1913): 159 (commercial). See also 843—American Club of Paris, Foreign Service Posts of the Department of State, Record Group 84, Entry no. 2452A, Paris (France) Embassy General Records, 1936–1941, 1936, NACP. See chapter 4 below on the American Chamber of Commerce in Paris.

82. Susman, "Pilgrimage to Paris," 175n17; ACC *Directory*, 1926, 34–37.

83. Anne Devanlay and Nicole Fouché, "La prohibition américaine à Paris: Le Harry's New York Bar, 1919–1939," *Histoire et anthropologie*, no. 20 (2000): 209–26.

84. Clare More de Morinni, "Miss Stein and the Ladies" (1967), in *Gertrude Stein Remembered*, ed. Linda Simon (Lincoln: University of Nebraska Press, 1994), 143 (enigmatic), 145 (black chiffon). The account is mistakenly attributed to the *New York Herald Tribune* (which did not yet exist). See "Gertrude Stein Pinch Hits for Fay," Paris *Tribune* [*CTEE*], December 9, 1933, in Ford, *Left Bank Revisited*, 72–73 (72, stepped manfully).

85. AWCP, *Bulletin* 2, no. 1 (October 1928): 46; Federation of American Women's Clubs Overseas, *The Years of FAWCO: From 1931 to 1991* (n.p., n.d.), 5; Benstock, *Women of the Left Bank*; Anne Firor Scott, *Natural Allies: Women's Associations in American History* (Urbana: University of Illinois Press, 1991).

86. AWCP, *Bulletin* 6, no. 10 (July 1933): 371–72 (1907 law), and see chap. 2 below; FAWCO, *Years of FAWCO*, 3 (Brown); Nora Faires, " 'Talented and Charming Strangers from across the Line': Gendered Nationalism, Class Privilege, and the American Women's Club of Calgary," in *One Step over the Line: Toward a History of Women in the North American Wests*, ed. Elizabeth Jameson and Sheila McManus (Edmonton: University of Alberta Press, 2008), 261–92.

87. On politics: AWCP, *Bulletin* 5, no. 11 (August 1932): 609 (dabble); no. 8 (May 1928), 617 (controversial); 3, no. 11 (November 1925): 463–71 (Twentieth Amendment); no. 5 (February 1928): 368–74, and 2, no. 5 (March 1929): 480 (Mussolini).

88. On motherhood: AWCP, *Bulletin* 2, no. 1 (October 1928): 47–48 (joy); 1, no. 18 (June 1924): 573.

89. AWCP, *Bulletin* 3, no. 11 (November 1925): 451.

90. AWCP, *Bulletin* 1, no. 16 (April 1924): 505 (jobs); 6, no. 1 (October 1932): 29 (razors); 4, no. 8 (May 1931): 584 (domestic troubles).

91. AWCP, *Bulletin* 6, no. 5 (February 1933): 181 (cake); 4, no. 3 (March 1926): 229 (American women); 5, no. 1 (October 1931): 42 (social center); cf. 1, no. 16 (April 1924): 517.

92. Tryphosa Bates-Batcheller, *A Short History of the Units of the Daughters of the American Revolution Outside of the USA* (n.p., n.d. [1948]), 8; minutes, Daughters of the American Revolution, Rochambeau chapter, Paris (hereafter "DAR minutes"), November 14, 1934 (statistics).

93. DAR minutes, March 20, 1934–March 27, 1940.

94. DAR minutes, report of November 1938 recapitulating several months' activities.

95. Tryphosa Bates-Batcheller, *Une amitié historique (France-Amérique)* (Paris: Plon-Nourrit, 1924); http://en.wikipedia.org/wiki/Tryphosa_Bates-Batcheller (accessed September 18, 2009).

96. Sylvia Beach, *Shakespeare and Company* (New York: Harcourt, Brace, 1956), 85 (Yankee), 105 (boisterous); Ernest Hemingway, *A Moveable Feast: Sketches of the Author's Life in Paris in the Twenties* (orig. 1947; New York: Charles Scribner's Sons, 1964), 35, 71.

97. ACC *Directory*, 1926, 40; Certificate of Protection, American Library in Paris, 1940, Class 300, NND775102, Foreign Service Posts of the Department of State, Record Group 84, Entry no. 2452A, Paris (France) Embassy General Records, 1936–41, NACP.

98. Mary Niles Maack, "Between Two Worlds: The American Library in Paris during the War, Occupation, and Liberation (1939–1945)," www.gseis.ucla.edu/faculty/maack/Documents/BetweenTwoWorlds.doc; a shorter version was published as "American Bookwomen in Paris during the 1920s," *Libraries and Culture* 40, no. 3 (Summer 2005): 399–415, 412 for the quotes; see also AWCP, *Bulletin* 5, no. 1 (January 1927): 126–30.

99. Laney, *Paris "Herald,"* 148 (headache); Charles L. Robertson, *The "International Herald Tribune": The First Hundred Years* (New York: Columbia University Press, 1987), 45 (labeur); William Shirer, *Twentieth Century Journey: A Memoir of a Life and the Times*, 3 vols. (orig. 1976; New York: Simon and Schuster, 1984), 1:258.

100. Advertisement in ACC *Directory*, 1926, 409.

101. *Chicago Tribune*, Army Edition, Paris, July 4, 1917, 1 (tent mate); Root, *Paris Edition*, 56 (lobster); advertisements in ACC *Directory*, 1926, 407, and 1931, 558–61; see also Robertson, *"International Herald Tribune,"* 121, 128–29, 154; Shirer, *Twentieth Century Journey*, 1:223; and Ronald Weber, *News of Paris: American Journalists in the City of Light between the Wars* (Chicago: Ivan R. Dee, 2006).

102. Root, *Paris Edition*, 169, 201 (circulation); Laney, *Paris "Herald,"* chap. 28, "The American Tide Ebbs"; Robertson, *"International Herald Tribune,"* 172 (comics).

103. Sutliffe, *Americans in Paris*, 12.

104. Henry James, *Parisian Sketches: Letters to the "New York Tribune," 1875–1876*, ed. Leon Edel and Ilse Dusoir Lind (New York: New York University Press, 1957), 6.

105. Young, *Around the World*, 1:136, 137.

106. 1906. Cited in Vajda, "Paris," 94.

107. Lease for 19 rue de Presbourg, November 8, 1934, Miscellaneous box, Archives 463, Blackmer, 1936–46, Law Offices of S. G. Archibald Archives, Paris.

108. Cf. Georges Mauco, *Les étrangers en France* (Paris: Armand Colin, 1932), 296, 293, 292.

109. Sutliffe, *Americans in Paris*, 62 (shortest), 9 (movement), 53 (San Francisco), 12–13 (moderation).

110. Edith Wharton, *A Backward Glance: An Autobiography* (orig. 1934; Everyman Edition, London: J. M. Dent, 1993), 116.

111. A. K. Sandoval-Strausz, *Hotel: An American History* (New Haven, CT: Yale University Press, 2007).

112. *Americans on the Côte d'Azur*, March 5, 1927, 2; F. Scott Fitzgerald, *Tender Is the Night* (orig. 1934; Everyman Edition, London: J. M. Dent, 1993); Mary Blume, *Côte d'Azur: Inventing the French Riviera* (London: Thames and Hudson, 1992); Jocelyne Rotily, *Au sud d'Eden: Des Américains dans le Sud de la France (1910–1940)* (Marseille: Editions ACFA, 2006).

113. ACC *Directory*, 1926, my count; *Résultats statistiques du recensement générale de la population*, 1926, vol. 1, pt. 5, p. 39.

114. Adam Gopnik, ed., *Americans in Paris: A Literary Anthology* (New York: Library of America, 2004), 182.

115. Ernest Hemingway, *The Sun Also Rises* (New York: Scribner, Simon and Schuster, 1926), 82.

116. Warrington Dawson to Herbert Barry, Esq., Oct. 27, 1910, 351.112D32, RG59, 1910–1929, NACP.

117. With many thanks to Carrie Landfried, who put in hours of work to help produce this line!

118. Tony Allan, *Americans in Paris* (Chicago: Contemporary Books, 1977), 10.

119. L. J. Keena, American Consul General, to Secretary of State, July 12, 1934, 351.1124 Waldberg, Patrick C., RG59, 1930–1939, NACP.

120. Fuller and Farrar both in 351.113/F24, RG59, 1910–1929, NACP.

121. Fabre, *From Harlem to Paris*, 121.

122. Helen Josephy and Mary Margaret McBride, *Paris Is a Woman's Town* (New York: Coward-McCann, 1929), 188.

123. Laney, *Paris "Herald,"* 147.

CHAPTER 2

1. American Chamber of Commerce in Paris (hereafter ACC), *Bulletin*, no. 63 (January 1908): 12.

2. I-Mien Tsiang, *The Question of Expatriation in America Prior to 1907* (Baltimore: Johns Hopkins University Press, 1942); "Opinions of the Heads of the Executive Departments, and Other Papers, Relating to Expatriation, Naturalization, and Change of Allegiance," in United States, Department of State, *Foreign Relations of the United States* (hereafter FRUS), 1873, pt. 2, 1188–1231; Elihu Root, "The Basis of Protection to Citizens Residing Abroad," *American Journal of International Law* 4 (1910): 517–28; Edwin M. Borchard, *The Diplomatic Protection of Citizens Abroad, or The Law of International Claims* (New York: Banks Law Publishing, 1915), 675–76; Nancy L. Green, "Expatriation, Expatriates, and Expats: The American Transformation of a Concept," *American Historical Review* 114, no. 2 (April 2009): 307–28; Nancy L. Green and François Weil, eds., *Citizenship and Those Who Leave* (Urbana: University of Illinois Press, 2007).

3. Patrick Weil, *The Sovereign Citizen; Denaturalization and the Origins of the American Republic* (Philadelphia: University of Pennsylvania Press, 2012).

4. ACC, *Bulletin*, no. 63 (January 1908): 12; see also no. 90 (January 1911): 9.

5. On women's citizenship in this period, see Candice Lewis Bredbenner, *A Nationality of Her Own: Women, Marriage, and the Law of Citizenship* (Berkeley: University of California Press, 1998); Nancy F. Cott, "Marriage and Women's Citizenship in the United States, 1830–1934," *American Historical Review* 103 no. 5 (December 1988): 1440–74, and *Public Vows: A History of Marriage and the Nation* (Cambridge, MA: Harvard University Press, 2000); Linda Kerber, "The Meanings of Citizenship," *Journal of American History* 84, no. 3 (December 1997): 833–54, and *No Constitutional Right to Be Ladies: Women and the Obligations of Citizenship* (New York: Hill and Wang, 1998); Rogers M. Smith, *Civic Ideals: Conflicting Visions of Citizenship in U.S. History* (New Haven, CT: Yale University Press, 1997); Marian L. Smith, "'Any Woman Who Is Now or May Hereafter Be Married . . .': Women and Naturalization, ca. 1802–1940," *Prologue Magazine* 30, no. 2 (Summer 1998), http://www.archives.gov/publications/prologue/1998/summer/women-and-naturalization-1.html, and naturalization-2.html (May 26, 2008).

6. Repatriation involved elaborate administrative procedures until the 1940s. On the limitations of the Cable Act, see esp. Cott, "Marriage and Women's Citizenship," 1464–71; Bredbenner, *Nationality of Her Own*, chap. 5; Edwin M. Borchard, "The Citizenship of Native-Born American Women Who Married Foreigners before March 2, 1907, and Acquired a Foreign Domicile," *American Journal of International Law* 29, no. 3 (July 1935): 396–422, 404–6.

7. Ernest Hemingway, *The Sun Also Rises* (New York: Scribner, Simon and Schuster, 1926), 120.

8. Ernest Earnest, *Expatriates and Patriots: American Artists, Scholars, and Writers in Europe* (Durham, NC: Duke University Press, 1968). Earnest contrasts the 1920s expatriates with the more genteel James and Wharton types who had preceded them before World War I.

9. Lilian Lida Bell, *The Expatriates: A Novel* (New York: Harper and Brothers, 1900, reprinted by Adamant Media, 2005), 69, 121; *Oxford English Dictionary*, 2nd ed., 1989.

10. In the *New York Journal*, January 14, 1900, quoted in Maureen F. Montgomery, *"Gilded Prostitution": Status, Money, and Transatlantic Marriages, 1870–1914* (New York: Routledge, 1989), 183.

11. Al Laney, *Paris "Herald": The Incredible Newspaper* (New York: Appleton-Century, 1947), 144. On expatriates as "derogatory social types" see Brooke Blower, *Becoming Americans in Paris: Transatlantic Politics and Culture between the World Wars* (New York: Oxford University Press, 2011), 214.

12. Vice Consul John R. Wood, "Summary of Protection Cases Handled by the Consulate General at Paris, France, during the Year 1925," February 20, 1926, 4–5, 351.11/2003, General Records of the Department of State, Decimal Files, Record Group 59 (hereafter RG59), 1910–1929, National Archives at College Park, MD (hereafter NACP).

13. John Russell Young, 139 (candles; sense of possession); on thin and thick citizenship see Charles Tilly, "Citizenship, Identity and Social History," *International Review of Social History* 40, supp. 3 (1995): 7–8; T. H. Marshall, *"Citizenship and Social Class" and Other Essays* (Cambridge: Cambridge University Press, 1950), 1–85.

14. Graham H. Stuart, *American Diplomatic and Consular Practice* (New York: D. Appleton-Century, 1936), 395.

15. Ibid., 398–99.

16. Luke T. Lee, *Consular Law and Practice* (London: Stevens and Sons, 1961), 116–19.

17. Philip Katz, *From Appomattox to Montmartre: Americans and the Paris Commune* (Cambridge, MA: Harvard University Press, 1998), 31, 47.

18. 35.11/365 [1914], RG59, 1910–1929, NACP; "The American Chamber of Commerce in Paris and the War," ACC, *Bulletin*, no. 128 (October 1914): 142–51; Charles Inman Barnard, *Paris War Days: Diary of an American* (Boston: Little, Brown, 1914).

19. T. Bentley Mott, *Myron T. Herrick, Friend of France: An Autobiographical Biography* (Garden City, NY: Doubleday, Doran, 1929), 188 (civilization), 127 (passport), 155 (relief).

20. Letter and memorandum, Ambassador to Secretary of State, November 12, 1914, 351.11/512, RG59, 1910–1929, NACP.

21. Mott, *Myron T. Herrick*, 145 (heart), 179–80 (treating Germans).

22. Joseph Wilson Cochran, *Friendly Adventurers: A Chronicle of the American Church of Paris* (Paris: Brentano's, 1931), 163.

23. American Consul-General to Secretary of State, concerning "Whereabouts of Miss Alice B. Toklar [sic]," September 27, 1915, 351.11/943, RG59, 1910–1929, NACP. Both quotes come from Gertrude Stein, *The Autobiography of Alice B. Toklas* (orig. 1933; New York: Vintage Books, 1990), 161.

24. E. E. Cummings, *The Enormous Room* (orig. 1922; Mineola, NY: Dover, 2002), 1. Cf. Charles A. Fenton, "Ambulance Drivers in France and Italy: 1914–1918," *American Quarterly* 3, no. 4 (Winter 1951): 326–43.

25. Edward Cummings to President Woodrow Wilson, December 8, 1917, 351.112B81, RG59, 1910–1929, NACP. The letter is reproduced in Cummings, *Enormous Room*, vii–ix.

26. Whipple to Adee, January 19, 1918, 351.112B81, RG59, 1910–1929, NACP.

27. Melvin Landsberg, *Dos Passos' Path to U.S.A.: A Political Biography, 1912–1936* (Boulder: Colorado Associated University Press, 1972), 58.

28. Telegrams between State Department and Embassy, Paris, July 10, 15, and 17, 1918, 351.11/1778a, 1779, 1795, RG59, 1910–1929, NACP. The incriminating letter is enclosed with dispatch 6481, confidential, August 1, 1918, 351.11/1797, ibid. On this episode, see also Landsberg, *Dos Passos*, 57–59, 64; and Virginia Spencer Carr, *Dos Passos: A Life* (Garden City, NY: Doubleday, 1984), 143–51.

29. L. D. Clark to State Department, August 28 [1914], 351.11/685, RG59, 1910–1929, NACP. Emphasis in original.

30. US Embassy in Paris to Secretary of State, June 24 and June 30, 1915, 351.11/816, 351.11/821 and 351.11/838, RG59, 1910–1929, NACP.

31. Westinghouse Air Brake Company to Secretary of State, March 9, 1916, and related documents, including newspaper articles, 351.11/1082/ and 351.11/1134 Westinghouse/Trube, RG59, 1910–1929, NACP; Donald Harper to Secretary of State, July 31, 1918, 351.11/1788, RG59, NACP. The expulsion order was suspended, but Trube was told not to return to France before the end of the war, and in spite of repeated efforts to clear his name in France, he (and the embassy) was unsuccessful. 351.11/1307; 351.11/1899 (February 2, 1919).

32. The consulate was given instructions to give her such assistance as might be possible and proper. Office of the Solicitor to the Consular Bureau, June 5, 1916, and letter from Mme. Jan Haeften-Hatch to Secretary of State, May 16, 1916, 351.11/1161, RG59, 1910–1929, NACP.

33. The government responded with instructions on how to file a claim against a foreign government. Thérèse Mayer to Monsieur le Ministre du Département d'État, February 18, 1918, 351.11/1687, RG59, 1910–1929, NACP.

34. The following exchange is found in telegram, Ambassador Sharp to Secretary of State, January 8, 1918, and memorandum, "RFW," Bureau of Citizenship, to Mr. Harrison, January 23, 1918, 351.11/1640; memorandum, RFW to Mr. Harrison, January 24, 1918, and telegram, Department of State to AmEmbassy, Paris, February 5, 1918, 351.11/1655; telegram, Ambassador Sharp to Secretary of State, August 15, 1918, between 351.11/1798 and /1804, all in RG59, 1910–1929, NACP.

35. Quoted in letter from American Consul General to Secretary of State, March 17, 1925, 351.1115—Brough, Elizabeth, RG59, 1910–1929, NACP.

36. Perkins: Wood, "Summary of Protection Cases"; 351.114H12, Nellie Hainer (1910), RG59, 1910–1929, NACP.

37. Letters, telegrams, and memoranda, May 6, 1910, to April 11, 1911, 351.111M61, RG59, 1910–1929, NACP.

38. ACC, *Bulletin*, no. 141 (July 1916): 92.

39. Wood, "Summary of Protection Cases."

40. All of the above are from ibid.

41. Ibid., 7, 16, 24.

42. Lodge & Shipley Machine Tool Co. to State Department, January 2, 1917 (and passim), 351.11/1347, re Harry Jones, RG59, 1910–1929, NACP.

43. All quotes except the last are from Osborne, American Consulate, Le Havre, to Secretary of State, April 7, 1913, 351.111B81, RG59, 1910–1929, NACP; last quote, Mr. Brown to Department of State, November 18, 1913, ibid.

44. April 10, 1938, from Mrs. G. R. Wood to Secretary of State, 351.1115—Wood, Charles M./6, RG59, 1930–1939, NACP.

45. Milton L. Schmitt, Attorney at Law, to William W. Corcoran, American Vice Consul, Boulogne-sur-mer, May 19, 1925, 351.1115-Noonan, Louella, RG59, 1910–1929, NACP.

46. Citing John Russell Young. Gerald Carson, *The Dentist and the Empress: The Adventures of Dr. Tom Evans in Gas-Lit Paris* (Boston: Houghton Mifflin, 1983), 81.

47. Gueydan de Roussel to "My dear Eugene" [Gueydan], December 24, 1910, 351.1112G93, RG59, 1910–1929, NACP.

48. Letter, Frank H. Mason to Secretary of State, July 27, 1911, 351.112C18/5, RG59, 1910–1929, NACP.

49. Mott, *Myron T. Herrick*, 313.

50. 351.1121/130—Wolinsky, Moses, RG59, 1930–1939, NACP.

51. Eli Joseph to Mr. Whitehouse, chargé d'affaires, American Embassy, October 26, 1927, 351.1156J77, RG59, 1910–1929, NACP.

52. 351.112 G93, RG59, 1910–1929, NACP.

53. 351.112T72, RG59, 1910–1929, NACP, especially 351.112T72/42: Office of the Solicitor (EMB) to Mr. Johnson, May 12, 1914; Trepionok to W. J. Bryan, Secretary of State, May 15, 1914; Trepionok to Miss Margaret Wilson, December 15, 1914; Trepionok (from Seattle, Washington), to Mrs. Woodrow Wilson (in Paris), June 6, 1919; and Mark Trepionok, *In the Land of Thieves* (n.p., 1911), esp. 9, 11, 20, 30, 32–33.

54. 351.1121 Turner, Blanche M., RG59, 1930–1939, NACP.

55. 351.111D28, RG59, 1910–1929, NACP.

56. Rent laws: *American Review*, January 31, 1929, 13; cf. FRUS, 1928, II, 832–37; FRUS 1933, II, 176–81; Jesuits: correspondence, November 21 to December 27, 1912, 351.111R98, RG59, 1910–1929, NACP. Cf. another request for release from a convent: 351.1115—Williams, Margaret Helen, n.d., RG59, 1910–1929, NACP.

57. On loan recoveries, continuing into the mid-1920s: 351.11/783a, 351.11/784a, 351.11/869, 351.11/1056. List of 73 persons owing money to the Treasury is under letter from Embassy to Secretary of State, July 12, 1916, 351.11/1200; for the Shanghai example (1918): 351.11/1764. All in RG59, 1910–1929, NACP.

58. Correspondence, April 1931, 351.1115/Barre Albina, RG59, 1910–1929, NACP.

59. John Torpey, *The Invention of the Passport: Surveillance, Citizenship and the State* (Cambridge: Cambridge University Press, 2000); Craig Robertson, *The Passport in America: The History of a Document* (New York: Oxford University Press, 2010).

60. Robertson, *Passport*, chap. 11.

61. Eli Joseph to US Ambassador, August 6, 1927, 351.1156 J77, RG59, 1910–1929, NACP.

62. 351.1153/1, RG59, 1910–1929, NACP; the US government disputed French interpretation of American citizenship in "Representations to the French Government Regarding Claims of American Citizens for Property Sequestered during the World War," FRUS, 1927, II, 707–17.

63. "Memorandum on the Citizenship of Mr. Emile Supper," July 27, 1915, from the American Consulate in Lyon to the Secretary of State, 351.11/890, RG59, 1910–1929, NACP. Files on Supper continue in 351.11/1105 and 351.11/1227.

64. Grace V. Carpenter to Ministry of Foreign Affairs [sic], Washington, DC, August 10, 1938, 351.1115—Carpenter Grace V. (Miss), RG59, 1930–1939, NACP.

65. 351.1115 Blandy, Mildred Arden, RG59, 1930–1939, NACP.

66. 351.112Sw7, RG59, 1910–1929, NACP.

67. Memorandum from Bureau of Citizenship and letter, Assistant Secretary of State to Howard Bowns [sic], June 19, 1915, 351.11/580, RG59, 1910–1929, NACP.

68. "Memorandum on the Rights and Duties of American Consular Officers in France in Respect of the Estates of Deceased American Citizens," 6–7, under cover letter from American Vice Consul DeWitt C. Poole Jr. to Secretary of State, August 24, 1915, 351.113/170, RG59, 1910–1929, NACP.

69. Unsigned letter, from Paris, August 1, 1910, to J. J. Morgan, Esq., in small address book, Box, "[mismarked] St. Christopher's Guild, 1930 . . . Jay Col. Nelson, Dean," American Pro-Cathedral of the Holy Trinity Archives, Paris.

70. E.g., 351.113—Bower, Lucy Scott, RG59, 1930–1939, NACP. In general, see "Memorandum on the Rights and Duties"; and decimal file 351.113 for Reports of the Death of an American Citizen, RG59, 1930–1939, NACP.

71. William O. Bullard to Secretary of State, August 10, 1915, quoted in Craig Lloyd, *Eugene Bullard: Black Expatriate in Jazz-Age Paris* (Athens: University of Georgia Press, 2000), 41.

72. Samuel Putnam, *Paris Was Our Mistress: Memoirs of a Lost and Found Generation* (New York: Viking, 1947), 48.

CHAPTER 3

1. Lucy Hamilton Hooper, *Under the Tricolor, or The American Colony in Paris: A Novel* (Philadelphia: J. B. Lippincott, 1880), 77–78; see also 70–71.

2. Sinclair Lewis, *Dodsworth* (New York: Harcourt, Brace, 1929), 87.

3. Whitney Walton, *Internationalism, National Identities, and Study Abroad: France and the United States, 1890–1970* (Stanford, CA: Stanford University Press, 2010). Cf. Alice Kaplan, *Dreaming in French: The Paris Years of Jacqueline Bouvier Kennedy, Susan Sontag, and Angela Davis* (Chicago: University of Chicago Press, 2012).

4. The founding text remains Sheri Benstock, *Women of the Left Bank: Paris, 1900–1940* (Austin: University of Texas Press, 1986).

5. Henry James, *The Ambassadors* (orig. 1903; New York: Signet Classics, New American Library, 1979), 57.

6. Patrice Higonnet, *Paris: Capital of the World*, trans. Arthur Goldhammer (Cambridge, MA: Harvard University Press, 2002), 325; cf. 320–21.

7. Helen Josephy and Mary Margaret McBride, *Paris Is a Woman's Town* (New York: Coward-McCann, 1929), 160.

8. "Parents' Protection Agency," *Paris Comet* 1, no. 13 (December 1927): 45–47.

9. Mildred Stapley, "Is Paris Wise for the Average American Girl?" *Ladies' Home Journal* 23, no. 5 (April 1906): 16, 54.

10. M. L. Girault, "Paris of the Distorted Vision," *Ladies' Home Journal* 23, no. 6 (May 1906): 38.

11. George Brereton to Hon. Wm. J. Ryan, Secretary of State, July 21, 1913, 351.11/1, General Records of the Department of State, Decimal Files, Record Group 59 (hereafter RG59), 1910–1929, National Archives at College Park, MD (hereafter NACP).

12. Report, Consul General Frank H. Mason, "American Young Women Art Students in Paris," September 17, 1913, 351.11/1, RG59, 1910–1929, NACP.

13. Girault, "Paris of the Distorted Vision," 38.

14. "Some Pitfalls in Paris," *New York Daily Tribune*, January 1, 1899.

15. Joseph Wilson Cochran, *Friendly Adventurers: A Chronicle of the American Church of Paris* (Paris: Brentano's, 1931), 219.

16. Ibid., 218.

17. Stapley, "Is Paris Wise," 54.

18. Ibid.

19. Letter, undated, Correspondence file, April 10–April 27, 1923, 351.1115—Tyler, Mrs. O. A., RG59, 1910–1929, NACP.

20. *For the 5000 American Students in the Latin Quarter*, fundraising brochure, File "American Students' and Artists' Center," Box "Altar and Processional Crosses (1922–27) . . . Funeral and Memorial Services," American Pro-Cathedral of the Holy Trinity Archives, 1.

21. "Les jeunes filles étrangères," *La vie parisienne*, May 11, 1878, 132–33, cited in Joanne Vajda, "Paris: Rendez-vous cosmopolite; Du voyage élitaire à l'industrie touristique, 1855–1937," doctoral thesis, École des Hautes Études en Sciences Sociales, 2005, 149.

22. Old-Nick Jr., "La colonie américaine à Paris," *La vie élegante* 1 (March 15, 1882): 250.

23. "Some Pitfalls in Paris," *New York Daily Tribune*, January 1, 1899, 7.

24. Gabrielle Houbre, "Demoiselles catholiques et *misses* protestantes: Deux modèles éducatifs antagonistes au XIXe siècle," *Bulletin de la Société de l'histoire du protestantisme français* 146 (2000): 49–68, 59–60.

25. Josephy and McBride, *Paris Is a Woman's Town*, 147.

26. Mary Louise Roberts, *Civilization without Sexes: Reconstructing Gender in Postwar France, 1917–1927* (Chicago: University of Chicago Press, 1994); Philippe Roger, *The American Enemy: A Story of French Anti-Americanism* (Chicago: University of Chicago Press, 2005), 186–87; Jacques Portes, *Fascination and Misgivings: The United States in French Opinion, 1870–1914* (Cambridge: Cambridge Universiy Press. 2000), chap. 9.

27. Anna Bowman Dodd, "The Expatriates: The American Colony in Paris," *Bookman* 25 (May 1907): 257.

28. Harvey Levenstein, *Seductive Journey: American Tourists in France from Jefferson to the Jazz Age* (Chicago: University of Chicago Press, 1998).

29. *Résultats statistiques du recensement général de la population*, 1901 (vol. 1, 311; vol. 2, 2); 1911 (vol. 1, pt. 2, 141; vol. 2, 2); 1921 (vol. 2, 1–2); 1931 (vol. 2, 1); 1936 (vol. 2, 1).

30. Georges Mauco, *Les étrangers en France* (Paris: Armand Colin, 1932), 175.

31. I have based the following statistics on the 1926 Residential List of *Americans in France: A Directory* (Paris: American Chamber of Commerce, 1926).

32. Alice Ames Winter, "Tribute," *Ladies Home Journal*, quoted in American Women's Club of Paris (hereafter AWCP), *Bulletin* 4, no. 2 (February 1926): 120.

33. "Josephine Baker Steps into New Role as First American Colored Countess," *Chicago Tribune European Edition*, June 20, 1927. He was apparently not a real count, but she did pose with him wearing a giant engagement ring. See (misdated) photo in Bennetta Jules-Rosette, *Josephine Baker in Art and Life: The Icon and the Image* (Urbana: University of Illinois Press, 2007), 149. See also GA Série étrangers, Carton 1, Baker, Frida, Josephine, Préfecture de Police Archives, Paris.

34. In the 1926 Residential Listing, 156 men had wives with French-sounding maiden names. American women listed with their non-American spouses were explicitly denoted with italics (175). An additional 63 women listed alone had French-sounding surnames. It is impossible to know whether men listed singly might be separated, divorced, or widowed from French wives.

35. The number of binational couples increased in the 1930s. There were 175 italicized couples in 1926, 311 such couples in 1931, and 262 in the 1939–40 volume.

36. Josephy and McBride, *Paris Is a Woman's Town*, 153–59.

37. Laura McProud, *American Students' Census—Paris, 1903* (Washington, DC: n.p., 1903), 82.

38. John Russell Young, *Around the World with General Grant: A Narrative of the Visit of General U. S. Grant, Ex-president of the United States, to Various Countries in Europe, Asia, and Africa, in 1877, 1878, 1879,* 2 vols. (New York: American News, 1879), 1:164.

39. The famous first line of *Pride and Prejudice* reads: "It is a truth universally acknowledged, that a single man in possession of a good fortune, must be in want of a wife." With thanks to Marianne Kac-Vergne for a timely discussion.

40. Hooper, *Under the Tricolor*, 73–74.

41. "She Pays All the Bills," *New York Times*, March 29, 1888.

42. Richard Harding Davis, *About Paris* (New York: Harper and Bros., 1895), 198.

43. American Chamber of Commerce, *Year-Book*, 1901, 17.

44. The quote is cited in Rogers M. Smith, *Civic Ideals: Conflicting Visions of Citizenship in U.S. History* (New Haven, CT: Yale University Press, 1997), 457. See also Candice Lewis Bredbenner, *A Nationality of Her Own: Women, Marriage, and the Law of Citizenship* (Berkeley: University of California Press, 1998), 74, 63; Dixon Wecter, *The Saga of American Society; A Record of Social Aspiration, 1607–1937* (New York: Charles Scribner's Sons, 1937), 386–427.

45. Maureen F. Montgomery, *"Gilded Prostitution": Status, Money and Transatlantic Marriages, 1870–1914* (New York: Routledge, 1989), chap. 9.

46. Cf. Arno J. Mayer, *The Persistence of the Old Regime: Europe to the Great War* (New York: Pantheon, 1981).

47. Isabella Singer, Isaac Merritt's widow, inherited five million francs at his death. Her two daughters, Isabelle-Blanche Singer (Duchesse Decazes) and Winnaretta (Princesse de Polignac) were worth ten million each, according to the *Gaulois* article. Both daughters were clearly considered American by the writer of the *Gaulois* article, due to their patrilineal inheritance more than their upbringing (largely in France with their French mother).

48. "Bloc-notes Parisien: Un milliard américain en Europe," *Le Gaulois*, May 14, 1895. There is a discrepancy within the article, which speaks at one point of sixteen women married to Frenchmen bringing in a total of 179 million francs, but Winnaretta Singer and her ten million seem to have been listed twice.

49. Michael de Cossart [*The Food of Love*], *Une Américaine à Paris: La Princesse Edmond de Polignac et son salon, 1865–1943* (Paris: Plon, 1979), 49; Sylvia Kahan, *Music's Modern Muse: A Life of Winnaretta Singer, Princesse de Polignac* (Rochester, NY: University of Rochester Press, 2003).

50. VD5, Archives 238 [1929] and 814 [1928], Law Offices of S. G. Archibald Archives, Paris (hereafter "SGA").

51. File "Draft Wills," ibid.

52. *Sic* punctuation marks. "Very Confidential Report," February 10, 1929, 2, VD5, 238, SGA.

53. "Very Confidential Report," February 11, 1929, 3, VD5, 238, SGA.

54. Gething Miller to Mme la Baronne, February 13 and 15, 1929. VD5, 238, SGA.

55. Note, 30/1/50, and Note, 1/2/50, VD5, 814, SGA.

56. Gething Miller to Harry Blackmer, September 7, 1928, 8, VD5, 814, SGA, (attached to "Note for Mr. Archibald"), noting the State Department's presumptions against residence abroad. On the question of domicile, legal scholar Edwin Borchard pointed out that administrative interpretation even went beyond the law in presuming residence abroad as a cause of expatriation. The 1922 law made a distinction for the first time between married women residing at home and those residing abroad. This was entirely repealed in 1930. Edwin M. Borchard, "The Citizenship of Native-Born American Women Who Married Foreigners before Mar. 2, 1907, and Acquired a Foreign Domicile," *American Journal of International Law* 29, no. 3 (July 1935): 404–6.

57. AWCP, *Bulletin* 6, no. 5 (February 1933): 175–76. On the French male-breadwinner model, see Laura Levine Frader, *Breadwinners and Citizens: Gender in the Making of the French Social Model* (Durham, NC: Duke University Press, 2008). On paternity law, see Rachel G.

Fuchs, *Contested Paternity: Constructing Families in Modern France* (Baltimore: Johns Hopkins University Press, 2008).

58. "How It Feels to Go Native—by One Who Has—with Reservations . . . ," *Paris Comet* 3, nos. 7–8 (January-February 1930): 23. For more recent figures, see Gabrielle Varro, *Sociologie de la mixité: De la mixité amoureuse aux mixités sociales et culturelles* (Paris: Belin, 2003), 98–99.

59. Henry James, *The Ambassadors* (orig. 1903; New York: Signet Classics, New American Library, 1979), 149 (possessions); 151 (respectability).

60. From a 1970s questionnaire, quoted in Mark Meigs, *Optimism at Armageddon: Voices of American Participants in the First World War* (Houndmills, Basingstoke, UK: Macmillan, 1997), 219.

61. Quoted in ibid., 117.

62. Susan Zeiger, *Entangling Alliances: Foreign War Brides and American Soldiers in the Twentieth Century* (New York: New York University Press, 2010), 14–17 (German foe); Adriane Lentz-Smith, *Freedom Struggles: African Americans and World War I* (Cambridge, MA: Harvard University Press, 2009), 83 (ruined Negroes); Meigs, *Optimism at Armageddon*, 139 (avalanche); Bernhard Ragner, "The Permanent A.E.F.," *Saturday Evening Post*, November 11, 1939, 28 (5,000); cf. Hilary Kaiser, *Des amours de GI's: Les petites fiancées du Débarquement* (Paris: Tallandier, 2004), 22 (6,000), citing *Stars and Stripes*, June 6, 1919. Cf. "Paths of French War Brides Are Rocky," *New York Times*, August 2, 1925.

63. Meigs, *Optimism at Armageddon*, 99, 131–34, 236n55; Yves-Henri Nouailhat, *La France et les États-Unis, août 1914–avril 1917* (Paris: Publications de la Sorbonne, 1979); Lentz-Smith, *Freedom Struggles*, 96–108.

64. Letter and telegram, June 3 and 6, 1939, 133—Collins, Ira Malcolm, Foreign Service Posts of the Department of State, Record Group 84, 2513, Paris Consulate General, 1936–1939, NACP.

65. Ragner, "Permanent A.E.F." Ragner himself fathered a Franco-American family. With thanks to Rebecca Rogers, American professor of French history at the Université Paris Descartes for some insight into her grandfather.

66. "Paris Now a Mecca of Divorce Hunters," *New York Times*, July 30, 1922. Diane Johnson's literary triptych on Franco-American liaisons begins with *Le Divorce* (New York: Dutton, 1997), followed by *Le Mariage* (2000), then *L'Affaire* (2003).

67. Joel Smith, *Edward Steichen: The Early Years* (New York: Princeton University Press, Metropolitan Museum of Art, 1999), 23.

68. Ibid., 29.

69. Ibid., 38.

70. Penelope Niven, *Steichen: A Biography* (New York: C. Potter, 1997), e.g., 249, 267, 279; on turtleneck, 133.

71. VD19, Archives 383, Mrs. [Clara] Steichen, SGA (hereafter VD19, 383, Steichen).

72. The poems are in Series I, Box 46, Folder 1086, Alfred Stieglitz / Georgia O'Keefe Archives, YCAL MSS 85, Beinecke Rare Book and Manuscript Library, Yale (hereafter "Stieglitz collection"). The publishers' letters rejecting Clara's poems are in Folder 1089.

73. Clara Steichen to S. G. Archibald, September 12, 1918, VD19, 383, Steichen.

74. Alfred Stieglitz to Clara Steichen, esp. March 1 and April 27, 1916, Folder 1087, Stieglitz collection; and, re dusting, Clara Steichen to Stieglitz, July 11, 1944, Folder 1088, ibid.

75. S. G. Archibald to Clara Steichen, March 7 and October 10, 1918, VD19, 383, Steichen; Emily Mitchell, *The Last Summer of the World* (New York: W. W. Norton, 2007).

76. Clara Steichen to Herman F. Gadd [of the Law Offices of S. G. Archibald], August 7, 1933; Clara Steichen to Gething Miller [also of the law firm], October 5, 1933, VD19, 383, Steichen; similarly, Clara Steichen to Alfred Stieglitz, January 15, 1935, Folder 1088, Stieglitz collection.

77. Gertrude Moulton to S. G. Archibald (hereafter GM to SG), September 18, 1934, Correspondence file, VD28, Archives 490, Mrs. Moulton, SGA (hereafter VD28, 490, Moulton); "New Yorker Weds Russian in Paris," *New York Times*, August 5, 1934.

78. GM to SG, July 7, 1935, VD28, 490, Moulton.

79. GM to SG, June 21, 1931; see also Gertrude Moulton to her brother William Wood, February 17, 1933; and GM to SG, July 10, 1935, ibid.

80. Arthur J. Moulton to S. G. Archibald, June 29, 1935, ibid.

81. GM to SG, July 10, 1932; see also May 14, 1932, "Comptes" file; and GM to SG, July 10, 1935, ibid.

82. Gething Miller to Henry Gadd, January 11, 1933; and S. G. Archibald to Gertrude Moulton, June 28, 1932, ibid.

83. GM to SG, June 27, 1935, ibid.

84. Arthur J. Moulton to S. G. Archibald, July 19, 1935, ibid.

85. GM to SG, September 30, 1935, ibid.

86. Gertrude to "Dear Arthur," July 27, 1933; Conner (Moulton's lawyer) to Archibald, May 4, 1933; Arthur to "My dear Gertrude," November 8, 1933; GM to SG, September 18, 1934; GM to SG, November 10, 1933; S. G. Archibald to Gertrude Moulton, November 13[?], 1933; GM to SG, November 18, 1933. All in ibid.

87. GM to SG, May 12, 1932, ibid.

88. GM to SG, September 30, 1935 (feeble), and GM to SG, October 26, 1936 (goat), ibid.

89. Gertrude Moulton to her brother William Wood, October 22, 1936, ibid.

90. GM to SG, October 15, 1936, and S. G. Archibald to Gertrude Moulton, October 19, 1936, ibid.

91. William Wood (her brother but also officer of the bank handling her transfer payments) to Gertrude Moulton, January 14, 1937, ibid.

92. S. G. Archibald to Gertrude Moulton, January 21, 1935, ibid.; and "Music" file, ibid.

93. Henri Bergson is on her list, but he had not (yet?) signed the proclamation.

94. GM to SG, November 10, 1933, VD28, 490, Moulton.

95. Gertrude Moulton to Dollfuss, November 15, 1933, ibid.

96. GM to SG, September 18, 1934, ibid.

97. From "my world" to "Schrecklichkeit: GM to SG, January 25, 1934; see also GM to SG, October 30, 1934, ibid.

98. GM to SG, March 30, 1935, ibid.

99. Letters, Grace Mikell to Secretary of State, August 18, 1929 and February 15, 1933, 351.1141—Mikell, Grace, RG59, 1930–1939.

100. Correspondence, May 2–8, 1922, 351.1115—Bove, Dr. Chas. F., RG59, 1910–1929, NACP. Cf. Charles F. Bove with Dana Lee Thomas, *A Paris Surgeon's Story* (Boston: Little, Brown, 1956), 42–43, 47.

101. E.g., *Le Figaro*, December 17, 1908.

102. Éric Mension-Rigau, *Boni de Castellane* (Paris: Perrin, 2008), 44–48.

103. *Le Figaro*, December 17, 1908. Boni, however, claimed that his mother liked his wife and was quite affected by the divorce, which was "contraire à ses sentiments religieux et à ses traditions." Boniface de Castellane, *L'art d'être pauvre* (Paris: Tallandier, 2009 ; comprising his two books *Comment j'ai découvert l'Amérique*, 1924, and *L'art d'être pauvre*, 1925), 321.

104. The love letter dates to 1870. Sylvie Brodziak, "Clemenceau et la culture anglo-saxonne," in *Georges Clemenceau et le monde anglo-saxon*, ed. Sylvie Brodziak and Michel Drouin (La Crèche, France: Geste Éditions, 2005), 33–51, 39–41, 50n16; Jean-Noël Jeanneney, *Clemenceau: Portrait d'un homme libre* (Paris: Mengès, 2005), 21–24, 73.

105. John R. Ellingston, "Paths of French War Brides Are Rocky," *New York Times*, August 2, 1925.

106. Tylver Stovall, *Paris Noir: African Americans in the City of Light* (Boston: Houghton Mifflin, 1996), 75, 113.

107. Ibid., 75–76.

108. Correspondence, 1922–1923, 351.1115—Scott, Mrs. George C., RG59, 1910–1929, NACP.

109. [December 3, 1938], 351.1115—Helm, Marie R., RG59, 1930–1939, NACP.

110. Internal memorandum by Assistant Secretary of Secretary of State, August 20, 1926, 351.1115—Jones, Mrs. Raymonde, RG59, 1910–1929, NACP.

111. G. A. Erickson to State Department, November 6 and 22, 1923, 351.1111—Erickson, G. A., RG59, 1910–1929, NACP; Zeiger, *Entangling Alliances*. For custody cases, see, e.g., 351.11/1927, 351.1115/15 and 19, RG59, 1930–1939, NACP.

112. Ragner, "Permanent A.E.F."

CHAPTER 4

1. American Chamber of Commerce in Paris (ACC), *Bulletin*, no. 64 (February 1908): 3.

2. See, however, Ronald Weber, *News of Paris: American Journalists in the City of Light between the Wars* (Chicago: Ivan R. Dee, 2006); Charles L. Robertson, *The "International Herald Tribune": The First Hundred Years* (New York: Columbia University Press, 1987); Waverley Lewis Root, *The Paris Edition, 1927–1934* (orig. 1987; San Francisco: North Point, 1989); Al Laney, *Paris "Herald": The Incredible Newspaper* (New York: Appleton-Century, 1947).

3. Weber, *News of Paris*, 9.

4. Ibid., 9 (Sevareid), 177 (Shirer).

5. Sylvia Beach, *Shakespeare and Company* (New York: Harcourt, Brace, 1956), 17.

6. Sheri Benstock, *Women of the Left Bank: Paris, 1900–1940* (Austin: University of Texas Press, 1986), 198, 389 (quoting Woolf); Laure Murat, *Passage de l'Odéon: Sylvia Beach, Adrienne Monnier et la vie littéraire à Paris dans l'entre-deux-guerres* (Paris: Fayard, 2003); Noel Riley Fitch, *Sylvia Beach and the Lost Generation: A History of Literature; Paris in the Twenties and Thirties* (New York: W. W. Norton, 1983); Mary Niles Maack, "American Bookwomen in Paris during the 1920s," *Libraries and Culture* 40, no. 3 (Summer 2005): 399–415.

7. Benstock, *Women of the Left Bank*, 208 (both quotes).

8. Beach, *Shakespeare and Company*, 179 (rape), 205 (disappointment), 201 (people imagined), 138 (pornography), 209 (bus tours); Sylvia Beach to Messrs. James B. Pinker & Son, July 4, 1931, Series I, Box 2, Folder 70, GEN MSS 112, Joyce Collection, Beinecke Rare Book and Manuscript Library, Yale.

9. Beach, *Shakespeare and Company*, 104.

10. Quoted in Fitch, *Sylvia Beach*, 180.

11. Bennetta Jules-Rosette, *Josephine Baker in Art and Life: The Icon and the Image* (Urbana: University of Illinois Press, 2007).

12. Bricktop with James Haskins, *Bricktop* (New York: Atheneum, 1983), 119 (worried), 126 (antics), 126-27 (Boyle), 118-19; Langston Hughes, *The Big Sea* (orig. 1940; London: Pluto, 1986), 157, 179; William A. Shack, *Harlem in Montmartre: A Paris Jazz Story between the Great Wars* (Berkeley: University of California Press, 2001), 109; and Craig Lloyd, *Eugene Bullard: Black Expatriate in Jazz-Age Paris* (Athens: University of Georgia Press, 2000), 91, 98.

13. Bricktop with Haskins, *Bricktop*, 99 (high-society), 116 (Prince), 166-68 (gangsters); Ada Smith Ducongé / aka Bricktop papers, Schomburg Center for Research in Black Culture, Box 4, envelope marked "1926 (3) 1920s-30(1)," New York City (address books); Tyler Stovall, *Paris Noir: African Americans in the City of Light* (Boston: Houghton Mifflin, 1996), 79.

14. Mary Niles Maack, "Exporting American Print Culture: The Role of Bookwomen in Paris during the 1920s," www.gseis.ucla.edu/faculty/maack/Papers.htm; Mary Niles Maack, "Americans in France: Cross-Cultural Influence and the Diffusion of Innovations," *Journal of Library History* 21 (Spring 1986), 315-33.

15. Edith Wharton, *A Backward Glance: An Autobiography*, Everyman Edition (orig. 1934; London: J. M. Dent, 1993), 173.

16. Weber, *News of Paris*, 240 (Thompson), 56-58 (Knight); Charles L. Robertson, *An American Poet in Paris: Pauline Avery Crawford and the "Herald Tribune"* (Columbia: University of Missouri Press, 2001).

17. Helen Josephy and Mary Margaret McBride, *Paris Is a Woman's Town* (New York: Coward-McCann, 1929), 187; Weber, *News of Paris*, 25.

18. Josephy and McBride, *Paris Is a Woman's Town*, 187; Regina Lee Blaszczyk, "Aux couleurs franco-américaines: Quand la haute couture parisienne rencontre la confection new-yorkaise," *Le Mouvement Social*, no. 221 (2007/4): 9-31.

19. Josephy and McBride, *Paris Is a Woman's Town*, 130, 190-91 (Scott), 183-84 (Wodery), 178-92 (more generally on American women in business in Paris); *Americans in France: A Directory* (Paris: American Chamber of Commerce, 1925-40, hereafter ACC *Directory*), 1926 (Scott in "Residential and Commercial Lists").

20. Josephy and McBride, *Paris Is a Woman's Town*, 178 (energy), 182 (cable), 192 (attitude).

21. Bernhard Ragner, "The Permanent A.E.F.," *Saturday Evening Post*, November 11, 1939, 38 (Sanua-Seymour).

22. Josephy and McBride, *Paris Is a Woman's Town*, 185-86 (Bendelari), 189 (White), 189-90 (Butler).

23. Lisa Schlansker Kolosek, *L'invention du chic: Thérèse Bonney et le Paris moderne* (Paris: Norma Editions, 2002), esp. 25, 78, 89, 154, 185 (with thanks to Mary Lynn Stewart for drawing this book to my attention); Josephy and McBride, *Paris Is a Woman's Town*, 188-89.

24. Josephy and McBride, *Paris Is a Woman's Town*, 126 (Wheeler), 187 (McDonald); ACC *Directory*, 1926–38 (Seemuller).

25. Fred S. Purnell to Secretary of State, September 7, 1929, 351.1115—Davis, John 26/1, General Records of the Department of State, Decimal Files, Record Group 59 (hereafter RG59), 1910–1929, National Archives at College Park, MD (hereafter NACP).

26. ACC *Directory*, 1926 (Babbitt); I calculated government jobs to be 4% of the Residential List in this directory; Ragner, "Permanent A.E.F." 31, 35.

27. Georges Mauco, *Les étrangers en France* (Paris: Armand Colin, 1932), 443–44.

28. 351.112 G93, RG59, 1910–1929, NACP, including his pamphlet *La magistrature gangrenée* (n.p., n.d. [1910]).

29. Commercial List, ACC *Directory*, 1930, (Leghorn), 1926–1940 (Sagdahl); Ragner, "Permanent A.E.F." 35 (Hogewoning, Van Riper, and De Ronde).

30. Josephy and McBride, *Paris Is a Woman's Town*, 163 (Sam's); American Women's Club in Paris, *Bulletin* 1, no. 10 (October 1923): 324 (grocery); "Who's Who Abroad: George Hull," *Chicago Tribune European Edition*, February 15, 1926; Laney, *Paris "Herald,"* 147 (undertakers).

31. Ragner, "Permanent A.E.F." 31.

32. Jean Baudrillard, *Amérique* (Paris: Grasset, 1986), 68.

33. Colin Jones, "Pulling Teeth in Eighteenth-Century Paris," *Past and Present*. no. 166 (February 2000): 139; Gerald Carson, *The Dentist and the Empress: The Adventures of Dr. Tom Evans in Gas-Lit Paris* (Boston: Houghton Mifflin, 1983).

34. René Rémond, *Les États-Unis devant l'opinion française, 1815–1852*, 2 vols. (Paris: Armand Colin, 1962), 1:227; Henry Blumenthal, *Americans and French Culture, 1800–1900: Interchanges in Art, Science, Literature and Society* (Baton Rouge: Louisiana State University Press, 1975), 436–44.

35. *Journal of the American Dental Club of Paris* 3, no. 4 (February 1935): 38; Carson, *Dentist and the Empress,* 172, 175–76; Alan Albright, "Thomas W. Evans: A Philadelphian 'Yankee' at the Court of Napoleon III," in *Les Américains et la Légion d'Honneur: 1853–1947*, ed. Véronique Wiesinger (Paris: Editions de la Réunion des Musées nationaux, 1993), also available at http://www.ourstory.info/library/1-roots/Evans2.html (accessed September 16, 2008).

36. ACC *Directory*, 1926, 25; Blumenthal, *Americans and French Culture*, 441 (1881 statistic).

37. William S. Davenport Sr., "The Pioneer American Dentists in France and Their Successors," *Journal of the American Dental Club of Paris* 3, nos. 4–8 (February-June 1935).

38. *Journal of the American Dental Club of Paris* 3, no. 1 (November 1934): 5–6 (would you); 3, no. 6 (April 1935): 1–2 (needle); 3, no. 3 (January 1935): 8 (no longer); 4, no. 4 (January 1936): 5 (aristocratic).

39. American Women's Club of Paris, *Bulletin* 3, no. 3 (March 1925): 88–89.

40. Hughes, *Big Sea*, 146; Michel Fabre, *From Harlem to Paris: Black American Writers in France, 1840–1980* (Urbana: University of Illinois Press, 1991), 64–65, 109; Stovall, *Paris Noir*, 45–47, 58.

41. Lloyd, *Eugene Bullard*, 75 (King of Noise), 102; Shack, *Harlem in Montmartre*, 30–31; Bricktop with Haskins, *Bricktop*.

42. Lloyd, *Eugene Bullard*, 91, 98; Wiesinger, *Américains et la Légion d'Honneur*; Charles Glass, *Americans in Paris: Life and Death under Nazi Occupation, 1940–1944* (London: Harper, 2009), chap. 4; Stovall, *Paris Noir*; see n12 above.

43. Ludovic Tournès, *New Orleans sur Seine: Histoire du Jazz en France* (Paris: Fayard, 1999); Stovall, *Paris Noir*, 84–85, 113, 240 (Depression); Shack, *Harlem in Montmartre*, 113 (Germans).

44. H. Gadd to Mr. McKinstry, February 7, 1936, VD9, Archives 326, Les Productions Fox-Europa, Law Offices of S. G. Archibald Archives, Paris (hereafter SGA).

45. Maurice Léon, "Foreign Lawyers in France" [1923], in "Office," VD6, Archives 299, SGA, 84 (frequently), 86 (interpreters).

46. Edmond Kelly, *The French Law of Marriage and the Conflict of Laws That Arises Therefrom* (London: Stevens, 1885; Paris: Galignani, 1885; Littleton, CO: F. B. Rothman, 1985); *American Register*, April 11, 1885, quoted in the second edition (London: Stevens and Sons, 1895).

47. Henry Cachard, *The French Civil Code* (London: Stevens and Sons, 1895); Charles Gerson Loeb, *Legal Status of American Corporations in France* (Paris: Lecram, 1922).

48. S. G. Archibald to D. L. Brown, November 16, 1938, and January 3, 1939; cf. Archibald to T. F. Hamilton, June 29, 1938, VD13, Archives 422, United Aircraft, SGA.

49. Virginia Kays Veenswijk, *Coudert Brothers, a Legacy in Law: The History of America's First International Law Firm, 1853–1993* (New York: Truman Talley, 1994); Léon, "Foreign Lawyers in France"; ACC *Directory*, 1929, 326–28; Charles P. Kindleberger, "Origins of United States Direct Investment in France," *Business History Review* 48, no. 3 (Autumn 1974): 382–413.

50. Veenswijk, *Coudert Brothers*, 56 (Kelly), 199 (Cachard and Robinson quotes), 204 (château).

51. Dumas Malone, ed., *Dictionary of American Biography* (New York: Charles Scribner's Sons, 1933), 10:307; "Edmond Kelly, a Memorial Read before the Association of the Bar of the City of New York by His Friend Paul Fuller, May 1910," "History," Box 3, file 28, "Edmond Kelly," SGA.

52. Edmond Kelly, *Memorandum re Raymond Seillière* (Paris: Dubuisson, 1887). On Seillière's case, see John Bassett Moore, *A Digest of International Law*, 8 vols. (Washington, DC: Government Printing Office, 1906), 3:850–53, 924–25.

53. Edmond Kelly, *Maxim contre Edison. Expertise: Dire pour M. Maxim* (Paris: Impr. de Chaix, 1886), 58.

54. George Haven Putnam, *Memoirs of a Publisher, 1865–1915* (New York: G. P. Putnam's Sons, 1915), 333–35; "Edmond Kelly, a Memorial Read"; William H. Ingram, ed., *Who's Who in Paris: Anglo-American Colony* (Paris: American Register, 1905); Boniface de Castellane, *L'art d'être pauvre* (orig. 1925; Paris: Tallandier, 2009), 300, 319; "Edmond Kelly Is Dead," *New York Times*, October 5, 1909; Edmond Kelly, *Twentieth Century Socialism: What It Is Not; What It Is; How It May Come* (London: Longmans, Green, 1910).

55. Henry Gadd to Les Productions Fox Europa, February 7, 1936, VD9, Archives 326, Les Productions Fox-Europa, January 1936, SGA.

56. VD36, Archives 910, National City Bank, 1931, SGA.

57. 1929 memorandum attached to letter, Gething Miller to Harrison Tweed, Esq., February 20, 1931, and billing cover letter of June 12, 1931, VD36, Archives 911, The Chase Bank,

January 1931, SGA; Lindell T. Bates, *The Divorce and Separation of Aliens in France* (New York: Columbia University Press, 1929), and "The Divorce of Americans in France," *Law and Contemporary Problems* 2 (1935): 322–28; memoir, Elisabeth Grosclaude, "The Law Offices of S. G. Archibald," April 13, 1983 (roly-poly).

58. VD5, Archives 271, Chrysler/Citroën, SGA.

59. Terkevorkoff letters, VD36, Archive 910, National City Bank, Correspondence 1931, SGA.

60. Arthur Vanson to P. Dormain, Swift, January 11, 1938, VD23, Archives 402, Swift et Cie. (inactivity); Vanson to Rowley, March 16, 1937, VD23, Archives 330, Palmolive, SGA.

61. Edwin C. Wilson to Secretary of State, July 29, 1938, 351.116 AM 31/19, RG59, 1930–1939, NACP. French officials approved the principle involved.

62. E.g., 850.4 and 851.2 in Foreign Service Posts of the Department of State, Record Group 84, entry 2513, Paris Consulate General, 1936–1939 (hereafter RG84-2513), NACP.

63. *Monthly Bulletin of the American Chamber of Commerce in France*, March 1939, 2; [S. G. Archibald] to Monsieur le Ministre du Travail, July 19, 1939, History Box 2, 22A, SGA; Béraud-Villars to Swift & Cie., February 9, 1939, VD23, Archives 402, Swift et Cie., SGA.

64. ACC *Directory*, 1926, 56; memorandum, May 15, 1936, 843, National Aeronautic Association of USA, Foreign Service Posts of the Department of State, Record Group 84, entry 2452A, Paris (France) Embassy General Records, 1936–41 (hereafter RG84-2452A), NACP.

65. ACC, *Year-Book*, 1896, 10.

66. ACC, *Annual Meeting of the American Chamber of Commerce in Paris* [first *Year-Book*], January 28, 1895, 5.

67. E.g., ACC, *Year-Book*, 1898, 49; ACC, *Bulletin*, no. 7 (May 15, 1899): 12; no. 36 (February 1905): 1; no. 46 (March 1906): 11–12.

68. Philip W. Whitcomb, *Seventy-Five Years in the Franco-American Economy: A Short History of the First American Chamber of Commerce Abroad* (Paris: American Chamber of Commerce, 1970), 12 (necessary); ACC *Directory*, 1926, 7 (international).

69. ACC *Directory*, 1926, 7 ; ACC, *Bulletin*, no. 21 (April 1903): 8–9; and *Year-Book*, 1928, 113, on other foreign chambers of commerce; and Claire Lemercier, *Un si discret pouvoir: Aux origines de la chambre de commerce de Paris, 1803–1853* (Paris: La Découverte, 2003).

70. ACC, *Year-Book*, 1895 ("The First Anniversary Banquet of the ACC of Paris"), 10–11.

71. ACC, *Year-Book*, 1923, 106, 108.

72. ACC, *Bulletin*, no. 8 (August 15, 1899): 16 (honest penny); no. 17 (March 1902): 13 (champion).

73. ACC, *Year-Book*, 1898, 17; Whitcomb, *Seventy-Five Years*, 11 (fanatic believer); "Dr. Stephen H. Tyng Dead," *New York Times*, November 18, 1898.

74. ACC, *Bulletin*, no. 17 (March 1902): 13 (preach); no. 15 (October 1901): 18 (disciple).

75. ACC, *Year-Book*, 1932, 74.

76. ACC, *Bulletin*, no. 17 (March 1902): 13.

77. ACC, *Year-Book*, 1939, 60–61, 77–78 (cheese), 61 (sardines).

78. ACC, *Bulletin*, no. 73 (March 1909): 26 (commercial fraternity). ACC, *Bulletin*, no. 111 (February 1913): 29 (freedom of trade); no. 147 (June 1918): 41, and ACC Annual Reports for Year of 1935 of the Committee on Importation, copy filed in RG84-2452A, NACP, 5 (world peace); ACC, *Year-Book*, 1936, 79 (taxation).

79. Joan Hoff-Wilson, *American Business and Foreign Policy: 1920–1933* (Lexington: University Press of Kentucky, 1971), 10; see also 99.

80. ACC, *Year-Book*, 1898, 17; cf. Nicole Fouché, "L'American Chamber of Commerce of Paris (1894–1919), est-elle aussi une institution ethnique?" *Bulletin du CENA-EHESS*, no. 5 (February 1999): 51–78.

81. ACC, *Bulletin*, no. 31 (July 1904): 2 (restricted).

82. ACC, *Year-Book*, 1929, 122 (vexatious visa); ibid., 1926, 119; Craig Robertson, *The Passport in America: The History of a Document* (New York: Oxford University Press, 2010), chap. 11.

83. ACC, *Bulletin*, no. 48 (May 1906): 13; no. 64 (February 1908): 11 (Shoninger); see also no. 73 (March 1909).

84. John D. McKinnon, "Tax History: Why U.S. Pursues Citizens Overseas," *Wall Street Journal*, May 18, 2012, *http://blogs.wsj.com/washwire/2012/05/18/tax-history-why-u-s-pursues -citizens-overseas/* (accessed August 7, 2012).

85. ACC, *Bulletin*, no. 146 (January 1918): 16; no. 147 (June 1918): 41–42; *Year-Book*, 1920, 97–98; Marc de Laperouse, "U.S. Expatriate Taxation: The Economic Recovery Tax Act of 1981," *International Law and Politics* 15 (1982): 127. See also ACC, *Bulletin*, no. 74 (April 1909), and no. 130 (January 1915): 11; memorandum, "French Taxes of Interest to American Citizens," 851.2 General, RG84-2513, NACP.

86. Alex Small, "Have Americans Taken Place of English as Most Ubiquitous Nationality?," *Chicago Tribune European Edition*, August 3, 1929.

87. Handwritten letter, Hartwell to US Consul General, Paris, France, May 10, 1938, 850.4—Hartwell, E.F., RG84-2513, 1938, NACP. The response was that unemployment was high in France; if he still wanted to come, he should contact the French consul in Chicago.

88. 850.4—Manson, Tina, RG84-2513, 1938, NACP.

CHAPTER 5

1. Reinhold Niebuhr, "Awkward Imperialists," *Atlantic Monthly* 145 (May 1930): 670.

2. American Chamber of Commerce in Paris (hereafter ACC), *Year-Book*, 1895 ("The First Anniversary Banquet of the ACC of Paris"), 33.

3. Niebuhr, "Awkward Imperialists," 671.

4. Mira Wilkins, *The Maturing of Multinational Enterprise: American Business Abroad from 1914 to 1970* (Cambridge, MA: Harvard University Press, 1974), esp. 414; Victoria de Grazia, *Irresistible Empire: America's Advance through 20th-Century Europe* (Cambridge, MA: Harvard University Press, 2005), esp. 3; Charles P. Kindleberger, *American Business Abroad* (New Haven, CT: Yale University Press, 1969).

5. De Grazia, *Irresistible Empire*, 210.

6. William Appleman Williams, *The Tragedy of American Diplomacy* (orig. 1959; New York: Dell, 1972); de Grazia, *Irresistible Empire*; Mira Wilkins, *The Emergence of Multinational Enterprise: American Business Abroad from the Colonial Era to 1914* (Cambridge, MA: Harvard University Press, 1970); Mira Wilkins, ed., *The Growth of Multinationals* (Aldershot, UK: Edward Elgar, 1991); Wilkins, *Maturing*. See also William Leach, *Land of Desire: Merchants,*

Power and the Rise of a New American Culture (New York: Pantheon, 1993); Gary S. Cross, *An All-Consuming Century: Why Commercialism Won in Modern America* (New York: Columbia University Press, 2000); and Charles P. Kindleberger, "Origins of United States Direct Investment in France," *Business History Review* 48, no. 3 (Autumn 1974): 382–413.

7. US Department of Commerce, Bureau of the Census, *Historical Statistics of the United States, Colonial Times to 1970*, 2 vols. (Washington, DC: Government Printing Office, 1975), 2:889–90, 903–7; Walter LaFeber, *The New Empire: An Interpretation of American Expansion, 1860–1898* (orig. 1963; Ithaca, NY: Cornell University Press, 1998), 18; Alfred E. Eckes Jr. and Thomas W. Zeiler, *Globalization and the American Century* (New York: Cambridge University Press, 2003), 19.

8. Frank Vanderlip, "The American 'Commercial Invasion' of Europe," *Scribner's Magazine* 31, nos. 1, 2, 3 (January-March 1902): e.g., 12, 17, 302, 305.

9. Wilkins, *Emergence*, 110, 200.

10. Matthew Simon and David E. Novack, "Some Dimensions of the American Commercial Invasion of Europe, 1871–1914: An Introductory Essay," *Journal of Economic History* 24, no. 4 (1964): 603 (witness), 604 (onslaught).

11. Frank A. Southard Jr., *American Industry in Europe* (Boston: Houghton Mifflin, 1931), xiii (migration), 119 (Shredded Wheat).

12. ACC, *Bulletin*, no. 8 (August 15, 1899): 17–19 (1900 Exhibition); Southard, *American Industry*, xiv (almost lose; 1,300 companies), 188 (exploited, undeniable, new technique), see also 189 and chap. 2; de Grazia, *Irresistible Empire*, 211 (lazy); Kindleberger, "Origins," 389 (failures). But see, e.g., Patrick Fridenson, "Business Failure and the Agenda of Business History," *Enterprise and Society* 5, no. 4 (December 2004): 562–82; Scott A. Sandage, *Born Losers: A History of Failure in America* (Cambridge, MA: Harvard University Press, 2005).

13. Allan W. Johnston, *U.S. Direct Investment in France: An Investigation of the French Charges* (Cambridge, MA: MIT Press, 1965), 43; Kindleberger, "Origins," 407, 107n.

14. Singer opened a sales office in Paris in 1880 but began local production only in 1937. ACC, *Year-Book*, 1898; Philip W. Whitcomb, *Seventy-Five Years in the Franco-American Economy: A Short History of the First American Chamber of Commerce Abroad* (Paris: American Chamber of Commerce, 1970), 11, 15; GA S19 Singer 89.917, Préfecture de Police Archives, Paris. Coca-Cola registered its logo in France in 1919. William Reymond, *Coca-Cola, l'enquête interdite* (Paris: Flammarion, 2006), first illustration page; Wilkins, *Maturing*, 43 (Westinghouse), 51 (Coca-Cola); Alphabetical Client Register, 1930–1965, Law Offices of S G. Archibald Archives, Paris (hereafter SGA) (Swift, Quaker, Sorbo, Dry Milk); André Kaspi, *Le temps des Américains, 1917–1918* (Paris: Publications de la Sorbonne, 1976).

15. Leach, *Land of Desire*, 99–100.

16. Kindleberger, "Origins," 396 (success); Charles-Edouard Haviland, *Les manufactures nationales et les arts du mobilier* (Paris: Impr. A. Quantin, [1884]), 23–25, 37; John Merriman, *The Red City: Limoges and the French Nineteenth century* (New York: Oxford University Press, 1985), 228 (strikers); Whitcomb, *Seventy-Five Years*, 15 (membership).

17. Kindleberger, "Origins," 393.

18. "The American Chamber of Commerce in Paris and the War," ACC, *Bulletin*, no. 128 (October 1914): 142–51.

19. Sidney B. Veit, "To American Manufacturers and Exporters," ACC, *Bulletin*, no. 132 (March 1915): 34–37; no. 137 (January 1916), 3 (vigilance).

20. ACC, *Bulletin*, no. 137 (January 1916): 17 (struggle; interests); no. 138 (February-March 1916), 32 (unbusinesslike).

21. David R. Foster, *The Story of Colgate-Palmolive: One Hundred and Sixty-Nine Years of Progress* (New York: Newcomen Society, 1975), frontispiece.

22. LaFeber, *New Empire*, 186.

23. ACC *Directory*, 1930, Commercial List, 530, 533–34, 578.

24. ACC, *Bulletin*, no. 16 (January 1902): 20.

25. Upton Sinclair, *World's End* [1940] (New York: Viking, 1943), 95.

26. Willard Bartlett to T. J. Macdonald, June 20, 1933, 651.113/129, General Records of the Department of State, Decimal Files, Record Group 59 (hereafter RG59), 1930–1939; cf. 300 — Bartlett, Willard, Correspondence, American Embassy, Paris, 1940, Class 300, Volume XIII, Foreign Service Posts of the Department of State, Record Group 84, entry 2452A (hereafter RG84-2452A), National Archives at College Park, MD (hereafter NACP).

27. Emily S. Rosenberg, *Spreading the American Dream: American Economic and Cultural Expansion, 1890–1945* (New York: Hill and Wang, 1982); cf. William H. Becker, *The Dynamics of Business-Government Relations: Industry and Exports, 1893–1921* (Chicago: University of Chicago Press, 1982). More generally, see Walter LaFeber's thoughtful preface to the 1998 edition of *New Empire*, xi–xxxiii. See also Melvyn P. Leffler, *The Elusive Quest: America's Pursuit of European Stability and French Security* (Chapel Hill: University of North Carolina Press, 1979), ix; cf. Wilkins, *Emergence*, 73–74; and William Barnes and John Heath Morgan, *The Foreign Service of the United States* (Washington, DC: Department of State, 1961), 197–98.

28. Secretary of State to Ambassador in Paris, September 9, 1914, 351.11/290a, RG59, 1910–1929, NACP (New York Life); Pacific Artificial Limb Company to Solicitor, Department of State, August 10, 1917, 351.11/1514, RG59, 1910–1929, NACP.

29. Joseph Ullmann to B. D'Anglade, Consul General de France, New York City, October 31, 1914; and letters to Secretary of State and Director of Consular Service in Washington, DC, October 17 and 31, 1914, 351.111U141, RG59, 1910–1929, NACP.

30. *Foreign Relations of the United States*, 1898–1940 [hereafter FRUS] (Washington, DC: GPO), 1922, 2:154–59.

31. 351.115Am33, RG59, 1910–1929, NACP.

32. ACC, *Bulletin*, no. 30 (June 1904); voluntary report, "The French Market for Toys," May 28, 1936, 867.1, RG84, entry 2513, Paris Consulate General, 1936–1939 (hereafter RG84-2513), NACP.

33. 866.12 Flushometer Company and 866.22 Kastor, Hugo (birch), RG84-2513, 1936, NACP.

34. M. S. Hodgson Jr. (Société Française des Breuvages Naturels-marque déposée Coca-Cola) to American Consular Service, September 23, 1936, 850.4 Powers, Steele, RG84-2513, NACP.

35. Bernard J. Shoninger and Arthur K. Kuhn, "Convention for the Reform of the Consular Service," ACC, *Bulletin*, no. 47 (April 1906): 3 (require); no. 146 (January 1918): 14 (legislation).

36. George S. Messersmith, *Some Aspects of the Assistance Rendered by the Department of State and Its Foreign Service to American Business* (Washington, DC: Government Printing Office, 1937), 10.

37. Ibid., 14 (baseless; well-informed).

38. Confidential letter, J. I. Straus to Secretary of State, June 2, 1936, 851.2—American Church of Paris, RG84-2452A, 1936, NACP.

39. "Franco-American Commercial Relations," ACC, *Bulletin*, no. 147 (June 1918): 33.

40. E.g., FRUS, 1934, 2:183; ACC, *Year-Book*, 1933, 75.

41. ACC, *Bulletin*, no. 140 (June 1916): 66; no. 143 (November-December 1916): 110–13; "Franco-American Commercial Relations," no. 147 (June 1918): 30–38.

42. Aide-Memoire, Memorandum, and Enclosure, American Embassy at Paris, under cover letter of July 27, 1933, 651.113/135, RG59, 1930–1939, NACP.

43. FRUS, 1932, 2:195–261; 1933, 2:165–66; 1934, 2:175–210: 1935, 2:211–45; 1936, 2:85–94; 1937, 2:275–85.

44. ACC, *Year-Book*, 1933, 77–78 (present time), 95 (rain), 97–98 (insects), and more generally 94–100; 1934, 77 (asparagus); 1935, 72 (war; paralyzation), 73 (patent leather).

45. *New York Herald Tribune* (*European Edition*), May 14, 1936, in 631—France United States (1936), RG84-2452A, NACP.

46. *Journal of Commerce* quoted in Paris *Herald Tribune*, May 8, 1936, "U.S. Press Favorable to French Trade Treaty," clippings in 631–France United States (1936), RG84-2452A, NACP.

47. Jens Ulff-Møller, *Hollywood's Film Wars with France: Film-Trade Diplomacy and the Emergence of the French Film Quota Policy* (Rochester, NY: University of Rochester Press, 2001); cf. Vanessa Schwartz, *It's So French! Hollywood, Paris, and the Making of Cosmopolitan Film Culture* (Chicago: University of Chicago Press, 2007); and de Grazia, *Irresistible Empire*, chap. 6.

48. Richard Abel, *The Red Rooster Scare: Making Cinema American, 1900–1910* (Berkeley: University of California Press, 1999).

49. Kristin Thompson, *Exporting Entertainment: America in the World Film Market 1907–1934* (London: British Film Institute, 1985). After 1945, the MPPDA became the Motion Picture Association of America.

50. Thomas H. Guback, "Film as International Business: The Role of American Multinationals," in *The American Movie Industry: The Business of Motion Pictures*, ed. Gorham Kindem (Carbondale: Southern Illinois University Press, 1982), 336–50; John Trumpbour, *Selling Hollywood to the World: U.S. and European Struggles for Mastery of the Global Film Industry, 1920–1950* (Cambridge: Cambridge University Press, 2002).

51. Thompson, *Exporting Entertainment*, 125; Jacques Portes, "Hollywood et la France, 1896–1930," *Revue française d'études américaines*, no. 59 (February 1994): 25–34, 31; Gerben Bakker, *Entertainment Industrialized: The Emergence of the International Film Industry, 1890–1940* (Cambridge: Cambridge University Press, 2008); Andrew Higson and Richard Maltby, eds., *Film Europe and Film America* (Exeter, UK: University of Exeter Press, 1999).

52. Kent to Knapp, March 24, 1934, VD28, Archives 492, Fox Europa c/Knapp, SGA (hereafter VD28-492, Knapp); David Puttnam and Neil Watson, *Movies and Money* (New York: Alfred A. Knopf, 1998), 122; Thompson, *Exporting Entertainment*, 72. Cf. Aubrey Solomon, *Twentieth-Century Fox: A Corporate and Financial History* (Metuchen, NJ: Scarecrow, 1988).

53. C. P. Sheehan to Knapp, May 8, 1934 (drastic), VD28-492, Knapp; memorandum, June 26, 1935 (accumulated loss), VD22, Archives 374, Fox Film, SGA; Vanson to Steinberg, November 6, 1936 (paper), VD9, Archives 326, Les Productions Fox Europa, SGA; Vanson to Stein-

berg, November 6, 1936, and Vanson to [S. G. Archibald], June 7, 1939 (losses), VD9, Archives 326, Les Productions Fox Europa, SGA; Miggins to Vanson, June 15, 1936 (Paramount), VD28-492, Knapp; Mike Walsh, "Options for American Foreign Distribution: United Artists in Europe, 1919–1930," in Higson and Maltby, *Film Europe*, 132–56.

54. René Jeanne, "L'invasion cinématographique américaine," *Revue des deux mondes* 100 (February 15, 1930) : 857.

55. ACC, *Year-Book*, 1935, 76; FRUS, 1928, 2:844–849; 1929, 2:1002–22; Thompson, *Exporting Entertainment*, 211–12.

56. "Surveillance des ressortissants États-Unis (1926–1932)," subfile "États-Unis—1930," sub-subfile "États-Unis, 1931," 4, June 14 [1931], F⁷13449, Archives Nationales, Paris.

57. Harold L. Smith to Harold L. Williamson (2nd Sec. of Embassy), January 16, 1936 (enemies); Smith to Williamson, January 2, 1936 (clique); Smith to Williamson, April 29, 1936 (dictatorial); Williamson to Smith, April 23, 1936, 840.6—France Motion Pictures, RG84-2452A, NACP.

58. Aide-Memoire, Memorandum, and Enclosure, American Embassy at Paris, under cover letter of July 27, 1933, 651.113/135, RG59, 1930–1939, NACP.

59. ACC, *Year-Book*, 1920, 97 (evil); Arthur Vanson to Mr. Eadie, May 19, 1948, VD102, Archives 641, SGA (bugbear).

60. Mitchell B. Carroll, "The Development of International Tax Law: Franco-American Treaty on Double Taxation–Draft Convention," *American Journal of International Law* 29, no. 4 (October 1935): 586–97.

61. Southard, *American Industry*, 121.

62. Charles Gerson Loeb, *Legal Status of American Corporations in France* (Paris: Lecram, 1921), ii.

63. "Americans Score on Double Taxes," *New York Times*, June 19, 1931; VD36, Archives 910, National City Bank, SGA.

64. Vanson to F. L. Horton, April 1, 1935, VD23, Archives 402, Swift et Cie, January 1935–November 1944, SGA. On the treaty and its aftermath, see FRUS, 1932, 2:262–73; 1934, 2:167–210; 1936, 2:99–120; 1937, 2:285–97. A second treaty on double taxation was signed in 1939, ratified in 1944.

65. W. J. Eadie to Vanson, January 12, 1937 (more lost); confidential letter, Vanson to Eadie, January 9, 1939 (agreed), VD22, Archives 374, Fox Film, SGA.

66. S. G. Archibald to Culbert, February 2, 1940, VD13, Archives 422, United Aircraft, SGA.

67. [S. G. Archibald] to Monsieur le Garde des Sceaux et Monsieur le Ministre de l'Économie Nationale, June 16, 1939, History Box 2, 22A, SGA.

68. VD13, Archives 422, United Aircraft; VD80, Archives 587, Thomas Hamilton ("Yacht Vagrant"), SGA.

69. F. P. Culbert to Robert D. Murphy, August 29, 1939, 300—United Aircraft Corp., RG84-2513, NACP, asking for instructions about evacuating United Aircraft personnel from Europe.

70. Timper to Culbert, December 14, 1938; Lechanteur, "Note," January 12, 1939, in inner "Timper" file, VD13, Archives 422, United Aircraft, SGA.

71. 851.2—Lanston Monotype Machine Company, RG84-2452A (1936), NACP.

72. Wilkins, *Emergence*, 45–46; cf. Southard, *American Industry*.

73. Southard, *American Industry*, 134; Kindleberger, "Origins," 402–3.

74. Southard, *American Industry*, 5.

75. VD3 [no archive number], Chewing Gum Français, "ancienne maison Théodore Muller"; VD29, Archives 493, American Express (France) en Formation, SGA.

76. VD23, Archives 402, Swift et Cie., SGA; Wilkins, *Maturing*, 9, 62, 94–95, 377n.

77. The question was raised in the context of whether to file a declaration under the Double Taxation Treaty. Personal and Confidential Letter, [S. G. Archibald] to P. Dormain, December 27, 1935 (camouflaged; mercy), VD23, Archives 402, Swift et Cie.; S. G. Archibald to Horton, April 25, 1936 (personnel file), VD23, Archives 402, Swift et Cie., 14, SGA.

78. [S. G. Archibald] to T. S. Wallace, March 4, 1949 (alter ego), VD217, Archives 726, Les Productions Fox Europa; Vanson to Trowbridge, April 24, 1936 (grandparent), VD23, Archives 330, Palmolive, SGA.

79. "Supplemental Memo in re: SOMPD [Société d'outillage mécanique de précision du Doubs]," August 5, 1940, VD16, Archives 372, Bulova Watch, SGA.

80. E.g., Vanson to S. G. Archibald, April 16, 1930, VD5, Archives 250, Equitable Trust and Chase National Bank of New York, SGA.

81. Loeb, *Legal Status*, 77.

82. S. G. Archibald to W. T. Annett, April 22, 1931; S. G. Archibald to S. Stern, June 3, 1931, VD36, Archives 911, The Chase Bank, SGA.

83. Confidential letter, Vanson to A. John Michel, June 24, 1936 (rapidly), VD22, Archives 374, Fox Film, SGA; [S. G. Archibald] to T. S. Wallace, March 4, 1949 (miracle), VD217, Archives 726, Les Productions Fox Europa, SGA.

84. Vanson to Carl F. Dixon, November 12, 1937, VD104, Archives 644, Studios Paramount, SGA.

85. Untitled memorandum by Vanson (AV/AC), June 7, 1939, VD23, Archives 330, Palmolive, SGA.

86. A. John Michel to Norman Steinberg, August 18, 1936, VD22, Archives 374, Fox Film, SGA.

87. Vanson to A. John Michel, September 22, 1936 (100%), VD22, Archives 374, Fox Film; Vanson to Mr. Steinberg, May 29, 1936, VD9 (if necessity), Archives 326, Les Productions Fox Europa, SGA.

88. E.g., Vanson to Rowley, September 2, 1938, VD23, Archives 330, Palmolive, SGA.

89. Vanson to Mr. Page, June 28 and July 5, 1937, VD21, Archives 392, Kodak-Pathé, SGA.

90. Southard, *American Industry*, 133, 125.

91. VD29, Archives 495, Joussein c/Max Factor, SGA (hereafter VD29-495, Max Factor).

92. Minutes, May 6 and 10, 1937 (*maquillage, fabriqué*); Joussein to Factor, May 3, 1937 (consider); on shades: undated memo, "For France"; minutes, January 18, February 6, May 10, 1937, VD29-495, Max Factor.

93. Minutes, July 22, August 2, 1937, VD29-495, Max Factor.

94. Klein to Joussein, September 2, 1937, VD29-495, Max Factor.

95. Annexes C (evolution) and D (Hollywood), letter from Joussein, November 4, 1937, VD29-495, Max Factor.

96. Judgment, rendered November 30, 1938, in the matter of Knapp v. Les Productions Fox Europa and Twentieth Century Fox Film Corporation, 5, VD28-492, Knapp; [S. G. Archibald]

to Maître Suzanne Blum, May 27, 1940, ibid. It won on this issue although not until after the war and the subsequent Blum-Byrnes accord that gave various advantages to American film companies. "Cour d'appel de Paris, 4ème chambre," May 24, 1950, VD217, Archives 726, Les Productions Fox Europa, SGA.

97. [Beekman?] to Allan Evarts, January 12, 1925, in "Gold Star Mother Pilgrimages, 1930–31 . . . Mission Work," File, "Legacies to the Cathedral," American Pro-Cathedral of the Holy Trinity Archives, Paris.

98. Vice President, Singer Manufacturing Company, to Secretary of State, November 22, 1915, 351.11/977, RG59, 1910–1929, NACP.

99. 351.11/435 (Union Sulphur Co. of NJ); 351.11/577 (Singer); 351.11/519 (Levi, Sondheimer & Co.); 351.11/565 (Baruch); 351.11/546 (Metzger), 351.11/538 (Mautner), RG59, 1910–1929, NACP.

100. The consulate did help. American Lead Pencil Company to Secretary of State, August 9, 1916, 351.11/1220 and 1231, RG59, 1910–1929, NACP; American Lead Pencil Company to Secretary of State and to Director of Consular Services, both dated October 28, 1916, 351.11/1288 and 1290, RG59, 1910–1929, NACP.

101. Loeb, *Legal Status*, 15–30; André Pepy, *De la nationalité des sociétés de commerce* (Paris: Sirey, 1920); see also discussion of the "arrêt Remington" discussed in Laurent Lévy, *La nationalité des sociétés* (Paris: Librairie générale de droit et de jurisprudence, 1984), 220–22, 291–94.

102. Joanna Vajda, "Paris: Rendez-vous cosmopolite; Du voyage élitaire à l'industrie touristique, 1855–1937," doctoral thesis, École des Hautes Études en Sciences Sociales, 2005, 557–60.

103. ACC, *Year-Book*, 1935, 85.

104. Michel Wlassikoff and Jean-Pierre Bodeux, *La fabuleuse et exemplaire histoire de Bébé Cadum* (Paris: Syros-Alternatives, 1990), 28; William Lee Sims II, *"150 Years . . . and the Future!": "Colgate Palmolive" (1806–1956)* (New York: Newcomen Society, 1956). According to colgate.fr, a famous French soapmaker, M. Landais, became the *directeur technique*. Note that the colgate.com and the colgate.fr websites differ significantly in their telling of the story. The American website ignores the Cadum story, and the French website notes that it was the discovery of a French machine at the St. Louis World's Fair that helped enable Palmolive's early success.

105. Marie-Emmanuelle Chessel, "Une méthode publicitaire américaine? Cadum dans la France de l'entre-deux-guerres," *Entreprises et histoire*, no. 11 (March 1996): 61–76; De Grazia, *Irresistible Empire*, 272–75; Brooke Blower, *Becoming Americans in Paris: Transatlantic Politics and Culture between the World Wars* (New York: Oxford University Press, 2011), 74. See also Marjorie A. Beale, *The Modernist Enterprise: French Elites and the Threat of Modernity, 1900–1940* (Stanford, CA: Stanford University Press, 1999); Stephen L. Harp, *Marketing Michelin: Advertising and Cultural Identity in Twentieth-Century France* (Baltimore: Johns Hopkins University Press, 2001); Richard Kuisel, *Capitalism and the State in Modern France: Renovation and Economic Management in the Twentieth Century* (Cambridge: Cambridge University Press, 1981).

106. Colgate-Palmolive France, *Notre usine l'espace d'une vie* (Courbevoie: Colgate Palmolive, 1990); cf. Wlassikoff and Bodeux, *Bébé Cadum*, 78; Wilkins, *Maturing*, 83.

107. "Memorandum of Agreement" stating that the French company operates as the agent of the US company, document file, VD23, Archives 396, Palmolive—Chiffre d'affaires, SGA (hereafter VD23-396, Palmolive); Vanson to Rowley, January 21 and 31, 1933; Decugis to Vanson, February 9, 1933, VD23-396, Palmolive. On summary of trademark issues: Arthur Johnston to Vanson, November 20, 1939; Vanson to Johnston, December 13, 1939, VD118, Archives 466bis, Morton/Palmolive fusion, SGA (hereafter VD118-466bis, Fusion). An earlier version of this trademark history are in Vanson to Rowley, January 31, 1933, and Vanson to Decugis, February 7, 1933, VD23-396, Palmolive. See also Decugis to Vanson, February 9, 1933; Rowley to Vanson, May 17, 1933, VD23-396, Palmolive.

108. VD23-396, Palmolive. See in particular, "Note," 27/9/34, and "Visit to Me. Coutard's," BV/BM 22.4.40, 3, "Notes et mémoires divers," Document File.

109. Vanson to Trowbridge, April 24, 1936, VD23, Archives 330, Palmolive, SGA; see also VD118-466bis, Fusion.

110. "Application for filing under Section 112(A) of the Internal Revenue Code," draft 10/22/51, Documents File, inner file "Autorisation américaine," VD118-466, Fusion ("Archives 683" stamped on cover).

111. Morton to Vanson, April 25, 1938, VD118-466bis, Fusion.

112. Vanson to Morton, August 25, 1938; Johnston to Vanson, November 20, 1939, VD118-466bis, Fusion.

113. Vanson to W. L. Sims, October 18, 1939, VD118, Archives 466bis, Morton/Palmolive fusion, SGA.

114. Inner file, "Autorisation américaine," draft 10/22/51, "Application for Ruling under Section 112(i) of the Internal Revenue Code," VD118-466bis, Fusion; Foster, *Colgate-Palmolive*, 18, although he put "merger" in quotation marks.

115. http://www.cadum.fr/#/histoire, Les années 2000 (accessed October 28, 2012).

116. "American Project in Paris," *New York Times*, December 17, 1904.

117. Kent to Knapp, March 24, 1934, VD28-492, Knapp.

118. "Note—Affaire enregistrement—Chase National Bank," no date, VD7, Archives 316, Chase-Equitable Merger, SGA.

119. Clark Eric Hultquist, "Americans in Paris: The J. Walter Thompson Company in France, 1927–1968," *Enterprise and Society* 4, no. 3 (September 2003): 471–501.

120. Yale & Towne Manufacturing Company to Secretary of State, August 28, 1913, 651.112/16, RG59 1910–1929, NACP.

CHAPTER 6

1. Samuel Putnam, *Paris Was Our Mistress: Memoirs of a Lost and Found Generation* (New York: Viking, 1947), 17.

2. Reported in "American Aid Society," American Women's Club of Paris *Bulletin* 2, no. 2 (December 1928): 240.

3. Henry James, *The Ambassadors* (orig. 1903; New York: Signet Classic, New American Library, 1979), 80.

4. Report, July 16, 1933, BA 2176, Consulat des États-Unis, 148.799.G (3), Préfecture de Police Archives, Paris (hereafter PdP).

5. No relation! 351.1121 Spaulding, General Records of the Department of State, Decimal Files, Record Group 59 (hereafter RG59), 1910–1929, National Archives at College Park, MD (hereafter NACP).

6. Alex Small, "Have Americans Taken Place of English as Most Ubiquitous Nationality?" *Chicago Tribune European Edition* (hereafter *CTEE*), August 3, 1929.

7. "Exile's Return," *Life*, October 10, 1949; Burl Noggle, *Teapot Dome: Oil and Politics in the 1920s* (n.p.: Louisiana State University Press, 1962), 182n7; "Colorado: Darling of the Gods," and "The Judiciary: Reckoning Day," *Time*, October 3 and November 14, 1949; VD152, Archives 463, Blackmer, 1936–1946, Miscellaneous Box, and VD152, Archives 758, Mr. Henry M. Blackmer (1947ff), Law Offices of S. G. Archibald Archives, Paris (hereafter SGA).

8. Gabrielle Houbre, *Le livre des courtisanes: Archives secrètes de la police des mœurs, 1861–1876* (Paris: Tallandier, 2006), 367–73, 484–85; Fanny Lear, *Le roman d'une Américaine en Russie* (Brussels : A. Lacroix, 1875).

9. G. Dallier, *La police des étrangers à Paris* (Paris: Arthur Rousseau, 1914), 88.

10. "Relief Work in France," August 22, 1918, 351.11/1808, RG59, 1910–1929, NACP.

11. F⁷14700—Coopération des polices française et américaine pour la répression des délits de droit commun dans lesquels sont impliqués des militaires américains, 1918–1919, Archives nationales, Paris; Harvey Levenstein, *Seductive Journey: American Tourists in France from Jefferson to the Jazz Age* (Chicago: University of Chicago Press, 1998), 218–24. Attending classes: Mark Meigs, *Optimism at Armageddon: Voices of American Participants in the First World War* (Houndmills, Basingstoke, UK: Macmillan, 1997), chap. 6; Whitney Walton, *Internationalism, National Identities, and Study Abroad: France and the United States, 1890–1970* (Stanford, CA: Stanford University Press, 2010), 31–38.

12. "La police américaine à Paris," *Le Matin*, January 27, 1919; "34 Murders Laid to Our Men in Paris," *New York Times*, January 28, 1919.

13. Charles N. Walker to A. A. Adee, November 28, 1921, 351.1121, RG59, 1910–1929, NACP.

14. Stevens L. Tyler, July 10, 1920 (gratitude); Lewis to Mamma and Papa, July 31, 1920 (misérable); Lewis to Mamma and Papa, July 2, 1920 (why did), 351.1121 T97, RG59, 1910–1929, NACP.

15. "American Boy Falls in Faint as Court Gives Him 10 Years," *Eagle*, undated clipping in 351.1121, RG59, 1910–1929, NACP.

16. 351.1121—Cibulsky, Louis, RG59, 1910–1929, NACP.

17. Charles Glass, *Americans in Paris: Life and Death under Nazi Occupation, 1940–1944* (London: Harper, 2009), 93.

18. 351.1115—Weitzenhoffer, Rosa, and Julia Kaufman, RG59, 1910–1929, NACP (Oklahoma); *CTEE*, July 29, 1926, 1 (Gates).

19. Anna Bowman Dodd, *The American Husband in Paris* (Boston: Little, Brown, 1901).

20. Miller to Jackson, Fuller, Nash & Brophy, December 6, 1934, VD52, Archives 518, Lanvin Claims (Vanderbilt) and Lanvin/Monteagle (motorcar), SGA.

21. Lanvin/Stewart et De Roussy de Sales subfile, VD52, Archives 518, Lanvin Claims, SGA; quote is from Walter Mills, introduction to Raoul de Roussy de Sales, *The Making of Yesterday: The Diary of Raoul de Roussy de Sales* (New York: Reynal and Hitchcock, 1947), v.

22. G. C. Miller to Messrs. Jackson, Fuller, Nash & Brophy, November 3, 1934, VD52, Archives 518, Lanvin Claims, SGA.

23. Graham H. Stuart, *American Diplomatic and Consular Practice* (New York: D. Appleton-Century, 1936), 396 (cigarettes); "In Our Pages, 1933: American Jailed in Paris," *International Herald Tribune*, July 2, 2008 (Chatterley).

24. Peggy Guggenheim, *Out of This Century: Confessions of an Art Addict* (orig. 1946; New York: Universe Books, 1979), 37.

25. Sylvia Beach, *Shakespeare and Company* (New York: Harcourt, Brace, 1956), 121.

26. "The Battle of Montparnasse," *New York Times*, July 20, 1923; http://www.gvsu.edu/english/cummings/Letters.html (accessed April 28, 2012); Malcolm Cowley, *Exile's Return: A Literary Odyssey of the 1920s* (orig. 1934; New York: Viking Compass, 1956), 167 (salaud).

27. GA-Dossier d'étranger, Carton 1, Sidney Bechet, PdP; Sidney Bechet, *Treat It Gentle* (New York: Hill and Wang, 1960), chap. 11; http://en.wikipedia.org/wiki/Sidney_Bechet#cite_note-KB01-3 (accessed April 26, 2012). On Montmartre and the Paris police, see Brooke Blower, *Becoming Americans in Paris: Transatlantic Politics and Culture between the World Wars* (New York: Oxford University Press, 2011), chap. 4, 66–69.

28. GA W1, Warner, Joan, PdP; *International Herald Tribune*, January 10, May 24, and July 18, 1935, reprinted in 2010 in the *IHT* column "100, 75, 50 Years Ago."

29. Reports, November 12, 1938, and March 1, 1940, GA W1, Warner, Joan, PdP.

30. GA M6, Miller, Henry, PdP.

31. GA T9, Thompson, Clarence, PdP; John Buehrens, "Famous Consultant and Forgotten Minister," UU World, http://www.uuworld.org/2004/01/lookingback.html (accessed April 18, 2012). Apparently Thompson was often taken for white. Clarence Bertrand Thompson, ed., *Scientific Management* (Cambridge, MA: Harvard University Press, 1914), and *Le Système Taylor* (Paris: Payot, 1919).

32. Report, May 11, 1935, 1W13 49620, Brownback, Henry, PdP.

33. 811.4 Leifer, Isaac [*sic*], Foreign Service Posts of the Department of State, Record Group 84, entry 2513, Paris Consulate General, General Records, 1936–1939; cf. "Held in Paris," *Milwaukee Journal*, August 3, 1938, available at http://news.google.com/newspapers?nid=1499&dat=19380803&id=MaVQAAAAIBAJ&sjid=EyIEAAAAIBAJ&pg=6663,2392613 (accessed April 28, 2012).

34. Putnam, *Paris Was Our Mistress*, 17.

35. Lucy Hamilton Hooper, *Under the Tricolor, or The American Colony in Paris: A Novel* (Philadelphia: J. B. Lippincott, 1880), 200–201.

36. Gerald Carson, *The Dentist and the Empress: The Adventures of Dr. Tom Evans in Gas-Lit Paris* (Boston: Houghton Mifflin, 1983), 170.

37. Episcopalian Church (later Cathedral) of the Holy Trinity: Annual Report of Mission Work, 1891–1892 ("country people"); Annual Report, 1894–1895, 6 (refinement); Registry, Applicants and Visits (Phillips), "'Dorcas Society' . . . Mission Work [1873–1933]," American Cathedral in Paris Archives. American Church: Albert Sutliffe, *The Americans in Paris* (Paris: Author, 1887), 149; Joseph Wilson Cochran, *Friendly Adventurers: A Chronicle of the American Church of Paris* (Paris: Brentano's, 1931), 118–19.

38. "Rim of the Limelight," *St. Petersburg Times*, September 19, 1926.

39. Ernest Hemingway, *A Moveable Feast* (New York: Charles Scribner's Sons, 1964), 125.

40. Waverley Lewis Root, *The Paris Edition, 1927–1934* (orig. 1987; San Francisco: North Point, 1989), 100–101.

41. Helen Josephy and Mary Margaret McBride, *Paris Is a Woman's Town* (New York: Coward-McCann, 1929), 128-29.

42. Claude McKay, *A Long Way from Home* (New York: Lee Furman, 1937), 253.

43. Alex Small, "Have Americans Taken Place of English as Most Ubiquitous Nationality?" *CTEE*, August 3, 1929.

44. List of claims against estate of late Philip A. S. Blair, n.d., 351.113/262, RG59, 1910-1929, NACP; Inventory, January 13, 1930, 351.113, Armstrong, Addison A., RG59, 1930-1939, NACP.

45. Frank H. Mason, "American Young Women Art Students in Paris," September 17, 1913, under letter of George Brereton to Hon. Wm. J. Ryan, July 21, 1913, 351.11/1, RG59, 1910-1929, NACP; 351.113/296, RG59, 1910-1929, NACP (Lord).

46. "Hard Up Americans Coming from Paris as Nation's Guests," *New York Times*, November 5, 1922.

47. GA S2 [Hally-]Smith, Daniel, PdP.

48. Preface, American Aid Society of Paris, 1924 report, enclosure, Myron T. Herrick to Secretary of State, January 20, 1925, 351.11/2001, RG59, 1910-1929, NACP; W. V. Cotchett to Department of State through American Consul General, September 30, 1931, 351.1115 Ruloff, Alexis, RG59, 1930-1939, NACP (mother-in-law).

49. 1926: The American Aid Society of Paris, Case Statistics Year 1926, enclosure, Cotchett to Herrick, April 26, 1927, 351.11/2008, RG59, 1910-1929, NACP. 2,780 figure: Herman Huffer to the President of the U.S., August 5, 1936, 351.1115/39, RG59, 1930-1939, NACP. Kathleen C. Burnett, "Needy Americans a Paris Problem," *New York Times*, September 29, 1929. See also William G. Bailey, ed., *Americans in Paris, 1900-1930: A Selected, Annotated Bibliography* (Westport, CT: Greenwood, 1989), 46.

50. Harvey Levenstein, *We'll Always Have Paris: American Tourists in France since 1930* (Chicago: University of Chicago Press, 2004), 6, 50.

51. American Aid Society to Wilbur Carr, October 4, 1923, 3551.1115—Scott, Mrs. Geo. C., RG59, 1910-1929, NACP.

52. L. V. Twyeffort to Secretary of State, July 28, 1923; M. K. Moorhead to Secretary of State, September 14, 1923, 351.1115—Chasselut, Louis A. and wife, RG59, 1910-1929, NACP; cf. Huffer to Ambassador Straus, July 8, 1935, 351.1115/27, RG59 1930-1939, NACP.

53. A. M. Thackara to Secretary of State, June 27, 1924; and John Farr Simons to Secretary of State, August 25, 1924, 351.1115—Bennett, H. W., RG59, 1910-1929, NACP.

54. Cotchett to Sheldon Whitehouse, January 16, 1925, enclosure, Herrick to Secretary of State, January 20, 1925, 351.11/2001; Cotchett to Herrick, April 26, 1927; Herrick to Secretary of State, May 4, 1927; and Memorandum, Passport Division, May 31, 1927, 351.11/2008, RG59, 1910-1929, NACP.

55. Document File Notes quoting letters of June 21, 1932, and November 7, 1934, from American Aid Society, 351.1115/17 and 22, RG59, 1930-1939, NACP.

56. 351.1115/23, RG59, 1930-1939, NACP.

57. R. Walton Moore to Addison E. Southard, September 8, 1936, 351.1115/39, RG59, 1930-1939, NACP.

58. Answer to American Aid Society, July 26, 1935, 351.1115/23, RG59, 1930-1939, NACP.

59. State Department to Huffer, August 5, 1936, 351.1115/39, RG59, 1930-1939, NACP.

60. Huffer to President of the United States, August 5, 1936, 351.1115/39; Jesse Isidor Straus to Secretary of State, February 12, 1935, 351.1115/23; and Addison E. Southard to Secretary of State, October 9, 1936, 351.115/42, RG59, 1930–1939, NACP.

61. *CTEE*, February 15, 1925, cited in Warren Irving Susman, "Pilgrimage to Paris: The Backgrounds of American Expatriation, 1920–1934," PhD thesis, University of Wisconsin, 1957, 154, and, more generally on living cheaply in Paris, 123, 147–60.

62. Lewis to My dear Mamma and Papa, July 31, 1920, 351.1121 T97, RG59, 1910–1929, NACP.

63. P. J. Philip, "Springtime Paris Thrills Visitors," *New York Times*, March 20, 1927.

CHAPTER 7

1. Sinclair Lewis, *Dodsworth* (New York: Harcourt, Brace, 1929), 125.

2. "Fourth of July in Paris," *New York Times*, July 22, 1900; Department of State, *Papers Relating to the Foreign Relations of the United States, 1900* (Washington, DC: Government Printing Office, 1900), 456–68.

3. On the "riot" see *New York Times*, July 20, 23, 24, 26–28, September 16, 1926; *Chicago Tribune European Edition* (hereafter *CTEE*), July 24, 1926; Ronald Weber, *News of Paris: American Journalists in the City of Light between the Wars* (Chicago: Ivan R. Dee, 2006), 177 (dapper); Harvey Levenstein, *Seductive Journey: American Tourists in France from Jefferson to the Jazz Age* (Chicago: University of Chicago Press, 1998), 257, 266–71; Ralph Schor, *L'opinion française et les étrangers en France, 1919–1939* (Paris: Publications de la Sorbonne, 1985), 467–76; Brooke Blower, *Becoming Americans in Paris: Transatlantic Politics and Culture between the World Wars* (New York: Oxford University Press, 2011), esp. her keen description of the tours, chap. 4, 154–55; William G. Bailey, ed., *Americans in Paris, 1900–1930: A Selected, Annotated Bibliography* (Westport, CT: Greenwood, 1989), 37–39.

4. Levenstein, *Seductive Journey*, 269.

5. *CTEE*, August 1 and 2, 1926.

6. Richard Harding Davis, *About Paris* (New York: Harper and Bros., 1895), 190–91.

7. Sylvia Beach, *Shakespeare and Company* (New York: Harcourt, Brace, 1956), 16 (plump), 106 (French customers), 210 (Gide).

8. *Journal of the American Dental Club of Paris*, no. 6 (April 1935): 9.

9. American Women's Club of Paris (hereafter AWCP), *Bulletin* 4, no. 8 (May 1931): 589.

10. *Americans in France: A Directory* (hereafter ACC *Directory*) (Paris: American Chamber of Commerce [hereafter ACC], 1926), 38; AWCP, *Bulletin* 6, no. 2 (February 1927): 126–30.

11. As summarized in the minutes, Daughters of the American Revolution, Rochambeau chapter, Paris, December 13, 1937, 60.

12. *Journal of the American Dental Club of Paris* 3, no. 3 (January 1935): 2, 7; 3, no. 4 (February 1935): 35, 37.

13. ACC, *Year-Book*, 1902, 41; 1918, 46; 1921, 114; 1923, 106, 108, 111–12; 1925, 75, 129; 1927, 120; 1928, 131; 1934, 68; 1935, 62, 64; 1937, 69; ACC, *Bulletin*, no. 137 (January 1916): 10; Philip W. Whitcomb, *Seventy-Five Years in the Franco-American Economy: A Short History of the First American Chamber of Commerce Abroad* (Paris: ACC, 1970), 38, 61.

14. ACC, *Bulletin*, no. 81 (March 1910): 35 (name); Albert Sutliffe, *The Americans in Paris* (Paris: Author, 1887), 56 (ingratitude); "Dorcas Society," Mission Work, American Pro-Cathedral of the Holy Trinity Archives, Paris.

15. VD56, Archives 527, Skerten, Law Offices of S. G. Archibald Archives, Paris; Alan Price, *The End of the Age of Innocence: Edith Wharton and the First World War* (New York: St. Martin's, 1996).

16. Evelyne Diebolt and Jean-Pierre Laurant, *Anne Morgan: Une Américaine en Soissonnais (1917–1952)* (Soissons, France: Association Médico-Sociale Anne Morgan, 1990); Evelyne Diebolt and Nicole Fouché, "1917–1923, les Américaines en Soissonnais: Leur influence sur la France," *Revue française des études américaines*, no. 59 (February 1994) : 45–63.

17. "1936 France Fetes Rockefeller," *International Herald Tribune*, June 30, 2011; Ludovic Tournès, *Sciences de l'homme et politique: Les fondations philanthropiques américaines en France au XXe siècle* (Paris: Classiques Garnier, 2011); François Cochet, Marie-Claude Genet-Delacroix, and Hélène Trocmé, eds., *Les Américains et la France, 1917–1947: Engagements et représentations* (Paris: Maisonneuve et Larose, 1999).

18. Tyler Stovall, *Paris Noir: African Americans in the City of Light* (Boston: Houghton Mifflin, 1996), 22; François Boucher, *American Footprints in Paris* (New York: George H. Doran, 1921), 164–66 (artists); AWCP, *Bulletin* 5, no. 3 (March 1927): 324 (farm); 3, no. 2 (November 1929): 142–43 (lighthouse).

19. AWCP, *Bulletin* 4, no. 3 (March 1926): 209.

20. Mary Niles Maack, "Americans in France: Cross-Cultural Exchange and the Diffusion of Innovations," *Journal of Library History* 21, no. 2 (1986): 319 (people), and "Exporting American Print Culture: The Role of Bookwomen in Paris during the 1920s," available at www.gseis.ucla.edu/faculty/maack/Papers.htm (statistic); Diebolt and Laurant, *Anne Morgan*; Diebolt and Fouché, "1917–1923"; http://www.adbdp.asso.fr/ancien/outils/histoire/biogr.htm#C.

21. Nicole Fouché, "Les Américains en France (XVIIIe-XXIe siècle)," http://www.histoire-immigration.fr/des-dossiers-thematiques-sur-l-histoire-de-l-immigration/les-americains-en-france-xviiie-xxie-siecle (accessed August 29, 2013); Sabine Chavinier-Rela, "Ambiguïté des relations du 'basket' français au 'basketball' américain," *Revue juridique et économique du sport* 86 (2008): 197–205.

22. Hélène Trocmé, "Un modèle américain transposé: Les foyers du soldat de l'Union franco-américaine (1914–1922)," in *Les Américains et la France, 1917–1947: Engagements et représentations*, ed. François Cochet, Marie-Claude Genet-Delacroix, and Hélène Trocmé (Paris: Maisonneuve et Larose, 1999), 5–23; Jean-François Boulanger, "L'aide américaine après la Grande Guerre vue de l'archevêché de Reims," *Bulletin de l'Institut Pierre Renouvin*, no. 4 (Fall 1997): 49–66; Diebolt and Laurant, *Anne Morgan*, 128–31; Philippe Roger, *The American Enemy: A Story of French Anti-Americanism* (Chicago: University of Chicago Press, 2005), 416–22.

23. Eugène Brieux, *Les Américains chez nous*, in *La Petite Illustration Théâtrale*, n.s. no. 11, February 7, 1920, act 2, scene 3, 16.

24. Ibid., act 1, scene 6, 6 (ouch); act 3, scene 1, 22 (cry); act 2, scene 3, 16 (living); act 2, scene 8, 21 (ancestral).

25. Ibid., act 2, scene 3, 15; ACC, *Bulletin*, no. 8 (August 15, 1899): 16.

26. ACC, *Year-Book*, 1902, 22 (D'Estournelles); Charles A. Martin, "Deux conférences de M. James H. Hyde," *Journal de la Société des Américanistes* 11, no. 1 (1919): 368–71, 371, http://www.persee.fr/web/revues/home/ (search for Hyde Journal Américanistes; accessed August 29, 2013).

27. ACC, *Bulletin*, no. 122 (February 1914): 51 (Panama); no. 147 (June 1918): 41 (go-ahead).

28. E.g., Emily S. Rosenberg, "Ordering Others: U.S. Financial Advisers in the Early Twentieth Century," in *Haunted by Empire: Geographies of Intimacy in North American History*, ed. Ann Laura Stoler (Durham, NC: Duke University Press, 2006), 405–24, esp. 420.

29. Gertrude Stein, *Paris France* (orig. 1940; New York: Liveright, 1970), 43.

30. Henry James, *The Ambassadors* (orig. 1903; New York: Signet Classic, 1979), 66, 93–94.

31. Guillaume de Bertier de Sauvigny, *La France et les Français vus par les voyageurs américains, 1814–1848*, 2 vols. (Paris: Flammarion, 1982–85), 2:67 (meat); 2:29 (drunks).

32. Michel Fabre, *From Harlem to Paris: Black American Writers in France, 1840–1980* (Urbana: University of Illinois Press, 1991), 31 (Douglass), 34–35 (BTW).

33. R. Malsagne, "M. Alexandre Joukowski [as it was spelled in France]," *Paris-Presse*, May 6, 1930, 1.

34. In ACC, *Bulletin*, no. 53 (December 1906): 9–13 (French industrial art); no. 134 (June-July 1915): 64 (happy exile).

35. John Russell Young, *Around the World with General Grant: A Narrative of the Visit of General U.S. Grant, Ex-President of the United States, to Various Countries in Europe, Asia, and Africa, in 1877, 1878, 1879*, 2 vols. (New York: American News, 1877, 1879), 1:142.

36. For some of the early visitors' complaints, see Bertier de Sauvigny, *France et les Français*, e.g. 1:75, 257, 76, 133. He titles one section "Les Américains pressés" (1:254). Emery Pottle, "The Expatriates," *Harper's Monthly Magazine* 116 (May 1908): 871 (fleas).

37. Young, *Around the World*, 1:161–62.

38. *Americans in Beautiful France*, no. 7 (August 1927): 5.

39. T. Bentley Mott, *Myron T. Herrick, Friend of France: An Autobiographical Biography* (Garden City, NY: Doubleday, Doran, 1929), 300, 299.

40. AWCP, *Bulletin* 4, no. 7 (June 1926): 613.

41. Dorothy Galantière, "Paris American Letters, Number Two," AWCP, *Bulletin* 4, no. 7 (June 1926): 611–14.

42. Langston Hughes, quoted in Fabre, *From Harlem to Paris*, 64–65. However, he ended with "Little old New York for me! But the colored people here are fine, there are lots of us."

43. Mary Bromfield, "Paris When One Lives There," *Vogue* 75, no. 1 (January 4, 1930): 37, 38, 39, 96, 102, 104, 106; Ivan Scott, *Louis Bromfield, Novelist and Agrarian Reformer: The Forgotten Author* (Lampeter, UK / Lewiston, NY: Edwin Mellen, 1998).

44. Cover memo, Department of State, May 27, 1935, 351.1141—Mullaney, Bernard J., forwarding two undated statements: "Lederlin vs. Pratt: A Statement of the Salient Facts" and "Lederlin vs. Pratt: A Statement of the Details by Mrs. Georgia Blackman Mullaney," General Records of the Department of State, Decimal Files, Record Group 59 (hereafter RG59), 1930–1939, National Archives at College Park, MD (hereafter NACP).

45. Mark Wyman, *Round-Trip to America: The Immigrants Return to Europe, 1880–1939* (Ithaca, NY: Cornell University Press, 1993); Marjory Harper, ed., *Emigrant Homecomings: The Return Movement of Emigrants, 1600–2000* (Manchester: Manchester University Press, 2005).

46. Reinhold Niebuhr, "Awkward Imperialists," *Atlantic Monthly* 145 (May 1930): 672.

47. Georges Simenon, *La tête d'un Homme* (Paris: Presses de la Cité, 1931), and *Les caves du Majestic* (Paris: Gallimard, 1942). With thanks to Jacques Sélamé, my faithful guide to Maigret episodes.

48. Frank Costigliola, *Awkward Dominion: American Political, Economic, and Cultural Relations with Europe, 1919–1933* (Ithaca, NY: Cornell University Press, 1984), 180–81; Blower, *Becoming Americans in Paris*, chap. 3; Moshik Temkin, *The Sacco-Vanzetti Affair: America on Trial* (New Haven, CT: Yale University Press, 2009), esp. chap. 3.

49. Blower, *Becoming Americans*, 93. On anti-Americanism since World War II, see Richard Kuisel, *Seducing the French: The Dilemma of Americanization* (Berkeley: University of California Press, 1993), and *The French Way: How France Embraced and Rejected American Values and Power* (Princeton, NJ: Princeton University Press, 2012).

50. Golda M. Goldman, "Paris Is Not America," *Outlook and Independent* 156, no. 10 (November 5, 1930): 372–73, 395–96.

51. Jacques Portes, *Une fascination réticente: Les États-Unis dans l'opinion française, 1870–1914* (Nancy: Presses universitaires de Nancy, 1990), translated as *Fascination and Misgivings: The United States in French Opinion, 1870–1914* (Cambridge: Cambridge University Press, 2000); Marie-Christine Granjon, "Sartre, Beauvoir, Aron: Les passions ambiguës," in *L'Amérique dans les têtes: Un siècle de fascinations et d'aversions*, ed. Denis Lacorne, Jacques Rupnik, and Marie-France Toinet (Paris: Hachette, 1986), translated as *The Rise and Fall of Anti-Americanism: A Century of French Perceptions* (New York: St. Martin's, 1990); Christine Fauré and Tom Bishop, eds., *L'Amérique des Français* (Paris: François Bourin, 1992).

52. Roger, *American Enemy*, 87.

53. Abel Hermant, *Les transatlantiques* (Paris: Arthème Fayard, n.d. [1898]).

54. Tony Allan, *Americans in Paris* (Chicago: Contemporary Books, 1977), 131; cf. Michael de Cossart, *Une Américaine à Paris: La Princesse Edmond de Polignac et son salon, 1865–1943* (Paris: Plon, 1979).

55. Boniface de Castellane, *L'art d'être pauvre* (Paris: Tallandier, 2009), 286. For some of his comments on Americans and America, see esp., 114–16, 265–71, 447–49. He described New York, for example, as a city constrained by two bodies of water that had had to grow vertically, which explains why people live in tall buildings on top of one other, as in dresser drawers (265).

56. Octave Noël, *The American Peril* (Paris: De Soye et Fils, 1899), 1 (brutal); Henri Hauser, *L'impérialisme américain* (Paris: Pages libres, 1905); Portes, *Fascination réticente*, chap. 14.

57. David Strauss, *Menace in the West: The Rise of French Anti-Americanism in Modern Times* (Westport, CT: Greenwood, 1978); Roger, *American Enemy*; Yves-Henri Nouailhat, *La France et les États-Unis, août 1914–avril 1917* (Paris: Publications de la Sorbonne, 1979), 345, 332.

58. Léon Laborde (M. le Comte), *De l'union des arts et de l'industrie*, 2 vols. (Paris: Imprimerie impériale, 1857); Emile Levasseur, *L'ouvrier américain*, 2 vols. (Paris: L. Larose, 1898).

59. André Siegfried, *Les États-Unis d'aujourd'hui* (orig. 1927 ; Paris: A. Colin, 1931), 2 (dispassionate); cover letter, February 4, 1932, transmitting report of talk by M. Siegfried (Americans everywhere), F[7]13449, "Surveillance des ressortissants États-Unis (1926–1932)," subfile 6, "États-Unis 1932," Archives nationales, Paris. See also Sean Kennedy, "André Siegfried and

the Complexities of French Anti-Americanism," *French Politics, Culture and Society* 27, no. 2 (Summer 2009): 1–22.

60. Georges Duhamel, *Scènes de la vie future* (orig. 1930 ; Paris: Arthème Fayard, 1934), 81 (masturbation); Numa Sadoul, *Tintin et moi: Entretiens avec Hergé* (Tournai, Belgium: Casterman, 1975), 99.

61. Robert Aron and Arnaud Dandieu, *Le cancer américain* (Paris: Edition Rieder, 1931).

62. Gustave Le Rouge and Gustave Guitton, *La conspiration des milliardaires*, 3 vols. (orig. 1899–1900 ; Paris: Union Générale d'Éditions, 1977).

63. F⁷13449, "Surveillance."

64. Levenstein, *Seductive Journey*, 263.

65. *Action Française* (far right), July 23 and 26, 1926; *L'Ère Nouvelle* (left), July 23 and 24, 1926; *La Croix*, July 24, 1926; "Tourist Booing Is Regretted by Paris Paper," *CTEE*, July 22, 1926 (*Paris-Midi*).

66. Roger, *American Enemy*, 310–20.

67. F⁷13449, "Surveillance des ressortissants États-Unis (1926–1932)," subfile 6b "Amérique, Dettes, Décembre 1932," Archives nationales, Paris.

68. Strauss, *Menace in the West*, 200 (role); Frank H. Simonds, "'Uncle Shylock' in Europe," *American Review of Reviews* 74, no. 440 (September 1926): 269–78, and the political cartoons reproduced in "Uncle Sam in Current Caricature," *American Review of Reviews* 74, no. 440 (September 1926): 252–57; Jean-Louis Chastenet, *L'oncle Shylock, ou L'impérialisme américain à la conquête du monde* (Paris: C. Flammarion, 1927).

69. "Latin Quarter Youths Boycott American Products and 'Spirit,'" *New York Times*, December 8, 1929.

70. ACC, *Year-Book*, 1939, 71–72.

71. Report 490 [by Taudière], Chambre des députés, session de 1932, annexe au procès-verbal de la séance du 11 juillet 1932, 860.2 Monopolies Concessions Contracts, United Shoe Machinery Company, Foreign Service Posts of the Department of State, Record Group G84, Entry 2542A, Paris Embassy General Records (1936), NACP.

72. Jean Bonnefon-Craponne, *La pénétration économique et financière des capitaux américains en Europe* (Paris: Imprimerie "Labor," 1930), 209 (outrance), 229 (danger).

73. Al Laney, *Paris "Herald": The Incredible Newspaper* (New York: Appleton-Century, 1947), 149.

74. Henri-A. Jules-Bois, "Contre l'anti-Américanisme," *Le Moniteur Franco-Américain* 18, no. 7 (October 1932): 8–9, 8.

75. Paul d'Estournelles de Constant, preface, 8, and Jean Jaurès, "La force pacificatrice de l'idéalisme américain," 47–49, *Conciliation internationale*, no. 3 ("L'amitié franco-américaine") (1912).

76. Brieux, *Les Américains*, act 3, scene 4, 26.

77. Patrick Fridenson, "Un tournant taylorien de la société française (1904–1918)," *Annales, E.S.C.* 42, no. 5 (1987): 1031–60; Don Reid, "La genèse du fayolisme," *Sociologie du Travail* 28 (April-June 1986): 75–93; Charles S. Maier, "Between Taylorism and Technocracy: European Ideologies and the Vision of Industrial Productivity in the 1920s," *Journal of Contemporary History* 5, no. 2 (1970): 27–61; Anson Rabinbach, *The Human Motor: Energy, Fatigue, and*

the Origins of Modernity (New York: Basic Books, 1990), esp. chaps. 9–10; Aimée Moutet, *Les logiques de l'entreprise: La rationalisation dans l'industrie française de l'entre-deux-guerres* (Paris: École des hautes études en sciences sociales, 1997); Yves Cohen, *Organiser à l'aube du taylorisme: La pratique d'Ernest Mattern chez Peugeot, 1906–1919* (Besançon: Presses universitaires franc-comtoises, 2001); Portes, *Fascination réticente*, chap. 13.

78. Emile Pouget, quoted in Rabinbach, *Human Motor*, 241 (exhaustion); Fridenson, "Un tournant taylorien," 1038 (we ask).

79. Frank A. Southard Jr., *American Industry in Europe* (Boston: Houghton Mifflin, 1931), 190 (Citroën); Stephen L. Harp, *Marketing Michelin: Advertising and Cultural Identity in Twentieth-Century France* (Baltimore: Johns Hopkins University Press, 2001).

80. [Hyacinthe] Dubreuil, *Standards: Le travail américain vu par un ouvrier français* (Paris: Grasset, 1929), 421. See also E. Servan [Emile Servan-Schreiber], *L'exemple américain* (Paris: Payot, 1917); Émile Schreiber, *L'Amérique réagit* (Paris: Plon, 1934).

81. André Tardieu, *Notes sur les États-Unis* (Paris: Calmann-Lévy, 1908), *L'Amérique en armes* (Paris: E. Fasquelle, 1919), and *Devant l'obstacle: L'Amérique et nous* (Paris: Editions Emile-Paul Frères, 1927); Richard Kuisel, *Capitalism and the State in Modern France: Renovation and Economic Management in the Twentieth Century* (Cambridge: Cambridge University Press, 1981), 90–92.

82. Robert W. Rydell and Rob Kroes, *Buffalo Bill in Bologna: The Americanization of the World, 1869–1922* (Chicago: University of Chicago Press, 2005); Jacques Portes, *Buffalo Bill* (Paris: Fayard, 2002); cf. David McCullough, *The Greater Journey: Americans in Paris* (New York: Simon and Schuster, 2011), 166–76 (Catlin).

83. ACC, *Bulletin*, no. 8 (August 15, 1899): 10–11 (Millerand: smiles); Old-Nick Jr., "La colonie américaine à Paris," *La Vie Élégante* 1 (March 15, 1882), 248 (exotic), 250 (rough; twisted); [William W. Davenport], *The Story of Reid Hall: An Old House in Paris* (Paris: Reid Hall, n.d.), 13, quoting *L'Intransigeant* (charming); Jacques Portes, *Fascination réticente*, chap. 9, "La belle Américaine."

84. *New York Herald*, May 31, 1923.

85. "Paris Eager to Greet American Legion," *New York Times*, February 4, 1927.

86. Consuelo Vanderbilt Balsan, *The Glitter and the Gold* (orig. 1953; Maidstone, Kent, UK: George Mann, 1973), 200.

87. *Les Américains et la Légion d'Honneur*, exhibit catalogue (Paris: Editions de la Réunion des Musées nationaux, 1993); lists in ACC *Directory*, e.g., 1926; Davenport, *Reid Hall*, 14; Joanne Vajda, "Paris: Rendez-vous cosmopolite; Du voyage élitaire à l'industrie touristique, 1855–1937," doctoral thesis, École des hautes études en sciences sociales, 2005, 382 (place de Bitche).

88. Stovall, *Paris Noir*, 68 (Apollinaire), 35 (soldiers); Fabre, *From Harlem to Paris*, 107 (critique); Ludovic Tournès, *New Orleans sur Seine: Histoire du Jazz en France* (Paris: Fayard, 1999).

89. "L'hospitalité de Paris," *Le Temps*, July 25, 1926; Wladimir D'Ormesson, "Les étrangers en France," *Le Temps*, December 16, 1934, 1.

90. Laney, *Paris "Herald*," 149; Charles L. Robertson, *The "International Herald Tribune": The First Hundred Years* (New York: Columbia University Press, 1987), 140; "Tourist Booing Is Regretted by Paris Paper," *CTEE*, July 22, 1926 (*Paris-Midi*).

91. William Leon Smyser, "French Critics of America," AWCP, *Bulletin* 6, no. 8 (August 1927): 855–61; see also Kennedy, "André Siegfried."

92. Arthur K. Griggs in AWCP, *Bulletin* 6, no. 8 (August 1927): 870 (Tardieu) and in AWCP, *Bulletin* 3, no. 3 (December 1929): 186 (Dubreuil).

93. "Rules for Social Guidance," in Sutliffe, *Americans in Paris*, 184 (church; egotism); 164 (self); 194 (speak softly).

94. Bromfield, "Paris When One Lives There."

95. [George Monroe Royce], *Americans in Europe, by One of Them* (New York: Tait, Sons, 1893), 51 (soil), 61 (prison), 40 (surrender), 240 (home-bred), 237 (conclusion).

96. Davis, *About Paris*, 178 (struggling), 190–91 (Lafayette). Cf. Lloyd Kramer, *Lafayette in Two Worlds: Public Cultures and Personal Identities in an Age of Revolutions* (Chapel Hill: University of North Carolina Press, 1996).

97. Cited in T. R. Ybarra, "'Americanization' Again," *Outlook*, November 6, 1929, 382 (gloomy).

98. T. R. Ybarra, "America's Conquest of Paris," *New York Times Magazine*, July 31, 1927, sec. 4, 1; see also Alexander Hume Ford, "The Americanization of Paris," *Independent* 59, no. 2953 (July 6, 1905): 23–30.

99. Ybarra, "America's Conquest of Paris," 1 (chase); Ybarra, "'Americanization' Again," 382 (sinister).

100. Goldman, "Paris Is Not America," 372 (Folies Bergères).

101. AWCP, *Bulletin* 5, no. 3 (March 1927): 330 (Opéra), 332 (ruin; never feared).

102. Bernhard Ragner, "The Permanent A.E.F.," *Saturday Evening Post*, November 11, 1939, 28, 36, 38.

CHAPTER 8

1. Tryphosa Bates-Batcheller, *France in Sunshine and Shadow* (New York: Brentano's, 1944), 71.

2. Ad in Paris *Herald* early 1929. Cited in Janet Flanner, *Paris Was Yesterday* (London: Virago, 2003), 73; and Al Laney, *Paris "Herald": The Incredible Newspaper* (New York: Appleton-Century, 1947), 267.

3. "Americans Whose Stock-Market 'Ships' Didn't Come In Now Seek Ships to Go Home," *Chicago Tribune European Edition*, October 29, 1929.

4. "Tales of the Comet: Dies Irae," *Paris Comet* 3, no. 6 (December 1929): 17.

5. William G. Bailey, ed., *Americans in Paris, 1900–1930: A Selected, Annotated Bibliography* (Westport, CT: Greenwood, 1989), 60.

6. American Women's Club of Paris, *Bulletin* 6, no. 8 (May 1933): 293.

7. Procès-verbal de la réunion du Conseil d'Administration, October 14, 1931, and Internal Memorandum, VD36, Archives 910, National City Bank, January 1931, Law Offices of S. G. Archibald Archives, Paris (hereafter SGA).

8. 351.1115/47 and /58, General Records of the Department of State, Decimal Files, Record Group 59, 1930–1939, National Archives at College Park, MD (hereafter NACP).

9. Notes, September 26, 1938 and July 8, 1939 ("Manifestation en l'honneur des Volontaires américains morts pour la France"), BA2176—Consulat des États-Unis, inner file no. 148.799.G (1) Affaires concernant l'Amérique: Informations (Rapports) 1932–1947, Préfecture de Police Archives, Paris.

10. Charles Glass, *Americans in Paris: Life and Death under Nazi Occupation, 1940–1944* (London: Harper, 2009), 9.

11. Black register and letter from Beekman, January 25, 1940, "Women's Auxiliary—Misc. Reports 1927–1940," American Cathedral in Paris Archives.

12. Bernhard Ragner, "The Permanent A.E.F.," *Saturday Evening Post*, November 11, 1939, 40.

13. Letter to Ragner [American Legion], May 4, 1939, and article from *Herald Tribune*, April 13, 1939, 300—Gas masks, Foreign Service Posts of the Department of State, Record Group 84, entry 2513, Paris Consulate General, 1936–1939, NACP (hereafter RG84-2513).

14. July 1, 1939, 300 Section II, Evacuation Plan, American Citizens, RG84-2513, NACP.

15. August 24, 1939, ibid.

16. August 28, 1939, United States, Department of State, *Foreign Relations of the United States: Diplomatic Papers* (hereafter FRUS) (Washington, DC: Government Printing Office, 1956), 1939, 1:592.

17. 300 Section II, Evacuation Plan, American Citizens, RG84-2513, NACP.

18. FRUS, 1939, 1:617. See also ibid., 574–655; 1940, 2:68–184.

19. Philip Bennett to E. de W. Mayer, Embassy, September 23, 1940, Class 300 (Protection of Interest)—Bennett, Philip, Correspondence, American Embassy, Paris, 1940, Volume XIII, 1940, RG84, entry 2452A, NACP (hereafter RG84-2452A). Protection certificates are filed alphabetically in RG84-2452A. They are sometimes marked 300–Section XI or 300-XI.

20. 300—Suzanne E. Bartlett, RG84-2452A.

21. 300—Beach, Sylvia; 300—Stein, Gertrude; and 300—Barney, Natalie, all in RG84-2452A. See also Laure Murat, *Passage de l'Odéon: Sylvia Beach, Adrienne Monnier et la vie littéraire à Paris dans l'entre-deux-guerres* (Paris: Fayard, 2003); Gertrude Stein, *Wars I Have Seen* (New York: Random House, 1945); Janet Malcolm, *Two Lives: Gertrude and Alice* (New Haven, CT: Yale University Press, 2007); Barbara Will, *Unlikely Collaboration: Gertrude Stein, Bernard Faÿ, and the Vichy Dilemma* (New York: Columbia University Press, 2011).

22. 300—Allen, Julian, RG84-2452A (Ketty); Rubinstein specified that she had been an American citizen for over twenty years by virtue of the naturalization of her former husband, Edward J. Titus. 300—Rubinstein, Helena, RG84-2452A; 300—Sanders, John B., RG84-2452A (Bertram).

23. George Balkema to Tyler Thompson, December 17, 1940; Tyler Thompson to George Balkema, December 23, 1940, 300—Balkema, George, RG84-2452A.

24. Stéphane Chapelier, le président, to "Excellence," William Bullitt, Ambassador, June 15, 1940, 300—American Society of Composers, Authors and Publishers, RG84-2452A.

25. 300—Les Artistes Associés, RG84-2452A.

26. E.g., Tyler Thompson to Mrs. Florence Armbruster, August 25, 1940, 300—Armbruster, Mrs. Florence, RG84-2452A. Variant, in brackets, was in letter to Helena Rubinstein, 300—Rubinstein, Helena, RG84-2452A. On the number of certificates: memorandum for Mr. Barnes, August 20, 1940, "Embassy Property Protection Activities," Class 350—American Property, RG 84-2452A.

27. Telegram, signed Matthews, October 22, 1940, Class 350—American Property, RG84-2452A; telegram, Barnes/Matthews to Secretary of State, December 6, 1940, 300-XI-1940, RG84-2452A.

28. 300—Altwegg, C. Albert, (car); F. J. Whittle to American Embassy, August 18, 1940 (ping pong), 300—Armour, Reginald, RG84-2452A.

29. 300—Benedict Bureau (Miss Margaret DeWitt Benedict), RG84-2452A.

30. "Tous les biens américains doivent être déclarés," *Le Matin*, January 15, 1942, VD52, Archives 519, File 520 Office—Correspondance 1940–1943, inner file, "Office Documents," SGA.

31. President [signature illeg.], American Chamber of Commerce in France to A. Lechanteur, September 21, 1942, VD52, Archives 519, File 520 Office—Correspondance 1940–1943, SGA.

32. Etta Shiber, *Paris Underground* (New York: Charles Scribner's Sons, 1943); Charles F. Bove with Dana Lee Thomas, *A Paris Surgeon's Story* (Boston: Little, Brown, 1956), 224–301.

33. I found the account, attached to a letter from Russell H. Porter (Hotel New Weston, NYC) to Mr. and Mrs. Leo Giraud, September 9, 1942, uncataloged in a cabinet in the American Cathedral in Paris Archives. Porter's son gave me permission to use it.

34. Interview, Russell M. Porter, Paris, March 9, 2000; 804.1—List of Lawyers, RG84-2513 (1938), NACP.

35. They were sent to Compiègne; many were released within three weeks. Glass, *Americans in Paris*, chap. 22. In the second roundup, on September 24, 1942, women were also interned and sent to Vittel. Ibid., chaps. 24, 29, 32.

36. Shiber, *Paris Underground*, 1.

37. Nancy L. Green, "Trans-frontières: Pour une analyse des lieux de passage," *Socio-anthropologie*, no. 6 (2nd semester 1999): 33–48; Laurent Vidal, "Les territoires de l'attente: De quelques éléments de réflexion," http://terriat.hypotheses.org/ (accessed November 8, 2012).

38. Peggy Guggenheim, *Ma vie et mes folies* (Paris: Plon, 1987), 178, 194; Shiber, *Paris Underground*, 14.

39. Bates-Batcheller, *France*, 71 (where to), 109 (peasant); 186–87 (Mr. Officer); Virginia C. Russell, *Daughters Overseas: A History of Units Overseas* (Washington, DC: National Society Daughters of the American Revolution, 1990), 35 (dangerous).

40. Bricktop with James Haskins, *Bricktop* (New York: Atheneum, 1983), 201–6.

41. William A. Shack, *Harlem in Montmartre: A Paris Jazz Story between the Great Wars* (Berkeley: University of California Press, 2001), 110; Tyler Stovall, *Paris Noir: African Americans in the City of Light* (Boston: Houghton Mifflin, 1996), 120–22; Glass, *Americans in Paris*, chap. 4; en.wikipedia.org/wiki/Eugene_Bullard (accessed August 10, 2012).

42. W. S. Scott, *A Crusading Dean: An Era in the Life of the American Colony in Paris* (Langham, UK: Herald, 1967), 73 ("mit smiles"). Unmarked clippings, Beekman file; Entry, November 26, 1940, Minutes of Vestry, January 17, 1936–October 18, 1944; Beekman's diary, June 9–12, 1940 ("stunning"), and letter from "Freddy" to "Dear Boys" (Amherst College, Class of 1893), October 22, 1940, unmarked group of papers from Beekman's World War II files, all of the above in American Cathedral in Paris Archives; Beekman, "Justice and Peace: An American View; The Dangers of Compromise," *Times*, quoted in Scott, *Crusading Dean*, 70–71, also 73–74. See also 300—American Cathedral Church, RG84-1940.

43. Richard L. Stokes, "Won Privileges for Prisoners: Organist of American Cathedral in Paris Was Freed after Giving Piano Concert at Prison Camp," *Post-Dispatch*, October 3 [dateline], 1944; letter of Beekman, from New York, November 20, 1944, quoting Whipp's October 2, 1944, letter; clippings on Whipp; "Case of the Missing Organist," *Time*, March 12, 1945;

Mrs. Beekman to the Editor, *Time*, March 9, 1945—all in unmarked group of papers from Dean Beekman's World War II files, American Cathedral in Paris Archives. See also Edward Tipton, "The Case of the Missing Organist," *Trinité* [American Cathedral magazine], Spring 2007, 10–12; Vaughan, *Doctor to the Resistance*, 56–59, 182.

44. The Chambrun legacy is mixed. Clara's son-in-law was Pierre Laval, prime minister in the Vichy government, executed for collaboration after the war. Glass, *Americans in Paris*, draws heavily on the Chambruns' memoirs but also critical newspaper reports, esp. chaps 3, 8, 9, 12, 18, 36, 47; Bennetta Jules-Rosette, *Josephine Baker in Art and Life: The Icon and the Image* (Urbana: University of Illinois Press, 2007); Shiber, *Paris Underground*. On Jackson, see Hal Vaughan, *Doctor to the Resistance: The Heroic Story of an American Surgeon and His Family in Occupied Paris* (Washington, DC: Brassey's, 2004); and Glass, *Americans in Paris*, esp. chaps. 6, 35, 39, 43–44, 46.

45. Vanson to Rowley, July 21, 1939, VD23, Archives 330, Palmolive, SGA.

46. Virginia Kays Veenswijk, *Coudert Brothers, a Legacy in Law: The History of America's First International Law Firm, 1853–1993* (New York: Truman Talley, 1994), 251–254; see also Robinson's testimony in *Schaposchnikoff v. Estate of De Gheest*, 362 Mo. 634 (Mo. 1951) 243 S.W.2d 83, http://www.loislaw.com/livepublish8923/doclink.htp?alias=MOCASE&cite=243+S.W.2d+83; Nancy L. Green with Rebecca Fite, "The Law Offices of S.G. Archibald: A Century of International Law Practice," unpublished manuscript, 2000, chap. 3.

47. VD63, Archives 548, Les Productions Fox Europa; VD9, Archives 326, Les Productions Fox Europa ; and VD218, Archives 792, Les Productions Fox Europa, Baux, inner file "Documents divers," SGA.

48. VD218, Archives792, Les Productions Fox Europa, Baux, SGA.

49. F. J. Scholl to Paul T. Culbertson, October 23, 1940; Guillo to Thompson, December 13, 1940, 300—Scholl Manufacturing Company, Sec. XI, RG84-2452A.

50. Lechanteur to Leroy, June 11, 1941, and March 26, 1942, VD23, Archives 402, Swift et Cie., SGA.

CONCLUSION

1. Elliott A. Kaplan to US consulate in Paris, June 8, 1938, 850.4 Kaplan, Elliott, A., Foreign Service Posts of the Department of State, Record Group 84, Entry no. 2513, Paris Consulate General, 1936–1939, National Archives at College Park, MD (hereafter NACP).

2. Christopher Sawyer-Lauçanno, *The Continual Pilgrimage: American Writers in Paris, 1944–1960* (New York: Grove, 1992). More recently, see Alice Kaplan, *Dreaming in French: The Paris Years of Jacqueline Bouvier Kennedy, Susan Sontag, and Angela Davis* (Chicago: University of Chicago Press, 2012).

3. Warren Irving Susman, "Pilgrimage to Paris: The Backgrounds of American Expatriation, 1920–1934," PhD thesis, University of Wisconsin, 1957, 125–26, citing Harry and Caresse Crosby's translation of *47 Lettres Inédites de Marcel Proust*.

4. Richard Kuisel, *Seducing the French: The Dilemma of Americanization* (Berkeley: University of California Press, 1993); Emily S. Rosenberg, *Spreading the American Dream: American Economic and Cultural Expansion, 1890–1945* (New York: Hill and Wang, 1982).

5. "Gertrude Stein Found," *New York Times*, September 2, 1944. But as Janet Malcolm noted, "it was a point of pride with Stein never to appear unhappy." http://www.newyorker.com/archive/2003/06/02/030602fa_fact2 [November 8, 2012].

6. Memos (both on one sheet), American Chamber of Commerce (ACC) in France, "Communications with the USA" and "Return of American Business Men to France," November 2, 1944; and circular and questionnaire, ACC in France, July 2, 1945, both in VD52, Archives 519, File 520 Office—Correspondance 1940–1943, inner file "Office Documents," Law Offices of S. G. Archibald Archives (hereafter SGA).

7. Erik Cohen, "Expatriate Communities," *Current Sociology* 24, no. 3 (1977): 12.

8. VD63, Archives 548, Les Productions Fox Europa, SGA (carpets); 300 [Section XI]—Train, Arthur, Correspondence, American Embassy, Paris, 1940, Volume XII, Record Group 84, entry 2452A, NACP.

9. Nelcya Delanoë, *Le Raspail vert: L'American Center à Paris, 1934–1994* (Paris: Seghers, 1994), 34; see also 73, 210.

10. http://theamericanclubs.com/alumni-clubs.html (accessed August 30, 2013).

11. Hilary Kaiser, *Des amours de GI's: Les petites fiancées du Débarquement* (Paris: Tallandier, 2004).

12. Phyllis Michaux, *The Unknown Ambassadors: A Saga of Citizenship* (Bayside, NY: Aletheia, 1996).

13. Dennis Riley, *Expatriates Employment Handbook: Seeing the World and Getting Paid for It!* (Boulder, CO: Paladin, 1990); Ronald L. Krannich and Caryl Rae Krannich, *The Complete Guide to International Jobs and Careers: Your Passport to a World of Exciting and Exotic Employment*, 2nd rev. ed. (Manassas Park, VA: Impact, 1992).

14. "Américaine et SDF [sans domicile fixe/homeless] à Paris," *Le Monde* 2, February 21, 2009.

INDEX

Max Factor Company, 170–74, 180, 225
Maxim, Hiram Stevens, 131
Maxim's, 203
Mayer, Thérèse, 56
McBride, Mary Margaret, 87, 119–20, 182
McCullough, David, 205, 265n2, 307n82
McDonald, Hortense, 121
McKay, Claude, 20, 38, 126–27; quoted, 22, 24, 25, 26
McKendrick, Mike, 189–90
Meigs, Mark, 96
Mercer, Mabel, 116–17
Messersmith, George S., 153–54
metric system, proposal to adopt, in United States, 135
MGM, 242
Michaëlis, Herbert, 177
Michaux, Phyllis, 259, 262, 312n12
Michelin, 177, 228
Mikell, L. Grace, 106
Mikell, Otto, 106
Militärbefehlshaber, 243
Miller, Gething J., 132
Miller, Henry, 21, 78, 114, 192, 207, 256
Miller, Warner, 59–60, 63, 74
Mitchell, Emily, 106
Mitchell, Louis, 127
mixed marriage. *See* marriage, international
mobility, 41–42
Monnier, Adrienne, 115, 206
Montesquiou, Robert de, 222
Montgomery, Maureen, 89
Montmartre, 13, 23, 26, 27, 108, 116–17, 118, 126–28, 183, 189–90, 231
Montparnasse, 22, 23, 25, 26, 27, 28, 43, 184; "battle of," 188–89
Morand, Paul, 208
Morgan, Anne, 210, 211, 230
Morgan sisters, 86
motherhood, 34, 90
Motion Picture Export Association, 157
Motion Picture Producers and Distributors of America (MPPDA), 158, 160

Motley, Archibald, 26
Mouillefarine, Mme (née Ethel Simon), 87
Moulton, Arthur, 100–103, 106, 258
Moulton, Gertrude (née Wood), 98, 100–106
Moveable Feast, 205
movies. *See* Hollywood
musicians, 49, 117, 198; African American, 13, 23, 26, 106, 108, 117; French, 21
Mussolini, 34, 105

Napoleon III (Louis Napoleon Bonaparte), 1, 15, 216
Nathan, Louis, 177
National Aeronautic Association of the USA, 135
National Cash Register, 145, 148
National City Bank, 132, 238
nationality of companies, 162, 174–76, 252–53
Negro Anthology, 83
neighborhoods, 40–43; Arc de Triomphe (Étoile), 40, 43; Belleville, 211; Grands Boulevards, 204; Opéra, 40, 203; Pigalle, 44. *See also* Latin Quarter; Montmartre; Montparnasse
neighborhoods, arrondissements: 6th, 41; 7th, 41; 8th, 41, 91, 230; 14th, 41; 16th, 35, 41, 43, 100, 106, 164, 188, 193, 195; 17th, 41
newspapers, 38–40. *See also individual titles*
New Yorker, 118
New York Herald European Edition (1887–1935), 22, 39, 40, 50, 114, 118, 124, 238
New York Herald Tribune European Edition (1935–67), 193, 238. See *International Herald Tribune*
New York Life Insurance Company, 151
Niebuhr, Reinhold, 143, 220
Nightwood, 83
Norton-Harjes Ambulance Corps, 54
Nouailhat, Yves-Henri, 96
novelists, 49
nurses, 18, 120

Red Cross, American, 2, 54, 55, 58, 118, 120, 185, 197, 209, 211, 212, 213, 219

Reese, Philip (née Philip A. S. Blair), 195–96

Reese Europe, James, 126, 127

Reid, Mrs. Whitelaw (née Elizabeth Mills), 29, 42, 230

Reid, Whitelaw, 1, 206

Reid Hall, 29

Reims, cathedral reconstruction, 146, 209, 210

relief, 34, 51, 194; for Americans, 14, 27, 32, 52, 68–69, 194, 197–98, 239; Federal Emergency Relief Administration (FERA), 200; for French, 53, 54, 209–10, 230; limitations on, 199, 200; workers, 57, 185. *See also* American Aid Society; American Legion Paris Post; Morgan, Anne; philanthropy; Red Cross, American; Stein, Gertrude; Toklas, Alice B.; Wharton, Edith

religion, 8, 102, 137, 151

Rémond, René, 125

Renault, 228

rentiers, 6, 17, 22, 113, 198

repairmen, 121–22

residence cards. *See* permits: residence

Resistance (World War II), 26, 230, 244, 250

Revue Nègre, 25, 127, 189

"riot," anti-American, 10, 13, 204, 224–25, 231

Riviera, 41, 42, 43

Robinson, John B., 130, 250–51

Rochambeau, 36, 137, 206, 207, 217. *See also* Daughters of the American Revolution (DAR)

Rockefeller, John D., Jr., 210, 212, 229

Rodin, Auguste, 98–99, 106

Roditi and Sons, 149

Roger, Philippe, 221, 222

Roosevelt, Franklin D., 9, 56, 99, 102, 103

Root, Elihu, 6

Rosenberg, Emily, 4, 151

Rotary Club, 8, 27, 144, 231

Roussy de Salès, Count Raoul de, 187–88

Royce, George Monroe, 232–33

Rubinstein, Helena, 40, 121, 171, 241, 309n22

Russell, Henry Tosti, 234

Russians in Paris, 8, 18, 82, 270n15

Sacco, Nikola, 10, 220, 229

Sagan, Princesse de. *See* Gould, Anna

Sagdahl, Hjalmer, 123

salonnières, 17, 21, 85

salons, 8, 11, 21, 33, 37, 78, 117, 222, 229

Salvation Army, 18

Samaritaine, La, 192

Sam's place, 124

Sanders, John B., 254

sardines, 139, 154

Sauna-Seymour, Mrs., 120

Savage, Augusta, 25

Sawyer-Lauçanno, Christopher, 255

Scholl Manufacturing Company, 252

Scott, George C., 109

Scott, Helen, 119, 121

Scott, Yvonne, 109

Seaman and Pendergast, 121

seamen, 51, 198

Sears, 149

secretaries. *See* stenographers

Seemuller, Mrs. H. E., 121

Seillière, Baron Raymond, 130–31

Seligman, William, 1, 89, 148

Seligmann art dealers, 122

Sevareid, Eric, 3, 114, 257

Seven Spades Band, 127

Sewell, William H., Jr., 267n22

sex, 8, 49, 84, 206; as gender, 31, 79, 84, 94, 107, 110; image of, 8, 78–82, 113

Shakespeare and Company, 38, 114–16, 206, 258

Sharon, Alfred, 42

Sharp, William Graves, 56, 58

Shaw, Constance Fish, 67

Shiber, Etta, 244, 247, 250

Shirer, William, 39, 114

Shoninger, B. J., 140, 209

Shoop, Max, 240